Praise for
GOOD MUSIC, BRIGHTER CHILDREN

"I have a premonition that one day soon we will wake up, like Woody Allen's character in the film *Sleeper*, to the realization that stripping instrumental music from our elementary schools was a true blunder of twentieth-century American education. Sharlene Habermeyer outlines why music is important to learning, and provides parents with excellent suggestions for launching and sustaining a musical influence in the lives of their children."
James S. Catterall, Professor of Education
and Co-Director of Imagination Project at UCLA

"Sharlene Habermeyer's book, *Good Music, Brighter Children*, is a very well-crafted look at the importance and many benefits of music in our children's lives at home and school. She weaves together contemporary brain research about how music affects the short- and long-term development of young children's minds, the very successful use of music—and truly all the arts— in supporting children who have learning exceptionalities, and the practical ways that parents can organize and support music education both in and after school. This is an enjoyable, lucid, and informative read for anyone who wants to better understand or make the case for the value of arts education in our schools."
Tim Seldin, President
The Montessori Foundation

"Music is a powerful and necessary tool for engaging students' hearts and minds. *Good Music, Brighter Children* provides educators, parents, and the community with critical information as well as the language to advocate for its rightful position within a child's complete education."
Joan Ashcraft, DMA
Director, Tucson Unified School District, Fine and Performing Arts
Opening Minds through the Arts (OMA)

"*Good Music, Brighter Children* provides extensive information in the area of brain research and offers a whole host of strategies for bringing music into the home or school. Children are our most important renewing natural resource, and any opportunities we can offer them to grow better brains benefits the entire world. We have no idea which child we encounter at a playground will grow up to be a scientist who develops the cure for cancer. Music has long been regarded as an enjoyable and educational pursuit for our children that most parents would readily agree benefits their children in many ways, but until recently we didn't have the scientific evidence to support making those assertions. With advances in neurosciences it is now possible to conclude that music does more than just 'enrich' our lives; it 'enriches' our brains. This text is timely, as it shows why we must continue to support music endeavors for all children even when budgets are tight. This beautifully written work presents the most compelling argument to date that supports why we as a society must continue to fulfill the cultural mandate of including music in the life of every child."

Kathleen A. Horvath, PhD
Associate Professor of String Education and Pedagogy
Director of Undergraduate Studies in Music Education
Case Western Reserve University

"An outstanding book that brings so much hope to families, particularly to children with disabilities. Music is indeed the best therapy in helping many children overcome their challenges, enabling them to accomplish so many things beyond our imaginations. Every parent and teacher should read this book to discover the hidden talents of their children, from as young as eighteen months old and particularly those with disabilities. Nothing is impossible if we strive to help our children through the power of good music, with our belief that every child can excel."

Miriam Choi
Suzuki Piano Teacher (Advanced)
Melbourne, Australia

"A great resource for both parents and teachers. Anyone interested in music or the overall well-being of children will not be able to put this book down."
     Lisha Papert Lercari, Director
     Music and the Brain

"This new book is an incalculable resource for family members, educators, and music-affiliated retailers alike. It is a road map, providing categorical stepping-stones for aiding children as they mature into well-developed and successful adults. I have kept Sharlene Habermeyer's first edition of *Good Music, Brighter Children* on my office desk for more than a decade, offering recommendations and testimonials to store visitors for building higher intellect in both children and young adults. It is a wonderful, thought-provoking book. Parents should immerse themselves in its message."
     Antoinette Purdon
     The Piano Company
     Leesburg, Virginia

"Sharlene Habermeyer's enthusiastic and informative guide explains the potential impact of music in the home and community and backs it up with academic studies and other evidence of music's exceptional capability to influence the lives of children for good. Carefully researched and highly readable, *Good Music, Brighter Children* is written for musicians and nonmusicians alike. The book describes the powerful benefits of music in a child's life and offers helpful ideas to keep children involved in music as they grow. It is filled with wisdom, insight, and helpful tips to bring music into the home for all ages and stages of childhood."
     Shauna Bird Dunn, JD, MPA
     Utah Young Mother of the Year, 2010

"*Good Music, Brighter Children* perfectly outlined for me how to brighten my children's lives through the magical world of music. I learned that children who receive a music education can evolve and possess critically important traits such as discipline, teamwork, creativity, and respect for themselves and others. My sincere thanks to Sharlene Habermeyer for *the* single most important resource I relied upon to be a confident mother whose children have 'evolved' and are not only accomplished students and musicians, but sensitive, intelligent, happy people as well."

Nancy Allen Naroff,
Mother of musicians Madeline and Dylan

"*Good Music, Brighter Children* is a refreshing and inspiring 'how-to' manual for parents who want to improve their child's life through music. Sharlene Habermeyer not only describes the 'whys' of using music, but explains the 'hows' of easily incorporating music into the lives of our children. Turn on the music and watch your child's mind grow!"

Michelle Whitesides
Mother and Young Violinist Chairperson
Palos Verdes Regional Symphony Orchestra

Habermeyer (*Good Music, Brighter Children*, 1999) updates her debut exploration of the importance of music in children's lives with enlightening new information.

After educator Habermeyer struggled to find a book on the benefits of music for children that included practical guidance for parents, she decided to write one herself. The result was a meticulously researched and crafted work—a blend of investigation, manual, textbook and inspiration—with careful scrutiny of the merits and implementation of music instruction. The updated edition brings in 21st-century scientific studies, laws and technological innovations, along with anecdotes about successful child musicians—all of which support the idea that music should be as fundamental to education as the three R's. With a scientist's eye and an artist's voice, Habermeyer examines everything from the benefits of music for the developing brain to music's ability to improve cultural awareness. "Music, like truth, is often felt before it is understood," the book notes. Similarly, Habermeyer's lucid writing tends to strike a chord before the reader has processed the wealth of data that supports it. Her book is never preachy or hyperbolic—it is instead well-reasoned and peppered with moments of science-backed epiphany—yet its effect is as moving as it is cerebral. It is also motivational enough to encourage many parents to sign their children up for lessons. And it provides tips and resources that can help, including lists of recommended books, DVDs and Internet sources, as well as clear explanations of which instruments might best suit children of different ages and personalities. It gives particular attention to the value of music in the lives of special needs children, a topic often slighted in books for a general audience. And it delves into important ancillary subjects, such as ways to support local arts or start an orchestra. This is an encyclopedic, invaluable resource for anyone who believes in music education. Habermeyer may be preaching partly to the choir, but that choir is ready to sing and start playing instruments. Even parents whose children are already taking lessons may find valuable recommendations.

A magnum opus, fact-filled and inspiring, on the benefits of music.

Kirkus Indie, Kirkus Media LLC

GOOD MUSIC
BRIGHTER CHILDREN

Simple and Practical Ideas to Help Transform Your
Child's Life Through the Power of Music

SHARLENE HABERMEYER

ISBN: 1484157311
ISBN 13: 9781484157312

Library of Congress Control Number: 2013908285
CreateSpace Independent Publishing Platform
North Charleston, South Carolina

Photograph on page xvii- Violin with music ©John Wood/Index Stock
Photograph on page 11- Ella playing the recorder ©Jason Habermeyer
Photograph on page 33- Matthew playing the guitar ©Jenny Oaks Baker
Photograph on page 61- Tyler playing the trumpet © Jason Habermeyer
Photograph on page 99- Audrey with piano teacher ©Ryan Habermeyer
Photograph on page 116- Let's Play Music © Josh Caldwell
Photograph on page 149- PVRSO Young Violinists © Shau-Lian Liao
Photograph on page 163- Collin playing violin © Mary Stewart
Photograph on page 197- Trevor playing the cymbals ©Mark Habermeyer
Photograph on page 229- Trenton sings with dad ©Mark Habermeyer
Photograph on page 269- Jason playing the oboe © Shau-Lian Liao
Photograph on page 271- Lillian Concertmistress playing violin ©Panfey Chen
Photograph on page 329- Julianna playing the harp © Timothy Hoopes
Photograph on page 331- Samuel and Mr. Jin playing bass ©Shau-Lian Liao
Photograph on page 353- Cassidy playing the oboe ©Timothy Hoopes

To my family:
my constant source of inspiration

CONTENTS

PART FIVE: FINALE

ACKNOWLEDGMENTS

Every aspect of bringing this book to publication has been a team effort. Even the countless hours writing were not spent in solitude. For those occasions, I received inspiration from Mozart, Beethoven, Handel, and others.

I am grateful to my husband, Mark, for his untiring support, patience, and consistent encouragement. I could not have completed this project without him.

I appreciate my spirited sons, Jason, Ryan, Brandon, Jarom, and Trevor, who are remarkable young men; compassionate, strong, and honest.

I'm especially indebted to my son, Ryan. Our history of writing together goes back to when he was in the sixth grade and learning, for the first time, to critically analyze literature. It was a difficult process for him, so I helped him by reading everything he read and then explaining it in a way so he could better grasp the concepts. He ended up falling in love with writing and literature, and today he is working toward his PhD in English. He is an exceptional writer with amazing critical thinking skills. Naturally, I had him read parts of the manuscript. His quick understanding of the material, his insights, his valid criticisms, and his lively comments were an inspiration and helped me to construct and reconstruct my ideas.

I am grateful to Antoinette Purdon, who has kept me abreast of musical events and stories that have crossed her desk over the last ten years. She is a trusted and treasured friend who loves music as much as I do. Thank you, Antoinette.

INTRODUCTION

I started taking piano lessons when I was five years old. When I was seven, my music teacher told my parents that it was a waste of her time and their money to have me continue studying.

"She hasn't learned the notes in two years, and musically she'll never amount to anything," she emphatically explained.

Before taking me out of lessons, my mother consulted my father, who asked, "Does she enjoy her music?"

"Yes," my mother said, "very much so."

"Then let her continue with another teacher," my father replied simply.

I will always be grateful for that decision—made by my parents at a time when I was too young to realize the broad implications of severing those music lessons. My parents, while observing the enjoyment I derived from the piano, sensed that my love of music was more important than my ability to play music. As far as my music teacher…she was partially correct in her estimation of my musical aptitude. I was obviously not a prodigy, and today my musical talent is certainly not on the virtuoso level (or remotely close!). But, I feel that my connection to music today—and the reason I took lessons through college and into adulthood, acquired a degree in the arts, started an orchestra in our community, and still continue to play, enjoy, appreciate, and love all kinds of music—is because of that early and consistent exposure.

Many years later, while raising our sons, the motivation to make music a legacy for our children was a direct result of the musical experiences my husband and I had while growing up. It is a natural desire to pass on to those we love the things we love.

Music has always been a central part of our home. I started playing music for each of our children when they were *in utero*, and once they were born, music activities and lessons enveloped their lives. Music was especially important for our son Brandon, who at the age of five was diagnosed with severe learning disabilities (discussed in chapter 8). For him, music became his lifeline to learning, with musical games and jingles a daily occurrence. Seeing how music was helping Brandon to learn, I began to seriously research the educational and brain benefits of music. During this time, the studies, research, and theories of psychologists, scientists, neuromusicologists, music researchers, and educators influenced and broadened my perception and educational appreciation of classical music. I read and gathered hundreds of articles from medical journals, periodicals, newspapers, magazines, dissertations, texts from biological music conferences, and national music organizations. I consulted and interviewed many experts in these fields. I joined music organizations to learn about their music philosophies, to participate in their conferences and workshops, and to see how their particular approach to music enhanced learning. This was a sixteen-year journey. I then searched for a comprehensive "how-to" book geared to parents on the far-reaching benefits of music to pass on to interested parents at my lectures. Finding nothing under one title, I decided to write this book.

Good Music, Brighter Children was originally published in 1999 and was translated into five languages. Over a year ago, I discovered the book was still generating activity, even though it was out of print. I was also getting e-mails from people all over the world trying to find the book. So, as a result of that "gentle nudging," I began the tedious process of revising and updating and getting it ready for republication. Every chapter has been updated—some more extensively than others. There are new chapters and deleted chapters. And except for a few examples, you will find that once again, I focus entirely on classical music. Certainly other kinds of music are inspiring, but because of the massive amount and variety of music available, the emphasis must be narrowed, and because of classical music's extensive educational benefits, the concentration is on classical music.

Here are some suggestions on how to read this book.

In section 1, I establish *why* classical music for you and your child. These chapters discuss the science, the research, and the influence of music throughout the ages. If you enjoy reading studies and research to confirm the importance of music, this section is a must.

Section 2 gives the nuts and bolts of *how* to accomplish the *why* by turning your home into a powerful musical training center. You will learn how to introduce your child to music from the time before he is born through high school and beyond. Choosing an instrument, finding a teacher, and getting your kids to practice, as well as values developed through music involvement, are among the topics included. If you are a parent, this section will act as a valuable guideline and a treasure trove of information.

Section 3 focuses on advocacy. It explains the importance of music education in the schools and how an education in the arts produces a well-rounded adult. It discusses the impact music has on children with various disabilities and how it becomes their link to the outside world. Creativity and its relationship to music and the global economy will be covered. If you are an educator and believe in an arts-integrated classroom, a parent with a special-needs child, or someone interested in the correlation between creativity, the arts, and the business world, these chapters will be useful.

Section 4 explains the role and need for music in the community and how families and individuals can become active supporters of the music community. It also covers the steps to starting an orchestra.

The finale, in my opinion, is the most important chapter in the book, as it will give you strong reasons, ideas, and keys in making music a lasting legacy in your home.

The resource section provides lists of music, CDs, MP3 downloads, DVDs, books, national music organizations, websites, and so forth and is a great tool to take to any music store or library or use while surfing the Internet.

You will find this book is chock full of stories. Why? Simply put, we remember stories. You may not remember the details of the research and studies I cite, but you will remember the poignant stories of people, schools, and communities that have been positively influenced by music. These narratives will become embedded in your brain and create a lasting influence in your life.

As you read this book, I hope you will look at and appreciate music in many different ways—a biological human need, an astounding art form that allows us to feel and experience a multitude of sensations, an extraordinary vehicle for enhancing intelligence, a medium for helping children with special needs, and a way to connect and unite people all over the world. Over the years, I have looked for a fitting definition of music that would demonstrate the influence it has on all of us. What comes closest is the following quote, spoken by Walter Damrosch in 1928, which elegantly portrays the power music has on human life while concurrently speaking of its divine origin:

> "Servant and Master am I: Servant of those dead, and Master of those living.
> Through my spirit immortals speak the message that makes the world weep and laugh and wonder and worship…For I am the instrument of God, I am Music."

Today, my sons are grown, married, and have families of their own. The legacy of music, started in our extended family generations ago, continues, as their children are now taking up the baton and finding joy in music.

PART ONE

WHY MUSIC

CHAPTER 1

Overture:
The Power Of Music

*"Superstring theory suggests that the microscopic landscape is suffused
with tiny strings whose vibrational patterns orchestrate
the evolution of the cosmos."*
Brian Greene, *The Elegant Universe*

Music has power to change us. The advanced civilizations of antiquity—the Greeks, the Romans, the Chinese, and others—viewed music as a powerful force that could change the character of an individual and influence the masses. Confucius believed that music was so far-reaching in its significance that it influenced much of what humans did in life and held potential power for both good and evil. He stated, "If you would know if a people are well governed, and if its laws are good or bad, examine the music it practices."[1] These cultures did not consider music a mere art form...they knew and understood its power.

Today, scientists and neuromusicologists—researchers who study how music affects the brain—are beginning to unravel the potential music has on the development of human beings. They know people are born musical, that is, music is a vital part of our biological makeup and is one of the ingredients that make us human. These observers agree that all human beings respond to music on some level, and it has an astounding influence on people's behavior, thinking, and being. Music is one of the first things that babies respond to at birth and one of the last things that people who are dying acknowledge. People who report near-death experiences sometimes tell of the presence of music.[2] We played music during the births of our sons and for my mother-in-law as she lay dying from a malignant brain tumor. In each instance, music created a calm peaceful environment—for one human being entering the world and for another leaving it.

Anthropologists believe that music had its beginnings with early man, and since then there has never been a time or a civilization without it. The first evidence of music in cave paintings dates back as much as seventy thousand years. Hundreds of cave drawings depict humans engaged in musical activities. Some of these paintings depict bows, which are thought by anthropologists to have been used as musical instruments as much as they were used as weapons of war.[3]

Anthropologists believe that music had its beginnings with early man, and since then there has never been a time or a civilization without it.

Flutes from thirty thousand years ago, found in southern France, the Pyrenees, and Russia, provide more evidence of music in early man's life. The positions of the tone holes on the flutes indicate that early humans probably created music of artistic significance. More than forty thousand examples of rock carvings illustrating man's involvement in music have been found in caves in Northern Italy, Africa, and other parts of Europe.

Universally, evidence shows that songs have been an integral part of the formation of cultures. Records in the form of hymns, chants, and songs have been discovered among the ruins of ancient civilizations. In Asia Minor and Sumeria, clay tablets have been found that contain writings discussing the place and importance of music in those societies.[4] The Greeks linked the creation of music and song to their goddesses, the Muses, who presided over the arts, literature, and the sciences and are told about in their mythology. Zeus created the world, and the gods viewed in silent admiration all its beauty and magnificence. Then Zeus asked if something was still missing. And the gods answered that one thing was still missing: the world was lacking a Voice, the ultimate voice which in words and sounds had the gift of expressing and praising all this magnificence. To make such a voice sound, a new kind of divine being was necessary. And thus the Muses were created, as the children of Zeus and Mnemosyne.[5]

This story continues. Calliope, one of the nine Muses, has a son, whom she names Orpheus. He is taught music and the art of singing by the Muses. His voice is so enchanting that his melodies have the power to make the trees follow him and wild animals lie down at his feet. Orpheus meets and falls in love with the tree nymph, Eurydice. On their wedding day, she is bitten by a viper and dies. Undaunted, he travels to the Underworld to rescue her. On the way, he captivates everyone with his beautiful singing, including Cerberus, the three-headed dog who guards the entrance to Hades. When Orpheus stands before the gods of the Underworld, he sings his pleas for Eurydice. Hades and the queen of the Underworld are moved by his voice and allow Orpheus to take Eurydice back to earth. But there is a condition: he cannot look back to see if she is following him. Orpheus sings as they travel over rugged terrain, never looking back at Eurydice. But as Orpheus sees the earth and sunshine, he fears for Eurydice and looks back to help her. She dies a second time and Orpheus is unable to rescue her. He mourns her loss for three years through song. And that is how singing—according to the ancient Greeks—became a part of this world.

Throughout the ages mankind has produced many forms of music and—whether for religious purposes, rituals, ceremonies, or enjoyment—the human need to create music seems basic to life.

Throughout the ages mankind has produced many forms of music and—whether for religious purposes, rituals, ceremonies, or enjoyment—the human need to create music seems basic to life.

A Musical Universe

We live in a musical universe. In 1772, Johann Bode, a German astronomer, measured the distance between the planets. His mathematical formula was so precise that it later became known as "Bode's Law." He stated that all of the planets possessed mean orbital distances from Mercury that become progressively greater by the ratio of 2:1 as the planets' distance from the sun increases. The ratio 2:1 means that each planet vibrates twice as fast as its predecessor vibrates and produces a sound with a pitch one octave higher than the previous planet. This ratio is the same as that of the musical tones in an octave, suggesting that the planets themselves form a chain of octaves, with each planet representing one octave. Within this octave, the planets, as they spin on their axis, have an actual tone created by their pitch-frequencies.[6]

To understand this concept, think of the toy tops that children play with. As the top spins around and gains speed, it begins to "hum," and a musiclike tone is produced. Scientists measured the tone of the earth in 1960 during an earthquake in Chile. Seismographs showed that the earth "rings" with deep vibrations that are exactly twenty octaves below the lowest sound that the human ear can hear.[7] Approximately every twelve years, the planets become somewhat aligned with one another. If we could hear the combination of these various tones at this time, they would most likely sound like a musical chord.[8] Imagine—the planets are like a gigantic musical instrument resonating in the universe!

Stars also produce tones. On August 27, 1998, scientists reported a blast of an unusual star in the earth's upper atmosphere. Kevin Harley of the University of California at Berkeley said that the star "rang" in x-rays for several minutes, producing an "unheard of" tone in the universe.[9] To explain how the star "rang," think of what happens when we strike a bell. The tone from the bell continues to vibrate, then slowly diminishes, just like the star burst and produced a tone for several seconds in space. (X-rays, like a musical note, are measured by frequencies.)

Our magnificent sun also creates musical vibrations. Astronomers have recorded "heavenly" music generated by the sun's atmosphere. In 2007, a study was presented at the Royal Astronomical Society's National Astronomy Meeting in Lancashire, England, revealing that "the looping magnetic fields along the sun's outer regions, called the corona, carry magnetic sound waves in a similar manner to musical instruments such as guitars or pipe organs."[10]

Musical patterns are also found in nature. Pythagoras—a philosopher and mathematician of ancient Greece—and his followers, the Pythagoreans, discovered that all music could be understood as numbers and mathematical ratios. More recently, Richard F. Voss of IBM's Thomas J. Watson Research

Center used mathematical formulas to find patterns of music in nature. Music, he says, resembles not the sounds heard in nature, but nature itself. Through a mathematical equation, he linked the underlying musical structure that is found in "flicker" noise (noise found in nature) to a landscape, a range of mountains, or a seascape. "Flicker" noise can be converted to a signature sound and can be compared to how a particular physical system changes over time. Every large mass (a building, a human, a mountain) resonates at a certain "background" frequency that can be measured. If external forces match that frequency, the mass will disintegrate. The Tacoma Narrows Bridge in Washington broke apart in a "frequency disturbance" as a result of winds. The structure was not engineered properly and was out of tune with its environment, literally. Every structure or mass has this background frequency, and it's referred to mathematically as "flicker noise." This noise is the fingerprint of that mass and all parts of the structure or mass.[11] Although this "noise" is unlike the music of a Mozart, it can still be judged distinctly musiclike. Voss has created realistic-looking artificial landscapes, planets, and clouds using similar equations as a part of the science known as "fractals."[12]

Animals and Music

Along with music in our universe and musical patterns in nature, it has been found that animals also respond to music—particularly classical music. In February 1985, as many as three thousand beluga whales were trapped under ice in the Senyavina Strait of Siberia, a narrow body of water across the Bering Strait from Alaska. There were only a few breathing holes in the ice, and the whales had to take turns surfacing for air. Food was running out, the whales were becoming exhausted, and some were even dying. When all seemed hopeless, a Soviet icebreaker, the *Moskva,* came to the rescue. The ship broke through the ice, making an escape path for the whales, but they wouldn't budge. Knowing that whales like music, they tried pop and jazz, but still the whales remained motionless. Finally, the crew tried classical music. It was then that the whales followed the music to the open sea and to freedom.[13] This touching story has been retold in a children's book entitled *A Symphony of Whales,* by Steve Schuch.

Birds also respond to classical music. A study by the late Stewart Hulse, an experimental psychologist trained in the field of animal learning at Johns Hopkins University, found that European starlings are able to recognize a simple melody in different keys. The researchers concluded that starlings respond to musical features just like humans.[14] Hulse was considered one of the founders of the field of animal cognition. During his tenure at Johns Hopkins his interest in acoustic perception in birds grew, and he offered a popular graduate-level course called the "Psychology of Sound and Music."

In another experiment by Debra Porter and Allen Neuringer at Reed College in Portland, Oregon, pigeons were trained to distinguish the music of J. S. Bach from the music of Igor Stravinsky. They were even able to correctly categorize music from other composers that sounded Bach-like or Stravinsky-like.[15]

Many animals communicate with one another through musical sounds. Baby emperor penguins rely on the sound of their parents rather than sight. When their parents go to sea to hunt for food, the baby penguins stay in penguin day-care centers called creches. Upon returning, the parents walk from creche to creche trumpeting at the top of their lungs. Ann Bowles, an expert on emperor communication, states, "Each bird's call is distinctive. When a child recognizes its parent's voice, it comes barreling out to meet it."[16] Dolphins use high whistles and clicks to "see" underwater and communicate with other dolphins. Whales use sounds that resemble songs to communicate with other whales. Frogs sing choruses when they are looking for mates or defending their territory. Elephants communicate with one another using rumbling sounds that are too low for humans to hear, but strong enough for us to feel. They can hear each other from miles away and listen to one another with their huge ears held open.[17]

Household pets also respond to music. In 2003, our family became foster parents to a mother cat and her four baby kittens through a foster-care program sponsored by the Society for the Prevention of Cruelty to Animals (SPCA). Since our own cats enjoyed classical music, we decided this cat family might also. We chose a variety of classical CDs to play

> *Many animals communicate with one another through musical sounds. Baby emperor penguins rely on the sound of their parents rather than sight.*

for them intermittently throughout the day. In the beginning, we found that lullabies and soothing tunes worked best for the baby kittens, but as they grew older, they enjoyed an upbeat tempo. They even played with one another to the beat of the music, much like a group of children on a playground interacting to a musical rhythm. These kittens grew into happy, very social cats, and when they were adopted, we included a classical CD for their new owners to play for them.

Music and Learning

Music goes beyond being a powerful force in our universe, a part of nature, and a communication vehicle between the animals of the earth. Proportionately, its greatest impact is on human beings—to our learning processes, brain development and organization, and the refinement of our entire neurological system. The late Dr. Gordon Shaw and Dr. Frances Rauscher, scientists at the University of California at Irvine and the University of Wisconsin at Oshkosh—and many others within the brain research community—have shown music to have extensive educational and brain-developing value. Listening to classical music can increase memory and concentration, and studying a musical instrument has been shown to increase spatial reasoning.[18]

Listening to classical music can increase memory and concentration, and studying a musical instrument has been shown to increase spatial reasoning.

When music in all of its forms (singing, playing a musical instrument, listening to classical music, and so on) is a part of the home environment, it creates a positive atmosphere, one which is conducive to learning and aids in the acquisition of early language. When music is taught comprehensively and sequentially in the schools, it increases math, science, reading, history, and SAT scores. It also reaches at-risk students by increasing their confidence and those with learning disabilities by making the learning process easier. Additionally, studying a musical instrument helps develop imagination, invention, creative thinking, communication, and teamwork skills—precisely those attributes needed for a twenty-first century global workforce.[19]

An education in music and the arts has been shown to be an essential ingredient for our children's future success, and with a collaborative effort between parents, schools, arts organizations, and corporations, music and arts education can become a reality for children in schools across our nation.

Communicating Emotions

But no matter what potential music has in developing the intellect, how it describes us as human beings, and its affect on us emotionally is by no means insignificant. Donald Hodges, editor of *Handbook of Music Psychology*, relates the following story: In 1978, when NASA was preparing to launch *Voyagers 1* and *2* into space, they called Carl Sagan to head up a special team. The team's job was to devise a means of communicating with extraterrestrials, should the spacecrafts be captured or discovered. The scientists agreed that because of the universal appeal of music, it would be the most effective way of communicating to aliens what humans are all about. The spacecrafts would show our scientific technological side, but music would show our emotional nature. Music from all over the world was recorded and sent aboard the *Voyagers* to explain to others what we are like as human beings.[20]

Why does music affect our emotions so profoundly? The 1990s were dubbed the "decade of the brain" because of the explosion in brain research, which helped us to see and understand the brain as never before. New and interesting data emerged indicating that instead of one brain, we actually have three—one in the head, one in the heart, and one in the gut. Scientific evidence shows that all three brains communicate with one another via a vast network of connections: biochemical (through hormones and neurotransmitters), biophysical (through pressure waves), and neurological (through the transmission of nerve impulses).[21] Although each brain has its specific functions, crossover and linking of duties and purposes can and do occur, particularly in the realm of emotions. For example, the brain in our head contains the cortex, which is responsible for intellectual functions and represents 85 percent of brain mass. The limbic system represents 15 percent of brain mass and is responsible for our emotions. The cortex's primary function is to take past experiences and transform that data into perceptions, thoughts, and, with the help of the limbic system, emotions. On the other hand, the brain in our heart processes information in a more intuitive way, making it open to new possibilities and forever seeking intuitive understanding. Thus the brain in the head "knows," but the brain in the heart "understands."[22]

If we were to appreciate music only from the perspective of the head-brain, or intellect, we would miss a great deal. We would detect the intricate and mathematical patterns of music, but miss the emotions and powerful feelings the music conveys. Music, like truth, is often felt before it is understood. When listening to a piece of music, a person may lack the ability to intellectually articulate the technical nuances of a piece with his or her head-brain, but still fully enjoy and emotionally understand the music with his or her heart-brain. Oftentimes our heart tells us what the mind has yet to understand.

When listening to a piece of music, a person may lack the ability to intellectually articulate the technical nuances of a piece with his or her head-brain, but still fully enjoy and emotionally understand the music with his or her heart-brain. Oftentimes our heart tells us what the mind has yet to understand.

The gut-brain also exudes emotions and feelings. According to Michael D. Gershon, MD, and author of *The Second Brain*, "the ugly gut is more intellectual than the heart and may have a greater capacity for "feeling."[23] Hence, the term "gut-level feeling" is not just an idiom, but a physical reality. Additionally, Gershon found that over 95 percent of the body's serotonin—the neurotransmitter that contributes to emotions of well-being and happiness—is made in the bowel, thus making this part of the body teem with emotions.

Interestingly, the ancient Hebrews understood what we are now scientifically unraveling about the gut. They regarded the bowels or gut as the literal center of feeling and emotion. The ancient prophet Jeremiah, when talking about the feelings of terror that would engulf the inhabitants of Judah as the Babylonian armies descended upon them, said, "My bowels, my bowels! I am pained at the very heart..." (Jeremiah 4:19). Although tragically poetic, he is confirming their time-honored belief that emotions are felt both in the heart and bowels. In our modern English vernacular, it seems odd to use "bowel or gut" to describe feelings or emotions, but the Old English definition of bowels is "inward affection, tender mercy, kindness, benevolence, compassion." Based on this data, it makes perfect sense that one of the reasons humans are so emotionally attached to music is that we feel it throughout our entire being.

Additionally, scientists feel that emotions may be vital to our very survival. Dr. Marian C. Diamond, professor of anatomy at the University of California at Berkeley, found that giving tender loving care to aging rats increased their life span.[24] These results implied that the emotional areas of our three brains are as necessary for the well-being of the individual as the intellectual side—if not more so. The late Dr. Paul MacLean, an American physician and neuroscientist of the National Institute of Mental Health, believed that the emotional side of our makeup is so powerful that it can either facilitate or inhibit learning and higher-order thinking skills.[25]

Because recent studies demonstrate that music seems to involve the brain and the heart at almost every level, music may be the key to providing, in part, this emotional balance. Anne Blood, who conducted studies at McGill University in Montreal, found that the 'neural mechanisms of music may have originally developed as a way of communicating emotion as a precursor to speech, offering insights into how the mind integrates sensory information with emotion and meaning.[26] The research indicates that music and the arts utilize both the emotional and intellectual areas of our brains. All are essential for learning that lasts and—as Diamond found—for our very survival. You simply cannot study music and the arts without feeling joy, happiness, love, tenderness, sorrow, humor, and so on, and when we allow these emotions to be a part of the learning process, our education becomes richer, more meaningful,

You simply cannot study music and the arts without feeling joy, happiness, love, tenderness, sorrow, humor, and so on, and when we allow these emotions to be a part of the learning process, our education becomes richer, more meaningful, and longer lasting, and has greater impact in our lives.

and longer lasting, and has greater impact in our lives. As Diamond suggests, "One without the other is only half an experience."[27]

Mark Jude Tramo, a neurobiologist with the Harvard University Medical School, concurs: "Music is biologically part of human life, just as music is aesthetically part of human life. In short, music is essential to human life."[28] Music has power.

CHAPTER 2

MUSIC AND THE BRAIN: NOTHING IS MINOR ABOUT MUSIC

"If I were not a physicist, I would probably be a musician.
I often think in music. I live my daydreams in music.
I see my life in terms of music."

Albert Einstein

Centuries ago Plato said, "Music is a more potent instrument than any other for education." Today, because of the advancement of technology, we can see more clearly why this statement is true. A growing field known as neuromusicology—the study of how music affects the brain—has advanced significantly in the last thirty years. Scientists have found that music has the ability to train the brain for higher levels of thinking—the kind of thinking involving problem solving, inference, arriving at conclusions, comparing and contrasting the similarities and differences between two or more objects, analyzing, synthesizing, and evaluating information. In 1994, a study found music to be a powerful tool for increasing spatial-temporal reasoning, which is the ability to perceive the visual world accurately and form mental images of objects. In other words, it is the mind's ability to see in very detailed pictures and to recognize, compare, and find relationships among the patterns and details of an object.[1] The temporal element involves children's ability to think ahead. In learning music, one must be able to play a note, then a series of notes, then a series of chords, and be able to look ahead at the music and determine where and what will be played next. Drs. Gordon Shaw and Frances Rauscher, scientists at the University of California at Irvine, conducted the experiment showing a causal link between spatial reasoning and music. They found that college students who listened to Mozart's Sonata in D for Two Pianos, K. 488 for ten minutes prior to taking a spatial IQ test scored eight to nine points higher than students who did not. Although the effect was temporary, the scientists believed that a particular organization of the elements in the music caused the improvement in spatial-temporal reasoning. This phenomenon was dubbed the "Mozart effect."[2]

The scientists wondered, if merely listening to music could cause an increase in spatial-temporal reasoning, could the effect be prolonged by studying a musical instrument? To find out, the researchers tested three-year-olds in a Los Angeles preschool—three-year-olds were chosen because the cortexes of their brains are still maturing.[3] They divided the children into two groups and provided eight months of keyboard and singing lessons to nineteen of the children. Fourteen of the children made up the control group and did not receive any music training. The spatial-temporal reasoning of those in the control group increased by only 6 percent, but those who had received the music training increased their spatial-temporal reasoning by an impressive 46 percent.[4]

Next the researchers took a group of seventy-eight preschool children and divided them into four groups. One group was given private daily piano lessons. A second group had ten minutes of private computer training each day. A third group of children had singing-only lessons; and the last group had no lessons. After six months of training, the four groups were tested. Those in the piano group had the most dramatic improvement in spatial-temporal reasoning—their scores increased by 34 percent.[5]

Again in 1998, the scientists explored how a computer math game called "Spatial-Temporal Animation Reasoning (STAR)" coupled with either piano lessons or English-language training affected students' performance in math. The four-month study focused on 170 second-graders from an elementary school in Los Angeles. One group of children studied the piano keyboard and the math video game, another group received English language training and studied the math video game, and a third group, the control group, had no exposure to these lessons. After four months, both groups of students who had received training in the computer game showed a 100 percent increase in their math skills as compared to the control group. Additionally, the students who had piano keyboarding along with the computer game showed a striking 127 percent increase on questions devoted to fractions and proportional math compared to those students who received training in English language and the math video game. Teachers of the group who studied the keyboard also reported that these students demonstrated better attention and concentration abilities.[6]

In 2003, a study involving thirty-one children found that the children who received keyboard instruction for two years beginning at age three continued to score higher on spatial-temporal and arithmetic tasks two years after the instruction was terminated.[7] They also found that the age at which the children began instruction affected the duration of extramusical cognitive outcomes. It was determined that at least two years of music instruction are required for sustained spatial abilities.[8]

The Importance of Patterns

This research brings up questions: How did the scientists determine there *could* be a link between spatial-temporal reasoning and music? And why is spatial-temporal reasoning important? To understand this link, it is important to realize the significance of patterns. Patterns are found throughout the universe and in the functions of our bodies. We see them in the frequency of lunar eclipses, in the changing of the seasons, in sunspots, in tree rings, in our heartbeat, in hormonal cycles, and in brain waves. Simply put, just about everything in life has connecting patterns. Music has been defined as an ordered *pattern* of sounds.[9] The structural patterns found in music and math are similar; in fact, so similar that the Pythagoreans considered music one of the four branches of mathematics.[10] In the sixth century BC, Pythagoras said, "There is geometry in the humming of the strings. There is music in the spacing of the spheres." Eric Wright, of the Irvine Conservatory of Music, who worked with Shaw and Rauscher, said, "When you look at music, it truly is a mathematical production."[11]

Many of the great composers enjoyed math and understood its pattern relationship to music. Bach loved mathematical structure, patterns, and order, which can be observed most readily in his music. It comes as no surprise that the first music to be put on the computer (an orderly, structured device) was the mathematical music of Bach. Mozart also loved math. Just before his sixth birthday, he discovered math, and "suddenly the house erupted with figures scribbled on every bit of space—wall, floors, tables, and chairs. This passion for mathematics is plainly in close alliance with his great contrapuntal facility."[12] Interestingly, musicologists refer to Mozart's music as a "science" and describe his music as "architectural" because it is built around the same mathematical proportion and elemental structure laws as are found in many famous cathedrals.[13] Confirming the relationship between music and math, neurologist Martha B. Denckla, MD, said, "Music and mathematics are very similar in that both are *par excellence*—when performed well—duets between the two sides of the brain."[14]

Confirming the relationship between music and math, neurologist Martha B. Denckla, MD, said, "Music and mathematics are very similar in that both are par excellence—when performed well—duets between the two sides of the brain."

Likewise, the patterns found in the brain and those found in music are similar. Researchers using data from SQUID—superconducting quantum interference devices, which measure the brain's electrical activity—determined that the arrangement of the tonotopic map in the auditory cortex of the brain is much like that of a piano keyboard, with equal distance between octaves.[15] Tonotopic maps are pathways in the brain and are involved in determining the pitch of a note played on a piano. Studies show that these "maps" are about 25 percent larger in musicians than nonmusicians, demonstrating that musical experiences during childhood influence the development of the auditory cortex.[16] Any activity that develops the auditory cortex is significant for reading ability.

When a child learns to read, he *first* uses his ears—an auditory cortex function—to decipher *how* to say the word. For example, if English is your primary language and I held up the word "apple" in Japanese,

Since music strengthens the auditory cortex, it should logically reinforce the reading process, and research indicates this.

you could look at it with your eyes all day, but you would not know how to pronounce it until I said the word to you. You would be using your *ears first* to understand *how* to say the word. This same process is used when a child first learns to read—ears first, eyes second. Since music strengthens the auditory cortex, it should logically reinforce the reading process, and research indicates this. In 2000, a meta-analysis of a set of twenty-four correlated studies, some involving over five hundred thousand high school students, found a reliable association between music instruction and strong reading test scores.[17] (In statistics, a meta-analysis refers to methods focused on contrasting and combining results from different studies, in the hope of identifying similar patterns.)

Dr. Shaw also found similar patterns in music and the brain. For over twenty-five years, he created computer models that map the mathematical patterns that neurons make when they fire in the brain. He found that the neurons are organized into patterned columns that "talk" to one another by sending out electrical impulses. Shaw and researcher Xiaodan Leng assigned musical tones to each of the columns and found that the brain was organized into what appeared to be musical themes. They then picked a piece of music that most closely resembled the musical themes on the computer model: Mozart's Piano Sonata in D for Two Pianos, K. 448. It was determined that if the music exercised the same brain circuits responsible for spatial reasoning, then spatial reasoning would naturally increase. When they tested the students, that is exactly what happened. The music—with the patterns and themes similar to those found in the brain—increased spatial-temporal reasoning. The results were even more dramatic when the students were given ongoing keyboarding lessons. The research showed that when children study music, patterns in the brain are affected, which has an impact on the way brain circuitry is developed in the first few years of life.[18]

"Music involves structured sequences of patterns," Shaw said.[19] The conclusion—music could enhance brain function. The music lessons led to a sustained improvement in certain spatial skills in young children, suggesting that both functions exercise the same brain circuits. So, as a child learns a musical instrument, he is exercising two functions at once: learning to play a musical instrument and increasing spatial-temporal reasoning skills.

Spatial-temporal reasoning is the kind of reasoning used in higher levels of math and science. Children with strong spatial-temporal reasoning enjoy chess and more abstract advanced mathematics, and have a greater understanding of science. For instance, they understand ratio and proportions better and consequently do better on proportional reasoning tasks. These elements are important in understanding many difficult math and science concepts that are taught in school.[20] Because musical training increases the ability to comprehend higher-level math, science, engineering, and physics concepts, it is considered essential for optimal thinking capabilities.[21]

The skills associated with spatial-temporal reasoning are found in many different professions. They are crucial elements in the worlds of the surgeon, the pilot, the artist, the scientist, and the engineer. Many of these people, because of their ability to visualize, can "see" three-dimensionally, or see the intricate details of an object in their mind. Dr. Ben Carson is one of the top pediatric neurosurgeons in the world. In 1987, he separated the Binder twins, who were joined at the skull. He talks about his ability to see three-dimensionally and how this acute inner vision has increased his capability to understand physical relationships between objects. People say he has "gifted hands" because of his visual abilities. Dr. Carson is also a gifted musician and mathematician.[22]

While flying, many pilots have an innate visual sense of direction, a mental map of where they are, even if they are surrounded by clouds. Artists and architects see and observe in their minds how the elements of space, line, shape, color, patterns, and balance come together to form a completed building or picture. Some people with strong spatial reasoning skills are daydreamers as they think, imagine, create, and invent pictures and ideas in their minds. Some don't necessarily do well in school, either. An example of one such person is found in the following description of a very spatially intelligent and scientific child.

> Once there was a boy who consistently made a poor adjustment to school. In fact, in his senior year of secondary school he got a certificate from his doctor stating that he should leave school for six months. He was not a good all-around student, hated tests and exams, and did not make high grades. He had no school friends and his speech was delayed. Some teachers found him a problem and described him as dull. His father was ashamed of his lack of athletic ability. Who was he? The theoretical physicist and Nobel Prize winner Albert Einstein, whose curiosity and perpetual sense of wonder lasted his whole life.[23]

Einstein was daydreaming—taking a ride through the universe on a beam of light—when he came up with his theory of relativity. It was his acute visual imagination, not his formal training in physics, that led to his discovery of one of the most significant theories of all time.[24] He was also a gifted violinist and felt that music helped him to think and organize his thoughts. Einstein's son, Hans Albert, acknowledged that his father used music to think and solve problems. He said, "Whenever he felt that he had come to the end of the road or faced a difficult challenge in his work, he would take refuge in music and that would solve all his difficulties." A friend of Einstein concurred, "He would often play his violin in his kitchen late at night, improvising melodies while he pondered complicated problems. Then suddenly, in the middle of playing, he would announce excitedly, 'I've got it!' As if by inspiration, the answer to the problem would have come to him in the midst of music."[25]

Historian Eugene Ferguson said, "Pyramids, cathedrals, and rockets exist not because of geometry, theories of structures, or thermodynamics, but because they were first a picture—literally a vision—in the minds of those who built them."[26] We will need visionary thinkers to solve the perplexing problems of the twenty-first century.

Thomas Armstrong, educator and author of *7 Kinds of Smart,* believes spatially intelligent people need to be more valued in society, that their skills and abilities of being able to see things so accurately in the mind's eye will be greatly needed for the challenges of our twenty-first century. He illustrates his point with the story of the space-shuttle disaster, demonstrating the impact spatially intelligent people can have in the world…if listened to. "Apparently, the *Challenger's* poorly designed O-rings failed to remain flexible in cold weather and thus allowed a leakage of fuel that led to the explosion that destroyed the spacecraft. This flaw was spotted by spatially intelligent technicians, but overruled by analytically oriented and politically motivated supervisors who were perhaps less able to visualize the consequences of the problem."[27]

Music for a Scientific Future

The discovery of the correlation between math, music, and spatial-temporal reasoning may have significant ramifications for the twenty-first century. For over twenty years, both the American Mathematical Society and the National Science Foundation have warned that the United States is headed for a shortage of science, technology, engineering, and mathematical (STEM) capability. They predicted that by the year 2010, the shortfall of doctoral-level and professional scientists and engineers would approach one million if current trends persisted.[28] In March 2008, Dr. Duane Cooper, associate professor of mathematics at Morehouse College, stated, "The United States is facing a shortage of American mathematics students in doctoral programs. We're underrepresented across the board in the sciences, engineering, and mathematics. We lose people in mathematics at every level, so by the time we get to the doctoral level, there are just not many of them left."[29] In December 2010, the Information Technology and Innovation Foundation reported that the United States graduated sixty-nine thousand engineers in 2008,

The discovery of the correlation between math, music, and spatial-temporal reasoning may have significant ramifications for the twenty-first century.

but the number of STEM graduates in the United States would need to increase by 20 to 30 percent between 2006 and 2016 to meet the country's projected growth in science and engineering employment alone.[30] In 2011, the US Chamber of Commerce reported that out of concern for our country's ability to "sustain its scientific and technological leadership, a group of fifteen prominent business organizations joined together with the goal of doubling the number of science, technology, and engineering and mathematics graduates with bachelor's degrees by 2015."[31] Today, to meet the current demand for these jobs, our country is forced to outsource to other countries. According to Accenture Institute for High Performance, our country relies heavily on high-skill foreign STEM talent. The United States awards more than 50 percent of engineering and computer science doctorates to foreign students, and many of these students, upon graduation, return home to work because of incentives offered by their own countries.[32] The grim picture: we're not developing enough of our own STEM talent, and foreign students are heading back to their own countries after completing math, science, and engineering degrees from American universities.

To add to the complexity of the issue, here is something interesting to think about: in 2008, the United States graduated sixty-nine thousand engineering majors compared to eighty-eight thousand visual and performing arts majors (a broad definition of visual and performing arts includes music, dance, theater, and painting).[33] If arts graduates are *increasing* despite nationwide school budget cuts to the arts, and STEM majors are *decreasing* despite additional school funding for these programs in some school districts, then what is the missing link(s)? This is an interesting question, and perhaps it can be solved if we consider two issues. First, genetic epistemology—the single most important theory of learning that emerged during the twentieth century. It was posed by Swiss psychologist Jean Piaget several decades ago and has been supported by research in education laboratories throughout the world. The theory basically says that children cannot learn abstract theories—they can only memorize details of the theories—*unless* those theories are preceded by *actual experiences* in their own lives.[34] In other words, if the United States wants more STEM majors, then education in these subjects must start very early, must include consistent hands-on experiences taught by qualified teachers, must continue over many years, and must include parental support and involvement.

Case in point: Shirley Ann Jackson, president of Rensselaer Polytechnic Institute and the first African-American woman to receive a PhD. When she was in elementary school in the 1950s, she would collect bumblebees, yellow jackets, and wasps. She bottled them in mayonnaise jars and tested which flowers they liked best and which species were the most aggressive. She meticulously recorded her findings and observations in a notebook and determined that she could alter their daily rhythms by putting them under the dark porch in the middle of the day. Jackson's parents strongly believed in education and supported her interests. Her father would work with her on science projects and would help her and her sister design and build go-karts. Her mother taught her to read early. She benefited from small classes, access to more resources, consistent and early hands-on learning, and strong teachers who focused on nurturing talent. Jackson went on to study particle and high-energy physics at the Massachusetts Institute of Technology.[35]

Second, when music—as opposed to science and math—is taught in kindergarten through high school, there is a big difference in approach and teaching methodologies. Music naturally follows genetic epistemology because, for the most part, it is an all-encompassing kinesthetic experience, as opposed to science and math, which many times are taught from boring textbooks. Music involves learning to play, experience, enjoy, and fall in love with a musical instrument. A student can touch her instrument, carry it to school, and feel a sense of ownership, whether it is sand blocks, a violin, or a saxophone. And if that experience eventually includes playing in a band or orchestra, she gets to show-off what she has learned in front of a rapt audience. STEM subjects can be taught in similar ways, but it depends on the school, the teacher, the program, and the parents.

For example, in Torrance, California, an after-school science academy, Experium, follows a true genetic epistemology approach. The program offers students in kindergarten through high school hands-on science experiences. Classrooms are filled with state-of-the-art equipment fit for a world-class research institution. The instructors all have advanced degrees in the sciences, and some have doctorates. The ratio of students to teachers never exceeds ten to one. Learning is exciting and includes such things as "a centrifuge for separating DNA components, a bomb calorimeter for measuring the number of calories in food samples, a 'fume hood' for watching dangerous chemical reactions unfold, and a floor-to-ceiling glass terrarium for viewing butterflies, ants, and other insects behaving naturally." The students don lab coats and goggles and dissect night crawlers, sponges, crayfish, squid, and sharks. They examine the brains of sheep, set floating bubbles of methane on fire, hatch chickens, and make biodegradable plastics and environmentally friendly cosmetics from scratch.[36]

Karen Shipherd, co-founder of Experium Science Academy, said that her idea came as a "happy coincidence." She was concerned about the rote aspects of learning and how best to promote critical thinking skills in children. She said, "We wanted to give children the opportunity to really think and think about why and how and what if."[37] At Experium, children use the scientific method of testing and experimenting to find answers to the why, how, and if. Emphasis is on scientific research. One fourteen-year-old student has spent the last eight months testing whether asparagus can inhibit population growth of yeast cells. She spends four days a week working with a mentor at the Experium lab. She is not just reading about scientific research, she is experiencing it firsthand.

Experium Science Academy is a playground for students to explore their curiosity in science and take this inspiration to the next level. Not surprisingly, student enthusiasm for science is high at the academy. The stimulating kinesthetic approach to learning biology, chemistry, microbiology, physiology, genetics, and forensics is working. Hopefully, with continued exposure, the students' love for scientific exploration will persist through college and beyond.

Shirley Ann Jackson fell in love with science and math in a similar way. She was not just reading boring, rote information from a math or science book. Nor was she taught by teachers who knew precious little about these subjects. On the contrary, much like the scientific offerings at Experium, Jackson had consistent kinesthetic experiences in science and math and was supported by dedicated teachers and supportive parents.

Keep in mind that music involvement does not promise to produce more scientists, mathematicians, or engineers. What the research indicates is that learning a musical instrument primes, prepares, and develops the brain in such a way that the child understands STEM subjects more easily, more comprehensively, and more thoroughly. For example, in 2003 it was discovered that nearly 100 percent of the past high school winners of the prestigious Siemens Westinghouse Competition in Math, Science, and Technology play one or more musical instruments. In 2004, as a result of those findings, the Siemens Foundation hosted a recital at Carnegie Hall featuring some of these young people. Afterward, a panel of experts debated the apparent science/music link.[38]

If Piaget is correct and we follow a genetic epistemology approach to teaching STEM subjects along with a comprehensive music education, we just may be able to avert what Jackson and others in the scientific community have called the "quiet crises." These "crises" include the slipping of US student scores on international achievement tests in math and science, failing to prepare young people for STEM careers, and underinvesting in talent and research and development.

Music and Brain Development

An increase in spatial-temporal reasoning is just one of the positive effects that music training has on brain development. Donald Hodges reports that magnetic resonance imaging (MRI) shows that certain areas of the brain—the *planum temporale* and *corpus callosum*—are larger in musicians than in nonmusicians and even more exaggerated for those musicians who started training before age seven. The *planum temporale* plays an important role in language and in early auditory processing. The *corpus callosum* transfers information from one hemisphere of the brain to the other. From this, the researchers concluded that music training can affect brain organization.[39] Neurologist Dr. Gottfried Schlaug of Beth Israel Deaconess Medical Center in Boston found that male musicians have significantly larger brains than men who have not had extensive musical training. He found that the cerebellum, which contains about 70 percent of the brain's neurons, is about 5 percent larger in expert male musicians. Dr. Schlaug believes that the cerebellum grows larger as a result of constant practicing by the musician as he develops those motor skills needed to play an instrument.[40] Dr. Frank Wilson, assistant clinical professor of neurology at the University of California School of Medicine, San Francisco, reports that learning to play an instrument refines the development of the brain and the entire neurological system. It also connects and develops the motor systems of the brain in a way that cannot be done by any other activity. Dr. Wilson believes that learning a musical instrument is vital for the total development of the brain and individual.[41] Another researcher, Dr. Jean Houston of the Foundation for Mind Research, concurs and believes that the brains of children not exposed to music arts education are actually being damaged because these nonverbal modalities help them with skills such as reading, writing, and math.[42]

> *Dr. Frank Wilson, assistant clinical professor of neurology at the University of California School of Medicine, San Francisco, reports that learning to play an instrument refines the development of the brain and the entire neurological system. It also connects and develops the motor systems of the brain in a way that cannot be done by any other activity.*

One of the most remarkable aspects of learning a musical instrument is that both sides of the brain are utilized. Psychologist Dr. Howard Gardner of Harvard University states, "Most musical capacities seem to be represented chiefly in the right hemisphere...but it is far too simple to conclude that music is principally a right-hemisphere function...as an individual becomes more skilled in music, capacities that were initially housed in the right hemisphere are found increasingly in the left hemisphere. It seems as if with musical training, a significant proportion of skills migrate across the *corpus callosum* into the linguistically dominant hemisphere."[43]

Dee Dickinson, former chief executive officer of New Horizons for Learning in Seattle, Washington, cites research showing that when a child listens to classical music, the right hemisphere of the brain is activated, but when a child studies a musical instrument, both left and right hemispheres of the brain "light up." Significantly, the areas of the brain that become activated are the same areas that are involved in analytical and mathematical thinking.[44] Dr. Wilson has cited data from brain-scan research studies performed at the University of California at Los Angeles. These data show that studying music involves more left- and right-brain functions than any other activities studied.[45] Dr. Lawrence Parsons at the University of Texas at San Antonio also found that music involves the entire brain. "We find that harmony, melody, and rhythm had distinct patterns of brain activity. They involved both the right and left sides of the brain," he said.[46] He found that melody affects both sides of the brain equally and that harmony and rhythm predominately activate the left side. The conclusion—music seems to involve the brain at almost every level, and when the entire brain is being utilized, learning is significantly enhanced. Additionally, because learning to play a musical instrument involves daily practice, studies show that coordination, concentration, and memory are heightened, which leads to greater visual and hearing acuity.[47]

Frances Rauscher advises, "It's important to involve children in music, the more the better. If you can't afford music lessons, get them a simple keyboard. If you can't afford a keyboard, sing to them."[48]

Music Enhances Memory

In 1982, at North Texas University, researchers Dr. Barbara Stein, C. A. Hardy, and Herman L. Totten conducted an experiment to see what effect, if any, certain music had on the memorization and retention skills of students. Using the *Water Music*—music that Handel created as a court composer at the request of King George I for his trips down the

Thames River—they tested graduate students' ability to visually learn twenty-five vocabulary words, either in silence or while listening to the *Water Music* being played in the background. The results of the test showed that those students who listened to the music while learning the words did remarkably better than those who learned the words in silence. The researchers believed that utilizing both sides of the brain dramatically increased learning.[49] They also examined elements in the music that could have caused the students to memorize the words more easily. They turned to the work of Georgi Lozanov, a Bulgarian doctor and psychiatrist who extensively studied music and memory. Lozanov found that listening to very specific music with a very specific rhythm, particularly music from the baroque period, caused the rhythms of the body—the heartbeat, the brain waves, and so on—to synchronize themselves to the beat of the music. When the heartbeat slowed down, the mind was able to work more effectively and efficiently. For years, psychologists have claimed that if we relax our body, we will be able to remember better what we study.[50] Lozanov also found that although the music caused the body to relax, the mind remained alert and able to concentrate on very strenuous mental work. With a slower heartbeat and an alert mind, the electromagnetic frequency of the brain changed to approximately 7.5 cycles per second.[51] This frequency is also referred to as the Schumann Resonance, alpha mode, or the range of meditative thought in the brain. Dr. Norio Owaki, a Tokyo researcher, did a ten-year study on specific kinds of sound patterns that can induce alpha brain waves. He found that music and sound could, indeed, change brain wave activity.[52]

In October of 2000, while working on my master's degree, I decided to conduct a parallel study based upon Lozanov's work. The purpose of the study was to explore the use of music in enhancing the absorption, retention, and retrieval of information—all components of memory. I was hoping to demonstrate to parents and educators the important role listening to classical music plays in helping students with verbal memory and learning. Rather than using vocabulary words, like the researchers at North Texas University, I presented a one-hour lecture to different groups of educators. Handel's *Water Music* played quietly in the background.

Pre- and post-lecture tests were given based upon the material from the lecture. The percentage increases between pre-and post-test scores were significant; the lowest increase being 7 percent and the highest being 85 percent. The results of my study and other similar studies seem to indicate that listening to classical music can help to encode information into working long-term memory and make the retrieval of information more readily available. During the learning process, it is essential that students move information from a sensory register to working memory. Many theorists believe that attention plays a key role. Whatever people pay attention to (mentally) moves into working memory.[53] It is critical that students pay attention to information the teacher wants them to learn. Attention is not just a behavior; it is also a mental process. It is not enough that student's eyes and ears are directed toward their classroom material. Their minds must be directed toward it as well. From my study, I found the same thing that other scientists and researchers have theorized: that although music causes the body to relax, the mind remains alert and able to concentrate on very strenuous mental work; that music improves listening skills; and that students listen, focus, and learn better after being relaxed through music.

In 2003, researchers found that children with musical training had significantly better verbal memory than those without music training. Additionally, they found that the longer the training, the better the verbal memory. Ninety boys between the ages of six and fifteen were studied. Forty-five boys were members of their school's string orchestra program and had been taking music lessons for five years. The other forty-five students had no musical training either at home or school. The students with musical training recalled more words in a verbal memory test than did the untrained students, and after a thirty-minute delay the students with

> *In 2003, researchers found that children with musical training had significantly better verbal memory than those without music training. Additionally, they found that the longer the training, the better the verbal memory.*

musical training retained more words than the control group. One year later both the students with musical training and beginners who had just started to learn to play an instrument showed improvement in verbal learning and retention.[54]

As far back as Bach, the effects of certain sound patterns and their ability to cause relaxation and concentration were understood. History relates an interesting story about a series of musical pieces written by Bach that were later used for Count Kayserling, who had constant problems with insomnia. After hearing this music played for a short time, the count was able to relax and felt less tense. These pieces have since been called the *Goldberg Variations*, in honor of the count's friend and musician, Johann Goldberg, who came and played the Bach music each time the count had difficulty relaxing or sleeping.

Try playing classical music as background music while your child is studying or doing other homework. (See the resource section for specific examples) According to the studies, he or she should be able to concentrate, focus, and memorize facts easier. However, don't expect your child to tell you how much easier it is to study with Bach playing in the background. In the beginning, the child may not notice—but you will. Many people have reported remarkable experiences using music from the baroque, classical, and romantic periods while studying. (The musical periods will be discussed in more detail in chapter 10).

Deborah Cave was teaching part time, tutoring, and attending law school. To help herself focus, concentrate, and block out the daily stresses while studying for her law classes, she played in the background music from the baroque period. She felt it made a significant difference in her effectiveness for memorizing and retaining the material. During law school, Deborah took two very difficult take-home exams. Both times, she played Handel's *Water Music* in the background. She states, "When the music stopped, I hit the repeat button. I found that the music was a critical factor in helping me to organize my thoughts." She ended up with the highest grade in the class on the first exam and a 97 percent on the second one, which was the second-highest grade in the class and her highest grade in law school. When she sat down to take the California bar examination, Handel's *Water Music* immediately began playing in her mind. She relaxed instantly and went on to successfully pass the exam on her first try. Deborah firmly believes the music made a significant difference in her ability to absorb, retain, and retrieve information during law school and was an important element in her ability to focus during the bar examination.

Joan Erzer Behrens, who is very organized and focused, was skeptical about whether music could help her. Usually when she listened to music in the background, she would analyze the music instead of concentrating on the task at hand, so she started out by playing the music very softly in the background. In a few days, she noticed that the music did indeed become "background" music, and she was able to focus and concentrate more effectively than ever before.

Lauren Smith was recently divorced, in her fifties, and had gone back to school to complete a master's degree. Overwhelmed by stresses, she was unable to focus on her studies and considered dropping out of school to wait until her life calmed down. Per my suggestion, she began playing Handel's *Water Music* in the background while she studied. Within days, she noticed a remarkable improvement in her ability to absorb, retain, and retrieve the information from her classes.

Even though Georgi Lozanov's research did not include the work of classical composer Franz Schubert, it was precisely the music of Schubert that helped my son Ryan when he was studying school lessons. He tried Lozanov's suggestions from the repertoire of Handel, Haydn, and Bach, but did not notice an increase of concentration or ease in memorization. But when he began playing Schubert, his mind relaxed and he was able to concentrate on his lessons. He particularly enjoyed Schubert's Piano Impromptu in E-flat major, Moment Musical in A-flat major, and Trout Quintet: Tema con variazioni. Today, Ryan is in graduate school, and the music of Schubert continues to be his "best friend" when needing to concentrate and memorize difficult information. Music can and does make a difference.

Through the use of sophisticated equipment, scientists are now able to see how the brain functions as never before. A baby's brain at birth contains one hundred billion neurons, which is as many nerve cells as there are stars in the Milky Way. At birth, the brain contains nearly all the nerve cells it will ever have, but the pattern of wiring between them has not yet stabilized.[55] This wiring depends on the rich sensory experiences the child is exposed to during the early years of life. If a child is deprived of a stimulating environment, the brain will suffer.

Researchers at Baylor College of Medicine have found that children who are not given opportunities to play or who are rarely touched develop brains that are 20 to 30 percent smaller than normal for their age.[56] The opposite can also occur. Researchers at the University of Illinois found that lab animals in an environment of stimulating activities developed 25 percent more synapses per nerve cell and 80 percent more blood vessels to nourish each cell. The conclusion—"rich experiences really do produce rich brains."[57] Scientists now realize that a baby comes into the world primed for stimulating environmental experiences that will shape her intellect and future. These facts have profound implications for parents. Hands-on parenting cannot be underestimated in its effect on young children and their brain development. As parents, we must provide numerous, ongoing, and enriching experiences that will nourish our children's brains. Music is such an experience.

As we have learned, all human beings are born musical and will respond to music. Because classical music, with its complex repetitive patterns, has far-reaching effects on the child and his brain development, it is the *perfect*

> *Hands-on parenting cannot be underestimated in its effect on young children and their brain development. As parents, we must provide numerous, ongoing, and enriching experiences that will nourish our children's brains. Music is such an experience.*

experience. As you read this book, you will learn specific ways to increase children's brain functioning, enlarge their capacity for learning, and profoundly enrich their lives—through classical music.

PART TWO

MUSIC IN THE HOME

CHAPTER 3

*H*OME:
SET THE TONE WITH MUSIC

"If the child is not filled at least once by the life-giving stream of music during the most susceptible period, between his sixth and sixteenth years, it will hardly be of any use to him later on. Often a single experience will open the young soul to music for a whole lifetime."

Zoltán Kodály

I grew up in Salt Lake City, Utah, and was the third of eight children. My life was somewhat void of material possessions, but rich in educational and cultural experiences. Whatever we lacked in worldly possessions, our parents made up for by exposing us to the arts. Music was an integral part of our home and lives. My parents took our family to the opera, ballet, symphonies, and art museums, many of which were free. Libraries were also a frequent destination. Somehow they afforded piano, flute, clarinet, violin, and saxophone lessons for all eight children. I learned to play the familiar childhood tunes of John Thompson on a wonderful old black upright piano that had belonged to my grandparents. I have many fond memories of practicing on that piano and listening to my father playing as he made the instrument come alive for me.

Music was important to my parents because they had grown up with musical experiences afforded by their parents. Their extended families abounded in musical talent, and among them were mandolin players, violinists, pianists, and opera singers. My parents did not get their eight children involved with music because research told them it was going to build "bigger, better brains." My parents never read a study on music. They exposed their children to music simply because they loved music. It was a natural course of events for them to pass on to their children their love for the arts.

One of the musical experiences I remember was the free concerts offered by the Utah Symphony Orchestra. Conductor Maurice Abravanel, a Russian Jew, was responsible for teaching thousands of children to appreciate music and follow proper concert etiquette. I distinctly remember how he would peer out over the audience with searching eyes before beginning the program, looking for anyone who was whispering or walking down the aisles. When he found an offender, he would emphatically point his baton at the person and yell, "Freeze!" The children in the audience learned very quickly to respect the musicians and their music!

My husband, Mark, was fortunate to have had a similar early exposure to music while growing up in San Francisco, California. Today, we both continue to love and enjoy music and the arts. Like the homes we grew up in, our home is also filled with music. When our children were growing up, we took them to concerts, ballets, and operas, thus passing on an important family legacy. Today, our sons are married and are passing the legacy of music and the arts to their children.

Whenever someone starts a new business, analysts say the three most important things to consider are "location, location, location." Likewise, the keys to having your children love and appreciate classical music are "exposure, exposure, exposure." The first exposure to music usually comes from the home—and the good news is that parents do not have to be musicians, or schooled in music, to introduce their children to music.

The first exposure to music usually comes from the home—and the good news is that parents do not have to be musicians, or schooled in music, to introduce their children to music.

Any home can become a musical training center. In this chapter, we will explore many ways to accomplish this with ease and pleasure. With parental help, children can reap many important benefits that come from early musical exposure and training such as early language, reading, and math development, as well as listening, memorization, and thinking skills.

As you begin to expose your children to music, you will find that they have an innate or natural capability for music. Dr. Frank Wilson confirms this and believes there are natural musical qualities that are a part of every human being. He said, "I am convinced that all of us have a biologic guarantee of musicianship. This is true regardless of our age, formal experience with music, or the size and shape of our fingers, lips, or ears...We all have music inside us, and can learn how to get it out, one way or another."[1]

The ideas given in this chapter are not difficult to follow. They do take a little time and effort, but the time you spend exposing your children to music and giving them opportunities to learn a musical instrument becomes a powerful investment in their future. Plus, as you progress in this labor of love, you will witness music's capability to positively affect your children socially, intellectually, physically, and emotionally. Let's begin by exploring different ideas you can use to accomplish this from prebirth through high school.

Prebirth (In Utero)

Glen Gould, the famous concert pianist, reports that his mother played the piano for him constantly while he was developing *in utero*. Sergei Prokofiev, the famous Russian composer who wrote *Peter and the Wolf,* was also exposed to music before he was born. His pregnant mother played the piano every day for him, exposing him to the music of Chopin and Beethoven. When world-famous Canadian conductor Boris Brott was asked when his interest in music began, he stated, "Before birth." His mother, a violist, practiced continually while pregnant with him. Today, scientists agree that a child's music development may start before he is born. Approximately twenty-two days after conception, a little heart begins to beat. This distinct rhythmic beat is similar to the mother's heartbeat and to the rhythmic patterns found in the symphonies of Mozart, Beethoven, and Brahms.[2] As the development of the baby continues, so does the rhythmic fashion in which the baby moves his arms, his legs, and his torso. Already the baby is producing music!

Studies have been done to determine whether the unborn fetus is able to hear sounds coming from outside the uterus. As early as 1925, researcher S. Peiper found that a five-week old fetus responds with sudden movements to loud sounds coming from outside the body of the mother, and by the twenty-fourth week, the fetus listens to sounds all the time.[3] Many pregnant singers report that their babies seem much quieter when they sing. Perhaps the fetus is responding much like the newborn does to his mother when she sings a soothing lullaby. Other mothers report that when they practice a musical instrument, their babies become more active.[4] When I was pregnant with my second and third sons, I was taking piano lessons and practicing daily. The pace of the song I was practicing determined whether or not my baby was calm or active. As newborns, both of my sons responded to music. When the stereo was playing, they would turn their heads in the direction of the music, and it would calm them when they were upset. Orchestral lullabies and soothing vocal music would help them fall sleep.

Over the last twenty years, expectant parents have been encouraged to not only talk and read to their unborn children, but to play classical music and sing to them as well.

Over the last twenty years, expectant parents have been encouraged to not only talk and read to their unborn children, but to play classical music and sing to them as well. When a mother sings and talks to her unborn baby, she is exposing her to the sound and nuances of her voice. Because of this daily exposure to singing, the baby will immediately recognize her mother's voice at birth. To support this, scientists have found that just moments after birth, a baby will turn in the direction of the mother's voice, and by the end of the first week she can identify her mother's voice from a group of female voices (much like the baby emperor penguins talked about in chapter 1).[5]

Today, many fathers are becoming involved in prenatal activities, too. Researcher Sarah Lopez from the University of California, San Diego, found that when fathers use a Pregaphone to talk to their unborn child, they reap big rewards. A Pregaphone is an instrument that has a mouthpiece to talk into, with a trumpet-shaped part that fits on the mother's stomach and can amplify the father's voice. With it, fathers are able to sing and talk to their child in utero. From this simple exercise, newborns recognize the father's voice as quickly as they do the mother's. Lopez calls this phenomenon "father presence."[6] It is not absolutely necessary to use a Pregaphone when communicating with an unborn infant; it is thought that just by singing and talking close to the mother's stomach, the baby will still hear.

Nearly thirty years ago, Rene Van deCarr said that prenatal infants are in a "prenatal university." He instructs parents to expose their prenatal child to music, poetry, and children's literature. He found dramatic developmental differences between those children exposed to music and literature in utero and their siblings who were not.[7]

Donald Shetler, professor emeritus of music education at the Eastman School of Music in New York, found dramatic increases in language development and memory skills in children exposed to music in utero. In the Eastman Pilot Study, headphones were placed directly on the stomachs of the expectant mothers, exposing the fetus to five to ten minutes of both sedating and stimulating music each day. Within four to six weeks after birth, he met with the mother and child to watch and observe the baby. Shelter noted that the most remarkable development was observed in the children between the ages of two and five. Their memory skills were stronger, and their speech patterns were developed earlier with greater articulation, sophistication, and organization than their siblings who were not exposed to music in utero. For example, a two-year old girl in the study was able to sing a thirty-two-measure song with chromatic intervals and key changes. She sang with excellent speech clarity and used expressive dynamics and gestures. Another little girl, not quite two, sang twelve songs from memory and was able to play the piano with independent fingering. She used excellent verbal articulation and expressed herself in complete sentences. A four-year-old boy in the study identified the sounds made by a wide variety of musical instruments that he was hearing for the first time. He played and improvised his own songs on various rhythm instruments. When his mother played different beats on a drum, he was able to imitate them.[8]

The experience we had with our firstborn son, Jason, supports the finding of this research. During this pregnancy, my husband was in graduate school, I was working, and we were living in an apartment. Not having a piano to play, we constantly sang, talked, and read to Jason as he was developing in utero. When he was only five months old, he said his first word; at nine months he was talking and singing in short sentences, and by the age of two he had taught himself to read. He memorized poetry and books with a strong rhythm very quickly. He also loved to sing and dance, and was able to correctly beat out different rhythms on his little drum.

Recent research suggests that babies, after birth, will recognize music that was played to them in utero. In 2001, a study by Dr. Alexandra Lamont from the Music Research Group at the University of Leicester School of Psychology in the United Kingdom, found that babies remember musical sounds they listened to in the womb. At the age of one, the babies still recognized the music they were exposed to three months before birth. This discovery diminishes the theory that babies only remember music exposure in utero for a month or two after birth and suggests that memory can last a great deal longer.[9] In the case of Canadian conductor Boris Brott, his musical memory lasted much longer than a few months. When learning to play new music, he was surprised to find that he already knew the pieces by heart, particularly the viola parts. He credits this ability to his mother's constant playing of the viola for him while in utero. In his book, *The Secret Life of the Unborn Child*, Thomas R. Verny found that the unborn child "can see, hear, experience, taste, and, on a primitive level, even learn in utero."[10]

Although musical studies on babies in utero are continuing, the research suggests that by singing, talking, playing classical music and lullabies, and reading to the unborn child, parents can give them a significant advantage in early language, memory, and music development.

In 2011, psychobiologist Carolyn Granier-Deferre of Paris Descartes University also found that babies can remember melodies heard in the womb. Scientists played music to fifty mothers three weeks before the birth of their babies and tested the babies one month after they were born. The babies' heart rates slowed at a greater rate when they heard the familiar melody, in comparison to a melody they had not heard in the womb. Based on these results, scientists understand better the effects of musical sounds heard in the womb, including how babies learn to perceive speech.[11]

Although musical studies on babies in utero are continuing, the research suggests that by singing, talking, playing classical music and lullabies, and reading to the unborn child, parents can give them a significant advantage in early language, memory, and music development.

MUSICAL EXPERIENCES FOR YOUR UNBORN CHILD:

- PLAY MUSIC EACH DAY: If you play a musical instrument, play it each day for your unborn baby for thirty minutes to an hour.

- HEADPHONES ARE OPTIONAL: If you have headphones, you may want to place them on your stomach during pregnancy and play ten minutes or more of classical music that is both calming and stimulating (see resource section for suggestions). Shelter found when mothers played stimulating music, their babies responded with sharp, rapid, or agitated movements. When the mothers played sedative music, the babies responded with rolling or soft motor movements. But, based on what other scientists have found, it is not necessary to use headphones because your child will hear the music regardless. My concern with headphones is getting the decibel level correct—what is too loud to us will be the same for your unborn child.

- DEVELOPMENT OF SPATIAL-TEMPORAL REASONING IN UTERO: In the car, at work, and at home, play the music of Mozart and other composers for your unborn child. Studies indicate it may increase their spatial-temporal reasoning, even in utero. In 1998, Dr. Frances H. Rauscher found that rats exposed to Mozart's Sonata (K. 448) in utero plus sixty days postpartum performed better in a maze learning environment than rats exposed to white noise, minimalist music, or silence. The rats were tested for five days in a T-maze, and by day three the rats exposed to Mozart in utero completed the maze more quickly and with fewer errors than the other rats. By day five the rats that listened to Mozart continued to outshine the other rats. The researchers believe that the patterns within the music can influence or rewire an animal's internal neural network.[12]

- SING TO YOUR UNBORN CHILD: You may not have an operatic voice, but your child doesn't care...to him you have the most beautiful voice in the world.

- PACK YOUR HOSPITAL BAGS WITH CLASSICAL MUSIC: Take classical music to the hospital to play while your baby is being born. It makes for a very relaxing, peaceful atmosphere for both mother and baby.

Infants (Premature Babies)

The definition of a "preterm" baby is birth before thirty-seven complete weeks of gestational age. A "premature" baby is one that has not yet reached the level of fetal development that allows for life outside the womb. Although both can have serious health issues, premature babies are especially fragile. Between weeks thirty-four and thirty-seven, several organ systems are maturing. One of the main organs affected by premature birth is the lungs. They are one of the last organs to develop in the womb, and because of this premature babies typically spend the first few weeks on a ventilator. Another hurdle facing the premature infant is his or her neurological inability to coordinate a suck/swallow/breathe response for oral feeding. Research to help these infants is ongoing because the effects of premature birth can be long lasting. Many of these babies grow up healthy, but many others suffer from disabilities, such as learning issues, chronic lung disease, vision and hearing problems, and even cerebral palsy. Unfortunately, premature birth rates are on the rise; between 1990 and 2006 there was an increase of more than 20 percent.

Interesting studies have been done to show that music—particularly classical music—can and does help these infants. In 2003, Jayne Standley, Florida State's Robert O. Lawton Distinguished Professor of Music Therapy, invented a device known as the Pacifier Activated Lullaby (PAL). It is a medical device that uses musical lullabies to help premature babies overcome the coordination required to suck, swallow and breathe. "Unlike full-term infants, very premature babies come into the world lacking the neurologic ability to coordinate a suck/swallow/breathe response for oral feeding," said Standley. She adds, "The longer it takes them to learn this essential skill, the further behind in the growth process they fall. PAL uses musical lullaby reinforcement to speed this process up, helping them feed sooner and leave the hospital sooner."

PAL works like this: it is a specially wired pacifier and speaker that provide musical reinforcement every time a baby sucks on it correctly. Since the musical lullabies are gentle and soothing to the infant, she will continue sucking so she can hear more of the music. Extensive clinical studies have been conducted at the following university hospitals: Tallahassee Memorial Hospital (TMH), University of Georgia Hospital in Athens, University of North Carolina Medical Center in Chapel Hill, and Women's and Children's Hospital in Baton Rouge, Louisiana. The studies have shown that infants will increase their sucking rates up to two and a half times more than infants not exposed to the musical reinforcement. Additionally the babies eat sooner, tolerate their feedings better, and are able to leave the hospital earlier. PAL has undergone extensive testing, has received a United States patent, and has been approved by the Food and Drug Administration.[13]

A study in Israel found Mozart's music to have a positive effect on premature babies. At the Neonatology and Pediatrics departments at Tel Aviv Sourasky Medical Center, medical researchers found

At the Neonatology and Pediatrics departments at Tel Aviv Sourasky Medical Center, medical researchers found that playing just thirty minutes a day of Mozart can help premature babies gain weight.

that playing just thirty minutes a day of Mozart can help premature babies gain weight. Dr. Dror Mandel and his colleagues found that when preemies listened to the music of Mozart, the amount of energy the babies expended was lowered. This means they were able to gain weight faster and, as a result, go home sooner.[14] Considering the enormous costs of caring for premature babies—in the United States, more than $26 billion a year, or $51,600 per preemie—this may have significant ramifications.[15]

Last, it has been suggested that music may reduce pain during circumcision and other medical procedures in premature babies. In 2001, a study conducted in the United States found that playing lullabies and nursery rhymes lowered pain levels in preemies. The babies' heart rates and oxygen saturation were measured using pain scales that gauged behavioral responses. Based on these scales, the babies who listened to the lullabies and nursery rhymes tolerated the procedures better.[16]

MUSICAL EXPERIENCES FOR YOUR PREMATURE OR PRETERM BABY

Although musical experiences are limited because of the delicate condition of preemies, there are still musical activities you can do.

- INFANT MASSAGE USING CLASSICAL MUSIC: Infant massage—also referred to as tactile/kinesthetic stimulation—includes various techniques for massaging the premature baby. Most of the data on the positive effects of infant massage come from studies on premature infants. The research indicates that 72 percent of massaged premature infants are positively affected. Most of these infants experienced greater weight gain and better performance on developmental tasks.[17] If you would like to learn infant massage for your premature baby or full-term baby, I highly recommend the International Loving Touch Foundation (ILTF). Also, include soothing classical music and lullabies to maximize your baby's experience. (See resource section for suggestions.)

- CLASSICAL MUSIC IN THE NEONATAL INTENSIVE CARE NURSERY: Take classical music and lullabies to the hospital for your baby to enjoy and relax with, especially when he has to undergo painful medical procedures such as circumcision, taking blood, inserting feeding tubes, and so forth. As the research indicates, it should help.

- AVOID SENSORY OVERLOAD: A neonatal intensive care unit by definition is an experience in sensory overload for the preemie. They are bombarded with buzzing machines, alarms going off, chatter of people, bright lights, and periodic adverse touch. Add sensory defensiveness—a tendency to react negatively and intensely to sensory stimuli that most babies consider nonirritating—and it's no wonder they make jerking movements, are restless throughout the day, and experience end-of-the-day fussiness. One researcher, after placing little earmuffs on a group of preemies, noticed that the babies breathed in more oxygen, breathed more slowly, slept longer and in a more quiet state, and appeared more relaxed and calm.[18] Like the earmuffs, classical music that includes soothing lullabies can help calm and pacify the infant. However, playing music all day long it not advisable unless it blocks out the white noise of the hospital or if you notice a positive difference in how your baby responds. For some preemies, a quiet environment supplied by earmuffs is best, but for others playing soothing lullabies or peaceful classical music is more calming. Bottom line—be observant to your baby's needs.

Infants (Birth to Age Two)

In the late nineteenth and early twentieth centuries, orphanages for babies were called foundling homes. The death rate in these homes was nearly 100 percent. Although the children received enough food, and the shelter and clothing were adequate, they still continued to die. When a baby came into the home, the caretakers would enter "condition hopeless" into the records, knowing all too well that eventually the baby would die. This condition became so prevalent that it was even given a name: "marasmus," a Greek word meaning "wasting away." No one could find the cure because they were unable to trace the cause of the malady. Then, quite by accident, both cause and cure were discovered. An elderly woman was hired in a German foundling home. Each day this loving woman went from child to child, holding them, talking to them, singing lullabies, and caressing them. Miraculously, the babies began to thrive. It was then that the authorities realized that these infants had been dying from a lack of love. Researchers now know that a baby less than one year old will die without enough love.[19]

Mothers throughout the ages have communicated love and warmth to their infant child through the singing of lullabies and songs, and through talking and touching. These simple activities also give the baby a feeling of security and protection. The late Peter Ostwald, professor of psychiatry at the University of California, San Francisco, found music to be a strong conveyer of love and security between mother and baby. In his research, he noticed that infants respond positively to the musical qualities of their mothers' voices. When the mothers sang lullabies to their babies, it signaled to the baby that it was safe to go to sleep. Ostwald also found that infants who are sung to by their parents will have a much stronger emotional bond to them.[20] More than forty years have passed since my husband's German grandmother sang lullabies to him as he slumbered. He was just a toddler, yet he clearly remembers the sound of her voice, the German language she spoke, and her hands gently rubbing his back as he drifted safely off to sleep.

Although mothers all over the world sing lullabies to their babies, the lullaby format can be very different from culture to culture. They do not necessarily need to be soft and soothing for a child to go to sleep or to feel secure. John Baily, an emeritus professor of ethnomusicology, Goldsmith College, University of London, and his wife, Veronica Doubleday, found

Whether the lullaby is soft and soothing or vigorous and highly rhythmic, singing regularly to your baby has significance in terms of early language development.

when studying the music systems in Afghanistan that even though lullabies are the first musical experience that Herati children are exposed to, the form is much different than lullabies sung in the United States. Women swaddle their babies as they *vigorously* rock them to sleep in their cradles. Instead of the lullaby being soft and lilting, these songs consist of highly rhythmic sounds and repeat the phrase "Allā Huwa," or "He is God."[21]

Whether the lullaby is soft and soothing or vigorous and highly rhythmic, singing regularly to your baby has significance in terms of early language development. Language occurs as a gradual process. First, the baby in utero moves in a rhythmic motion, much like the rhythms and cadences found in speech. After birth, a baby hears and responds to the musical tones of the mother's voice as she communicates with her tiny infant. "Motherese" is a term that some psychologists use to describe the speech patterns a mother uses when she talks to her baby. It is a highly rhythmic musical jargon between parent and baby and not only strengthens the child emotionally, but helps with his budding language development.[22] As a mother pats and sings to her infant, he will wave his arms and kick his legs in rhythm to the mother's voice. As a mother coos and talks to her baby, the infant will respond with noises and coos similar to the mother. Researchers have found that babies less than six months old are actually able to "sing" back pitches and simple melodies sung to them.[23] Patricia Kuhl, a professor of speech and hearing sciences and co-director of the Institute for Brain and Learning Sciences at the University of Washington in Seattle, discovered this to be true in a study that she and her colleagues completed. They found that the mother's singsong melodious cadence with fluctuating pitches is nature's way of teaching the beginning of language to the receptive infant.[24] Remarkably, studies have also found that babies as young as four months can recognize out-of-tune notes and changes in melodies, all of which adds to early language development.[25] Dr. Robert Garfias, professor of anthropology at the University of California at Irvine, believes music can have a tremendous impact on language development in children. Through research, he has found that music and language are inseparably linked as a single system in the brain. This system is acquired in the earliest stages of infancy and continues as the child processes the sounds of human voices around him.[26] Additionally, singing songs to infants may influence how quickly the child later learns math and languages. The late Eric Oddleifson, former chairman for the Center of the Arts in the

Basic Curriculum (now known as Arts Learning at Walnut Hill School), talks about a Japanese master mathematics teacher whose almost two million students have demonstrated math abilities beyond their years. The teacher was asked, "What would you say is the most effective way of heightening children's mental ability at the earliest possible stages?" He answered, "The finest start for infants is to sing songs. This helps to elevate their powers of understanding, and they register astounding speed in learning math and languages."[27]

MUSICAL EXPERIENCES FOR YOUR INFANT (BIRTH TO AGE TWO)

- CONTINUE SINGING: Sing or play songs to your newborn as often as possible throughout the day, especially while you are bathing, dressing, and feeding him.

- NIGHT MUSIC: At night, play soothing classical music or vocal lullabies as he falls asleep. Choose a variety and watch and see which ones your child prefers (see resource section).

- MUSICAL GAMES: Play musical games and fingerplays. Clap the beat as you sing, and take his hands and clap the beats along with him. He will be able to pick up the rhythm very quickly. There are many wonderful fingerplays—*Where is Thumbkin; The Farmer in the Dell; The Brave Old Duke of York; The Wheels on the Bus; Trot, Trot to Boston; Where is the Beehive,* and so on.

- INVEST IN MUSIC TOYS: Purchase age-appropriate musical toys and rhythm instruments. Xylophones, bells, and rattles are wonderful beginning instruments.

- SING UP THE SCALE: As you sing to your child, vary the tempo, the pitch, the softness, and the loudness. Make your voice go up and down from low sounds to high sounds.

- MUSIC MIMICRY: Encourage him to mimic the musical sounds and songs you sing to him. The Papouseks, developmental researchers from West Germany, found that infants as young as two months old were able to imitate the pitch and intensity of the songs their parents sang to them.[28]

- MUSIC IN THE COMMUNITY: Expose him to age appropriate musical experiences and classes offered in the community.

- MAKE MUSICAL HISTORY: Videotape your musical experiences together, no matter how insignificant they may seem. Later, your children will love watching themselves creating music as infants.

- *BABY EINSTEIN* SERIES: A compilation of wonderful DVDs to play for your child (ages one month to thirty-six months) is the *Baby Einstein* series, which includes *Baby Mozart, Baby Bach, Baby Beethoven*, and so forth. Originally these DVDs were developed by Julie Clark, a former teacher in Colorado, but are now part of the Disney Corporation. The DVDs combines color, shape, texture, and the music of Mozart, Bach, Beethoven, and so forth to create a dazzling visual and audio experience for your young child. This DVD series is a *must* for babies! (See resource section.)

Preschoolers (Ages Two to Five)

Research indicates that music continues to have a powerful influence on a preschooler's language development, as well as his motor, listening, and memory skills. Sally Rogers, assistant professor of psychiatry at the University of Colorado Health Sciences Center, believes that giving your preschool child a chance to

Research indicates that music continues to have a powerful influence on a preschooler's language development, as well as his motor, listening, and memory skills.

experience a wide variety of musical activities can enhance his learning of language—which develops rapidly between the ages of fifteen months and three years—and at the same time teach him valuable motor skills.[29] As a child learns to clap to the beat of the music, or as he uses triangles, blocks, and sticks to beat out the rhythms, or as he marches to different cadences, his physical coordination, his timing, and his thinking develop, according to Dr. Carla Hannaford, author of *Smart Moves*. She states, "Movement is an indispensable part of learning and thinking."[30] He will also gain memory skills as he learns to sing a variety of songs with different rhythms. Aural, or listening skills will be developed as he listens to the varying pitch, rhythm, and harmony of a multitude of songs, and various pieces of music. Dancing to the music, marching, singing, whistling melodies, humming tunes, and playing musical games with other children all boost the child's growing language, listening, and motor skills. "These early musical experiences can help children develop physical coordination, timing, memory, visual, [listening], and language skills," confirms Dr. Frank Wilson. "When they work to increase their command of music and exercise musical skills in the company of others, they gain important experience with self-paced learning, mental concentration, and a heightened personal and social awareness."[31]

Preschoolers can also develop early math abilities when learning a keyboard instrument. Drs. Frances Rauscher and Gordon Shaw found that preschoolers who had eight months of keyboard lessons had a greater ability to work mazes, draw geometric figures, and copy patterns of two color blocks—all important spatial skills that later help with higher forms of math. "If you're working with little kids," says Shaw, "you're not going to teach them higher mathematics or chess. But they are interested in and can process music."[32] Clearly, early music education offers a pleasurable and effective way to prepare a child for the learning tasks of school.

MUSICAL EXPERIENCES FOR YOUR PRESCHOOLER (AGES TWO TO FIVE)

- PRESS FORWARD: Continue with all the musical activities previously mentioned.

- PURCHASE RHYTHM INSTRUMENTS: Provide all kinds of rhythm instruments for your child to experiment and play with. Making rhythm instruments with your child can be a fun and creative experience, but keep in mind that rhythm instruments that are purchased will have a much better tone quality to them. These pure sounds are important for your child to hear and experience.

- INVEST IN EQUIPMENT: Purchase age-appropriate CD players, CDs, and/or MP3 downloads, and teach your child how to use them. Let your child start her own classical music collection. Also, use your local library as a resource to borrow CDs.

- GET CREATIVE: Give children scarves, feathers, or ribbons, turn on classical music, and let them dance, sing, and improvise to the music.

- CLAPPING AND RHYTHM GAMES: Play clapping games to see if they can match a variety of simple and complex rhythms.

- RHYME AND READ: Read to and help your child memorize all kinds of poems and Mother Goose rhymes that have a strong musical rhythm.

- READ MUSIC BOOKS: Read stories about great composers, instruments of the orchestra, and general music books—*The Nutcracker, The Magic of Mozart,* and so on. (See resource section for more suggestions.)

- MARCHING MUSIC: Play marches in the morning as your child is getting ready for the day. She will enjoy marching to the bath, to dress, or to eat.

The strong rhythmic beat will help her accomplish these tasks with ease, as well as keeping her focused on the task at hand.

- ABSOLUTE MUSIC MUSTS: Play music for your child throughout the day. "Absolute musts" include:
  Saint-Saens: *Carnival of the Animals*
  Prokofiev: *Peter and the Wolf*
  Britten*: The Young Person's Guide to the Orchestra.*
  Tchaikovsky: *Nutcracker*
  Dukas*: The Sorcerer's Apprentice*

- A LITTLE NIGHT MUSIC: Play classical music while your child is going to sleep at night and when she's getting up in the morning. A favorite is the "Classical Kids" series that include recordings such as "Mr. Beethoven Lives Upstairs" or "Mozart's Magnificent Voyage." (See resource section for list.)

- A GREAT MUSICAL SERIES: Another excellent series to play at night and in the morning is called "The Musical Lives of the Great Composers," with A. A. Hannes as the narrator and the Vienna Symphony Orchestra. This series gives interesting facts and stories about the composer, as well as playing a variety of music written by the composer. (See resource section.)

- GROUP MUSIC LESSONS: Enroll your child in group music classes, appropriate for her age and development.

Elementary (Ages Five to Twelve)

By the time children enter kindergarten, they start the momentous task of learning to read. Prior to entering kindergarten and while in kindergarten, exposure to music can help with this task and make it significantly easier. An explanation of how this happens will make the connection clear. As children memorize the lilting tunes of Mother Goose rhymes, use rhythm instruments, and play musical games and fingerplays, they are learning about the patterns that formulate the sounds, rhythm, and blending of syllables that make up words. This is a one-skill learning pattern necessary for beginning readers. In her book *Endangered Minds,* Jane Healy confirmed the importance of early rhymes and music when she said, "Reading specialists tell us children's ability to discriminate and create rhyming words, as well as their sense of rhythm, are closely related to early reading ability. A child who has absorbed over and over—through the *ears,* not the eyes—such common word parts as 'fun, sun, run,' or 'fiddle, diddle, middle' as well as the *melody* of their language is statistically destined to have an easier time learning to read."[33]

> *As children memorize the lilting tunes of Mother Goose rhymes, use rhythm instruments, and play musical games and fingerplays, they are learning about the patterns that formulate the sounds, rhythm, and blending of syllables that make up words.*

Before your child enters kindergarten, exposing him daily to a variety of songs and Mother Goose rhymes will make the evolution of reading easier for him. Once he is in kindergarten, continue teaching him songs with a strong rhythm. The *Alphabet Operetta,* by Mindy Manley Little, is wonderful; uses alliteration (the repetition of usually initial consonant sounds in two or more neighboring words or syllables); is fun for the child to sing along with; and is a great way to learn the sounds of letters, syllables, and words. Frequently reading poetry that has a clear musical rhyme is also helpful to children's language and reading skills. Hearing the combination of sounds, syllables, and rhyme further enhances reading ability. The poetry of Jack Prelutsky is an excellent example. It is not only filled with humor, but has wonderful rhyming words and phrases, too. Try "singing" his poetry and you will be amazed at how quickly your child is able to memorize twenty or thirty lines of poetry as music, rhyme, and language come together. "Bleezer's Ice Cream," from *The New Kid on the Block,* is a great Prelutsky poem, and children immediately hear and *feel* its strong rhythm—"Cocoa Mocha Macaroni, Tapioca Smoked Baloney, Checkerberry Cheddar Chew" are some of the delightful rhyming word combinations.

While your child is in elementary school, have her memorize a fun poem and song each week. Choose poems and songs that have a well-defined rhyme, such as *I Point to Myself*, *Itisket, Itasket*; and *Little Rabbit Foo Foo*. You will start an educational (and fun-filled) tradition in your home, as well as increase your child's reading, language, vocabulary, and memorization skills. These exercises will also confirm to you the power that music has in developing those skills necessary for language and reading. Dr. Hannaford believes that the most natural way for children to learn when they are starting school is through "image, emotion, and spontaneous movement," all of which are found in these simple and fun musical activities.[34]

Elementary age children are great imitators. If they see their parents listening to classical music, they will want to listen to it. Parents can also lead the way by reading books to their children about classical composers and musicians, taking them to local concerts, or playing musical games with them. These activities will have a significant influence on their attitude toward music, particularly classical music. They will grow up knowing that good music should be a part of their life and that it makes life more rewarding and interesting. In homes all over the world where music has a significant, long-lasting impact on the child, the parents are active participants. In Afghanistan, for example, children born into musical homes are exposed to the sounds of music and encouraged to engage in musical activities at a very early age. The parents set the example by taking the children to musical celebrations where the parents themselves are involved playing musical instruments. In these settings, the child is given access to musical instruments and opportunities to observe his parents' and older siblings' musical skills. It is through imitation and experimentation that young Afghan boys and girls learn to play an instrument. These children grow up believing that music is what life is all about.[35] Parents in every part of the globe can have the same influence on their child. Example and parent participation speak volumes to the child. Musical involvement by the parent starts a cycle that can repeat itself for generations, bringing enjoyment and pleasure into the lives of countless family members.

> *Elementary age children are great imitators. If they see their parents listening to classical music, they will want to listen to it.*

It is usually sometime in the elementary years that children begin private music lessons. (In the next chapter, we will discuss how to choose an instrument and teacher.) This is a big step as far as the commitment required from both child and parent. Realizing that learning a musical instrument is valuable to the child in multiple ways will make this commitment easier. When a child learns a musical instrument, most of his senses are being utilized. For example, a child learning the piano is using his eyes to read the music, his ears to hear the correct notes, his hands to play the notes, and his feet to coordinate and play the pedals. All of this requires a level of concentration, memory skills, motor coordination, and symbol recognition. Both sides of the brain, as well as the front and back portions of the brain, are being used to accomplish this incredible feat. Not only is the child experiencing the enjoyment that comes from learning a musical instrument, he is also learning skills that will help him succeed in school and beyond.

MUSICAL EXPERIENCES FOR YOUR ELEMENTARY AGE CHILD (AGE FIVE TO TWELVE)

- PRESS FORWARD: Continue with all of the musical ideas previously suggested, making them age appropriate.

- SING YOUR POETRY: To help your child with his reading skills in the early elementary years, continue to sing and memorize songs and poetry with a strong rhythm and rhyme. Besides the poetry of Jack Prelutsky, check Tom Glazer's songbooks, *Eye Winker, Tom Tinker, Chin Chopper,* and *Do Your Ears Hang Low?*

- MORE MUSICAL GAMES: Play musical games with your child involving math, spelling, and reading. Young children learn their ABCs faster when singing the ABC song. As you drill your child on his math facts, sing the facts to a rhythm. He will learn them much faster and with greater ease. Fifth-graders can learn all fifty of the United States more quickly and easily when they learn the song "Fifty Nifty United States." Kathleen Carroll, a former science teacher in Washington, DC, developed a CD called *Sing a Song of Science,* which helps students learn science material. She developed the CD after watching her students respond to a little jingle she had made up about matter. She noticed the children writing down the jingle in their notebooks (a first!) and then coming back to school the next day singing it. Carroll knew she was on to a very positive learning experience for her students and, as a result, developed this CD. By using this CD at home, your child will learn many interesting things about science that he or she can then share at school. (See resource section.)

- Name that tune: While driving in the car, play musical guessing games. Call it "Name That Tune" (after the popular TV show). Use either the classical music station on the radio or a classical CD that you can play in your car. Try to identify the piece of music, the composer, and what period the music was written: baroque, classical, romantic, or twentieth century. Some wonderful CDs to help your child recognize musical periods and the composers of those periods are *Mozart TV, Bibbidi Bobbidi Bach,* or *Heigh Ho! Mozart.*

- Recognize instruments of the orchestra: Play guessing games that require recognizing the different instruments of the orchestra. Once your child knows them by their individual sound, have him or her try to categorize them into their correct "family," such as the strings, woodwinds, percussion, and brass. Listen many times to *The Young Person's Guide to the Orchestra* to become familiar with each instrument's distinct sound. You will be amazed how your child's listening skills will improve by playing this simple game.

- More games: Play the game "Twenty Questions." Possible categories include musicians, composers, or instruments of the orchestra.

- Private lessons: Continue with your child's group music lessons until you decide to enroll him in private lessons. Although every child is different, a good time to begin private lessons is between the ages of three and eight.

- SHARE MUSICAL EXPERIENCES: Invite someone from your neighborhood who is taking music lessons to come to your home and share a piece of music or a song with your child.

- SUPPORT YOUR MUSIC COMMUNITY: Take your child to age-appropriate symphonies, musicals, ballets, or chamber orchestras. (See chapter 10 for more information.)

- WATCH MUSIC DVDs: Rent DVDs about music and musicians and watch them together as a family. Examples: *Mr. Beethoven Lives Upstairs, Amadeus, Mr. Holland's Opus.*

- TALENT SHOWS: Organize a yearly talent show in the neighborhood. It should be a low key, noncompetitive get-together where the kids on the block can have fun just sharing their talents. Who knows, this may encourage others in the neighborhood to work at developing their talents. Don't forget to videotape these events for future memories.

- MUSIC AND HOMEWORK: As children are doing their homework, play music from the baroque or classical periods in the background. As research suggests, the music will help with concentration, absorption, and organization of information. We call this our "study music," and some favorites include Handel's *Water Music,* the *Mozart for Your Mind* CD, and any of Bach's *Brandenburg Concertos.* (See resource section.)

- THE POWER OF PRAISE: Compliment your child for all of his musical efforts.

Junior and Senior High School (Ages Twelve to Eighteen)

Academic Preparation for College: What Students Need to Know and Be Able to Do is a handbook published by the College Board to help high school students prepare for college. It states, "Preparation in the arts will be valuable to college entrants whatever their intended field of study. The actual practice of the arts can engage the imagination, foster flexible ways of thinking, develop disciplined effort, and build self-confidence."

By the time your child is entering junior and senior high school, competition for her time becomes more intense, but do not let her give up her music. Remember, keeping your child involved in music is an investment in her future. You may rationalize, "OK, Jenny has had a few years of piano lessons. It's been good for her, but now life is going to get very busy with school, sports, and other activities. She won't have time to practice, and I'm not going to waste money on unprepared lessons. Besides, she's not going to be a concert pianist. I guess it's time to quit." Wrong! Children don't have to become concert pianists to gain the lasting benefits that come from continuous study of a musical instrument. Today, as well as in years past, parents understand the importance of their children furthering their education by going to college, but the competition is getting more and more difficult. It is a well-documented fact that students involved in music do better in school. They are more responsible, dependable, and have a greater degree of self-discipline. They tend to be far more creative and innovative, and their critical-thinking skills are considerably more advanced. Additionally, the College Entrance Examination Board has found that students involved in the arts continue to outperform their non-arts peers on their SATs (Scholastic Achievement Tests). The accumulation of data is ongoing, but from 2006 through 2010 students enrolled in fine arts courses scored between 11 and 13 percent higher on the SAT.[36]

In Texas, a five-year study revealed that Texas All-State musicians scored 22 percent higher than the national average and 25 percent higher than the Texas average on the SAT.[37] In terms of standardized tests, students in high quality school music programs (particularly top-quality instrumental

> *By the time your child is entering junior and senior high school, competition for her time becomes more intense, but do not let her give up her music. Remember, keeping your child involved in music is an investment in her future.*

programs) have higher math and English scores in comparison to students in schools with deficient music programs. And this is regardless of the socioeconomic level of the school or school district.[38] Last, schools that have music programs also have significantly higher student attendance rates and higher graduation rate than those schools without music programs—90.2 percent as compared to 72.9 percent—*and* lower dropout rates.[39]

All of these reasons, plus others that will be discussed later, should be sufficient motivation for parents to keep their children actively involved in music throughout their high school years. Their chances for making a lifelong commitment to music will be stronger if they continue with it during the high school years. Recall that Dr. Wilson believes *all* children are born with an innate musical nature, and with nurturing it can blossom, giving enjoyment and satisfaction their entire life. I repeatedly told my children, "When you're eighty years old you're not going to be out kicking a soccer ball, but when you are eighty you can still enjoy music and play an instrument." My father is proof of that. When he turned eighty, he was still playing the piano and finding enjoyment from his music.

MUSICAL EXPERIENCES FOR YOUR JUNIOR AND SENIOR HIGH SCHOOL STUDENT (AGES TWELVE TO EIGHTEEN)

- THE POWER OF EXAMPLE: Encourage older children to be an example to younger siblings in regard to practicing their instruments. After seeing the movie *Shine*, my son Ryan (who was sixteen at the time) became very enthusiastic about his music. He wanted to play more difficult pieces and, as a result, began to practice more. His enthusiasm was electrifying to his younger brothers. They followed his example and began practicing more and asking their piano teacher for more difficult pieces. Pretty soon, the three of them were fighting over practicing time on the piano. Example is powerful.

- ATTEND MUSIC CONCERTS: Take your child to more sophisticated concerts. Check the local newspaper and community and local colleges for a variety of choices. If possible, arrange for a backstage tour. If it is an opera or a musical, children will gain much more from the experience if they understand some of the details that make the actual performance seem flawless. (More on this in chapter 10.)

- MEET THE COMPOSER: If possible, arrange for your child to meet with a real composer. Network with other parents and on the Internet to find composers in your area. See if they are child friendly and would welcome the opportunity to meet and encourage another budding musician.

- GIVE GIFTS OF MUSIC: For holidays and other special occasions give musical gifts—subscriptions to concerts, plays, symphonies. Encourage grandparents to give tickets to a symphony or musicals.

- FAMILY MUSIC RECITALS: Hold family music recitals and invite the grandparents and any other extended family. It will give your child a chance to "show off" in front of family and friends in a nonthreatening environment.

- COMPOSER HALL OF FAME: Start a "Hall of Fame" in your home with either miniature statues or pictures of famous composers. Talk regularly about the greatness and strength of these men and women and their dedication to the arts. As a family, choose a composer each week and enjoy an evening together listening to his or her music and discussing interesting facts about his or her life. Thomas Carlyle said in his book *Heroes and Hero Worship,* "Great men taken up in any way are profitable company, for we cannot so much as look upon a great man without gaining something from him."

The ideas presented here can be your guide to making your home a musical training center, and your consistency in implementing them will ensure its success. No matter the ages of your children, you can start now to build musical traditions in your family. You will find that these traditions will become valuable treasures that can be passed down from generation to generation.

CHAPTER 4

$\mathscr{M}$AKING SOUND CHOICES:
CHOOSING AN INSTRUMENT
AND TEACHER

*"Musical training is a more potent instrument than
any other for education."*

Plato

In 2003, a survey conducted by The Gallup Organization found that
54 percent of all United States households had a member that played
a musical instrument and that 48 percent of those instrument-playing
households had at least one additional player. It was also discovered that
64 percent of individuals began their music study between the ages of
five and eleven and 18 percent between the ages of twelve and fourteen.
Last, it was found that 97 percent of parents polled believe that children
benefit from a music and arts education by becoming more creative and
imaginative.[1] Thousands of statistics like these are available to illustrate how
far-reaching music is in our lives. Music provides a meaningful, lifelong
learning experience. It gives our children a critically important outlet for
their emotions and feelings; it helps to develop their sense of creativity and
wonderment, and gives them sensitivity to the world and people around
them. Because music develops the whole child, it will have a profound
influence on whatever he decides to do in life. In addition to music helping

our children learn in school, it can bring joy, beauty, and happiness into their personal lives. These three elements alone will contribute to our children having richly rewarding lives.

Getting Started

Early involvement in a group music class enlarges a child's musical experiences and prepares him for the concentration and commitment required for private lessons when the time comes.

When children are young, parents can provide them with the many meaningful musical experiences previously discussed, but eventually parents will need the help of professionals to further their children's music education and enjoyment. Music lessons, both group and private, are readily available in most communities. Early involvement in a group music class enlarges a child's musical experiences and prepares him for the concentration and commitment required for private lessons when the time comes.

MUSIC PHILOSOPHIES

In the music community, you will find a variety of methods and philosophies regarding how best to introduce a young child to music. The five most well-known music philosophies are Dalcroze, Kodály, Orff-Schulwerk, Yamaha, and Suzuki. The following sections offer a brief description of each.

Dalcroze (www.dalcrozeusa.org)

Dalcroze was started in Switzerland by Emile Jaques-Dalcroze. In a Dalcroze class, children move their bodies to the beat of the music in a very systematic, rhythmic way called eurhythmics. The body is trained like an instrument. Attention, concentration, and memory are required. Dalcroze teaches a child to understand complex rhythms.

When the child hears the music, she moves her body in sync with the rhythms. By merging the senses of seeing, hearing, feeling, and moving to the music, the child enjoys a complete musical experience. The training to become a Dalcroze instructor is both extensive and intensive, and, as a result, there are only a few licensed teachers in the United States. The principles of Dalcroze also form the foundation for both the Kodály and the Orff philosophies.

Kodály (www.oake.org)

Zoltán Kodály developed the Kodály method in Hungary, utilizing singing, reading, writing, and creating music. Singing is the core of the Kodály method. Kodály himself said, "I sang before I could speak, and I sang more than I spoke." He taught that through singing a child learns relationships between sounds. Children learn to sing on pitch and eventually are able to look at a piece of music and sing it with perfect pitch without the aid of any instrument. The Kodály method calls this type of singing *solfege*, and it takes a great deal of practice. While singing, the children use certain hand signals called *curwen* that reinforce their learning. Seeking to preserve the cultural and national heritage of Hungary, Zoltán Kodály, along with his colleague Bela Bartók, gathered together thousands of folksongs from villages and towns all over their country. Part of the Kodály philosophy includes teaching children these folksongs, as well as those from other parts of the world.

Several years ago, I attended a conference in Provo, Utah, for the Organization of American Kodály Educators (OAKE). At the conference, I heard a Kodály children's choir perform. It was some of the most beautiful singing I've heard from a young chorale group. These children understood music and how to make perfect musical sounds. They lived in different parts of the United States and had come to the conference to perform for educators. Although they had rehearsed together only briefly, their voices blended in perfect pitch and harmony, and they sang as if they had been singing and performing together for years. It was both impressive and inspiring.

Orff-Schulwerk (www.aosa.org)

Orff-Schulwerk was started by German composer Carl Orff and his associate, Hunild Keetman. Orff's philosophy is, "Out of movement, music; out of music, movement."[2] Clapping, stamping, patting the hands on the lap, and finger snapping are the four body movements that make up the Orff experience. Through play activities and the use of rhythm instruments such as drums, sticks, blocks, and bells, children learn music patterns and how to keep a beat. Orff's melody instruments include wooden xylophones and metal glockenspiels (glockenspiel means "bell play" in German). This method is a group experience, and the children learn to be team participants through songs, games, rhymes, and dances. The Orff-Schulwerk program has been translated into eighteen languages and is taught all over the world using the traditional music and folklore of the country in which it is taught. There are more than ten thousand Orff teachers in the United States.

Yamaha (usa.yamaha.com)

Genichi Kawakami of Japan founded the Yamaha method. He said, "If the education method is correct, the same results will be obtained anywhere in the world." His method requires parents to be actively involved in their children's music experience. Young children are taught musical pitches, rhythm patterns, and harmonies. Using an electronic keyboard, students learn keyboarding and sight playing. They are also involved in such activities as singing, ear training, group performance, music arranging, sight singing, and theory. Later, the children are encouraged to compose and perform their own music. The program usually starts at age three. The Yamaha method has been established for more than thirty years and is in over forty countries worldwide.

Suzuki (www.suzukiassociation.org)

Suzuki was founded by Shinichi Suzuki in Japan. He believed that, given the proper musical learning environment, all children could learn and reach their potential. His approach to teaching music is based on how children learn language. First, they listen to the sounds, and then they try to imitate those sounds. Eventually, they mimic words, then phrases, and finally whole sentences. Using this same method in music, Suzuki students first listen to a note, then they imitate that, and then the process is repeated with a musical phrase and, finally, an entire piece. With patience, love, and encouragement, parents and teachers teach the child to play the violin, cello, viola, flute, or piano. Each step is mastered with constant repetition. Suzuki believed talent is no accident of birth, but is developed through hard work, effort, and education.[3]

CHOOSING THE RIGHT PROGRAM FOR YOUR CHILD

When choosing a music program for your child, consider her personality and interests and the philosophy that would make the best fit. If one particular program or philosophy does not work for your child, try another. There are many music programs in communities all over the world that embrace several philosophies successfully. Perhaps a combination, rather than just one method, may work best for your child. A group class is a good way to start a one- to five-year-old. Here are some things to consider.

- RESEARCH LOCAL MUSIC CLASSES IN THE COMMUNITY: Check your community to see what music classes are available. Try local universities, community arts and music facilities, recreation centers, and children's education programs.

- NETWORK, NETWORK, NETWORK: Network with other mothers to see what music classes their children have enjoyed and why. Seek opinions from parents whose children are similar to yours in personality and temperament, but remember that what works for one child does not necessarily work for another child.

- Observe the teacher and the program: Prior to enrolling your child, attend a class and observe the teacher, the program, and the other students. First, does the teacher seem happy to be there? Does she seem to enjoy teaching? Is she responsive and positive to the children? Does she relate equally well to both girls and boys? Does she have control over the class? Keep in mind that a class is only as good as the teacher who teaches it.

- Learn the philosophies and goals: Observe the program after educating yourself on its philosophy and goals. Ask yourself, does it meet my expectations? Does the program provide varied and interesting experiences for my child? Does the program accomplish its goals?

- Observe the children in class: Observe the other children in the class. Do they seem happy? Do they seem to enjoy what they are doing? Are they having fun, or do they seem bored?

- Choose age-appropriate classes: If the program is for children ages one to three, select a class that includes movement, rhythm, singing, dancing, listening, and the use of rhythm instruments. By age four, enroll them in classes that include an introduction to the instruments of the orchestra, notation, keyboarding, and learning about the lives of the great composers.

After exposing your children to group lessons for a few years, they will be prepared to take the next step: *private lessons.*

Private Music Lessons

Deciding when to begin private music lessons, selecting an instrument to study, and choosing the right teacher can be challenging and fun. Scientists talk about "windows of opportunity," meaning the optimum periods of time that children learn. Although humans are learning constantly throughout their lives, there are times when scientists believe learning is much easier. For music, that window is between the ages of three and ten. The brain is primed in such a way that it is able to process new information quickly and effectively. By introducing music lessons to the child during this time, brain circuits

> *Although humans are learning constantly throughout their lives, there are times when scientists believe learning is much easier. For music, that window is between the ages of three and ten.*

become permanently wired, and the child never forgets how to play that musical instrument.

Pediatric neurobiologist Harry Chugani, M.D., of Children's Hospital of Michigan has had personal experience with this theory. He started taking piano lessons with his young daughter. Although she learned easily, he did not. However, as a child, he had taken guitar lessons, and when he went back to the guitar he was excited to find that he was able to recall what he had learned many years prior and, in his own words, "the songs [were] still there."[4]

Does this mean that if you have a child over ten, she won't learn a musical instrument easily and that you should forget the idea of giving her music lessons? Definitely not! In his book, *Never Too Late: My Musical Life Story,* John Holt, an educator and musician, advocates that learning is a lifelong process. At the age of fifty, he took up the cello and, by practicing intensely, was able to join a chamber orchestra and string quartet. Says Holt: "Teachers say that if we don't learn to play musical instruments as children we will never be able to learn as adults…not so. Of course, it is nice, if we come freely to music, to come to it young, but if we don't come to it then, we can later. It is never too late."[5]

Joseph Sparling, who coauthored *Learningames*, agrees: "You want to say that it is never too late, but there seems to be something very special about the early years. And yet, there is new evidence that certain kinds of intervention can reach even the older brain and like a microscopic screwdriver, rewire broken circuits."[6]

Although scientific research shows that a young child can learn to play a musical instrument more easily when she is young, don't panic if you miss the "window of opportunity." Just start lessons as soon as possible.

The challenge then becomes choosing a musical instrument and the right teacher to teach that instrument.

Choosing an Instrument

According to a Gallup poll on instrument popularity among the sixty-two million amateur musicians in the United States, the piano is the instrument of choice of 34 percent. Twenty-two percent chose the guitar; 6 percent, drums; 5 percent, flute; 4 percent each, clarinet, organ, saxophone, and keyboard; and 3 percent, trumpet and violin.[7]

Before your child chooses an instrument to learn, it is fun and worthwhile to listen to some of the music that "features" that instrument. This will allow both you and your child to hear what the instrument sounds like, its range of versatility, and how it is combined with other instruments of the orchestra to produce its varied and unique sound.

Before your child chooses an instrument to learn, it is fun and worthwhile to listen to some of the music that "features" that instrument.

Below are some of the things to consider when selecting an instrument to study and a repertoire sampling of music that "shows off" the particular group of instruments, along with interesting stories and anecdotes about people, instruments, and compositions of music.

Vocal

The human voice is considered an instrument and is actually the first instrument we learn. It is regarded as the most beautiful and perfect of all instruments. Long ago, instrument makers tried to make instruments where the sound most resembled the human singing voice. The term "voice" is still used by instrument makers and tuners today as they make adjustments in improving the sound of an instrument.[8] Likewise, it is possible for our voices to sound like instruments of the orchestra, as illustrated by the following story.

In the early 1940s, three young Dutch sisters, Antoinette, Helen, and Alette Colijn, living in the Netherlands East Indies, were sent to a woman's Japanese prison camp on the island of Sumatra. The world was experiencing war, and people everywhere were affected. At the camp, conditions were horrible—the food scant, the guards brutal, and disease rampant. Desperately wanting to lift the morale of the women prisoners, an Englishwoman, Norah Chambers, who had studied at London's Royal Academy of Music, decided to form an orchestra made up of human voices. Among the participants were Antoinette and Alette. On the day of their performance, excitement filled the air as thirty women, wearing ragged prison attire, stood before the other women prisoners prepared to sing. Another Englishwomen, Margaret Dryburgh, stepped forward and said, "This evening we are asking you to listen to something new: a choir of women's voices producing music usually performed by an orchestra. The idea of making ourselves into a vocal orchestra came to us when we longed to hear again some of the wonderful melodies that uplifted our souls in days gone by. So close your eyes and imagine you are in a concert hall hearing a world famous orchestra."[9]

They began to sing the largo from Antonin Dvořák's *New World Symphony*. No words were used by the singers, only the musical syllables "ah," and "loo" to imitate the various sounds of the orchestra. They continued to sing such pieces as Chopin's "Raindrop Prelude," Handel's "Pastoral Symphony" from the *Messiah*, and Debussy's "Reverie." The prisoners were spellbound, overtaken by memories of better times and places.

That night in the barracks, the women talked of the seeming miracle that had taken place. It was learned that Margaret Dryburgh had written down all the music and Norah Chambers had arranged the music to be performed by voices instead of instruments—and all from memory. The choir performed four more concerts that year, each time uplifting the prisoners from their brutal conditions.

After the liberation in 1945, the three Colijn sisters moved to America. Thirty-five years later, in 1980, Antoinette Colijn found her precious sixty-eight-page booklet of the vocal orchestra scores sung in the prison camp. Having sung in a church choir at Stanford University in Palo Alto, California, she decided to donate the music to the university for preservation. Because of the moving story behind the music, the Peninsula Women's Chorus of Palo Alto began practicing the music for a special "Song of Survival" concert. In 1983, nine of the original prison-camp singers flew to California to witness the performance, among them Norah Chambers.[10] It was a riveting emotional experience for the survivors.

Today, in all parts of the world, women's choirs have performed "Song of Survival" music, and in 1997, the movie *Paradise Road* brought the story to millions. This story illustrates not only the power of music to lift our spirits in the most desperate of circumstances, but the tremendous versatility of the human voice.

Interest in choral singing is growing and is especially significant today as we increasingly rely on Internet-based communications rather than face-to-face interaction. Robert Putnam, Harvard University's Kennedy School of Government scholar, believes that the significance of choral singing goes beyond music making and the arts. Group performing, he asserts, contributes directly to the social trust that is basic to civic engagement, and the mere existence of choral groups helps to foster America's democratic culture.[11]

> *Interest in choral singing is growing and is especially significant today as we increasingly rely on Internet-based communications rather than face-to-face interaction.*

Considerations for Selecting Vocal Training

- GROUP SINGING: If your child enjoys singing, get her involved in group singing classes, school choirs, church choirs, or children's chorale groups. Serious vocal training does not come until later.

- VOCAL TRAINING: Intense vocal training usually starts between the ages of twelve and fourteen for girls and fifteen and sixteen for boys. Starting lessons too soon can damage a child's voice. (This does not include the kind of singing mentioned above.) More and more young people are seeking out vocal training because programs such as *American Idol* and *Britain's Got Talent* have made the art of singing enormously popular. The talented voices of Paul Potts, Susan Boyle, Jacqueline Marie "Jackie" Evancho, and duo Jonathan Antoine and Charlotte Jaconelli have inspired would-be vocalists all over the world.

- JOIN A CHILDREN'S CHOIR: The American Chorale Directors Association in Laughton, Oklahoma, reports that children's choirs are forming across the nation as more music programs are cut in the schools. Presently, there are over seven thousand children's choirs nationwide, and the number is growing. Look into opportunities in your community for choirs your child can join. They may be affiliated with churches, schools, community programs, or the local university. Here are examples of two exceptional children's choirs, located in Virginia and Alaska, respectively.

The World Children's Choir was started in 1990 in McLean, Virginia, under the direction of Sondra Harnes and her husband, James Selway. Both studied at the Juilliard School in New York City. The formation of the choir was an inspirational experience. Harnes states, "The choir owes its creation to the spirit of *glasnost*. In December 1989, just weeks after the Berlin Wall was torn down, the Soviet Union's Red Army Chorus sang at the Kennedy Center. It was the emotional reaction of the Concert Hall audience to their astounding promise of international friendship through song that led to the World Children's Choir. In that moment, I had a vision of children from all over the world singing together for peace."

The WCC features a professionally trained children's choir for ages four through eighteen. All students are trained in the Italian *bel canto* style of singing that originated in Italy in the late seventeenth century and focused on the development of a solo-quality singing voice. Along with helping children develop a solo voice, WCC's goal is to bring young people together to promote friendship and peace through music and serve as a voice for children. WCC has performed at the White House and Kennedy Center for national and international dignitaries and has helped to raise money for children's causes worldwide. Harnes states, "My personal mission is to train children to sing beautifully and artistically so they may open the hearts of people everywhere to what is possible if we come together as one family to make a better world."[12]

The Alaska Children's Choir was founded in 1979 and is located in Southcentral, Alaska. It is for children ages five through eighteen. The focus of the choir is to educate and train Southcentral Alaskan children in choral music with an emphasis in classical, opera, and folk music. In addition, children learn music theory, harmony, vocal techniques, sight-singing, and concert etiquette. Under the tutelage of choir director Janet Stotts, the choir has performed locally with the Anchorage Opera and the Anchorage Symphony. Nationally, they have performed in Washington, DC, New York, San Francisco, Seattle, and Chicago and internationally in Australia, New Zealand, and throughout Europe. Over the years, they have received numerous awards at choral festivals. Some include: first place children's choir in the Nineteenth International Youth and Music Festival (Vienna, Austria); second place children's choir in the International Oskarshamn Festival (Oskarshamn, Sweden); and second place awards in both children's and youth competitions at the International Kathaumixw in British Columbia.

Marg Kruse has been involved with the choir for over twenty years both as a choir parent and currently as choir manager. She has observed how involvement in the choir changes the participants. Kruse says, "Being a member of the choir is demanding and the children have to push themselves and budget their time. Our tour choir gives a minimum of four hours of their time each week for rehearsals. Having to juggle school, sports, and a demanding choir schedule, these high-school students develop an amazing ability to manage time. There is something special about all the children involved in this choir. I've watched them grow into disciplined professional performers as well as independent, confident people."[13]

Although different, each choir shares a common goal—a life-changing musical experience for young people.

Famous and not-so-famous singers

Franklin Roosevelt, the thirty-second president of the United States, sang soprano in his school choir, and Woodrow Wilson, the twenty-eighth president of the United States, sang tenor in his college glee club.[14] Research indicates that choral singers are more aware of current events and more involved in the political process...perhaps there is a correlation.[15]

Vocal Repertoire Suggestions

Mozart: "Pa-Pa-Pa-Pa" (*The Magic Flute*)
Humperdinck: "Brother Come Dance With Me" (*Hansel and Gretel*)
Offenbach: "The Doll Song" (*The Tales of Hoffmann*)
Mozart: Queen of the Night's aria—"Der Holle Rache" (*The Magic Flute*)

PIANO

The piano, the heaviest of all musical instruments, is considered a percussion instrument because the strings are struck by hammers. The early pianos came in many shapes and sizes, with the makers always striving for elegance and beautiful tone quality.

> *The piano, the heaviest of all musical instruments, is considered a percussion instrument because the strings are struck by hammers.*

One of the most popular pieces of children's music ever written for two pianos (and a few strings) is Camille Saint-Saëns's *Carnival of the Animals*. Not only was Saint-Saëns a composer, he was also a writer of poems, plays, and books. He composed *Carnival of the Animals* in 1886, under the title *Grand Zoological Fantasy*. It was actually composed as a private joke and performed at a Mardi Gras concert for a few of the composer's friends. The original music was scored for two pianos and a small instrumental ensemble, but was later changed and orchestrated by the composer for a larger instrumental group. Interestingly, Saint-Saëns refused to let the score be performed in public or published during his lifetime. Two months after his death in 1922, the Colonne Orchestra in Paris, with Gabriel Pierne, conducting, performed *Carnival of the Animals* to the delight of hundreds. Some conductors felt that the reason Saint-Saëns did not want the music published while he was alive was that serious audiences would not understand the humor he was trying to portray in the music. There are fourteen sections describing lions, hens, roosters, wild asses, tortoises, elephants, kangaroos, fish, cuckoos, birds, fossils, pianists, (early pianists are dangerous beasts!), and swans. In the late 1940s, Columbia Records commissioned American poet Ogden Nash to write a series of humorous verses for *Carnival of the Animals,* and these are still included in recordings today. In 1995 Bruce Adolphe, composer and music scholar, updated Nash's verses and wrote another version of the kid-friendly poems for *Carnival of the Animals.* They were later narrated by his friend, Itzak Perlman, and recorded on the CD *Classical Zoo.* Adolphe wrote the new poems, he said, "simply to get more laughs as a narrator." Children love *Carnival of the Animals* and have a great time mentally visualizing the animals Saint-Saëns musically describes. It also gives piano students an opportunity to appreciate the versatility of the piano.

Considerations for Selecting the Piano

- PIANO—A GREAT FIRST CHOICE: The piano is a wonderful first instrument for many children to learn. It is one of the easiest instruments to play and sounds good immediately for two reasons. First, when you push down a middle C, that's what you hear. With string instruments, you have to have a good ear to "find" the correct note. Second, in a short time your child can "sound" good because pianos play many sounds at once, unlike the woodwinds and brass, which play one tone at a time.

- Relationship between piano keyboard and musical scale: In learning the piano, children can see a direct linear relationship between the keyboard and the musical scale, which is not true for learning stringed instruments.[16]

- No accompanist needed: A pianist rarely needs an accompanist, unless she is performing a piano concerto, in which case she is accompanied by an orchestra. It is pretty much a solo instrument and one that sounds wonderful by itself.

- Not necessarily a group experience: Pianists do not usually play with other musicians. A child learning the piano will not have the ongoing group experience that she would get from playing band or orchestra instruments. For some children, the group experience is very important, so take into consideration your child's personality when choosing the piano to study. In today's business world, teamwork skills are very important, and a child learns teamwork skills when playing in a band or orchestra. However, there are music organizations that offer piano students a group experience. The Fairfax-Loudoun Music Fellowship, located in Loudoun, Virginia, is such a place. Twenty-five years ago, they began sponsoring the *Piano Ensemble Festival*, a concert performed by piano students playing duets or trios on six grand pianos all at the same time, thus providing an excellent "team" opportunity. Each year approximately two hundred piano students participate and learn duet or trio music that can be rehearsed with a partner. Frank Conlon of Washington, DC, conducts the concert, and students learn how to follow the conductor and play music simultaneously with twelve to eighteen other pianists.[17]

- Disadvantage of playing the piano: A possible disadvantage in playing the piano is that in a performance setting—such as playing at an assisted living home, or for a funeral—your child is at the mercy of the piano that is available. A piano can be out of tune, have keys that stick, or have other problems that make it difficult to play. I have personally experienced all these problems in the past. Many times people who arrange a musical program do not understand the importance of performing on a quality instrument. A rather humorous story is told of Count Basie, the famous bandleader, who told a club owner whose piano was always out of tune, "I'm not returning until you fix it." A month later, the owner called Basie and told him everything was fine. However, when he returned to the club, the piano was still out of tune. "You said you fixed it!" an angry Basie exclaimed. "I did," the club owner replied. "I had it painted."[18]

The famous and the not-so-famous who play or have played the piano

The piano is a popular instrument. A number of presidents, statesmen, and celebrities have played this instrument, including former United States Secretary of State Condoleezza Rice. As a youth, she trained as a concert pianist. At fifteen she performed Mozart's Piano Concerto in D minor with the Denver Symphony Orchestra. In 2002, when cellist Yo Yo Ma received a National Medal of the Arts, he requested that Rice accompany him. During her term as US secretary of state, Rice was considered the most prominent amateur musician in the world.

Richard Nixon, the thirty-seventh president of the United States, was a classically trained pianist. Harry Truman, the thirty-third president of the United States, also played the piano.[19] Actor, writer, and director Kelsey Grammer, known for his role as Dr. Frasier Crane in the sitcoms *Cheers* and *Frasier*, studied the piano at Juilliard for two years. And actors Clint Eastwood, Jamie Foxx, Anthony Hopkins, and Dustin Hoffman play the piano.

Piano Repertoire Suggestions

Saint-Saëns: *Carnival of the Animals*
Chopin: Waltz, op. 64, no. 1 "Minute Waltz"
Mozart: "Rondo alla Turca"
Beethoven: "Fur Elise"
Rimsky-Korsakov: "Flight of the Bumblebee" (from *The Tale of Tsar Sultan*)

STRING: VIOLIN, VIOLA, CELLO, DOUBLE BASS

The stringed instruments had a rather shady beginning in the early seventeenth century, with the fiddlers of the time referred to as "scurvy thrashing scraping mongrels."[20] But time has changed that perception, and today the stringed instruments serve as the front position in a symphony orchestra, with the violin considered the king of instruments.

> *The stringed instruments had a rather shady beginning in the early seventeenth century, with the fiddlers of the time referred to as "scurvy thrashing scraping mongrels."*

The exquisite violins created by Nicola Amati and Antonio Stradivari in the seventeenth and eighteenth centuries continue to be in demand today because of their beautiful tone quality, which amazingly gets better with age. Today, a Stradivari can cost over $3 million! The secret of how these violins were made died with the creators themselves, and although scientists have studied the varnishes, the thickness and shape of the wood, and the molecular composition of the wood under powerful microscopes, no one can explain what makes these violins so unique.

Fascinating stories abound of priceless Amati and Stradivari violins stolen from their owners, only to turn up decades later at the deathbeds of the thieves. One remarkable story is that of Vahan Bedelian, who in 1915 was to be sent to his death in what is now the Syrian Desert. It is there that 1.5 million Armenians died at the hands of the Turks. Bedelian defended himself with neither gun nor sword. On the eve of his appointed journey to death, Bedelian picked up his violin and performed mournfully and passionately before a Turkish general. The general listened and then, with champagne in hand, said, "A talent like you we need. You should not be sent to the desert." Bedelian's life was spared, and he lived to teach the violin to many, including his son, Haroutune, who attended London's Royal Academy of Music at age fifteen and became an accomplished violinist.[21]

Considerations for Selecting a Stringed Instrument

- A HIGH-DEMAND INSTRUMENT: The strings are a high-demand instrument. An orchestra usually needs a combination of at least sixty violins, violas, cellos, and basses.

- LARGE REPERTOIRE: There is a wonderful, large repertoire written for the stringed instruments.

- PATIENCE REQUIRED: The first few years of learning a stringed instrument can be difficult and will require patience and encouragement from parents.

- A GOOD EAR: Playing a stringed instrument requires a good ear. Because there are no frets to mark where the fingers are placed, the violinist must learn exactly where to put his fingers to play "in tune."

The famous and the not-so-famous
who play or have played string instruments

The popularity of the string instruments is well known, and many presidents, statesmen, and celebrities have played these instruments. Thomas Jefferson, third president of the United States, was an accomplished violinist who played chamber music, especially baroque trio sonatas, throughout his political career. He also played the cello and clavichord. American diplomat and statesman Benjamin Franklin played a variety of musical instruments, including the violin. Abraham Lincoln, the sixteenth president of the United States, played the violin.

String Instrument Repertoire Suggestions

Beethoven: Violin Concerto in D Major, last movement
Brahms: Concerto for Violin and Cello, last movement
Dvořák: Concerto for Cello

Dittersdorf: Concerto for Double Bass in E-flat Major
Debussy: String Quartet, Second Movement

WOODWIND INSTRUMENTS: FLUTE, PICCOLO, BASSOON, CLARINET, OBOE, SAXOPHONE

The wind instruments are varied in their sound and appearance. Some are made of wood, while others are made of silver, gold, or other metals. In an orchestra, there are usually three flutes, one piccolo, three oboes, three clarinets, and three bassoons. There are also an English horn, a bass clarinet, and a double bassoon. They are considered nonresonating instruments because once the musician has stopped blowing, the sound stops. Good breath control is very important when playing all of the wind instruments.

A delightful example of a piece of music that is beloved by children everywhere and that uses several wind instruments for solo passages is Sergei Prokofiev's *Peter and the Wolf.* Prokofiev, the Russian composer, is probably best known for this children's work, which he called "a present not only to the children of Moscow, but also to my own." Although a very controversial figure, Prokofiev had the innate ability to look at the world through a child's eyes. He loved fairy tales and imaginary play. Realizing that children love and intently listen to music, he wrote a number of pieces for them, his most popular and engaging one being *Peter and the Wolf.* Being rather childlike himself, Prokofiev understood how children think and was able to bring exciting characters and events into this work. Each character and its personality are memorably represented by an instrument of the orchestra, with most of them being from the wind section. The excitable bird is represented by the flute; the waddling duck by the melancholy sound of the oboe; the cat's graceful gliding steps by the clarinet; Peter's grandfather by the rich sound of the bassoon. The wolf is portrayed by the growling sound of the brass, the hunters by the bass drums, and Peter is played with loving warmth by all the strings of the orchestra. *Peter and the Wolf,* in typical fairy-tale fashion, addresses itself to a child's sense of courage, adventure, and risk taking (and a little bit of disobedience), with, of course, a happy ending as Peter saves the day and marches triumphantly with the other characters at the end.[22]

Considerations for Selecting a Woodwind Instrument

- A GROUP EXPERIENCE: The child has a group experience when learning to play a wind instrument.

- CARRY THE MELODY: Winds get to play many solo passages in an orchestra, as they often carry the melody. Their tone both blends and contrasts with the strings.

- LEARN THE "SISTER" INSTRUMENTS: Woodwind players are often called upon to play their "sister" instruments as well. For instance, a flutist can be asked to play the piccolo; the oboist, the English horn; and the bassoonist, the larger contrabassoon. The saxophone and clarinet players also are able to easily switch from an alto sax or bass clarinet. And, in rare instances, musicians are able to play more than one woodwind at a time. Saxophonist Chang-Kyun Chong plays tenor, alto, and soprano saxophones simultaneously. He has always liked the big band sound and, not having his own orchestra, he decided to improvise. He started out playing two saxophones, which he found to be fairly easy, but they still lacked the sound he was looking for. By adding a third saxophone, he achieved his goal, but it was quite difficult blending three instruments with different tones and in different keys. Practicing two hours a day at a local park helped him hone his skill. Audiences are skeptical when he wraps his lips around three mouthpieces and spreads his arms around three horns and his fingers over six sets of keys, but the sound he produces impresses everyone.[23] So if your child decides to play more than one woodwind simultaneously, remember the success of Chang-Kyun Chong and rest assured that anything is possible.

- LEARN WINDS IN SHORT AMOUNT OF TIME: A child can learn to play the winds in a short amount of time with positive results.

- NOT AS EXPENSIVE: Wind instruments are not as expensive as the string instruments

The famous and the not-so-famous who play or have played the wind instruments

Sixth president of the United States John Quincy Adams played the flute. Bill Clinton, the forty-fourth president of the United States, plays the saxophone, as does Alan Greenspan, former chairman of the Federal Reserve.[24] Celebrities who play the saxophone include director Steven Spielberg and actress Jennifer Garner. Entertainer and comedian Bob Hope played the saxophone, and actress Julia Roberts plays the clarinet and oboe. Ian Anderson from Jethro Tull plays the flute. And, of course, James Galway is a famous classical flautist.

Wind Instrument Repertoire Suggestions

Prokofiev: *Peter and the Wolf*
Debussy: "Syrinx," for unaccompanied flute
Weber: Bassoon Concerto in F Major
Mozart: Clarinet Concerto in A Major, last movement

BRASS INSTRUMENTS: TRUMPET, TROMBONE, FRENCH HORN, TUBA, CORNET

The brass instruments were originally made from the horns of beasts, elephants, bulls, and boars. Consequently, these instruments have been associated with great strength and power. A famous biblical story is told of how Joshua, leader of the Israelites, and his army blew on their horns as they marched around the city of Jericho.

The brass instruments were originally made from the horns of beasts, elephants, bulls, and boars. Consequently, these instruments have been associated with great strength and power.

So great was the sound that the walls tumbled to the ground and the Israelites took possession of the city.

Today, brass instruments have gained wide popularity and are used in jazz, dance, and brass bands. A piece of music that is both brilliant and jubilant and is scored for nine trumpets, nine horns, twenty-four oboes, twelve bassoons, a contrabassoon, three pairs of timpani, and assorted drums is Handel's *Music for the Royal Fireworks.* King George I of England commissioned Handel to write the music to commemorate the signing of the Treaty of Aix-la-Chapelle. A huge victory pavilion was built to serve as the place for this event and the spectacular fireworks display. The king, of course, wanted equally spectacular music for the occasion, so he requested that Handel use only military-type instruments and no strings. At first, Handel was concerned, but in the end he was able to give the king the electrifying sound he wanted. The event took place on April 27, 1749, with Handel's monumental music the most exciting part of the evening. The overture is magnificent, with a marvelous interplay between the wind and brass instruments.[25]

Considerations for Selecting a Brass Instrument

- GROUP EXPERIENCE: The child has a group experience when learning to play the brass instruments.

- VERSATILE INSTRUMENTS: Brass instruments are very versatile—they can play both loud and soft melodies of music.

- BRACES ARE PROBLEMATIC: Children wearing braces will have a hard time playing these instruments.

- AN OVERBITE IS A GOOD THING: Children with an overbite do very well with this instrument, but those children with an underbite have difficulty.

- EMBOUCHURE AND A STIFF UPPER LIP: Children learning a brass instrument will develop a "stiff upper lip" and will learn about the concept of embouchure, which is how you hold your lips around an instrument. The mouthpiece is held against the upper lip, and the muscles of the lip control the pitch. If the lip becomes tired and limp, the notes will split or crack.

The famous and the not-so-famous that play or have played the brass instruments

Warren Harding, the twenty-ninth president of the United States, organized "The Citizen's Cornet Band." He once remarked, "I played every instrument except the slide trombone and the E-flat cornet!"[26] Astronaut and Senator John Glenn played the French horn. Actor Richard Gere played the trumpet in high school. TV personality and anchor Harry Smith plays the tuba, and Otto Graham, NFL Hall of Fame quarterback, plays the trombone.

Brass Instrument Repertoire Suggestions

Handel: *Music for the Royal Fireworks*
Handel: *Water Music*, alla hornpipe
Mozart: Horn Concerto no. 4, last movement
Mussorgsky: *Pictures at an Exhibition*
Rossini: Overture, *William Tell*

PERCUSSION INSTRUMENTS: CYMBALS, DRUMS (TIMPANI), MARIMBA, XYLOPHONE, BELLS, CHIMES, TRIANGLE, AND OTHERS

The percussion section is made up of many different instruments that are either banged together or banged on with a stick or sticks, but they do not necessarily have to have a loud sound. The drums can be used to emphasize the music's rhythm and how it changes. Cymbals, castanets, chimes, and triangles can be used to add an interesting and added dimension to the music, such as what you would hear in Tchaikovsky's *Nutcracker Suite*. Although the history behind each of the percussion instruments is fascinating, the cymbals have the longest history and date back to the second millennium BC. Today, the best cymbals come from either Turkey or China and are made by a secretly guarded formula of copper and tin. After the percussionist of the orchestra clashes the cymbals, he holds them high in the air so everyone can see them and to allow the sound to resonate throughout the hall.

An excellent way to hear all the individual percussion instruments (and other instruments as well) is by listening to Benjamin Britten's *The Young Person's Guide to the Orchestra*. This recording is considered the most popular symphonic work of the twentieth century. According to Ted Libbey of National Public Radio, "This 1946 score by Britten has made more friends than any other work of English music, with the exception of Handel's *Messiah*."[27] Using Henry Purcell's *Abdelazer* as the main theme, Britten demonstrates how each instrument of the orchestra plays an important part in a musical score. The theme is first heard with all the instruments of the orchestra playing, and then each section of winds, strings, brass, and percussion instruments is played. Individual instruments in each section have an opportunity to have the "spotlight." The percussion section includes such instruments as the kettle drums, bass drums, cymbals, tambourine, triangles, side drum, Chinese blocks, xylophone, castanets, gong, and whip. The percussion instruments play separately and then together to show how the individual sounds complement one another. In the end, Britten, using his fugue and Purcell's theme, brings all the instruments together for a dramatic climax. (A fugue is a composition with three or more musical lines that enter at different times in the piece, creating a counterpoint with one another.)

Considerations for Selecting Percussion Instruments

- A steady sense of rhythm and a good ear: A percussionist can learn to play all of the percussion instruments, but it is important for the player to have a steady sense of rhythm and a very good ear. Most percussionists start by playing the bells. Playing the mallet instruments requires the ability to read music.

- Versatile instruments: Percussion instruments can play melodies, solos, and accompaniments.

- Popular drums: The most popular percussion instrument is the drum. The technique involved in playing drums takes time to learn well, and a percussionist must have a strong sense of rhythm and be able to read music rhythm patterns. In an orchestra setting, the person playing timpani, or kettle drums, is usually an individual who has had a great deal of experience playing with an orchestra and understands how the drums contribute to the music. It is definitely not as simple as one would think.

The famous and the not-so-famous that play or have played the percussion instruments:

Johnny Carson, an American comedian known for hosting *The Tonight Show*, played the drums. Richard Feynman, an American physicist and a winner of the 1965 Nobel Prize in physics, played the bongo drums. Evelyn Glennie of Scotland is a world-class percussionist despite being profoundly deaf.

Percussion Instrument Repertoire Suggestions

Tchaikovsky: *Nutcracker Suite*
Tchaikovsky: *1812 Overture*
Britten: *The Young Person's Guide to the Orchestra*
Grieg: *Peer Gynt* Suite no. 1
Gounod: *Funeral March of a Marionette*

GUITAR

Although the guitar is considered a string instrument, it is discussed separately from the other string instruments because of its versatility and association with both classical and rock music. The first known guitar existed as early as 1000 BC among the ancient Hittites. The Moors introduced it into Spain in the twelfth or thirteenth century, and the early form of the guitar as we know it today was made in Spain in the sixteenth century. The guitar is often used to accompany singing. In 1860, the guitar began a decline and was not accepted in musical circles as a serious instrument. There were several reasons for this. First, despite the fact that there was a great deal of music for the guitar, it had not been written by any of the great composers. Both Franz Schubert and Hector Berlioz were guitarists, but they wrote very little music for the guitar. Second, the music that was written for the guitar could not compare to the quality of music written for other instruments. As a result, serious classical musicians did not play the guitar.

It was Andrés Segovia, a self-taught guitarist, who brought the classical guitar up to the same standing as the other serious classical instruments, and he dedicated eighty years to do so. He accomplished this by exposing people to the music of the guitar in concerts and by extending its repertoire. As he traveled around the world performing in concert, people everywhere were astounded not only by his talent

> *It was Andrés Segovia, a self-taught guitarist, who brought the classical guitar up to the same standing as the other serious classical instruments, and he dedicated eighty years to do so.*

as a musician, but also by the brilliance of the guitar in the hands of someone who knew how to play it skillfully. Next, he focused his energies on convincing prominent composers to write music for the guitar. One of the first great composers to do this was Manuel de Falla. Many others followed, including Villa-Lobos, Paganini, and Weber. Segovia also worked tirelessly with guitar makers to improve the quality of sound and volume of the instrument. In 1947, because of Segovia's influence, Albert Augustine developed the nylon guitar string. Finally, Segovia went to colleges, universities, and music conservatories, convincing them of the importance of establishing a seat for the classical guitar. Because of his efforts, music departments today have both included the guitar in the curricula and have professors of guitar. Today, classical guitarists the world over owe a debt to Andrés Segovia for establishing the guitar as a serious and respected instrument.[28]

The guitar is a very popular instrument with teens. They especially like the electric guitar (introduced in 1936) because of its association with rock n' roll bands. They also like the fact that they can increase the volume on an electric guitar because it can be used with an electric amplifier.

Considerations for Selecting the Classical Guitar

- INVEST IN THE BEST: Invest in a good guitar teacher so your child does not pick up any bad habits. Don't just allow children to "teach themselves" the guitar. (Many teens just want to learn the guitar from a friend.)

- LEARN OTHER FRETTED INSTRUMENTS: Once a child learns the guitar, he can transfer these skills to other fretted instruments, such as the banjo or ukulele.

- LEARN ON A NYLON STRING: When she is first starting lessons, encourage your child to learn on a nylon-string or classical guitar as opposed to an acoustic guitar. By starting on a classical guitar, your child will develop a good technique foundation, which will give her greater versatility to play with either a band or an orchestra.

- A POPULAR INSTRUMENT: If you have a child who is getting tired or bored with the instrument he is now playing, or if you are concerned about your child wanting to quit music lessons, try the guitar. It is a very social and popular instrument. Jenny Oaks Baker, an accomplished violinist and mother of four, started her son Matthew taking violin lessons, but quickly saw that it was not the instrument for him. He balked at practicing and complained about lessons, so she switched him to the classical guitar. He loves it! He loves practicing, he loves taking lessons, and he loves performing with his mother and siblings. What could have been a frustrating experience is now a success story.

The famous and not-so-famous that have played guitar and other fretted instruments

American diplomat and statesman Benjamin Franklin played several instruments, including the guitar.[29] Actor Kevin Bacon plays the guitar and is part of the Bacon Brothers band. Andy Griffith, best known for his role in *The Andy Griffith Show*, earned a bachelor of arts in music from the University of North Carolina and played the guitar. Steve Martin, director, actor, and comedian, is a brilliant musician. He plays the banjo and is an excellent bluegrass picker. Nobel Prize-winning chemist Linus Pauling played the guitar.

Guitar Repertoire Suggestions

Vivaldi: Guitar Concerto in D
Andrés Segovia: *Macarena*
Villa-Lobos: *Bachianas Brasileiras no. 5*
Schubert: *Fifteen Original Dances* (for flute, violin, and guitar)

After carefully weighing the advantages and disadvantages of each instrument, make a decision with your child on which instrument would be best suited for him or her. Once this decision is reached, the next step is finding a good teacher.

Choosing a Teacher for Private Lessons

A good teacher is worth his or her weight in gold. He or she can make all the difference between a child having a positive feeling about music, and

> *A good teacher is worth his or her weight in gold. He or she can make all the difference between a child having a positive feeling about music, and not wanting to have anything to do with learning a musical instrument.*

not wanting to have anything to do with learning a musical instrument. I will never forget our sons' first piano teacher. Wendy Waring was a dedicated and inspiring teacher with the rare gift of relating to all children. She literally made every lesson fun and exciting, but she was also a tough taskmaster and insisted on pieces played musically. Wendy helped them to understand the music by telling them stories about the composers, their music, and the circumstances of when and why they wrote these pieces. Timing and correct rhythm were of utmost importance. Clapping, singing, and tapping were all forms of helping them to "feel" and play the correct beat.

Each week while waiting for their lessons, Jason and Ryan were given crayons, paints, and markers for creative expression. The teacher's weekly exuberance was electrifying, and the boys loved piano lessons because of Wendy's unique style. Wendy also became involved in her students' lives and was interested in their hobbies, school, and friends. She planned outings at the tide pools, the beach, and at parks along with her other students. She was sensitive to their moods when they came for lessons and listened to their opinions regarding pieces they were interested in playing, or not playing. Unfortunately, after three years of an ideal situation, she stopped teaching to have more time to spend with her son, a very gifted vocalist. But for our sons, it was a phenomenal experience. After Wendy, I went through a period of "trial and error" before finding another teacher who related well to our sons and had high musical standards. Although Kenner Bailey's style was much different, I found him to be the perfect personality for teens. He knew when to be fun, when to be serious, when to be tough, and when to lighten up. I believe that because of Kenner's influence and personality, our boys continued with their music during the tumultuous teen years and into adulthood.

The importance of a good music teacher—either a school music teacher or a private music teacher—cannot be overstated. Their influence can be felt by young people throughout their lives. Barry Trobaugh of Munford, Tennessee, is such a teacher. He has been the "director of bands" at Munford High School (MHS) in Munford, Tennessee, for the past nineteen years in a career spanning thirty-three years. He is responsible for 479 students in grades nine through twelve who are involved in the extensive music programs offered by the school. The program includes two concert bands, two jazz bands, a basketball pep band, symphonic ensembles, a choir, and "The Pride of Tipton County: Munford High School Marching Band," which is one of the most highly recognized groups in the Southeast.

Trobaugh's interest in his students goes beyond their music-making abilities. His goal is to teach them responsibility and maturity that will flow into their other school studies on campus and in their personal lives at home and at work. He states, "My students are revered as the most responsible and focused students on campus. I'm tough on them and expect them to perform their best academically. They score two points higher on national testing; their GPAs are a half-point higher than other students; their attendance figures are extremely high, and discipline problems are nonexistent. But my expectation for them is more than what they accomplish at school and in band—I expect them to represent what they have learned in my program at home, at church, on the job, and in the community. I get glowing comments from parents and employers about the discipline and responsibility these students manifest outside the classroom. Our alumni constantly remind me that their years with MHS Marching Band provided them with the ability to take on challenges and complete them with superior results."

Loralee Shoffner, a current MHS Marching Band member, summed up Mr. Trobaugh's impact on her life by saying, "Mr. Trobaugh has helped me to build my life and has opened my eyes to the many paths which I can choose. Every time I have needed help with anything, he has always been there. He cares about all of his students, not just for our musical abilities, but for the people we are. He gives us the chance to succeed and pushes us to our maximum potential by creating an atmosphere of perfection. He has given me, as a section leader, the opportunity to lead, has offered advice from time to time, but lets me figure out my leadership style. With all of his students he instills lifelong values, such as dedication, responsibility, passion for an idea, and accountability."[30]

Chris Niswonger, an alumnus of MHS Marching Band, concurs. "Mr. Trobaugh gave me the goals to pursue and the tools to achieve that goal. He showed the band members the importance of pursuing perfection through hard work; he taught us leadership skills, team-building skills, and the importance of communication. I would not have the success I have today if it was not for those life lessons I learned from Mr. Trobaugh and by being a member of the Munford Band."[31]

In 2011, MHS Marching Band was named USSBA National Champions after competing at the US Naval Academy stadium in Annapolis, Maryland. The United States Scholastic Band Association (USSBA), now known as USBands, is the nation's largest judging circuit for marching bands, with over one thousand bands participating yearly in this competition. In 2007 and 2010 the band was named USSBA State Champions. At the USSBA National Championship in 2009, they received the highest visual score, highest percussion score, and the United States Marine Corps Esprit de Corps award.

Trobaugh's accolades are many. In December 2011, he was touted as one of "the Top Fifty Directors Who Made a Difference" in *School, Band, and Orchestra* (*SBO*) magazine. In 2008 he was named Munford High School Teacher of the Year and Northwest Tennessee Teacher of the Year. Summing up the importance music plays in the lives of young people, he says, "Music is the best way to reach the youth of America, and, through music, it is the best way to help them develop into adults that appreciate the arts as well as the lives of others within today's society."[32] Without a doubt, Barry Trobaugh has impacted the lives of his students.

American-born Dorothy DeLay taught violin at Juilliard School of music in New York and was considered to be the best violin teacher in the world. Some of her students have included Midori, Itzhak Perlman, Cho-Liang Lin, and Nadja Salerno-Sonnenberg. What made her so special? She shares some of the very same qualities that make Wendy Waring an extraordinary piano teacher and Mr. Trobaugh an outstanding band teacher. She loved her students and showed it, was very patient and understanding of their feelings and moods, was involved with other aspects of their life, and knew how to get the very best musicianship from her students.

Of her, Itzhak Perlman said, "When you get right down to the nitty-gritty, it's that she believed in me. There was a time when my parents and Miss DeLay were the only people in the world who believed I could have a career. The fact that I was disabled—a lot of people looked at me with distorted vision. And she never did. She was able to see."[33]

Showing that Miss DeLay respected her students' independence, Midori said, "Unless it's really strange (the music), Miss DeLay lets me do what I want."[34]

Miss DeLay had high expectation of her students and, although she was very patient, she expected them to work hard. Nadja Salerno-Sonnenberg came to lessons for seven months without her violin because she just wanted to spend the time talking. Miss DeLay was very patient and then finally said to her, "If you don't come in next week with your violin and a piece prepared, you're out of my class and I'm kicking you out of Juilliard. I'm not kidding."[35] This scared Nadja enough that for her next lesson she had learned the entire Prokofiev Violin Concerto. After that, she started practicing thirteen hours a day and reached her goal of winning the 1981 Naumburg Competition.

Isaac Stern, who knew Miss DeLay for many years, summed it up when he said, "What Miss DeLay does is to give an enormously solid physical base to her students, but also allows them to keep a measure of their individuality instead of stamping them. She has a sense of responsibility to young psyches and an ability to arouse in them a devotion, which she returns tenfold. The result is that she's the most effective violin teacher in the world."[36]

Dorothy Delay passed away in 2002. She left behind an astonishing musical legacy as a master violin teacher.

Last is the example of my own piano teacher, Dorothea Alpert of Rancho Palos Verdes, California. I started taking piano lessons from Dorothea in 1978. I had graduated from college, was married, and wanted to continue with my music. She was referred to me by a trusted friend, and I set up an appointment for an interview. Meeting and talking to Dorothea was a life-changing experience. I sensed immediately that she was a very special, very remarkable, and very talented woman. I knew she was going to impact my life in more ways than music.

Dorothea Anseen was born March 1912 in Oakland, California. Growing up, her home was filled with music. Her mother was an exceptional lyric soprano and was the choir director and piano soloist at St. Paul's Lutheran Church in Oakland. Her father was the minister at the church. Music was important to her parents, and they instilled within Dorothea at a very young age a love for music and singing. When she was six years old, she began taking piano lessons. She studied under a number of excellent music teachers, including Louise Mansfield for voice and Esther Hjelte and Frances Knigge (of the University of Southern California) for piano. Over time, she became an expert musician and played the piano, pipe organ, and harpsichord, but her passion was teaching and imparting musical knowledge to budding musicians.

At the age of sixteen, Dorothea began teaching students. Her influence on promising musicians has spanned a lifetime. Like other influential music teachers, she was genuinely interested in her student's lives—their interests, their hobbies, and their aspirations. Over the last eighty-four years, she has developed hundreds of close personal friendships with each of her students and continues to keep in touch with many of them today. It has been gratifying for her to watch these young people go on to college and excel in a variety of professions.

Dorothea fondly remembers her student Stephen Benedict. He was twelve years old, a talented musician, and Dorothea adored him. Benedict went on to become a speech writer for the White House during the Eisenhower administration. Today, Benedict is in his eighties, living in Ohio, and their friendship continues.

Helena Sudgren was eight years old when she started taking piano lessons from Dorothea. She was an extremely talented musician and, under Dorothea's tutelage, was accepted to the Juilliard School of music in New York and became an accomplished pianist.

Long before science discovered the importance of music and brain development, Dorothea noticed the difference music made in the lives of her students. She says, "When playing the piano, many mental and physical operations are happening simultaneously: the feet are working the pedals, the fingers are playing both black and white keys, the eyes are watching the music, and the ears are listening for harmony—it is a brain stimulation, and that is why young people who study piano or any musical instrument do so well in college—they are sharp!"

Dorothea's methods of getting her students to practice were not out of the ordinary. She set up point systems and rewards for practicing, but for the most part she did not have problems inspiring her students to practice—the music was its own reward. She says, "My students were musical people, and they practiced because everything they did musically was stimulating to them—the music they were learning, the performances they were giving, and the peer recognition—all of these things were powerful motivators."

My own lessons with Dorothea were inspiring and included music interpretation, style, technique, theory, analyzing what the composer was saying, and so forth. Her teaching techniques always left me feeling excited about music. As one of her adult students, I participated in Friday evening music programs, recitals, and excursions that she planned. Even today, she continues to see a few of her adult students every Wednesday evening; discussing musical pieces, playing duets, and living life to the fullest.

In March 2012, Dorothea reached a milestone—she celebrated her one-hundredth birthday! She is still full of life, intellect, compassion, and understanding and credits her longevity to her strong gene pool and her involvement with music. I recently asked what music has meant to her in her life, and she said, "Music has invaded my life from early childhood until now. It is a very nurturing art. The emotions you feel when you listen to music are challenging. You peruse the writing and the composition from the standpoint of how that music is affecting you and why it is affecting you—there is a very intense and sensitive connection with one's feelings for music and how you impart it to others; particularly as a teacher."[37]

Dorothea remains one of the most influential people of my life, and I feel fortunate to have had her as my teacher and always as my friend.

Wendy Waring, Barry Trobaugh, Dorothy DeLay, and Dorothea Alpert are four very different teachers, but what unite them are their love for music and their love of teaching.

Wendy Waring, Barry Trobaugh, Dorothy DeLay, and Dorothea Alpert are four very different teachers, but what unite them are their love for music and their love of teaching. It is not easy to find teachers with their level of passion, but as you begin this process of choosing a teacher look for the following qualities:

- TEACHER WITH A DEGREE IN MUSIC: Find a teacher who has a degree in music. Consider teachers belonging to such organizations as the Music Teachers National Association, but do not rule out teachers who do not belong to such organizations. It is possible to find excellent teachers who do not affiliate with music organizations.

- INTERVIEW: Interview several possible music teachers. Ask questions regarding their length of time teaching, their expectations, and methods of teaching.

- QUALITIES OF A GOOD MUSIC TEACHER: Keep in mind that a concert musician does not necessarily make a good teacher. Instead, look for qualities that make any teacher outstanding: passion for the subject, dedication to his or her craft, patience, and wanting to make a difference in the lives of budding students.

- ATTEND A RECITAL: Ask to attend a recital so that you can observe the musical abilities of the students. If the teacher doesn't have recitals, find another teacher. Recitals motivate the child to complete and polish his or her music. They also help to keep student enthusiasm at a high level.

- INVOLVE STUDENTS IN MUSIC COMPETITIONS: Ask the teacher if she involves the students in music competitions. Skilled teachers know when, how, and if they should involve a student in a competitive musical atmosphere.

- COMPLEMENT TO YOUR CHILD'S PERSONALITY: Choose a teacher that will complement your child's personality. A teacher with lists of credentials and glowing recommendations may not be right for your child. One teacher may relate to one of your children, but not another. Consider finding another teacher for the other child. It may mean the difference between that child sticking with her music or quitting.

- TRUST YOUR INTUITION: Trust your instincts with teachers. If it doesn't "feel" right, it probably isn't right. A rather interesting incident occurred while I was interviewing a teacher for one of my sons. As she was telling me about her own two daughters, she suddenly exclaimed (obviously without thinking), "I have two little girls, and I'm so glad because I hate boys." Because I am a mother of five sons, the last person I want involved with my child is someone who hates boys.

- CHILD HELPS SELECT MUSIC: As a child gets older, he may want to help select the pieces he plays. Make certain the teacher is flexible and will listen to the student when making these decisions.

- RHYTHM AND COUNTING IMPORTANT: Question the teacher on what emphasis she places on counting and rhythm. If a child doesn't play the correct rhythm, he or she is just playing notes on a page. Students who struggle with the music are usually having difficulty with the timing. Many teachers have the student tap or clap out the rhythm before he or she starts playing the piece. Counting out loud should be part of the process. Rhythm and timing are probably the most important aspects of the music and should be emphasized by the teacher.

- KNOW THE EXPECTATIONS: Discuss with the teacher the length of the lesson time, as well as how much time your child should be practicing each day.

- MAKE THE RULES OFFICIAL: Get in writing the policy and procedures of the teacher regarding absences, vacations, sicknesses, tardiness, makeups, and payment schedule. It is important that you understand the rules and are willing to abide by them.

- SHOW CONSIDERATION AND APPRECIATION: Once you have carefully decided on a music teacher, give him or her every consideration. Teachers are professionals trying to make a living by bringing music into the lives of your children. They need parental support and help. Show the teacher every courtesy that you would any professional. Take the time to express your appreciation. It is one of the greatest needs of human beings.

With the right teacher and instrument, your child is ready to embark on an exciting musical journey.

$\mathscr{P}$RACTICING: KEEPING THE TEMPO

> *"If I don't practice for one day, I know it; if I don't practice
> for two days, the critics know it; if I don't practice for
> three days, the audience knows it."*
>
> Jan Paderewski

"**M**om," wailed Jason from the piano bench, "how long do I have to practice?"

"Until you're eighteen," I replied, "so keep practicing!"

This scenario is a familiar one in many homes. Getting a child to practice consistently can be a challenge. Few children enjoy practicing day after day, except perhaps Mozart, who hated to *stop* practicing. Midori, one of the great violinists of our day, loved to practice the violin for hours each day when she was barely four years old. Then, of course, there was Handel, whose mother hid a clavichord in the attic so that at night he could secretly practice without his father knowing. (Handel's father wanted him to become a lawyer and *not* a musician.) But, unlike Mozart, Midori, and Handel, most children need encouragement and gentle prodding to practice their musical instruments.

Additionally, there may be reasons why children do not want to practice. When I was growing up, our piano was down in the basement, and it was dark and scary. I was only six and hated to practice by myself in a place that was frightening to me. When I was in junior high school, I started taking organ lessons, and, because my family didn't have an organ, I practiced on the one at our church. The building was huge, and for security reasons I had to lock myself in. It didn't help that I was in a church; I was still frightened. I couldn't concentrate on the music and spent most of the time paralyzed with fear. As a result, I was never thoroughly prepared for my organ lessons, and I felt uncomfortable telling my parents about my fears of being alone in a big church building.

Finding out why your child does not like to practice does not necessarily solve the problem, but knowing why can be helpful as you seek to find ways to motivate and encourage her. In this chapter, we discuss some ideas on motivating children to practice that have worked for different families across the nation.

Getting Your Child to Practice

When raising our sons, my husband and I had only three laws in our home that were nonnegotiable. We felt that a few well-placed rules can be very powerful and that too many rules lose their effectiveness. One of these nonnegotiable laws was that each one of our sons choose a musical instrument, or instruments, and learn to play it, through consistent practice, until he entered college. Our goal was not to produce musical virtuosos, but rather to help our sons gain a deep appreciation and love for music and to instill within them certain values and skills that learning an instrument can teach. If our sons wanted to continue music lessons in college (and they did), my husband and I continued to support them.

From the outset, we allowed our sons to choose what instrument they wanted to play and what instrument they would be willing to practice and learn. Next, we set down the rules for practicing while our sons were excited about this new adventure of learning a musical instrument. Before the first lesson, my husband and I drew up a contract explaining the terms of practicing, commitment, and expectations. Once everyone agreed with the rules, my husband and I and each of our sons signed the paper. A copy of the contract was given to each son, so he would have something he could see, hold, and look at whenever he wanted to. For young children, this is important because "seeing is believing." The contract was now binding and could not be broken until they left for college.

For many children, about three or four months into the lessons, the fun and excitement begin to wane. "This is hard work," "I don't like this anymore," and "I think I want to quit" are typical comments heard when this happens.

When this happened at our house, I would whip out the contract and say, "Sorry. Talk to me when you're eighteen, when the contract becomes null and void."

Losing enthusiasm about practicing is a very common occurrence with children because they are experiencing the discipline of doing something each day, which is not easy. When your child sends you this message, it is time to seriously look at ways to support, motivate, and convince her that learning a musical instrument can bring big dividends and is worth the sacrifice, even though the benefits seem intangible and distant.

Losing enthusiasm about practicing is a very common occurrence with children because they are experiencing the discipline of doing something each day, which is not easy.

It is important to remember that in life there are many things we do that start out fun and exciting, but that eventually become difficult and frustrating. Developing a talent, doing homework, working at a job, learning a difficult subject, and practicing an instrument are all things that have their challenging moments. For instance, in the early years, learning math and science involves many fun hands-on activities and the use of manipulatives (such as pattern blocks, algebra tiles, and fraction bars), but sooner or later the student must learn the complexities and abstractions of the subjects that take *real* studying and commitment. Oftentimes when this happens, students lose interest, become overwhelmed, or their grades drop, particularly if there is no one to give the help and support they need. Many educators understand this dilemma. George Tressel of the National Science Foundation, addressing teachers of the nation, said, "At an early age, you try to develop the enthusiasm, but then in high school there does come a time when science is not easy. Science is hard." And, according to John Tyrell, senior science advisor for the Boston City schools, "Theories abound as to why kids lose interest [in science]. Basically, the high schools blame the elementary schools, and the elementary schools blame the parents."[1]

In many ways, learning a musical instrument can be compared to learning science or math. It starts out rather simply when learning the basics, but eventually gets more challenging and sometimes the interest wanes. When this happens, absolutely do not throw up your hands and let your child quit, no matter how much he complains, nags, or whines. Stick to your original mutual commitment, keeping in mind that in the long run, your child will be happy he stuck with it. By not allowing your child to give up, you are teaching him valuable lessons of life—perseverance and commitment. How many adults do you know who, when looking back at their childhood, wish their parents had not allowed them to quit their music? When I speak to audiences about this subject, invariably, many people share stories of unfulfilled dreams of learning a musical instrument. They quit because it got difficult, and their parents allowed it.

You wouldn't allow your child to stop going to school if he got discouraged or didn't like the homework, would you? So, what do you do when discouragement is at a high and enthusiasm is at a low? Research indicates that in order for children to succeed at something, they need a combination of volition (willpower) and motivation (inspiration or incentives). If not, the best laid plans can backfire. That is why it is important from the outset that you allow your child to choose his or her musical instrument, which increases his or her willpower and motivation to practice it. But even then, disciplined practicing is not easy. (Think dieting!) Incentives to increase motivation and willpower are also an option and can be many and varied. For some children, a parent sitting with them during practice sessions and offering help, encouragement, and support acts as an incentive and supplies the willpower and motivation not to quit. For other children, tangible incentives work. Tangible incentives need to be something they ask for and not something that you, the parent, feel they should have or would be an exciting reward for them. If the parent decides on the particular reward or motivation, it usually doesn't work. Let them decide what they want and are willing to work for. Some children want a trip to the ice cream store, to see a movie with a friend, or some money. Keep in mind, too, that there will always be children who will consistently practice their musical instrument because they love to, but they tend to be the exception and not the rule. All of our sons started out loving to practice, but they *all* went through a period when they hated it and wanted to quit.

In the beginning, I sat with our sons during practice sessions, and occasionally they asked for a specific tangible reward. It was usually in the first two years that they needed these little boosts of encouragement. After that, they no longer seemed interested in rewards. What changed? By this time they were reading the music well and were practicing successfully on their own. They were involved in music recitals, and their confidence had increased through achieving a substantial level of musical proficiency. In short, the music had become its own reward.

Many parents have shared similar experiences about both their struggles and successes in getting their children to practice. It seems that children who are the most successful at consistent practicing have parents who consistently help and encourage them. For example, Grammy-nominated artist Jenny Oaks Baker of Fairfax, Virginia, is considered one of America's most accomplished classical violinists.

It seems that children who are the most successful at consistent practicing have parents who consistently help and encourage them.

She began playing the violin when she was four years old. Growing up, she did not like to practice, so her mother practiced with her every day until she was twelve years old. She states, "I never enjoyed practicing until I was mature enough to realize that it was necessary in order to achieve my musical goals. Even today, I do not love to practice, but I do it knowing how important it is. In college I practiced six to ten hours daily, but today, with four children to care for, I simply do not have that kind of time." Baker received her bachelor's degree in violin performance from the Curtis Institute of Music in Philadelphia and her master's of music degree from Juilliard School of music in New York City. She has performed all over the world, and her album *Wish Upon a Star: A Tribute to the Music of Walt Disney* earned a nomination for the fifty-fourth Grammy Awards for best pop instrumental album. Today, although she continues to perform throughout the world, her focus is centered on passing the legacy of music to her four children and motivating them to practice as her mother encouraged and motivated her. Laura June is eleven years old and plays the violin, Hannah Jean is nine and plays the piano, Sarah Noelle is seven years old and plays the cello, and Matthew Dallin is five years old and plays classical guitar. Her children accept practicing as part of their daily activities, much like eating or taking a bath. Baker looks for ways to make practicing rewarding, offering incentives and fun activities when it is accomplished. She also enlists others to help her, such as her husband, and she makes certain that the practicing is always high quality, effective, and efficient.

"Because my children are performing with me on a regular basis, they see the benefits of practicing and how they are improving daily," she says. Baker also recognizes that each of her children is different; therefore, she supports their practicing in individual ways. She states, "I used to practice with Laura, but not anymore. She is a very strong-willed girl and I'm a strong-willed mother—so I remove myself from practicing with her—but I do remind her to practice. Hannah loves to practice the piano and usually practices for hours each day on her own, but Sarah and Matthew are still young and require my daily support and help. Each child is different, and I look for ways to inspire and help them individually."[2]

As a result, her children are not only becoming excellent musicians, but they also understand the meaning of hard work at an early age and that hard work pays off. They do not waste time on video games or watching television; instead they take advantage of every moment of life and understand the importance of time management. Playing music together as a family has increased their love and commitment to one another. (See Jenny Oaks Baker playing with her four children: http://youtu.be/0YmbZc7PQnY.)

Kevin Hsieh of Rancho Palos Verdes, California, started playing the piano at the age of five, the violin at the age of seven, and the upright bass at seventeen. His mother supported him right from the outset. He states, "I was lucky enough to have a really stubborn mother who would often sit by me while I practiced. At lessons, she took a notebook and took notes on what the teacher said. Each day when I practiced, we would review the notes together. She was probably more valuable to my development as a musician than most of my teachers. When you are young, you do not have the foresight to realize that developing a talent such as music will have such a profound effect on your life later on. I have friends who deeply regret not continuing with their music." Kevin was often a first-place winner at the Southwest Music Festivals in California. In 2001, he won the "Artist of the Future" competition and was invited to perform the Mozart Piano Concerto in G with the Beach City Symphony. In 2009, he was invited to attend the Betty Carter Jazz Ahead residency at the Kennedy Center. Kevin graduated from Columbia University in New York and spent a year at Juilliard School in the master's program for jazz bass, studying under Ben Wolfe.[3]

Mikel Poulsen of Wenatchee, Washington, has been playing percussion since the fourth grade. His parents bought him a $60 used snare, and Mikel was on his way. Practicing each day was not always an easy task. His mother, a nonmusician, found that Mikel liked her to sit with him, even if it was for only ten minutes. Through the interest she showed and her generous praise of what he was accomplishing, Mikel felt validated.

She states, "It was not really a big sacrifice; I enjoyed sitting with him and listening to him play. I didn't play a musical instrument when I was young, and I wanted this for my children. It gave me great pleasure seeing how much he enjoyed it." Mikel's mother also suggests attending all their music concerts in elementary, junior, and senior high school. She says, "When you show continued support and interest in your child's music, the child will motivate himself, even when you think you can't stand to hear 'Hot Cross Buns' played one more time." In high school, Mikel played in percussion ensemble, jazz band, jazz combo, wind ensemble, and marching band. He won the regional contest for snare drum and marimba solo and went on to compete in the state competition, where he placed in the top ten for snare. Along with his mother's support, Mikel also had a very supportive private drum instructor who had a significant influence on his musical development. Mr. Richard Everhart pushed, encouraged, and demanded perfection from Mikel and insisted on high-quality, daily practicing. Mikel relished both the challenge and his friendship with Mr. Everhart, and, as a result, he practiced very hard. Mikel says, "I can honestly attribute most of my musical successes to Mr. Everhart. He was instrumental in helping me through various challenges in my life. I even wrote my final English paper in college about the life-altering musical experiences with Mr. Everhart." Mikel continued to play during college and was actively involved with the university's orchestra, jazz band, and percussion ensembles. He eventually received an associate degree in performing arts and went on to graduate with a bachelor's degree in business management and finance. Today, at thirty-three, Mikel is married, has three daughters, and owns an independent financial and investment firm. His passion and love for music have never waned, and even as an adult with a hectic lifestyle, he still finds time to take advanced jazz drumming lessons.[4]

In all of the examples, the parents took an active role in their children's music development by being involved and interested and by being there when their children needed encouragement and support.

When a child is learning a musical instrument, he is learning long-term perseverance. It is a different kind of perseverance than completing a homework assignment for school or finishing a project for work; most of these tasks are done within a few days or weeks. The kind of perseverance learned from practicing a musical instrument day after day, year after year, communicates to the child that some talents take years to develop and can only be realized through daily practice and patience, but that the results are definitely worth the effort. Consider the following ideas as your child begins to play an instrument.

> *When a child is learning a musical instrument, he is learning long-term perseverance.*

- THE CHILD CHOOSES THE INSTRUMENT: From the outset, let your child choose what instrument he wants to learn. By your child making this choice, it becomes a motivating factor in his willingness to practice.

- DRAW UP A CONTRACT OF EXPECTATION: Establish rules of practicing and a statement of commitment regarding the study of the instrument. By putting it in writing, you will avoid any misunderstanding later on. Be sure to give a copy to your child to keep. The importance of consistent practice is illustrated in Shinichi Suzuki's comment, "You don't have to practice every day…only on the days that you eat."

- A DAILY ROUTINE: Establish a time each day for practicing. For consistency, try to make it the same time every day.

- SIT WITH YOUR CHILD DURING PRACTICE SESSIONS: Even if you cannot read music, be there for support and encouragement. The key to a child's early musical success requires the parent and child to become a unit. Think back when your child was first learning to read. Didn't you listen to him each day to encourage and praise him for his successes and efforts? Learning a musical instrument can be similar to learning to read. To a beginner reader, words and letters can look foreign. The same is true with music. Those black notes on the page look like a foreign language to a beginning music student. The only time it is not a good idea to sit with your child when he practices is if you tend to get frustrated or angry while working with him. In this case, do not sit with him and do not feel guilty about it. It would be counterproductive if you were to sit there and criticize him for every mistake he makes. A possible alternative could be to have your spouse or an older sibling sit with him, or you can listen to your child practice…from another room.

- SUCCESSFUL LEARNING IS A GROUP EFFORT: Children need support, encouragement, and help from parents, teachers, grandparents, and other family members in the learning process. It is particularly important for fathers to support their children's efforts. The United States Department of Education found that children whose fathers were actively involved in their school activities did significantly better in their schoolwork and were less likely to repeat a grade or get expelled. And this is regardless of parents' income, race, ethnicity, or education.[5] The same can be said about learning to play a musical instrument. When the father becomes part of the supportive team, the child will work even harder to learn a musical instrument and will be less likely to give up. A child senses when parents are united in helping him to accomplish a task. Those children who develop their talents to a high level almost always have a support group that is deeply committed and involved in what they do.

- PERFORMING FOR THE FAMILY: Have your child regularly put on performances for the family. It is a way for her to experience the enjoyment and fun that comes from sharing her hard-earned new skills with an audience with whom she's comfortable with.

- PRAISE YOUR CHILD: As always, be generous with praise. Cognitive theorist Kurt Fischer says that a child's innate problem-solving ability is enhanced 400 percent by practice combined with praise from an adult. When children receive praise for their efforts, their learning and musical skills are tremendously accelerated.[6]

- BE PATIENT: Learning to play a musical instrument involves learning many complex skills at once, and your child will need to receive a great deal of patience and love.

Each day as your child practices her instrument, the discipline required for consistent practicing becomes easier as habits are formed and valuable lessons are learned. One of these lessons is that hard work and discipline pay off, especially when a performance goes well at a recital, school talent show, or family gathering where people applaud her obvious talents. Quickly forgotten are the tedious hours of practice, and the motivation to continue to work hard is revitalized.

> *Each day as your child practices her instrument, the discipline required for consistent practicing becomes easier as habits are formed and valuable lessons are learned.*

Trombonist James Kraft of the National Symphony describes practicing like this: "Practicing is like putting money into the bank. Performing is like taking money out of your bank account."[7] This statement becomes a truism for any endeavor that the child pursues in life, and the best part is that he learns these lessons from the most influential of teachers...experience.

The Virtuoso

When our son Jason was eighteen months old, he would climb on a chair, reach up to the stereo, and put music on to sing and dance to. By the time he was three, he was studying the violin and taking group music lessons, which he immensely enjoyed. At seven, Jason started taking private piano lessons. Eight months later, with positive comments from the judges, he won second place in the duo division at the Southwest Music Festival at California State University, Dominguez Hills. At eleven, he performed from memory an hour-long recital on piano and organ. At twelve, he lost this intense interest in the piano. He continued taking piano lessons until he went to college, but not with the same focus. Today, at thirty-six, he still loves and appreciates all kinds of music and is practicing law in Northern California.

There were many reasons why Jason lost interest in seriously studying the piano, but regardless of the reasons, my husband and I did not feel he would have ever become a concert pianist, nor were we grooming him for such. The willingness to put in megahours to become a concert pianist was simply not there. The goals for children studying music should not be to transform them into virtuosos, but rather to help them realize their full potential in all aspects of life and to instill in them a love of music.

Henry David Thoreau said, "The woods would be very silent if no birds sang except those that sang best." What Mark and I wanted, and what we saw happen, was that Jason learned many valuable lessons, such as responsibility, perseverance, and dependability, that carried him through life's challenges. Additionally, Jason acquired increased inner confidence in his abilities and a love for the arts, which forever will enhance the quality of his life—and he didn't need to become a virtuoso to do so.

Many parents who see signs of genius in their young child feel compelled to relentlessly develop those talents immediately, fearing that if they do not, the child's potential, however dramatic it may be, will be lost…forever. This potential could be in music, sports, math, or any other subject in which the child shows exceptional talent at an early age. Actually, nothing could be further from the truth.

Lauren A. Sosniak, an associate professor of education at the University of Illinois at Chicago, conducted a study that gives a very clear outline on how exceptional talent is developed. Twenty-one concert pianists were interviewed to find out what was involved in developing outstanding achievement in music and how this relates to the overall development of talent. The data that formed the basis of her study was drawn from a much larger project entitled *Development of Talent Research Project*, by B. S. Bloom, and involved thousands of gifted individuals with many different talents. Ms. Sosniak found the following:[8]

- Development of a talent takes a long time—an average of seventeen years of hard work from the time the child begins training until she receives international recognition.

- All of the pianists interviewed started out playing a musical instrument with no intention of becoming concert-level performers.

- Surprisingly, they did not show any unusual talent at an early age. Their parents gave them lessons because, like many parents, they felt that learning a musical instrument was a positive thing.

- It wasn't until they were thirteen or fourteen, after spending several years taking lessons and practicing daily, that the teacher or parent realized they could accomplish more with their music. At this point, the focus of their music changed.

- From that point, the pianists started spending a lot more time practicing, giving serious attention to the details and technicality of the music.

- They got involved in musical competitions, summer camps, auditions, and public musical activities.

- Eventually, after working with some of the finest piano teachers and developing a music style uniquely their own, they reached their goal of concert status.

The musicians in the Sosniak study did not start piano lessons with the intent of becoming concert pianists—it was a natural evolution. If their parents saw talent, they did not push it. Some of the parents were not even musical themselves. By the time the students realized they wanted to seriously pursue music, they were also willing to work hard. Violinist Isaac Stern confirms this gradual process of music development and said, "Somewhere along the line, the child must become possessed by music, by the sudden desire to play, to excel. It can happen at any time between the ages of ten and fourteen. Suddenly the child begins to sense something happening, and he really begins to work, and in retrospect the first five years seems like kinderspiel, [or] fooling around."[9]

Yo-Yo Ma is an excellent example of the evolution of a virtuoso. Ma began playing the cello at age four, and six months later he was playing Bach suites. His father taught him but was careful not to put too much pressure on his young son. In fact, he insisted that young Ma practice only thirty minutes a day, learning only two measures of music, but playing them technically perfectly. By following this system, he had memorized three Bach suites at the young age of seven. When Ma was fourteen, it was obvious to people in the music business in New York that he was virtuoso material, but his father wanted his son to be "normal." Therefore, Ma did not enter competitions, and he rarely gave concerts. He said, "My father wanted us to be educated, good people first and musicians second." It was while he was at Harvard pursuing a liberal arts degree that he began to realize how very important music was in his life. It became clear to him that his first desire and priority was music. Today, he is internationally recognized as one of the greatest cellists in the world.[10]

Another example of emerging musical talent is Wynton Marsalis, the famous jazz/classical musician. He was raised in a musical home, and his father was an accomplished musician. His mother, understanding the importance of music, took the time to expose her children to music programs offered in the community. Marsalis was six years old when he started to play the trumpet. His father did not force him to practice, but rather encouraged his young son and made lessons available to him. When Marsalis turned twelve, he realized that music was something he was very interested in, and he began practicing every day. He learned about "shedding," which is what jazz musicians call "burning the midnight oil" and practicing hard. He began "shedding" up to six hours a day. With serious dedication to his music, along with parental encouragement and help, Marsalis has become a nationally renowned musician.[11]

Extraordinary musical talent, such as demonstrated by Wynton Marsalis and Yo-Yo Ma, is not forced but evolves gradually with the support, patience, and encouragement of family, friends, and teachers. Howard Gardner said, "The challenge of musical education is to respect and build upon the young child's own skills and understanding of music, rather than simply to impose a curriculum that was designed principally to ensure competent adult musical performances. The ready exploration of bits and the intuitive sense of the form and contour of a piece are precious experiences, which should not be scuttled if a full flowering of musical talent is to occur in later life."[12]

Additionally, it takes serious dedication and hard work from the child. All great composers through the ages have known and practiced this simple formula of perseverance and eventual success. As Johann Sebastian Bach put it, "I was obliged to work hard. Whoever is equally industrious will succeed just as well." Thomas Edison believed the same. He said, "Talent is 99 percent perspiration and 1 percent inspiration." Children everywhere who are developing their musical talents will agree that it takes their own personal commitment of working hard to achieve any amount of success.

A well-known study on music and talent that supports the critical link between hard work and musical greatness was conducted by K. Anders Ericsson and Neil Charness in the early 1990s at Berlin's elite Academy of Music. They discovered that innate talent in music or any subject area is not necessarily a criterion in producing a virtuoso or elite musician. What distinguished a good performer from an elite performer was nothing more than how hard he worked as opposed to innate talent. By the time elite music performers were twenty years old, they had amassed ten thousand hours of practice on their instrument—an enormous amount of time and translates into well over thirty hours per week of practice. In contrast, the good performers had totaled only eight thousand hours. None of the elite musicians soared effortlessly to the top of their field; they simply worked much, much harder than everyone else. It was a lot like the adage "practice makes perfect." Researchers now believe that the magical number for developing true expertise and greatness in music or any field of endeavor requires ten thousand hours of hard, diligent work, or what is referred to as "the Ten Thousand Hour Rule."[13]

The musical journey will be different for each of our children. Some will achieve concert status; some will enjoy playing a musical instrument with the school band, while others will enjoy listening to music with a deep love and appreciation. Whatever musical road your child chooses, the evolution and process involved take the time and patience of parents and child. This concept is illustrated in nature by the indra swallowtail butterfly. Laboratory scientists have carefully chronicled its life cycle. An egg is laid at just the right spot on the food plant, and within five days it hatches and grows into a black caterpillar with yellow-orange dots. When it reaches maturity, the caterpillar creates its own chrysalis. Most emerge after two years, but some take up to seven years to come forth out of the chrysalis. Unexpectedly, it begins to emerge, no longer the spotted caterpillar, but a gorgeous black butterfly. Scientists and observers understanding the indra swallowtail growth patiently wait and give time a chance.[14] As you watch your child emerge musically, encourage him or her to work hard, enjoy the journey, and, finally, appreciate the destination.

> *Whatever musical road your child chooses, the evolution and process involved take the time and patience of parents and child.*

©Josh Caldwell

$\mathscr{N}$OTEWORTHY:
LEARNING VALUES THROUGH MUSIC

*"Music is immensely important in the awakening of sensibility,
in the forging of values and in the training of
youngsters to teach others."*
Maestro José Antonio Abreu, *founder of El Sistema*

Many articles have been written on the importance of and necessity for young people to develop marketable skills for their future endeavors. In 1991, the US Department of Labor issued a report urging schools to teach for the future workplace. The report was relevant in 1991 and is still relevant today. Some of the areas the report recommended to be incorporated within the curriculum instruction were working in teams, self-esteem, communication, creative thinking, imagination, and invention. Interestingly, these qualities all grow out of the acquisition of the basic values of hard work, diligence, perseverance, self-discipline, and so on. In the past, these traits and values were formed as children worked, lived, and developed their talents within the family unit and community. In turn, these became qualities that sustained and enriched families, neighborhoods, communities, and the nation. But change comes and not always to our benefit. The traditional home with two parents, extended family, such as grandparents, and other family members is no longer the "norm." The nucleus of the family is changing because many families for many years now have found it necessary for both parents to work. Parents today are balancing hectic schedules, trying to provide for the basic needs of the family, leaving little time for teaching values to their children. Many feel there are simply not enough hours in the day, or they are too tired to put forth the additional effort after working all day, then facing a myriad of household duties to keep the family running. There are also parents who worry *how* best to teach basic values that will enable their child to lead a balanced, productive life. Because values are being taught "hit and miss" in the home, the schools have tried to pick up the slack by adopting programs for the classroom that teach values. But those programs are "hit and miss" as well and, furthermore, reading, discussing, or hearing stories about values does not teach them effectively. It takes actual experiences with the discipline of daily routines, disappointments, challenges, problem solving, and difficulties to teach children values and traits that they can utilize in a future job, as a future parent, and as a contributing member of society.

Confucius said, "Hear…and forget. See…and remember. Do… and understand." It is through this simple "do" where the learning sticks and the values take hold. Thomas Stanley, Ph.D., who coauthored *The Millionaire Next Door: The Surprising Secrets of America's Wealthy,* says that wealth is built on hard work, perseverance, planning, and, most of all, self-discipline.[1] Remarkably, when children learn to play a musical instrument, they acquire these values and traits, as well as others that will benefit them in their future work and will help them to be successful, be it financially or otherwise.

Character Education Partnership (CEP) is a nonprofit organization in Washington, DC, and teaches young people character education in schools, districts, and communities throughout the United States. In 2008, they published a paper that divided character education into two categories: moral character and performance character. Ethical or moral character includes recognizing what is right and having integrity. Performance character includes such traits as responsibility, creativity, diligence, and perseverance.[2] This chapter discusses what CEP would define as "performance character:" character traits such as how one learns to work hard, to persevere, and to be self-disciplined, as well as how one acquires many other skills and values needed to achieve success in life, all through the process of music education. Character values are not easily measured scientifically and rely on anecdotal examples for relevancy. So, I have included many stories to support how these values and character traits can be developed through participation in music.

The Value of Hard Work

The amount of energy we put into developing a talent—such as learning a musical instrument—determines its strength, force, and impact in our lives. Will it become a talent that we enjoy throughout our lives, or merely something we will say we briefly experienced? To accomplish the former requires diligent effort.

When children expend the consistent effort required to learn a musical instrument, they discover that the discipline of this day-to-day task will affect how they approach their other responsibilities in life, such as the effort they put into their school studies or the degree of diligence they give to the development of other talents. Through this hands-on experience, they come to realize that success in anything is the result of consistent hard work. The great composers learned that hard work was the key to creating beautiful music that would last through the ages. Bach credited hard work to the prodigious amount of music he composed in his lifetime. Haydn, a deeply religious man, worked hard composing music, not only mentally but also spiritually. If he began to have difficulties organizing his musical ideas, he would stop and pray to God, asking if

> *When children expend the consistent effort required to learn a musical instrument, they discover that the discipline of this day-to-day task will affect how they approach their other responsibilities in life, such as the effort they put into their school studies or the degree of diligence they give to the development of other talents.*

he had sinned or erred in any way and, if so, would God forgive him. In the words of a well-known saying, "he worked as though everything depended on him and prayed as though everything depended on God." George Frideric Handel, who wrote *Messiah,* the most famous oratorio of all time, did not write this monumental work easily. Even though it took him only twenty-four days to compose 260 pages, Handel never left his house during that time, and rarely left his room or stopped to eat. He was completely absorbed and obsessed with the task at hand, feeling driven and inspired to complete the work. Sir Newman Flower, one of Handel's biographers, said, "Considering the immensity of the work and the short time involved, it will remain, perhaps forever, the greatest feat in the whole history of music composition." After his first performance of *Messiah,* Handel was congratulated by Lord Kinnoul on the excellent "entertainment." Handel very simply replied, "My lord, I should be sorry if I only entertain them. I wish to make them better."[3]

Although most of us will never reach the level of talent of these great men of music, we can all benefit in many areas of our lives from the consistent hard work we put into developing our own potential. The Odessa Philharmonic Orchestra is an example of how hard work equals success. The Odessa Philharmonic Orchestra in the Ukraine was, at one time, a very successful orchestra that played to packed audiences, but under stifling Soviet rules, it had languished. Some members had become discouraged and had even thought of leaving and going to other orchestras. Then in 1991, a young American, Hobart Earle, seeing great potential in Odessa and needing a new challenge in his life, accepted the post as conductor for $50 a month. He knew that in order for this orchestra to regain the success it once had, hard work was essential. His first task was to raise money for desperately needed musical supplies for the musicians. With $3,000 collected from family and friends, he purchased bow hair to refit the entire string section and mutes for the brass and string sections. His next goal was to help each of the musicians earn the necessary money to live, which they could do by touring abroad. To do this, they needed to perfect their skills up to a world-class level of performance. Hard work was expended as each musician worked with a fervor and purpose he or she had never before experienced. Individual rehearsals with each section, plus four-hour practice sessions with the complete orchestra, were a daily routine and reinforced their one desire and goal: to perform abroad in the West. In late 1991, their first opportunity to perform outside the Ukraine presented itself. They went to Austria and performed the marches of John Philip Sousa, Gershwin, and others for the Bregenz Spring Festival. It was an enormous success, and people loved the unique experience of hearing a Ukrainian orchestra performing American music. This moment also became a turning point for each member of the orchestra. By putting forth the necessary effort, they eventually reached their goal and performed throughout the United States, with their dream performance in New York at Carnegie Hall.[4]

Since 1992 the Odessa Philharmonic Orchestra with Hobart Earle has made over fifteen trips abroad to twelve different countries, performing in some of the most prestigious concert halls in the world. In June 2001, Leonid Kuchma, the president of Ukraine, signed a decree granting national status to the Odessa Philharmonic Orchestra, thus making the orchestra the first performing arts organization in Ukraine to acquire national status. It is also the only performing arts organization in the entire country to go from regional status to national status since the independence of Ukraine in 1991.[5]

The Odessa Philharmonic Orchestra is a perfect illustration that individual and team effort, coupled with hard work, results in great rewards. (Watch the Odessa Philharmonic at the Twentieth Anniversary Concert of US–Ukrainian Relations: http://www.youtube.com/watch?v=VDApX-hQKs8.)

Gaining Perseverance and Determination

We live in an age of instants: instant photocopies, instant food, instant photos, instant communications of all sorts, and more. Although many of these instants make our lives easier, they also can give our children a distorted view of life and how goals are achieved. Many children grow up expecting instant results in life, never learning to work for or wait for a reward. When things don't come easily or immediately, they give up. For this reason, studying a musical instrument becomes a priceless lesson. As a child begins to learn to play the flute, for example, she soon realizes that this is not going to be done in an "instant." It will take time, patience, perseverance, determination, and the ability to stick to the task, day after day, year after year, to play the flute with any degree of proficiency. Learning to read notes, to develop hand-eye coordination, to listen, and to count rhythms is a process involving perseverance.

Learning to read notes, to develop hand-eye coordination, to listen, and to count rhythms is a process involving perseverance.

As she works through the difficulties and challenges of learning an instrument, she soon learns that determination and perseverance equal success. Likewise, the perseverance a child learns by practicing her instrument can be, as the experience of many demonstrate, transferred to other areas of her life. For instance, when subjects in school are difficult, she will continue to try her best until the assignment is completed, confident that eventually she will be successful. When life throws her a curve she will not give up, but will work harder with even greater diligence and perseverance until she reaches her goal.

Although most of the great composers suffered personal adversity, they persevered and went on to write beautiful sonatas, symphonies, and operas. Beethoven, despite his progressive deafness at an early age, wrote perhaps his greatest music after going completely deaf. Bach suffered blindness and diabetes, yet continued to compose music. George Frideric Handel suffered a debilitating stroke that put him in a rest home. The world felt that a great life had come to a close. With dogged persistence, he shuffled his way to the organ each night after everyone had gone to bed, forcing his fingers to slowly play each key on the organ. The nuns who heard him were amazed at his unfailing courage and determination. Eventually, he made a complete recovery and went on to write many great pieces of music.

Although the composers of past eras experienced and rose above adversities through determination and perseverance, so have many of the great musical people of our day, such as opera singer Denyce Graves. Graves grew up in poverty in Washington, DC, in the 1970s with her mother and two siblings. Although they lacked material possessions, their home was filled with singing and music. At an early age, Graves had a strong, clear voice that impressed her teacher, Judith Grove, who encouraged the young girl to audition for acceptance into the Duke Ellington School of the Arts. Grove was impressed with Graves's voice, but even more so with her perseverance and determination, which Grove believed would be her key to success. Graves was accepted to Ellington, and there she decided to become an opera singer. By working hard, she was able to graduate early from Ellington. She went to study voice at Oberlin Conservatory of Music in Ohio, and from there she went to the New England Conservatory to study voice. As Graves was preparing to compete for the National Council Auditions of the Metropolitan Opera, she began noticing phlegm in her throat and a pain in her vocal cords, which forced her to withdraw from the competition. After visiting dozens of specialists, she was finally diagnosed with a thyroid condition and was given medication that cleared up the problem. Free to pursue her goal, she went to the Houston Grand Opera, playing the part of Emilia in *Otello*. But in the back of her mind was her lifelong dream to perform at the Metropolitan Opera House in New York. Finally, that day arrived, and on October 7, 1995, she played the lead role in Bizet's *Carmen*. Years of determination and perseverance had paid off as she received a standing ovation from a spellbound audience. The *New York Times* said of Graves, "Few Carmens bring such beauty and sensuality to the role."[6] (Watch Denyce Graves on YouTube sing the *Habanera* from *Carmen*, by Bizet: http://www.youtube.com/watch?v=2V9woZuVIO4.)

An old saying illustrates the tenacity, perseverance, and determination of those like Graves, Handel, Bach, and Beethoven: "Man is like a postage stamp. He may get licked, depressed, stuck in a corner, and sent from post to post, but he will always succeed and arrive in the right place if only he will stick to it."[7]

Learning Self-Discipline

No matter the goal a person wants to attain—be it in music, sports, or business—it requires mastering the art of self-discipline. Self-discipline is one of the core traits of human behavior. It means that you do your work before you play; that you work on a task each day—no matter the difficulty—until proficiency and success are achieved. Self-control is a sister of self-discipline. The Greek word for self-control is *egkrateia*. It is made up of two roots: *en*, meaning "infused with," and *kratos*, meaning "vigor, dominion, power, and strength." To have *egkrateia* is to have great strength and a very strong will, but one firmly held in rein. In other words, to have self-discipline or self-control is to have strength and power over oneself and one's actions.

> *Self-discipline is one of the core traits of human behavior. It means that you do your work before you play; that you work on a task each day—no matter the difficulty—until proficiency and success are achieved.*

While perseverance is learned over time, self-discipline is exercised daily, such as in the day-to-day task of practicing an instrument. For many children, this is not easy. It takes self-discipline to work on the difficult measures of a piece. Instead of viewing those measures as something to avoid, a child over time learns that they are a challenge that can be solved by breaking the piece into workable parts. As he masters these difficult areas in the music, he is able to transfer that learning to other life situations.

Tina Tom of Alhambra, California, understands how self-discipline is learned through studying a musical instrument. She also understands how this skill can be transferred to other life situations. Tom began playing the violin in the fourth grade through her elementary school music program and continued playing until she graduated from high school. For Tom, one of the most important lessons she learned from playing the violin was self-discipline. She says, "Music demands self-discipline, particularly in the realm of listening with intent. My orchestra teacher, Curt Richardson, insisted that we listen carefully to the musicians sitting next to us, and to the music as a whole in order for us to create the sound he wanted. It required enormous self-discipline to listen in this way and coordinate my musical efforts with the other musicians. I transferred this skill to my other classes in middle school and high school, and, as a result, I was more disciplined when it came to paying strict attention in all my classes. When I graduated from college the recession had hit, but I needed a job. So, I transferred what I learned from years of playing the violin—self-discipline and determination—into finding a job. It paid off. When most of my peers were struggling to find something, I was offered three jobs. Music taught me the value of disciplined effort."[8]

Self-discipline is a quality that helps children not only start a task, but also finish it. In life, we often admire the person who has the self-discipline to never lose sight of his goal. Likewise, we have little respect for those individuals who never get past dreaming about their "good intentions." The difference between the person who daydreams about goals and the person who accomplishes his goals is self-discipline.

Young Dat Nguyen, a blind Amerasian orphan from Saigon, is not one who daydreams about his musical goals. In fact, despite a physical handicap, he has demonstrated self-discipline beyond his years. As a beggar on the streets of Saigon, he met a man named Mr. Truong, one of Saigon's finest music teachers and who, like Nguyen, was also blind. Mr. Truong, feeling sorry for the young boy, took Nguyen and his sister into his home and cared for them. Mr. Truong taught Nguyen the piano, several string instruments, and how to read in Braille, which required tremendous self-discipline from the boy. When Nguyen was eighteen, he heard a radio performance of Andrés Segovia playing the classical guitar. Later, when reflecting on the experience, he said, "I totally connected with…what he played. It was love at first sound." Nguyen knew instantly that he wanted to learn to play the guitar like Segovia, so Mr. Truong began teaching him. Being blind, it took time and self-discipline, but was worth the effort. In 1991, Nguyen and his sister were given the opportunity to come to the United States under a program that brought Amerasian children to the country. He was sent to live in Orange County, California, under the sponsorship of Thanh Vu, who had fled Vietnam in 1975. Nguyen attended California State University at Fullerton and, while there, met David Grimes, who headed the university's classical guitar program. Grimes encouraged Nguyen to enter the Southern California American String Teachers Association contest. In preparation, Nguyen practiced eight hours a day. On the day of the competition, Nguyen nervously wondered why he had ever decided to compete against so many talented people, but after playing the first few notes of *Nocturno*, by Federico Moreno Torroba, he became so absorbed in the music that he forgot everything and everyone around him. Nguyen won the competition and went on to win the statewide American String Teachers Association competition. Self-discipline paid off! He continues to work hard and has composed songs to raise money for Vietnamese refugees in the Philippines to come to the United States.[9]

Today, Nguyen has performed for audiences all over the world, and he continues to be an inspiration to the Vietnamese community and to others struggling with physical challenges. His message and example to aspiring musicians: self-discipline and hard work can surpass a visual or physical impairment one may have. If you were to ask him, "How does a blind man learn a score?" he would reply, "With difficulty!" There actually exists a Braille code for musicians, and Nguyen learned to read the Braille music system in Vietnam. "It is a very complicated system," he says. "I use letters and they translate into music." He uses a two-part process to compose music. First, he writes the lyrics in Braille and then he records the music on tape—time consuming and tedious, but worth the effort.[10]

Self-discipline has paid off for Dat Nguyen. He graduated from the University of California at Fullerton and went on to receive numerous recognitions and awards, including first-prize winner of the California ASTA Solo Guitar Competition, a national finalist of the Very Special Arts Program, the Disney Creative Challenge Award, and the National Panasonic Young Solo Artist Competition. (Watch Dat Nguyen perform on YouTube: http://www.youtube.com/watch?v=YPUmEAkBJGE.)

In a speech given at the National Symposium for Music Education in Washington, DC, the importance of self-discipline and its relationship to learning a musical instrument was noted. "As a child begins to understand the connection between hours of practice and the quality of a performance, *self-discipline* becomes self-reinforcing. It is only a short jump from that realization to making the connection between self-discipline and performance skill in life."[11]

The Benefits of Responsibility

"I'm the one that writes my own story—
I decide the person I'll be.
What goes in the plot, and what does not,
Is pretty much up to me."[12]

We are "pretty much" responsible for what we accomplish in our life—the decisions we make, as well as the talents we develop. Music teaches responsibility effectively over time. It is a gradual process that develops as a child grows in maturity and inner motivation. Responsibility comes in music training when the child realizes that ultimately he alone is accountable for any successes he will have with his instrument. It is shown in his willingness to practice consistently each day, even when no one is checking up on him. When he eventually masters various musical skills, he demonstrates that he has taken responsibility for solving difficult musical passages. If he plays in a band or orchestra, he is confronted with the responsibility of not only learning his part of the music, but also performing it well with the other musicians.

> *Responsibility comes in music training when the child realizes that ultimately he alone is accountable for any successes he will have with his instrument.*

As a child matures, so does his understanding of responsibility. He will enjoy taking charge of his life and actions. He will learn not to blame others or find scapegoats when thing go wrong with his musical performances. He will face his challenges, explore them, and take responsibility for the outcome. As a result, his confidence and self-worth will soar.

Bundit Ungrangsee is a world-renowned symphony conductor, a cultural ambassador, and a 2002 laureate of the inaugural Maazel-Vilar International Conductors' Competition. He is also a firm believer that success and taking personal responsibility for one's life and actions go hand in hand.

Born in Had Yai, Songkhla province, in southern Thailand, Ungrangsee grew up in Bangkok. "We were very poor when we moved to Bangkok and lived in a one-room apartment for many years," he says. "All seven of us slept in the same room—my mother and father, my four younger brothers, plus me."

As a teen he was influenced by the Beatles and began taking music lessons. His music teacher taught him mostly a classical repertoire, and he fell in love.

At eighteen, after seeing the New York Philharmonic perform in Bangkok under the direction of Indian Maestro Zubin Mehta, he decided that it *was* possible that even he, a Thai, could become a conductor. "It is so rare in Thailand to see Thais in leadership positions over Westerners; it is always the other way around. Seeing his example made me think it was possible."

This was precisely the motivation Ungrangsee needed, and he began reading and studying everything he could about conductors and conducting. He studied in Australia completing a double major in business and music composition and a master's degree in conducting at the University of Michigan in Ann Arbor.

During this time, he was working extremely hard and took advantage of all the necessary training to ensure success, honing his skills and securing music opportunities in the United States. He says, "I was a study animal as a young conductor. I would schedule every single minute of my day, right down to the ten-minute ice cream breaks."

But there were also bumps in the road and times of frustration and discouragement. He continued to be rejected from competitions in the international community. This was disappointing, because in order to be recognized and conduct on a local and international level, he needed to compete. Finally, his break came. His wife, sensing his discouragement, found an application for a prestigious new competition. She filled it out, he signed it, and she sent it in. He was accepted and in the end was named co-winner of the Maazel-Vilar Conductors' Competition. This achievement opened important doors for him, one being the opportunity to conduct a public concert at New York's Carnegie Hall.

Today, Ungrangsee and his wife, Mary Jane, are living in Bangkok and raising their four daughters. His career now includes music opportunities in Asia, Europe, Australia, and the United States, not to mention his near rock-star celebrity status in Thailand. In addition to his conducting responsibilities and his family, he is working with the mayor of a province in Thailand to create a similar music program to El Sistema of Venezuela that can be replicated all over Thailand. As a result of his varied experiences, he understands more than ever the importance of responsibility. "What I've realized is the more famous one becomes, the more responsibility one has. Therefore, I try to be a good example to younger generations of Thais," he says. Ungrangsee has written several bestselling books which discuss the fundamentals of success, leadership, and responsibility he has learned throughout his career. "I talk a lot about how we have to take responsibility for our lives," he says. "I would like young Thai people to see the value in constant personal improvement and help them understand that ambition and personal responsibility can be great things."[13] Bundit Ungrangsee has personally witnessed the power music has in teaching responsibility. (Watch Bundit Ungrangsee conduct Felix Mendelssohn's *A Midsummer Night's Dream* at Carnegie Hall: http://www.youtube.com/watch?v=UTa5gGO08e8.)

Years ago, William Ernest Henley commented on personal responsibility in his poem *Invictus*. He wrote, "I am the master of my Fate/I am the captain of my soul." We *are* the masters of our fate and the captains of our souls. It really is up to us to do, to become, and to be. Therefore, even if personal responsibility were the only benefit derived from music training, it would be worth any amount of effort and sacrifice to provide this valuable learning experience for your child.

The Value of Teamwork

In the United States, we tend to be an "I" culture. We prize the individual over the group. Most cultures outside of the United States are "we" cultures. Cooperation and collaboration are the rule where people move together or not at all. There is a saying in Japan that goes, "The nail that stands up gets hammered down." In many "we" cultures, to be singled out is an embarrassment and praise for the group is the standard.

Actually, there is strength in both philosophies, but the balance of the two is the most powerful of all. Playing a musical instrument encompasses both philosophies. In a band or orchestra, each musician is responsible for how he or she plays individually, but the group must work together as a team to create a beautiful blended sound. By doing so, they learn cooperation, team spirit, and the power that comes from working together for the greater whole. If you think about it, nearly every aspect of our life requires a certain amount of team effort: activities at school, home, and work. Certainly one of the top qualities that employers look for in potential employees is their ability to work as part of a team.

More and more colleges and universities are looking at prospective applicants who have been involved in activities where they learned and demonstrated team skills. These are young people who set themselves apart from the rest by being organized, working well with others, and accomplishing more with their time. Studies have shown that successful college students are those who show a high level of achievement and teamwork in their high school activities and not necessarily from their SAT scores, class rank, and grades in school.[14]

Studies have shown that successful college students are those who show a high level of achievement and teamwork in their high school activities and not necessarily from their SAT scores, class rank, and grades in school.

Fred Hargadon, former dean of admissions for Stanford University, said, "We look for students who have taken part in orchestra, symphonic band, chorus, and drama. It shows a level of energy and an ability to organize time that we are after here. It shows that they can carry a full academic load and learn something else. It means that these particular students already know how to get involved and that's the kind of campus we want to have."[15] Additionally, social scientists believe that social intelligence is more valuable than academic intelligence. You could be a genius, but if you can't cooperate and work with others, your intelligence will not be your greatest asset.

El Sistema, a music organization in Venezuela, is an astounding example of the power of teamwork. In 1975, in a parking garage in Caracas, Venezuela, Dr. José Antonio Abreu, an economist and musician, gathered together eleven children to play music. Thirty-eight years later, "El Sistema," or "The System," has graduated over eight hundred thousand music students; boasts almost two hundred youth orchestras, thirty-one symphony orchestras, and dozens of choruses; and currently teaches nearly four hundred thousand of Venezuela's poorest children how to play music. And not just any music—the main repertoire is classical music of the great composers. What makes El Sistema such a rousing success in Venezuela? Music education is considered a *social* program rather than a cultural one, and, as a result, El Sistema is financed in excess of $100 million each year by the government.

The success of El Sistema has not only created incredible musicians such as Gustavo Dudamel, the music director of the Los Angeles Philharmonic Orchestra, and Edicson Ruiz, a double-bass player who at seventeen became the youngest member of the Berlin Philharmonic Orchestra, but it has also dramatically changed the lives of thousands of Venezuela's neediest children. Many of these children are from the barrios, and some have special needs, but almost all are accepted into the program and are given instruments, meals, and, in some cases, transportation.

Starting at age two and progressing into their teens, children attend what is called a *núcelo* or music school, six days a week for three to four hours after school. Kids of preschool age learn body expressiveness and rhythm, and by the age of five they are playing a recorder and percussion. At the age of seven students begin to play their first string or woodwind instrument. Learning to sing is also emphasized. Early instruction focuses on a single note to develop a quality sound. Three levels of daily practice include full ensemble work, section work, and private lessons given by teachers deeply committed to their students' success.

Above all, teamwork is the "byword" as students work together to create not just beautiful music, but an extraordinary sound. Abreu himself was drawn to music as a social activity. As a boy, he never liked solitary practicing. In his words, "It was the teamwork, the high I got from playing with others, that was my love." Because of Abreu's experience, the kids in El Sistema do not practice alone. They work together in teams as they learn to play in kiddie and youth orchestras. Part of this team effort includes a mentoring system where the older, more experienced musicians help coach the younger ones. A combination of daily rehearsals, honing and perfecting their skills, and regular performances teach these musicians a highly committed form of teamwork: they consider El Sistema their *family*.

Along with cooperation and teamwork between musicians and teachers, there is also an emphasis placed on the much-needed team support of parents. Teachers make home visits and help parents understand the level of commitment required by the program. Parents are taught how to best support their child's practice schedule at home. They are taught the most effective ways of giving feedback and encouragement to these budding musicians.[16] Next, the community is involved. Importance is placed on creating a community that supports the people that make up the community. Teachers, students, and parents have an invested interest in both personal and community success. This creates a place where not only the children of El Sistema feel safe, but grow into adulthood feeling challenged, capable, confident, and valued.

Today, the concept of El Sistema can be found in over fifty cities in the United States, with Los Angeles, California, boasting the biggest Venezuelan-inspired initiative. Under the umbrella of the Los Angeles Philharmonic, nearly five hundred children in two neighborhoods are enrolled in the program, with expansion plans under way to include another neighborhood by 2013.[17]

The Harmony Program at the City University of New York is also modeled after El Sistema and provides about one hundred elementary-school students with daily after-school music lessons, instruments, books, and the opportunity to attend cultural events. Some of the students in the program have already advanced to the level to play alongside members of the New York Philharmonic.[18]

The united endeavors of many have made El Sistema the success it is today, and it is revolutionary proof that given the right opportunity and team effort, everyone has a capacity for music. (Watch "Gustavo Dudamel lead El Sistema's Top Youth Orchestra performing Shostakovich's Symphony No. 10, Second Movement," http://www.ted.com/talks/astonishing_performance_by_a_venezuelan_youth_orchestra_1.html.)

Developing Creative Thinking, Imagination, and Invention

Nothing can match the human mind when it comes to thinking, creating, imagining, dreaming, and inventing. When we are young, we dream about castles in the air and what our future may hold. As we get older, our dreams just get better planned. It was imagination that showed young Albert Einstein how to measure the distance an object travels through space at the speed of light. The world of light, power, and communication were the inventive thoughts of Thomas Edison. Thomas Jefferson followed his own creative and innovative thoughts when he wrote the United States Constitution. (Coincidentally, all three were musicians.) It was Michelangelo's imagination that saw a statue in every block of marble he chipped away at, and Leonardo da Vinci, one of the most creative men that ever lived, dreamed dreams never known before in science, music, art, math, and engineering. He was the embodiment of the Renaissance spirit of intellectual curiosity and creativity.

Every great achievement is at first and for a time only a dream and a part of someone's creative imagination. The story of sculptor Gutzon Borglum, who was working on a head of Abraham Lincoln, is an excellent example. As he chipped away at the marble, a cleaning woman swept up the pieces and threw them away. She was amazed as she watched the head of Lincoln emerge from the stone under the sculptor's hand, until at last the work was finished. She could no longer hold her wonder and said, "Mr. Borglum, how did you know that Mr. Lincoln was in that stone?"[19]

When we think of someone who is creative, we usually think of a person who is talented in the arts. But Pablo Picasso said, "Every child is an artist. The challenge is to remain an artist." Young children, uninhibited and easygoing, freely express creativity in their play with others. As children grown older, their natural creativity will wane unless it is nurtured. That nurturing can be accomplished through music education. Studying a musical instrument teaches and reinforces creativity in young children. As we have learned, the brain, like a muscle, can be developed through exposure to a rich environment of learning experiences. The mental process of learning music utilizes the whole brain. Music students are developing those areas of the brain that expand human creativity. They broaden their thoughts of originality, independence, curiosity, and flexibility as they interpret, analyze, and break apart the music in new and interesting ways. Creativity then becomes the natural process behind approaching situations in life in innovative ways.

> *Music students are developing those areas of the brain that expand human creativity. They broaden their thoughts of originality, independence, curiosity, and flexibility as they interpret, analyze, and break apart the music in new and interesting ways.*

Music through the ages has been a way for young musicians to creatively express and communicate their feelings, thoughts, and concerns to others. In 1792, Josef Haydn used an innovative way to convince his boss, Prince Nicolaus, that he and the other court musicians were in need of a vacation. Haydn composed a piece of music that conveyed their feelings. He called it the "Farewell Symphony." During the music, the musicians, one by one stopped playing and walked quietly out of the room with the music under their arms. The prince got the hint and gave them a vacation.

Creative musicians have also launched new musical genres. Despite critics' condemnation, Igor Stravinsky was a highly creative composer, willing to defy the traditions of musical composition by introducing an entirely new direction in music. He attained instant fame with his two ballets, *Firebird*, a ballet based on a Russian legend, and *The Rite of Spring*, which premiered in Paris on May 29, 1913. During the performance of *The Rite of Spring*, a riot broke out in the theater. Some people cheered, while most screamed and threw things. Despite this initial reaction, *The Rite of Spring* became an enormous success and was credited with changing the whole course of music. His fame spread worldwide. Stravinsky's actions demonstrate that creative people have the courage to "slay the sacred cow" of tradition by using their talents in innovative ways and thereby raising the level of creative expression to new heights.

Creativity will become one of the most important skills for people in the twenty-first century. As information rapidly expands and changes, people will need to be flexible and able to apply their knowledge, skills, and experiences in many different directions. Those individuals who have honed their creative skills through participation in the arts will be able to do this with greater ease.

Building Confidence

The Norwegian Research Council for Science and the Humanities found that students who study a musical instrument, or who are involved in the arts, are more likely to succeed in school because their confidence in themselves is higher.[20] When a child masters the complex task of learning a musical instrument or singing with a chorale group, his confidence begins to soar. Confidence can also come from something as simple as playing well in a recital. A successful performance at a recital gives a child an inner sense of accomplishment and satisfaction. Through the self-expression afforded in musical participation, he sees himself as unique and talented. A child cannot be gifted in every area, but he needs a chance to discover his uniqueness, on which confidence is built.

Have you ever observed a child post recital? If so, you might have seen a child who was bursting with confidence and excitement and could hardly wait to pick out a new piece to learn. Dan Rather talked about the confidence he felt as a young boy performing on woodblocks in a recital: "It is thrilling to be sitting in a group of musicians playing (more or less) the same piece of music. You are part of a great, powerful, vibrant entity. And nothing beats the feeling you get when you've practiced a difficult section over and over and finally get it right. (Yes, even on the wood block.) And you think *you're* excited when you get that song right: imagine how you *mother* feels. You can see it in her face: relief and pride. Big pride."[21] And this confidence continues to build upon itself with each new piece mastered.

Children who study a musical instrument oftentimes demonstrate their confidence by doing better in school and also in their future jobs. In the workforce, confident, self-assured individuals are often the leaders and strength of an organization. Instead of trying to "keep up with the Joneses," they *are* the Joneses! They set the standards that others try to emulate.

> *Children who study a musical instrument oftentimes demonstrate their confidence by doing better in school and also in their future jobs.*

Confidence stems from an inner belief in oneself and one's abilities. A child with confidence in his abilities demonstrates optimism and is not devastated by challenges or setbacks. In this life, no one has the luxury of escaping difficulties. Just like rain and sunshine affect everyone, so does adversity. But having confidence in oneself helps navigate successfully the inevitable bumps in the road. The following story is a poignant reminder of how confidence oftentimes grows from adversity.

The Acholi is an ethnic group living in war-torn Uganda whose way of life has been changed by music. As a consequence of the civil war, many displaced Acholi families live in the Patongo refugee camp under military protection from the terrorist group Lord's Resistance Army (LRA). For the past two decades, over thirty thousand children—some as young as five— have been abducted from villages by these militant rebels and forced to join the LRA. The boys are turned into soldiers and forced to kill family members and neighbors, while the girls are turned into sex slaves. The children are at once the victims of the LRA militancy, and eventually become rebels themselves.

The 2007 documentary film *War Dance* follows a group of Acholi school children from the refugee camp in northern Uganda to a national music competition in the capital city Kampala. The film focuses on three children who use music to piece together their lives in the aftermath of civil war tragedies: Nancy, a fourteen year-old dancer, who takes care of her siblings after her father is murdered and her mother abducted; Rose, the thirteen year-old choir singer who witnesses her parents' murder; and Dominic, a fourteen year-old former child soldier whose passion is playing the xylophone. Despite a lifetime of violent circumstances, music becomes an outlet for reducing the pain and suffering of their lives and giving them confidence and hope for their futures.

Each year in Uganda, twenty thousand schools compete for the right to represent their tribe at the National Music Competition in Kampala. As the documentary illustrates, for the first time Patongo Primary School wins the regional competition and is eligible to compete in the national championship with five thousand other students. Their chances of winning at the national level, however, are slim. They come from a war-ravaged area with limited resources and funding. In the overcrowded refugee camp there is no electricity or running water, and disease and malnutrition are rampant. Moreover, the children are ostracized from their southern rivals, who know that many of them were part of the LRA and were forced to commit unspeakable acts. But, despite these odds, the children confidently believe that music is the key to overcoming obstacles and accomplishing great things.

With help from music teachers outside the camp, the children begin the arduous task of preparing for the event. Instruments are practiced daily, dance routines are meticulously choreographed, and vocal cords are strained with intense rehearsal. In the process, music allows the children to—at least momentarily—escape the challenges of refugee life. As Nancy says, "Songs make me forget about what is happening in the camp…all the disease, no food, people dying…Dancing is like closing my eyes and being with friends. It feels like home." Music even assuages the grief of lost loved ones. Rose, who finds solace in singing, says, "Before my father died, he told me singing was a great talent. When I sing, I think of him."

Finally the day arrives for the children to leave for the competition. The two-hundred-mile bus journey to Kampala takes two days and requires a military escort since much of the area is teeming with rebels. Despite the threat, the children arrive in the bustling city of Kampala filled with excitement and ready to compete.

Of the eight competition categories, the film focuses on three: Western choral performance, instrumental music, and traditional dance. Nancy's category is traditional dance. She performs the ancestral "Bwola"—a royal tribal dance at least five hundred years old reflecting core cultural features of Acholi identity. Nancy speaks proudly of her cultural identification with the Bwola: "I am proud to be an Acholi when I dance. You have to be fearless like a warrior. When I dance, my problems vanish. The camp is gone. I can feel the wind. I can feel the fresh air. I am free and I can feel my home."

After a strenuous week, the competition comes to an end and a new anxiety fills the air as the children anxiously await the awards ceremony. Who will be the winners and have the honor of carrying home trophies to families and villages? The children of Patongo are not disappointed. Dominic is awarded "Best Musician" for his superb performance on the xylophone and is given a new xylophone as his prize. He proudly says, "I want to be a musician because playing the xylophone is a gift from God. Without music, there would be no life."

The biggest excitement is reserved for receiving the top award in the Traditional Dance category. It is a significant achievement that will bring respect and honor to all those, both young and old, living in the refugee camp. In a moment of confidence and cultural pride Nancy sums up their collective exhilaration: "There is no other group who has ever brought a trophy back for winning the Bwola dance. We did not just win for Patongo. We won for our entire Acholi tribe."

The ride back to the camp is filled with confident, exuberant children. Music has been the catalyst for change in their lives. It has forever transformed how they view themselves, how they will solve problems, and how they will face the challenges of the future. Confidence shines on the face of every child.[22] (Watch an excerpt from the movie: www.wardancethemovie. com.)

Developing Critical Thinking and Problem-Solving Skills

Critical thinking has been on the lips of educators now for at least thirty years. During this time, teachers have flocked to seminars, classes, workshops, and educational conferences to learn how to teach the rising generation to think, analyze, and problem-solve. Not surprisingly, they are finding that students who play musical instruments are better thinkers than those who do not. This is because the very process of learning a musical instrument requires, if not demands, critical-thinking skills. A child may start out learning notes on a page, but eventually rhythm, syncopation,

Music is not just developing hand-eye coordination or symbol recognition, but interpretation, thinking, and problem solving as well.

phrasing, the use of different "voices," or parts of the music, all have a critical part in making the music, musical. Music students need to carefully analyze how the composer may have wanted the piece to be played. Decisions are made regarding interpretation of phrases and passages. They analyze, take apart, and evaluate each piece. Music is not just developing hand-eye coordination or symbol recognition, but interpretation, thinking, and problem solving as well. Developing these skills while they are young gives them the tools they need for the future.

Today, many teachers lament the fact that children today simply cannot think or problem-solve. Alarmingly, this is fast becoming a common thread, weaving itself throughout our nation's schools. The future for young people who cannot think is a dismal one, because employers are looking for people who have the abilities to think and solve problems to meet the challenges of a progressive twenty-first century. At the Nashville

Music Forum, Susan Driggers of Bell South Corporation said, "At perhaps no other time has music and arts education been more important. Apart from their obvious benefits, music and the other arts produce critical thinkers, people who are decision makers. In the information age, our company needs people with the critical thinking skills to analyze data and make judgments."[23]

The much-needed critical thinking and problem-solving skills are at work in Cateura, Paraguay. It is an inspiring story about one man, Fabio Chávez, who saw a need and used music as the catalyst to help.

Cateura, Paraguay, sits on top of a landfill and is home to twenty-five thousand people. Their lives are filled with pollution, poverty, drugs, and alcohol. Every day the landfill receives over fifteen hundred tons of solid waste, which has caused serious pollution to the most important water source in the country. Because of their poverty, most of the families, including the children, are employed by the landfill as recyclers. Thirty-seven-year-old Fabio Chávez has worked beside these families for years as an ecological technician at the landfill. These families are his friends, and he wanted to do something that would bring happiness and hope to their difficult lives.

In 2007, Chávez decided to teach the children music. He opened a tiny music school at the Cateura landfill, hoping to keep the children out of trouble, but he had only five instruments and there were many children wanting to learn. Then an idea came to him. Chávez explains, "One day it occurred to me to teach music to the children of the recyclers and use my personal instruments. But it got to the point that there were too many students and not enough supply. So that's when I decided to experiment and try to actually create a few [instruments]."[24] But where could he find the materials to make the instruments? The solution—use recycled materials from the landfill. Chávez enlisted the help of Nicolas Gomez, one of the trash pickers, to take the recycled materials and make musical instruments. He asked another man, Tito Romero, who repairs damaged trumpets, to turn galvanized pipe and other scavenged metals into flutes, clarinets, and saxophones. The instruments from recycled materials begin to take shape. A classical guitar was made from two big jelly cans. Used x-rays became the skins of a drum set. A battered aluminum salad bowl and strings tuned with forks from a table became a violin, and bottle caps became keys for a saxophone.

Today, a chamber orchestra of twenty children performs the music of Beethoven, Mozart, Henry Mancini, and the Beatles on instruments fashioned from recycled materials. It took fifteen-year-old Rocio Riveros a year to learn how to play her flute made from tin cans. "Now I can't live without this orchestra," she says. They call themselves "the Orchestra of Instruments Recycled from Cateura," and in 2012 they performed in Brazil, Panama, and Colombia. Future plans include performing at the Musical Instrument Museum in Phoenix, Arizona. "We want to provide a way out of the landfill for these kids and their families. So we're doing the impossible so that they can travel outside Paraguay, to become renowned and admired," says Chávez.[25] A documentary is currently under way to tell of the story of these children. The title: *The Landfill Harmonic: A film about people transforming trash into music: about love, courage and creativity.* (Watch the trailer at: http://vimeo.com/52711779)

The construction of musical instruments from recycled materials illustrates how critical thinking can solve complex problems using creative solutions.

Lifelong Learning

At School Sisters of Notre Dame in Mankato, Minnesota, is a rather unique group of elderly nuns who are exceptionally active and alert. Their average age is eighty-five, with many of them in their nineties and some one hundred and older. Their secret to productive longevity: disciplined, lifelong learning! Interested in their remarkable vigor, scientists have studied this order of nuns and have found that their activities, which include earning college degrees, teaching, reading, doing puzzles, playing musical instruments, studying politics and current events, working math problems, and writing in journals, are constantly challenging their minds. In short, exercising the brain is a way of life at the nunnery.

The nuns' way of life was summed up by Dee Dickinson, who said, "In order to prepare human beings to be lifelong learners in a world of escalating change and uncertainty, it is essential that they become not just knowledgeable, but as fully intelligent as possible."[26] The sisters' accomplishments clearly show us that through the process of lifelong learning, we can remain active and alert well into old age. Arnold Scheibel, head of the Brain Research Institute at the University of California at Los Angeles, says, "Anything that's intellectually challenging can probably serve as a kind of stimulus for dendritic growth, which means it adds to the computational reserves in your brain."[27]

Scientists at the Salk Institute for Biological Studies in La Jolla, California, and at Princeton University discovered that intense mental exercise could spur the growth of new brain cells throughout our lives. Mental challenges that required spatial relationships and timing (which are required in learning a musical instrument) had the greatest effect in developing new brain cells.[28]

Studying a musical instrument—which works the sides, front, and back portions of the brain—can act as a high-powered stimulus for dendritic growth. Many musicians and composers have kept their brains alert by actively playing and composing music throughout their lives. Stephane Grappelli is one such musician who, throughout his eighty-nine years as a French jazz violinist, performed for audiences all over the world. He once said, "I will play until the final curtain."[29] And he did just that! Until he died in December 1997, he was performing with precision and classic beauty—"an advertisement for the sheer joy of playing jazz."[30]

> *Studying a musical instrument—which works the sides, front, and back portions of the brain—can act as a high-powered stimulus for dendritic growth.*

George Stevens, at the age of ninety-one, was still singing with the oldest nonuniversity men's singing club in the nation, which began in 1888. Stevens joined in 1928, when he was twenty-two years old, and, except for a hiatus during World War II, sang with this group his entire life.[31]

Even "younger" musicians, realizing the importance of music to their mental well-being, are making lifelong commitments to the study of music.

Case in point: Carolyn Allen of Torrance, California, is sixty-seven years old and recently started taking drum lessons. An unused drum set sitting in the corner of her garage—abandoned since her son graduated from high school—stirred an epiphany within her, and she took the plunge. She said that her drum teacher showed restraint and professionalism when he saw her for the first time, but Allen assured him that she didn't expect him to prepare her to try out for Neon Trees, or any other band. She was just there to "have fun and build brain cells." After her first lesson she said, "You mean each arm and each leg will all have to play in rhythm, but each with a different beat? That's like patting your head, rubbing your stomach, stomping your feet, and whistling at the same time." Undaunted, she decided, "Hey, I can do this. There are four year-olds, after all, playing drums on YouTube!" Allen has every intention to continue her lessons until the final curtain call, but she says, "Don't look for me on the Grammys anytime soon. But if you could see me in my garage, you would see me 'in the pocket,' smiling and loving this new addition to my life's experiences."[32]

Another example is Caduceus: The Doctors Band in Springfield, Missouri. This band was formed in 1989 by fifteen physicians and two medical administrators, who created the group out of a need for entertainment at an employee Christmas party. Their first performance was such a success that they now give performances throughout the community, despite their hectic schedules. They have produced one tape recording and three CDs. Their common bond is their love for music, and they have every intention of keeping their group together well into old age! (Watch the band performing Duke Ellington's "Take the 'A' Train": http://www.youtube.com/watch?v=h8_drBziu4g)

Forty-seven year old Roy Niederhoffer is founder and president of R. G. Niederhoffer Capital Management in New York. He began learning the violin at the age of four, and today he plays violin with New York's Park Avenue Chamber Symphony. Niederhoffer also helps to raise money for the music program, Harmony Program, and finds time to help his children practice their instruments.[33]

NAMM, the National Association of Music Merchants, in Carlsbad, California, is hooking up inactive musicians with other musicians in their locale in the Weekend Warrior program, giving them an opportunity to enjoy, utilize, and share their musical talents with others. After just four short rehearsals, these musicians are ready for a performance at a local venue!

You may conclude that if you want to remain mentally active and alert throughout your life, one sure way to do it is through an ongoing, lifelong study of a musical instrument. As the nuns of Mankato have proven, learning can continue throughout life, and, as Arnold Scheibel's research has shown, it *should*. Scheibel notes, "All of life should be a learning experience, not just for the trivial reasons, but because by continuing the learning process, we are challenging our brain and therefore building circuitry. Literally. This is the way the brain operates."[34]

Lifelong learning is not just a catch phrase of the twenty-first century, but can be an actual physical reality. Scientists now know that humans experience another growth spurt at about age thirty, particularly in regard to the refinement of muscle movement in the hands and face. Fine motor coordination increases, and pianists and violinists are able to move their fingers with greater agility. Vocalists are able to command a greater range with their vocal cords, and actors are better able to subtly control their facial muscles and express any emotion just with their face.[35]

> *Scientists now know that humans experience another growth spurt at about age thirty, particularly in regard to the refinement of muscle movement in the hands and face.*

Leif Ove Andsnes, winner of the 1998 Gilmore Artist Award, said this regarding this later refinement of growth: "I was fed the myth that basic technique must be mastered before twenty, but to my surprise, I've developed as much in the last couple of years. My capacity for learning is greater now because of a larger frame of reference."[36] So, we can expect patterns of growth throughout our life. We are a work in progress as long as we keep developing, striving, and learning. On a higher level, there is a deep satisfaction and knowledge that comes from continuous involvement with the arts that cannot be calculated. The quest for knowledge and self-improvement is endless. It seems that the more we know, the more we want to learn, and the more we realize there is so much yet to know.

Appreciation, Sensitivity, and Love of the Arts

Historian Arthur M. Schlesinger said, "If history tells us anything, it tells us that the United States, like all other nations, will be measured in the eyes of posterity not by its economic power nor by its military might…but by its character and achievement as a civilization." The arts give beauty and meaning to our lives, and they are the means by which the character and achievement of a civilization are measured. Monuments fall, civilizations perish, but artistic creations survive. One cannot study a nation without studying the music, art, and literature of that nation. It is through the arts that we understand and appreciate both the individual and the culture. For this reason, it is always interesting to visit a history, art, or science museum. The artifacts behind glass speak of the artistic talent of civilizations of bygone years and give us a picture of their daily life. It does not matter if we are looking at examples of an early musical instrument, pottery of the Incas, or Viking weapons of war—they all possess elements of creativity and artistic design and tell us much about the people who made them.

Music speaks to the inner reaches of the soul, giving solace to the mind as well as the body. It has the power to uplift us when life is collapsing around us. The poignant true stories that follow are moving examples of music's power.

Vedran Smailovic, a cellist with the Sarajevo Opera, watched as a bomb fell and killed twenty-two starving people while they waited in line to get bread. Using music to fight back his emotions, he dressed in full concert attire and played the cello each day for twenty-two days in the crater that the shell had made. With bombs exploding around him, he courageously played Albinoni's mournful Adagio in G minor for those who died so senselessly. Miraculously, he was never hurt. People in the village responded with love and brotherhood, as did the rest of the world. "The Cellist of Sarajevo" and his music became a universal symbol of hope and peace. His act illustrates the power of music to communicate love and sorrow for the victims in this war-torn country filled with hatred, and its power to help heal the wounds.[37] A wonderful children's book based on this story is *The Cello of Mr. O*, by Jane Cutler.

Herbert Zipper's life was changed in an instant when the Nazis marched into Austria in March 1938. He was a talented Viennese musician and conductor who enjoyed the life of the cultural elite. Rounded up and sent to Dachau along with many of his musician friends from the Munich Philharmonic, his life became a brutal existence. Determined to make things better, he and others began to make roughly hewn violins and other instruments from spare wood. They formed a secret orchestra and, on Sunday afternoons, performed for the other men in camp. Astonishingly, they were never caught.

Zipper said, "I realized in Dachau that the arts in general have the power to keep you not just alive, but to make your life meaningful even under the most dreadful circumstances."[38]

Zipper and his friend Jura Soyfer wrote a song entitled "Dachau Song," and in a few short months all one thousand inhabitants of Dachau knew the song. It spread from camp to camp and became "one of the powerful and tightly embraced resistance songs during the Holocaust."[39]

United States Air Force pilot Clair Cline was a prisoner at Stalag Luft I in Germany during World War II. As a child, he had learned to play the violin, but he had also loved fixing the broken violins and other stringed instruments of neighbors. As he languished in prison, desperately trying to combat boredom, he decided to make a violin made from wooden bed slats. Using a small pocketknife, a table knife, and a piece of broken glass for fine scraping, he began his project. From spring until late November, he worked feverishly until finally, the violin was complete. Because it was close to Christmas, he began learning some carols. On Christmas Eve, he pulled the violin from under his bunk and began playing some of the carols. A few of the men hummed along. When the guards ordered silence in the prison, the room grew quiet, but then Cline began to play softly "Silent Night" as the men lay quietly in their bunks, thinking of home, peace, and better times.

On April 30, 1945, the prisoners of Stalag Luft I were freed. Two months later, Clair Cline arrived back home with the beloved violin. "Today, over fifty years later, the violin sits in a display case on the Clines' living-room wall in Tacoma,"[40] a reminder of the power of music.

We cannot appreciate the arts unless we become involved with them on some level, and one cannot become involved with music without becoming immersed in *all* of the arts. Music, drama, the visual arts, and dance all have the power to uplift, inspire, and edify the human spirit. Our children's ongoing association with the arts will enhance their lives immeasurably. One might ask the question, can our children learn these same values and skills by playing a sport, or being involved in leadership opportunities, or other similar activities? The answer, of course, is yes, but there is something unique about the skills and values that are developed when children study a musical instrument, or otherwise become immersed in the arts on some level. It is simply this: their involvement with the arts will grow with them, as do the skills and the values associated with them, building and flourishing year after year, becoming a part of who they are and how they view themselves. It is rather unlikely that a person will be throwing a football around when he is eighty years old, but he can play in a band or orchestra, or sing in a choral group, throughout his entire life. Instead of dreaming about past glories and honors, he can still be actively achieving musically as he continues to hone and perfect those skills and values that will bring joy and satisfaction into his life and the lives of others.

We cannot appreciate the arts unless we become involved with them on some level, and one cannot become involved with music without becoming immersed in all of the arts.

PART THREE

A NEED FOR ADVOCACY: MUSIC EDUCATION IN THE SCHOOLS

CHAPTER 7

𝒜 DYNAMIC MOVEMENT: MUSIC'S POWER TO EDUCATE

"When we teach a child to draw, we teach him how to see.
When we teach a child to play a musical instrument,
we teach her how to listen.
When we teach a child to dance, we teach him how to
move through life with grace.
When we teach a child to read and write, we teach her how to think.
When we nurture imagination, we create a better
world, one child at a time."

Jane Alexander, *"Imagine"*

Lauren Blevins is a classically trained violinist. Her first introduction to music was through a school music program. She was nine years old and in the fourth grade at Flanders Elementary in Farmington, Michigan. As happens in many school music programs, Lauren was allowed to choose the instrument she wanted to learn. She chose the violin. It was love at first sound. When Lauren was twelve years old she attended Power Middle School. Her school music teacher, Sandy Vargo, recognized her musical talent when she discovered that Lauren was sight-reading Vivaldi concertos in bass clef that she borrowed from her violist friend. She also realized that Lauren needed more instruction than what the school could offer, so she talked to her parents about private lessons. Her parents, also recognizing her love of music, made the arrangements and she began taking private violin lessons. Lauren's passion for music blossomed under the tutelage of her music teachers, and her proficiency on the violin accelerated. While in middle school, she played in the school orchestra and was involved in school music performances. During this time, she also spent two summers at Blue Lake Fine Arts Camp. Between private lessons and school music opportunities, Lauren was on her way to becoming a classically trained violinist.

At Farmington High School, additional opportunities broadened her musical talent and awareness. She was concert mistress of the school symphony orchestra and became involved in leadership symposiums sponsored by Bands of America. She taught master classes, and by her senior year, she had opportunities to conduct the school orchestra under the direction of the school symphony conductor, Eric Banks. After graduating from high school, Lauren attended Michigan State University (MSU). She continued to play violin and eventually graduated from the Eli Broad School of Business at MSU with a degree in marketing. From there she attended the Fashion Institute of Design and Merchandising (FIDM) in Los Angeles and graduated with a business degree in the beauty industry. Although Lauren did not pursue a career in music, she firmly believes that her music involvement has contributed to every aspect of her life, including her career choice. She says, "Music enhanced every aspect of learning and led me to pursue what I found challenging and rewarding. Music helped me synthesize information and have a voice. Music helped me develop 'taste.' Music helped me develop characteristics of self-discipline and perseverance. Music gave me emotional awareness and will always be an important part of my life."

Although supportive of all her music activities, Lauren's parents are not musical themselves; therefore, her first beginnings in music came from the schools. If Lauren had not received this introduction to music in school, more than likely music would not be a part of her life today. It was the school music program that started her on her musical path. She says, "I retained so many universally applicable lessons in the chairs of a musical ensemble and very firmly believe a *healthy school music program* should not be wholly separate from daily education. Plus, adolescence is too rough to not have a source of solace and emotional fine-tuning."[1]

My husband, Mark, began his musical training in a similar way. He was introduced to the trumpet as a fourth-grader at Pippin Elementary in Sunnyvale, California. Neither of his parents was musical, but they were supportive of his involvement. He loved playing the trumpet. He loved his daily music classes in school, and he enjoyed the camaraderie and budding relationships with his music friends. His family had a piano, and Mark asked his parents if he could take piano lessons. Seeing his obvious love of music, they enrolled him in private piano lessons. His siblings soon followed in his footsteps.

In junior high school, he was part of the school band called the Mango Marauders and had many opportunities to play at school functions. At Fremont High School, he continued playing trumpet in both the band and the marching band, as well as taking private piano lessons. Music gave him a sense of belonging, and, since he was rather shy, it opened up doors of opportunities to make like-minded friends. While in high school, Mark joined with some of these like-minded music friends and they formed a band called the Tijuana Tacos. There were seven members playing the trumpet, trombone, clarinet, drums, guitar, bass guitar, saxophone, and keyboard. Their music was inspired by Herb Alpert and the Tijuana Brass, and they wore matching attire when they played. The Tijuana Tacos performed at high school football games, Boy Scout programs, New Year's Eve parties, community events, and Band Day at Stanford University. Not only did it give them all something valuable and worthwhile to do with their time, it was just plain fun.

When Mark went to college he stopped playing the trumpet, but continued on with piano. Eventually he only played these instruments for fun, but after I started an orchestra (see chapter 11), he dusted off his trumpet and, once again, began to play seriously.

For Mark, music began with a school music program and became the catalyst for his success in many other areas of his life. He says, "Music was an important part of my schooling beginning in elementary school and progressing through high school. It gave me a sense of belonging to something bigger than myself. Music surrounded me with great friends who had high goals and high standards. Music gave me a feeling of accomplishment and gave me the discipline I needed in other areas of school and life. High school is not necessarily an easy experience, and music gave me a safe haven to successfully endure those growing years. Music also gave me a voice in high school. I was quiet and rather nerdy, and music helped me to feel accepted. It was a way to express myself and be accepted by my peers."

Like Lauren Blevins, Mark's first exposure to music was a school music program. School music programs do make a difference in many young people's lives. They are not an expendable frill—they are an essential ingredient not only for academic success, but also for students grappling their way through school dealing with issues of acceptance and responsibility. For Lauren, Mark, and many others, school music programs become the overture to music involvement and the catalyst for future success.

This chapter is to convince you of the importance of having music programs in our schools. It will also establish the reasons *why* music and the arts matter and the research to back it up. Hopefully, after reading this chapter, you will agree that an education in the arts is worth establishing in *all* schools for *all* children across the nation.

The Mandates

An education in music and the arts has not only been shown to be an essential ingredient for our children's future success, but was mandated with the passing of two federal laws: Goals 2000: Educate America Act in 1994 and, more recently, the No Child Left Behind Act (NCLB) in 2001. Both documents nationally recognize the importance of arts education and specifically list the arts—music, visual, and performing arts—as core subjects students

An education in music and the arts has not only been shown to be an essential ingredient for our children's future success, but was mandated with the passing of two federal laws: Goals 2000: Educate America Act in 1994 and, more recently, the No Child Left Behind Act (NCLB) in 2001.

are to learn in school. The No Child Left Behind Act states that "the term 'core academic subjects' means English, reading or language arts, mathematics, science, foreign languages, civics and government, economics, *arts* [emphasis added], history, and geography."[2] The term "core" is defined as "as a small group of indispensable persons or things."[3] Core subjects are topics or areas of education that every student needs to learn, no matter his or her future occupation. Listing the arts as one of the core subjects was an important designation that was meant to give the arts distinction in the classroom and qualify school arts programs for a variety of federal grants.

In 2003, a report from the National Association of State Boards of Education, *The Complete Curriculum: Ensuring a Place for the Arts and Foreign Languages in American Schools,* called for stronger emphasis on the arts and foreign languages. The report included a sizeable body of research substantiating the benefits of the arts in the curriculum.[4] In 2007, another report, *The Value and Quality of Arts Education: A Statement of Principles*, recognized the place of arts in the classroom. The opening statement from this report states, "Every student in the nation should have an education in the arts." This document was compiled by ten of the most important educational organizations, including the American Association of School Administrators, the National Education Association, the National Parent Teacher Association, and the National School Boards Association.[5] In 2007–08, the Arts Education Partnership (AEP) noted that forty-eight states have arts-education standards, forty-seven states have arts-education mandates, and forty have arts requirements for graduation from high school.[6]

Since arts education was mandated by law, was espoused by decision-making educators, and nearly all fifty states have arts education standards, it would seem logical that every student in our nation's schools would be receiving a comprehensive, sequential education in the arts. Unfortunately, this has not been the case. Contrary to the reports and statistics, music, visual, and performing arts education has been relegated to the sidelines or narrowly eliminated in most schools nationwide.

For example, on April 2, 2012, the US Department of Education issued a report titled *Arts Education in Public Elementary and Secondary Schools, 1999–2000 and 2009–2010.* This report was based on a nationwide survey regarding the conditions of arts programs in schools across the nation. During the 2009–10 school years, the report showed that a striking 91 percent of the nation's public elementary and secondary schools provided music education taught by a licensed music teacher and that 57 percent of American high schools require arts classes for graduation.[7] But don't roll out the band just yet—it's important to look at the fine print. Richard Kessler, dean of Mannes College the New School of Music and former executive director of the Center for Arts Education, explains the fine print: "The disparity between what schools offer and what students actually receive can be enormous," he says. "What the data isn't telling you is that you have schools where there is one music teacher and one thousand students. Some of those students are going to get music and some of those students are not."[8]

If you dig deep into one of the 165 supplemental tables in the DOE study, you will find that Kessler is right. For example, table 70 shows that 81 percent of secondary schools with an enrollment under five hundred offer music, as compared to 98 percent of secondary schools with a thousand students or more who do not. Using these figures to calculate, the number of students receiving no music instruction comes to over 2.1 million children across the country, with students in the lowest socioeconomic quartile (25 percent) faring the worst. Over the last decade, students in high-poverty secondary schools have suffered a 20 percent drop in music instruction. This is unfortunate, because from 1999 to 2000, 100 percent of these schools had music programs. Today, only 81 percent do. What's more, the support music specialists receive is marginally adequate. Elementary music specialists rated their support as "somewhat or very inadequate" in funding, facilities, materials, equipment, tools and instruments, and instructional time in the arts. The secondary level shows equally discouraging data.[9] Much of this unfortunate situation can be traced back to the No Child Left Behind act.

The NCLB act has created a host of issues, including pressure to raise test scores, which, in turn, has reduced classroom time devoted to the arts. With the passing of this law, the federal role in public education was expanded to include annual testing, annual academic progress, report cards, teacher qualification, and funding changes. Think about it for a minute. Mandates are one thing and implementation in the classroom is another. Whatever these laws say about the importance of the arts, standardized tests measure achievement through math and language arts scores and not music or arts proficiency. As a result, school districts focus on these tested subjects and little else. That is how they get their funding, so that is what they are going to emphasize, even at the expense of the arts and any other subject that is not formally tested, such as science, history, or foreign languages.

In 2006, five years after the enactment of NCLB, a national survey by the Center on Education Policy, an independent advocacy organization in Washington, DC, found that 44 percent of elementary school districts had increased instruction time in English language arts and math and decreased time spent on other subjects like the arts and sciences. A follow-up study in February 2008 showed that 16 percent of districts had reduced elementary school class time for music and art by an average of 35 percent, or fifty-seven minutes each week.[10] In California, the numbers are even more dismal. The Music for All Foundation, after examining the California Department of Education data, issued a report, "The Sound of Silence," that shows a 46 percent decline in music participation from 1999 to 2000 through 2000 to 2004.[11] Despite standards set by the California Board of Education regarding what children should know and be able to do in music, visual arts, theater, and dance, a 2006 study found that 89 percent of kindergarten through grade twelve schools failed to offer courses of study in all four disciplines.[12]

Scott Schuler, president of the National Association of Music Educators, sums it up: "While policymakers pay lip service to balanced education, they continue to enact legislation that effectively narrows curriculum."[13] The mandates and policies for the inclusion of the arts have become nothing more than empty talk as districts zero in on test scores and incrementally eliminate the arts.

The Evidence

The question remains—are the arts important to a child's education, brain development, and future success? Do the arts really build a bigger, better brain? Do the arts help children learn academic concepts more easily? Does an education in the arts increase a child's chances for future success? Should parents, teachers, and educators fight for arts programs or for better quality arts programs in their local schools? The evidence says, "Yes."

Hundreds of studies have been conducted to show the significant role music plays in brain development and in the learning processes of our children. In the book *Handbook of Music Psychology,* more than four hundred studies on the educational benefits of music are reviewed in one chapter alone.[14] It is interesting to note that although these studies repeatedly illustrate the importance of music and the arts to a child's education, the three *R*s—reading, writing, and arithmetic—need no studies to back their validity. They are automatically accepted as vital subjects for children to learn. You never see these subjects fighting for survival and a veritable position in the educational hierarchy (nor should they). Yet, the ability to learn math, or the ability to learn how to read or how to write, is enhanced and understood better when it is coupled with arts education. Jeffrey T. Schnapp, professor of romance languages and literatures at Harvard University, believes that reading, writing, and arithmetic are coextensive with art as to be inseparable. He states, "Reading involves navigating the complexities of books and an emerging cluster of new media that merge text, moving or still images, and sound. Writing is the ability to state arguments and create narratives and thereby master the rules of written communication. To say that even everyday writing isn't an art is to accept the cliché that art refers exclusively to works of the fictional, visual, or musical imagination. Arithmetic is the domain of calculation and logic…and a domain where the highest aspiration of a proof, formula, or

> *Hundreds of studies have been conducted to show the significant role music plays in brain development and in the learning processes of our children. In the book Handbook of Music Psychology, more than four hundred studies on the educational benefits of music are reviewed in one chapter alone.*

algorithm is to be recognized as 'beautiful.'"[15] In order to equip students with the kind of thinking and expression Schnapp suggests, the arts, like the three *R*s, deserve a genuine position on the educational ladder.

Although many studies regarding music's effect on brain development have been discussed in other chapters, below is a partial list of other studies that demonstrate the importance music plays in the education process.

Music enhances the learning process: The very systems that music nourishes—our integrated sensory, attention, cognitive, emotional, and motor capacities—is the driving force behind all other learning.[16]

Music develops the brain and improves memory skills: Young children who take music lessons show different brain development and perform better on memory tests that are associated with general intelligence skills such as literacy, verbal memory, visiospatial processing, mathematics, and IQ.[17]

Music in the classroom equals increased academic performance: The arts can provide effective learning opportunities for students by increasing academic performance and better skill building and reducing absenteeism.[18]

Music in the classroom equals better math performance: Students involved in orchestra or band during their middle and high school years performed better in math in grade twelve. The results were even more significant when comparing students from low-income families. Students who were involved in orchestra or band were more than twice as likely to perform at the highest levels in math as their peers who were not involved in music.[19]

Music training increases the ability to learn foreign languages: A team of researchers at the Auditory Neuroscience Laboratory at Northwestern University found that people who study a musical instrument are better able to process foreign languages because they are able to hear differences in pitch and strengthens the auditory cortex. Kraus explains, "Music training is akin to physical exercise and its impact on body fitness; music is a resource that tones the brain for auditory fitness."[20]

Music improves the processing of spoken language: At Stanford University two studies showed that mastering a musical instrument improved the way the human brain processes parts of spoken language. When students have ongoing musical experiences throughout their lives, they are able to detect small differences in word syllables and are able to distinguish split-second differences between rapidly changing sounds—two components essential to processing language.[21]

The results of these two studies follow what many people anecdotally report when learning foreign languages. For Sol Jang of Seoul, Korea, music was the vehicle for her learning English. She began studying the piano at the age of three. Her elementary school, Seoul Insu, offered three different music programs that included training in violin, flute, an ocarina, a recorder and chorus. She took advantage of these school programs and eventually studied and became proficient on the flute, clarinet, cello, violin, viola, and double bass. Her favorite instrument is the double bass. "I can feel the sound of this instrument. It feels like it is holding and hugging my body. It is a wonderful feeling," she says. Sol also discovered that music helped her when learning English. She continues, "My involvement in music helped me develop very acute listening and concentration skills. I hear intricate sounds and pitches that many people miss. When I was learning English, I always had music playing in the background. It helped me to learn English much faster because it increased my levels of concentration. Also, I believe my music training helped me to hear delicate nuances of the English language."[22]

Learning the arts nurtures motivation: Students involved in the arts had increased sustained attention and were more persistent and willing to take risks—qualities needed for success in future jobs. They also had increased educational aspirations.[23]

The arts contribute to an increase in self-esteem and problem-solving skills: For at-risk youth, the arts contribute to lower recidivism rates, increased self-esteem, the acquisition of job skills, creative thinking, and problem solving and communication skills.[24]

Music program equals higher attendance rate: Schools with music programs boast a higher attendance rate than those without programs: 93.3 percent compared to 84.9 percent.[25]

Music equals higher standardized test scores: Students in high-quality music programs score higher on standardized tests regardless of socioeconomic levels. Students scored 22 percent higher in English and 20 percent better in math than students in deficient music programs.[26] Another study, "Different Ways of Knowing," was a three-year program for high-risk elementary students that focused on using the arts to teach. Elementary students with one year in the program gained eight percentile points on standardized language arts tests; students with two years in the program gained sixteen percentile points; and students not in the program showed no percentile gain. Students with three years in the program outscored nonprogram students with considerably higher report card grades in the core subject areas of language arts, math, reading, and social studies. A total of 920 students in fifty-two classrooms in Los Angeles, south Boston, and Cambridge, Massachusetts, were studied in this program.[27]

Music equals higher SAT scores: Students of the arts continue to outperform their non-arts peers on the Scholastic Aptitude Test (SAT). In 2006, SAT takers with experience in music performance scored fifty-seven points higher on the verbal portion of the test and forty-three points higher on the math portion than students with no experience in the arts. Scores for those with coursework in music appreciation were sixty-two points higher on the verbal portion and forty-one points higher on the math portion.[28]

Music in the classroom equals higher graduation rates: Schools with music programs have significantly higher graduation rates than those without music programs: 90.2 percent as compared to 72.9 percent. Exceptional music programs have an even higher rate of graduation: 90.9 percent.[29]

Eric Oddleifson said, "Teaching arts every day in the core curriculum of elementary schools is the single most powerful tool presently available to educators to motivate students, enhance learning, and develop higher-order thinking skills."[30] When the arts are included in the curriculum, learning is significantly enhanced. As the evidence linking the arts to learning continues to mount, some researchers are referring to the arts as the "Fourth R."[31] The question now is—how do children learn through the arts?

When the arts are included in the curriculum, learning is significantly enhanced. As the evidence linking the arts to learning continues to mount, some researchers are referring to the arts as the "Fourth R."

How Children Learn through the Arts

One of the biggest breakthroughs in education came in the early 1980s. The work of psychologist Howard Gardner gave educators and parents a greater understanding about intelligence and how children learn. In his book *Frames of Mind,* he introduced his "Theory of Multiple Intelligences." Until Gardner's research, educators believed that children are born with a fixed intelligence that is measured through an IQ test. Not so, said Gardner, there are *many* ways to be intelligent. Originally he identified seven different areas of intelligence and said that these seven areas develop at different times and to different degrees in different individuals.[32] He later identified an eighth intelligence, that of the naturalist. We have within us capabilities of all eight types of intelligence. Contrary to the fixed or predetermined intelligence notion of the past, we have a tremendous capacity for learning a variety of things throughout our lives. The possibilities are enormous in terms of what we can accomplish.

The bad news is schools only reward two of the types of intelligence identified by Gardner: the verbal/linguistic and logical/mathematical. The six other areas are equally important, though not necessarily acknowledged in school. These include musical, bodily/kinesthetic, visual/spatial, interpersonal, intrapersonal, and naturalist. The good news is that musical intelligence is so powerful that by learning a musical instrument and studying the arts, the other seven types of intelligence can be developed at the same time. Speaking to this idea, Eric Oddleifson says, "Music education at the elementary school level appears to be a necessary ingredient for children to realize their potential in mathematics and reading. Visual arts appear to be necessary for children to realize their potential in science. Similarly, other arts, such as creative writing, dance, or drama, appear to be necessary for development of one's abilities to fully express oneself, whether in writing or in interpersonal communications, both of which are requisite for being an effective member of a highly technological society."[33]

The chart on pages 164-167 identifies the eight types of intelligence and how they relate to music and the arts. (The definition of the "arts" includes the disciplines of music, the visual arts, drama, dance, and creative writing.)

The Eight Types of Intelligence

Intelligence	Definition
Verbal/Linguistic	Uses words well, enjoys writing and reading, good at entertaining through the spoken word.
Logical/Math	Loves numbers, is logical, able to reason, sequence, see pattern relationships.
Visual/Spatial	Visualizes in pictures and images. Able to create what he mentally sees, good at drawing, sketching in detail, understands three-dimensional space.
Bodily/Kinesthetic	Aware of his body, has control over his body movements. Able to use his hands skillfully.
Interpersonal	Able to work with and understand other people. Good team player. Able to view the world from another's perspective.
Intrapersonal	Knows and understands who he is; aware of his feelings, emotions. He enjoys meditation, contemplation. He is self-disciplined, independent, goal-oriented.

How intelligence relates to music and the arts

Students involved in drama learn to express themselves, memorize lines, and speak in front of an audience. Creative writers use the written word to articulate thoughts and ideas.

When learning music students also learn fractions, ratios, pattern relationships, sequencing, and repetitions. Children learn to count the correct beats in a measure, identify patterns and repetitions of a musical theme, and understand different forms of music, (rondo form, etc.). Music strengthens understanding of certain concepts of math.

Spatial intelligence is increased when studying a musical instrument. Child mentally sees in pictures and visual images. Is able to physically reconstruct his visual world. Artists constructing a mural understand spatial relationships to get it proportionally balanced. Drama students use spatial skills in staging a dramatic performance.

Dancing increases physical coordination, dexterity, and development of large and small muscles as children move their bodies to the music. Artists and craftsmen use their hands to create artistic masterpieces. Students playing musical instruments learn finger and arm dexterity and movement.

In orchestra, drama, and dance, students learn the importance of teamwork. They interact with one another and thrive on their involvement with their peers. Orchestra members must cooperate and listen to each other in order to play successfully together. Drama students work together painting scenery or performing a play. The artist critiques another's artwork, etc.

In the creation process artists are independent thinkers and creators. A musician independently composes music. Artists "find" themselves through individual expression of their artwork. Through the process of studying music and the arts students come to "know thyself."

The Eight Types of Intelligence (*continued*)

Intelligence	Definition
Musical	Understands and produces melodies, rhythms. Can sing in tune, enjoys music, plays a musical instrument.
Naturalist	Is sensitive to the natural world and enjoys spending time outdoors. He notices relationships in nature and sees connections and patterns within the plant and animal kingdoms.

Gardner's theories have dramatically shown that music may help children learn more and more readily, beyond the limited contexts in which their musical intelligence is generally put to use.

How do children learn? Primarily by hearing, seeing, doing, or a combination of the three. Lynn O'Brien of Specific Diagnostic Studies showed through research that students who are auditory learners, or those who learn by *hearing* information, comprise only 15 percent of the population. And yet, lecturing is the most popular way of teaching in our sixteen thousand school districts nationwide. Students who are visual learners are those who learn by *seeing.* They need diagrams, charts, graphs, or pictures to understand the information. They comprise 40 percent of the population. Brain research shows that the visual cortex of the brain is five times larger than the auditory cortex.[34] In other words, it is already established in the brain that a child is able to learn more easily and more effectively by *seeing* a picture of a dinosaur rather than just hearing about one. Those students who need to *touch, feel, experiment, or move* in order to understand information comprise 45 percent of the population. To

How intelligence relates to music and the arts

Helps a child in reading and mathematics. Stimulates creativity, imagination. Helps in learning foreign languages, memorization of facts, retention of ideas. Children think more clearly and more critically by studying a musical instrument.

These individuals find the sounds in nature—birds, wind, rushing water, rain, thunder, and so on—musiclike. (Many CDs have been made using the sounds of nature.) They find art expressed in nature through the changing of the seasons and the varying size, shape, and colors of plants, animals, clouds, and oceans. Through their lenses, outdoor photographers see art and beauty in the earth's natural surroundings. Artists find the varying patterns of natural objects perfect for creating artistic pieces. Musicians find patterns and themes in a fugue, symphony, and so on.

personalize these types of learning, ask yourself, "Could I learn to use the computer by *hearing* someone lecture on it? Would I understand it better if I drew a detailed picture of a computer and its operations? Or, would I understand the computer best by sitting down and actually working on it?" Most of us would have a difficult time learning how to operate a computer just by hearing about its many functions. But by drawing a detailed picture of a computer, using a computer, or building a mock computer, we would learn to use the computer.

So, how do music and the arts incorporate these three ways of learning? Simply put, children use their hands, feet, eyes, ears, and sometimes mouth as they learn a musical instrument. Learning a musical instrument involves the entire brain and helps in its total development and organization. All

> *Learning a musical instrument involves the entire brain and helps in its total development and organization.*

of the senses are being utilized as they hear, see, and touch the instrument.

The result: the child retains information and can transfer learning to other subjects.

Another example of how the arts incorporate the three ways of learning is found in Anne Green Gilbert's book *Teaching the Three R's Through Movement.* She is the director of Kaleidoscope, a modern dance company of young people, and has shown how music, movement, and dance are the keys to learning. Gilbert taught her third-grade class to spell by forming the letters with their bodies. The children expressed the feeling of sentences and punctuation marks through movement. They learned multiplication by moving in sets of threes and fours, discovered the difference between lunar and solar eclipses through planet dances, and choreographed their way across the Oregon Trail. Later, through a federally funded grant, she recorded the progress of 250 students from four elementary schools as they studied language arts using movement, music, and dance. She studied the students for twenty weeks and found that these third-grade students increased their standardized test scores by 13 percent from fall to spring, while the districtwide average showed a *decrease* of 2 percent. Gilbert made a most significant observation in the research: she found a direct relationship between the amount of movement the classroom teacher used and the percentage increase in the students' test scores.[35]

Arts-based education is a win-win situation because a child involved in music and the arts increases her ability to learn and understand other subjects. Her individual learning style is also enhanced. When she learns through her strengths, processing, understanding, and retaining information is easier. Let's look at how three teachers use the arts in their classrooms to boost a child's learning style.

Arts-based education is a win-win situation because a child involved in music and the arts increases her ability to learn and understand other subjects.

Kristin Leidig-Sears, a seasoned sixth-grade teacher at President Avenue Elementary in Harbor City, California, is an advocate of the power of the arts for stimulating learning in children and for helping them to comprehend subjects. For every subject she teaches—math, history, social studies, science, reading, and language arts—the arts are infused. When studying rituals used in ancient Egypt, students create their own rituals using music and musical instruments. When teaching fractions and ratios, Leidig-Sears demonstrates the correlation between fractions and musical "straight eights," quarters, and sixteenths. When teaching science and the food web, students create huge murals depicting the various methods of feeding connections (what eats what) in an ecosystem community. They write songs that feature the various ecosystems found in a rainforest, a tundra, a desert, grasslands, or indigenous forests. When studying one of the ten energy sources, students write original songs representing solar, hydropower, geothermal, biotic, wind, petroleum, coal, natural gas, propane, or nuclear energy. Afterward, they teach their songs to the entire class. One student, when writing a song about energy forces, wrote (to the tune of "Grandma Got Run Over by a Reindeer"), "Grandma got blown up by Old Faithful/While walking in a park called Yellowstone/Now you may say there is no such things as geysers/But I wouldn't walk out in the fire zone!"

Each year students design a city that utilizes total immersion of music, math, science, and social studies. They create laws, renewable energy sources, water sources, income sources, and self-sustaining practices. By stimulating their creative juices, students artistically and musically create this city, thus making the project more realistic.

For the past two years, she has taught character classics through the use of J. R. R. Tolkien's *The Hobbit*. Since Tolkien created a culture, her students also create a society using their own poetry, music, artifacts, and art to describe their make-believe civilization.

Leidig-Sears has witnessed firsthand the power of infusing the arts into subjects. "When you use the arts to teach, learning sticks," she says. "My students really understand what they are learning because they not only visualize concepts—they create them three dimensionally. The arts stimulate all their learning modalities: visual, auditory, kinesthetic. I have seen the arts help kids of all academic levels come together, work cooperatively, and be excited about learning. I have also seen music and the arts help kids that would otherwise slip through the cracks. There is nothing like the arts for helping students totally immerse themselves in school subjects. And best of all, the arts teaches them that learning is fun."[36]

Allison Hickmann is a music specialist at Banting Elementary in Waukesha, Wisconsin. Although time for music is limited, Hickmann makes use of every minute—including before school and at lunchtime. Banting is known for its school choir, and Hickmann has over seventy students in grades four and five who sacrifice their lunch to sing in the choir. Throughout the week, she teaches kindergarten through fifth-grade students various combinations of music theory, instrumental, Orff, percussion, recorder, and singing. Hickmann also works closely with the classroom teachers to musically complement their social studies and science units. For example, when third graders study the planets, she teaches them songs such as "The Planet's Chants." Using rap songs, fourth and fifth graders learn what it means to be a part of community and a responsible citizen. Hickmann reinforces simple math concepts of counting and subtraction by teaching songs such as "Five Little Apples" to kindergarten and first-grade students.

Banting Elementary has what is called a "Duel Language" (DL) program where the students are instructed in both English and Spanish. By third grade, most students are bilingual. To complement this program, Hickmann teaches songs in both English and Spanish, thus facilitating the speed in which students learn both languages. Each year, the students perform three thematic concerts in different languages. She prepared first- and second-grade students for a concert about food. They learned English and Spanish songs such as "Soy Una Pizza," as well as "Peanut Butter and Jelly."

Hickmann understands the important role music plays in a child's education. She has also seen how music can reinforce learning. She says, "Music can incorporate and reinforce so many things that children do every day in their regular classroom by allowing them to see some of the same concepts and ideas in a different light. There is nothing better than seeing students making connections across the curriculum. If I hear 'I know that word,' or 'We learned about this in science!' I know that I've helped a student create a deeper understanding through music."[37] Hickmann recognizes that for learning to stick, it must be reinforced, and music is the vehicle for that reinforcement.

As a young teen, Nicolas Ferroni's teachers used iconic protest songs to teach students about the antiwar movement of the 1960s and '70s. It was one of his favorite classes and helped him to understand what was happening to the nation and the political views of the era. This type of engaging learning made a stronger impact on him than any textbook or lecture could or did. Today, Ferroni is an educator as well as a film and TV writer. And, like the songs that impacted his learning, he, too, uses music to teach his students.

As a history teacher, Ferroni incorporates songs and the creation of soundtracks to teach historical events. For instance, he uses "In the End," by Linkin Park, to teach the Reformation and humanist movements and "Jesus Walks," by Kanye West, to teach the Protestant movement. The lyrics of each piece are studied and dissected to find connections in history and current events. He also encourages his students to pick pieces of music to explain historical events or to imagine what types of music historical figures would have on their iPod playlist. He asks them, "What kind of music would Christopher Columbus have on his iPod (if he had one)?" Sparking creative juices in his students, they reply with "Gold Digger," by Kanye West; "Down with the Sickness," by Disturbed; and "A Whole New World," by Peabo Bryson and Regina Belle. This approach to learning, Ferroni believes, is not just relegated to the history class, but can be used to teach English, math, and social studies. Ferroni has found music to be a powerful tool for not only engaging students in their own learning, but for helping them to form historical connections and associations they will remember long after they have left his classroom.[38]

Learning through music and the arts not only allows the child to develop all of the types of intelligence that lie within her, but also allows the child to express her uniqueness as a person, thereby promoting a strong inner confidence and self-worth.

The Success Stories: The Arts-Integrated Classroom

Despite a dismal picture nationwide showing the elimination of the arts, a new picture is slowly emerging. With renewed enthusiasm and dedication, schools and educators across the nation are realizing the importance of the arts and are making the necessary sacrifices to include them in the curriculum. There are striking examples of academic success in US schools where music and the arts are shown to be an integral part of the learning process. In these schools, the arts do not take priority over reading, writing, math, or science, but are skillfully integrated into the basic curriculum, as well as being taught as separate subjects. Some schools are partnering with outside music organizations, nonprofit organizations, or businesses that are helping to bring music programs into their community schools. The following examples are a small sampling of three elementary schools and one middle school that have had tremendous success using an arts-based curriculum and/or extensive music programs. The result is increased learning and achievement in all subject areas.

With renewed enthusiasm and dedication, schools and educators across the nation are realizing the importance of the arts and are making the necessary sacrifices to include them in the curriculum.

WOODROW WILSON ELEMENTARY SCHOOL: BARTLESVILLE, OKLAHOMA,
MUSIC SPECIALIST: DARLYS LICKLITER
ARTS SPECIALIST: KANDA HILL
OKLAHOMA A+ SCHOOL

At Woodrow Wilson Elementary school in Bartlesville, Oklahoma the arts are a daily part of every child's learning. Creativity is experienced at each grade level. Children discover things rather than being told things. They learn to think using self-discovery and experimentation. Excitement for learning is felt the moment students step on campus. Third graders created a "Michelangelo's Sistine Chapel" mural under the awning of the school's entrance to greet students as they enter. It is a bright beautiful sky that has clouds depicting Howard Gardner's eight different intelligences with a sun in the middle boasting an "A+." The day begins with teachers, children, and administrators gathering together to sing songs and recite poetry.

Wilson is one of fifty-two schools in the Oklahoma network of A+ Schools. The program was founded by a group of educators wanting to see improved academic achievement and a balance of arts education in schools. The result was the A+ model. This initiative is based on Howard Gardner's theory of multiple intelligences, which taps into every child's potential through a variety of learning strategies. It emphasizes a whole-school commitment that includes the engagement of the arts in every classroom. In 2002, the Oklahoma network was started, with the Oklahoma A+ Schools acting as the nonprofit organization that provided the training, supplies, support, and ongoing professional development needed by the school and faculty to meet these goals.

Kanda Hill has been the school's art specialist for the past nine years and is the A+ coordinator. She serves as an advocate for arts education and keeps teachers abreast of arts-integrated professional development training. She assists classroom teachers with arts projects and creates, along with other classroom teachers, dozens of lessons that incorporate the arts (visual, music, dance, drama, creative writing) into the curricula. The school's resource room is filled with art and music supplies, instruments, dance mats, art prints, puppets, costumes, math manipulatives, CDs, and other hands-on materials to help children learn better. Each Wednesday the teachers meet with Hill and other specialists to align the curriculum vertically (upper and lower grades) and horizontally (between grade levels and specialists) to create the best arts-learning environment. For example, fifth-grade students, when studying cultural diversity, sewed "Pillow People for Peace," then wrote short stories about their characters. Fourth-grade students dressed up in costumes to act out the Trail of Tears and the expulsion of Native Americans from the Southeastern United States. Kindergartners learned about different instruments used in jazz bands, then created a colorful jazz musician holding an instrument. Using butcher paper, the children made a stage, carefully assembled their musicians on the stage, and gave their jazz band a name.

Hill also works with the Bartlesville Symphony Orchestra in bringing music programs to the school that complement learning in the classroom. One year, the symphony performed Saint-Saëns's *Carnival of the Animals*.

Students throughout the school created artwork of the French impressionists. Another year, the symphony presented Prokofiev's *Peter and the Wolf.* Fifth-grade students created plaster masks of their favorite character and wrote stories about *Peter and the Wolf* from the perspective of the animals.

Hill has observed how the arts help children to learn. She says, "Children who are involved in the arts are happier, more involved, and more excited to be in school. They learn to express themselves through music, art, writing, dance, and acting. School is no longer boring. Students are more aware that they can learn and succeed in multiple ways. Through the arts, classroom subjects come alive and encourage more critical thinking. Students are not just a test score or a number. Through the arts, we are teaching the whole child."[39]

Along with arts integration in each classroom, music is also taught as a separate subject. Darlys Lickliter has been the music specialist at Wilson for the past twenty-two years. She is also the music coordinator for the six elementary schools in Bartlesville. Lickliter was recently named Teacher of the Year for her extensive work in bringing music into the lives of children. Her program is designed for prekindergarten through grade five and includes Orff, Kodály, recorder, drumming circles, rhythm instruments, a keyboard lab, and an eighty-five-person school choir. She is also responsible for the daily "Rise and Shine—Wake Up, Wilson" morning assembly where the entire school gathers together to sing a variety of songs, learn character words, and recite the Pledge of Allegiance. Each grade level is given a turn to conduct the morning ritual. This activity builds a spirit of camaraderie and sends a message to teachers and students that each person is important and contributes to the success of Wilson.

Since Wilson became an A+ school, Lickliter has noticed a difference in the students. She says, "Our school has gotten away from worksheets. Learning is now focused on experimenting and hands-on activities. Teachers are utilizing different learning styles to help all children learn and be successful. We use art, drama, and music to teach math, reading, social studies, and science. Teachers have found that the children are learning better and that comprehension and retention are improving."[40]

Wilson has a large population of low-income families, yet test scores have made the highest gains in the district and attendance is 94 percent.

State test results show that A+ schools score above average for their districts in reading and math. The results of an independent evaluation in Oklahoma City public schools showed that students in A+ schools outperform demographically matched students in other schools. Lickliter has seen the academic improvements of students. She says, "We have kids that come to our school who struggle academically, but know they are going to be okay and succeed. The reason? We give kids the opportunity to learn in the way they learn best and the result is success both in and out of school." And the way children learn best is engaging the mind and imagination through the arts.

PEORIA ELEMENTARY SCHOOL: PEORIA, COLORADO
MUSIC SPECIALIST: ELVA JEAN BOLIN

Elva Jean Bolin has been the music specialist at Peoria Elementary school in Aurora, Colorado, for the past fourteen years in a career that spans forty-two years. In September 2000, she started the Peoria Violin Program at Jamaica, a kindergarten-through-third-grade school. The inspiration came from the movie *Music of the Heart*—a true story about Roberta Guaspari, who, on a shoestring budget, starts a violin program at a tough Harlem elementary school in New York City and changes the lives of children. Principal Harry Chan, after seeing the movie, asked Bolin if she could replicate a similar program at Jamaica. Her reply—"Sure. Got violins?" A $10,000 grant from the Texaco Foundation enabled them to purchase twenty violins. In addition, the Colorado Youth Instrument Program donated eight violins. Bolin then recruited thirty-two students from kindergarten through grade three, and the program was officially launched.

Today, the Peoria Violin Program boasts eighty violins in six different sizes with fifty students participating. A free violin of the appropriate size and free violin lessons are provided for interested students in the low-income neighborhood school. Several of her advanced students in grades five through seven help her with the younger grades. Once students start the program, many continue until they graduate from high school. Bolin teaches the students modified Suzuki in both English and Spanish, and except for a small stipend from the school district, her time teaching the classes is donated. Why? "Because," she says, "I always remember that if I had not had a free violin and free lessons at my elementary school, I would not be a violinist today."

Although the school does not keep separate testing data for the violin students, the difference in these students has been obvious to both Chan and Bolin. They see improved academic performance, attendance, and behavior. Additionally, Bolin has noticed that these students have better concentration and more enthusiasm toward learning.

She also teaches general music classes to the 522 children at Peoria. They learn music expression (singing and playing), music theory (reading and writing music), aesthetic evaluation (music evaluation), and creating music on keyboard, recorder, and percussion instruments. "I'm fortunate to teach in a district that is very supportive of the arts," says Bolin, "Every school has a music teacher, art teacher, and physical education teacher based on the number of students attending that particular school."

In 2011 Bolin was named one of "Fifty Directors Who Make a Difference" by *School Band and Orchestra* magazine (*SBO*). In 2008, she was inducted into the Colorado Music Educators Association Hall of Fame as well as receiving a twenty-five-year service award. And in 2001, she received the Channel Seven Everyday Hero Award for her work with the violin program. Summing up the past forty-two years of teaching music to children, she says, "The energy I have invested in the lives of my students has been paid back one-hundredfold by their excitement, love, and enthusiasm for music."[41] Elva Bolin is one of those teachers whom her students will remember long past the fading strains of the final musical note.

LEE EXPRESSIVE ARTS ELEMENTARY SCHOOL, COLUMBIA, MISSOURI
MUSIC SPECIALIST: ELIZABETH TUMMONS

Learn, explore, express
At Lee we do our best.
We paint and sing and dance,
We learn to take a chance.

Chorus:
Lee School
A school unlike the rest
Where learning with the arts,
Helps us be our very best.

Verse Two
Our head, our hands, our voice
We learn to make a choice,
We read and write and speak,
We learn we are unique.

Chorus
(School song: Lee Expressive Arts Elementary)

Lee Expressive Arts Elementary (formerly Robert E. Lee Elementary) is a kindergarten-through-fifth-grade school where learning is enhanced through the arts. It is a small public school of three hundred children, and although Lee is not an arts magnet, it has both an art and dance specialist and full and part-time music specialists. Each week, extra time is allocated to the arts. Every student receives eighty minutes of music instruction every four days. Students are also instructed in the visual arts, dancing, and drama. The arts programs at Lee are supported by the district, but additional partners—the University of Missouri, Stephens College, Assistance League of Mid-Missouri, the PTA, the Columbia Art League, and Rag Tag Cinema—are also involved.

Elizabeth Tummons has taught music for thirteen years and is the full-time music specialist. She also collaborates with a part-time music specialist who helps with the extended music program. Students are taught Orff, Kodály, keyboard, and singing. Drumming classes are available to fourth and fifth graders, who work with percussionists from the University of Missouri. A school choir for fourth and fifth graders is offered both before and after school.

Tummons supports classroom teachers by aligning part of her music program with their curricula as well as assisting them when infusing the arts into their science, social studies, math, or language arts lessons. Kindergarteners studying weather patterns, such as precipitation and evaporation, learn songs relating to the weather. They create rainstorms on various musical instruments and perform dances pretending to be a cloud, raindrop, or snowflake that slowly evaporates. First graders study fairytales and learn songs from opera. They create a fairytale reader's theater, make shadow puppets, and play instruments for sound effects. Second graders study the jazz era. They draw timelines of different jazz genres, learn to dance the cakewalk and the swing, write poems about the blues, and go on field trips to see jazz concerts. Third graders study nonfiction and research. They design colorful trading cards of artists and music composers that include pictures, facts, and examples of the artist's paintings or musical works written by the composers.

In addition to her work with the classroom teachers, Tummons and the other arts instructors prepare the students for musical programs that are presented throughout the year. The popular schoolwide sing-along features specific songs for each grade as well as group songs involving the whole school. Each month on a rotating basis, every grade level performs at school assemblies. The Drumming Ensemble joins with the Percussion Ensembles of the University of Missouri for percussion concerts. The Drumming Ensemble and Choir perform for the yearly school fundraising events. The highlight of the year is the school musical presented by fourth and fifth graders, who work hard throughout the year preparing for this seminal event. One year, they performed "Princess and the Pea," to delighted audiences.

Tummons has seen what happens to students when they are engaged in the arts. She says, "When students create music, they learn to problem-solve. When students create music they learn about discovery and how things connect. When they are practicing and preparing for a program, they learn that hard work pays off. I want my students to be 'tuneful,' happy people. I hope that someday they will sing lullabies to their children, thus passing to another generation the importance of music as a language and a source of immense joy."[42]

Wiley H. Bates Middle School: Annapolis, Maryland
Arts Specialist: Laura Brino

Wiley H. Bates Middle School is located in Annapolis, Maryland. For many years the school had experienced problems: low student achievement, low test scores, and discouraged teachers. In 2007, Anne Arundel County Public Schools (AACPS) along with Bates administrators made an important decision. They decided to adopt a whole-school reform initiative where arts would take center stage. They would be fully integrated into the core curriculum and taught as separate subjects. This decision literally brought the school back from the brink of failure. At the time, Diane Bragdon was the principal, and with the blessing of her school superintendent, Kevin Maxwell, they applied for a four-year grant: Supporting Arts Integrated Learning for Student Success (SAILSS) from the US Department of Education. The grant was awarded to AACPS, and Bates was one of fifteen districts and schools to receive it. Today, Wiley H. Bates is an arts integration school with an arts magnet program, is home to eight hundred students, and is a success story.

Since starting the program in 2008, the school has seen a 23 percent drop in referrals and suspensions schoolwide, proficiency in math has grown four times, and reading has increased five times more than the state's average. They have also benefited in ways that are hard to measure, such as willingness for healthy risk taking; more cooperation and collaboration amongst students and teachers; students appreciating the differences of others; and parent and community involvement. School arts specialist Laura Brino has seen huge differences in students. She says, "It is gratifying and exciting to see what integrating the arts has done for our students. Bates used to be a tough school filled with a lot of angry students. Today, the school is filled with positive students who are fully engaged in their learning, who are willing to take risks, and who feel confident about their achievements. Witnessing this transformation is close to a miracle."[43] Clearly the arts have been the energizing medium that created the miracles experienced by Bates students and faculty.

Arts integration is a teaching strategy that works. By weaving the arts into the standard curricula, student learning is enhanced, and comprehension and retention are increased. At Bates, eighth-grade students combine the art of puppetry and science as they explore phases of the moon and weather systems, such as global winds, air masses, and jet streams. One girl dresses up as a full-body puppet and becomes a tornado. Sixth-grade science students studying the solar system choreograph a dance using locomotor and nonlocomotor movements to show their understanding of rotation versus revolution of the planets. Seventh graders in social studies class create a "Dance of the Economies" to kinesthetically express their understanding about various economies, such as free market, mixed, command, and barter. They create four thirty-second music clips to illustrate the moods of each economy. Finally, they add dance movements to show what each economy does. For instance, when communicating how a mixed economy works, they all dance together.

Arts integration is a teaching strategy that works. By weaving the arts into the standard curricula, student learning is enhanced, and comprehension and retention are increased.

Seventh-grade math students plot quadrants on a large grid on the floor and then become the points on the grid—much like a human chess board. They engage in dance movements to express various geometric figures. They compose original rap songs to both explain and learn the area of a triangle, square, and rectangle. To the tune of "La Cucaracha," eighth-grade students write original songs to help them learn and remember how to multiply and divide exponents. During the test, students quietly sing the song as they answer test questions.

By incorporating the arts into the learning quotient, students discover that it is easier to learn challenging subjects and that, once learned, they are never forgotten.

Along with seamlessly emerging the arts standards with core curricula, Bates also teaches the arts as separate subjects. It has four full-time music teachers: a choral director, band teacher, string teacher, and one general music teacher. Together they teach all aspects of music, instrumentation, and singing. Additionally, the school offers a rich variety of elective classes in the arts: visual and digital art classes, dance and high-level dance, dramatic and creative writing, and drama. They also offer a Liberal Arts Chorus, Music Goes Global, Performing/Visual Arts (PVA) Chorus, and Jazz Band. In these classes, students learn that dance can communicate ideas, feelings, and experiences. Dance has its own content, vocabulary, skills, and techniques. Music conveys emotions, has a mathematical structure, and employs rhythm, harmony, and melody. Art is built upon basic design principles of texture, form, line, space, contrast, and balance. Students discover that learning about the arts is as important as being engaged in the arts and is transferable to other school subjects.

Principal Paul DeRoo sums up the success of Bates: "We believe that arts integration is so effective that it is basically an institutionalized teaching practice in our school which benefits all kids in all subject areas. Our staff has developed what we refer to as an 'arts culture' in the school, where everyone works as a team. As each teacher becomes a part of the team, they adopt the arts integration as part of their teaching." He continues, "I am proud of the arts integration because it involves all kids and not just students who are high-interest arts. It influences the best teaching practices amongst all our teaching staff."[44] Wiley H. Bates Middle School is an example of what happens when a rich, creative learning experience is fashioned from the arts. Kids have fun learning. And it is learning that sticks.

TUCSON UNIFIED SCHOOL DISTRICT
TUCSON, ARIZONA

Of the many success stories of schools using arts-based education, one of the most remarkable is that of the Tucson Unified School District in Arizona. It is an inspiring story of how music and the arts can change the lives of students, a school district, and a community.

In the 1990s, the Tucson Unified School District was experiencing low achievement and troubled schools. Looking for solutions, district leaders spent a year researching the connections between brain development, music, and the arts. They found a striking correlation between arts-based education and sustained learning. As a result of their findings, the district started a program called Opening Minds through the Arts (OMA). The foundational structure of the program is based on brain research of how children learn best. By infusing the arts into academic subjects, studies showed that student achievement would increase exponentially. In 1999, the district partnered with the University of Arizona on a pilot program which included Howard Gardner's multiple intelligences and arts integration. The results were immediate: students were more focused, more excited about learning, and they understood math better. The research was correct.

Based on these results, they applied for and received two federal grants from the US Department of Education. They also received support from angel investor H. Eugene Jones, who eventually gave more than $1 million to the program. In 2000, OMA was officially launched in three elementary schools and one middle school. Currently there are eighteen elementary schools with OMA. In 2014, the goal is to have some form of the program in sixty-one elementary schools and ten middle schools. "My goal is to get the arts into every elementary school in Tucson," says Dr. Joan Ashcraft, the co-creator of OMA and director of fine and performing arts.

Formal testing to measure the effects of the program on basic subjects has been ongoing since its inception in 2000. The first three years, the nonprofit research firm WestEd tracked six OMA schools with demographically matched controls. All of the schools had high percentages of low-income students, English language learners, and children of transient families. In every case, OMA students significantly outscored their counterparts in reading, math, and writing. Today, test results continue to show notably better test scores for OMA students.

In a "think outside the box" decision, the district worked with Arizona Testing Incorporated (ATI) and arts educators to devise a test to measure what is learned from music and the visual arts. A pilot test was given, and the results showed that students involved in the arts are better at critical thinking and problem solving—all needed attributes for the twenty-first century. The test questions were not "circle the correct answer," but rather questions that required critical thinking, problem solving, and short answers. For example, one question focused on Dorothea Lange's famous photograph "Migrant Mother." Students were asked to explain the mood of the image based on the elements of art and compare/contrast it to other similar pieces of art. They were required to view it as a story and create a scenario on what would happen next and what questions they would ask the woman. Their answers needed to be in relationship to the time period and subject matter of the piece. Last, they had to decide how they would change the photo from black and white to color. What colors would they choose and why? Elements of analyzing, synthesizing and evaluating were necessary to answer the questions. These were not college students majoring in art. These were fourth-grade students taking the test. Nor was this a "let's teach to the test" scenario. This was the first time students had seen the photograph.

To have a test that quantifiably measures the results of arts-based learning is revolutionary! The reason so many schools expunge or nearly eliminate the arts is because they are not tested and therefore not tied to funding. This groundbreaking decision has the potential of paving the way to making arts-based learning visible and concrete not only in Arizona schools, but in school districts nationwide. Today, Tucson Unified School District stands as a leader in a national movement to integrate arts education. They have also created the testing methodology to measure its merit.

OMA in the Classroom

Each fully implemented OMA school has an arts integration specialist and a team of seven artists who work alongside classroom teachers to fuse the arts into core subjects. They employ more than forty artists from the Tucson Symphony Orchestra, the Arizona Opera Company, the University of Arizona Schools of Music and Dance, and other arts organizations to teach thirty- to forty-five-minute classes twice a week. Kindergartners, first, and second graders receive Orff instruction, sing, and learn percussion instruments. Third graders learn the recorder. Every fourth grader learns the violin, and all fifth graders learn a band or orchestra instrument.

The foundation and design of the program is based on a child's neurological maturation. The following examples briefly illustrate some of the neurological development that occurs at each age and grade level and how OMA supports and strengthens these neural connections.

Kindergartners come to school with a natural ability for rote memory. They positively respond to and can quickly memorize songs with a strong musical rhythm.

Kindergartners come to school with a natural ability for rote memory. They positively respond to and can quickly memorize songs with a strong musical rhythm. The OMA curriculum uses the rhythms found in songs and nursery rhymes as a tool to develop their listening, reading, and memory skills. They meet with various music ensembles, such as the Tucson Symphony Orchestra. Listening to classical music played by the orchestra trains the ear to hear and recognize sounds and patterns, which strengthens oral language and literacy skills. To support this maturation, Melissa Callahan, the arts integrated specialist (AIS) at Kellond Elementary, teaches kindergartners songs based on nursery rhymes such as "Hickory Dickory Dock" and "Old King Cole," as well as songs that teach them to count by twos, fives, and tens. The songs' strong rhyming pattern helps phonemic awareness—the ability to hear and identify individual sounds in words. Along with singing, the children learn kinesthetic movements and beat out rhythms on Orff instruments. Singing, dancing, moving are all activities that reinforce the letter/sound relationships and speech development.

The arts are also used to make connections to other subjects. For example, at Lineweaver Elementary, AIS Karen Fields works with classroom teachers and kindergartners to produce the musical *The Gingerbread Cowboy*. It is a story about a gingerbread boy who meets desert animals and learns all about the flora and fauna of desert life. Students make connections to social studies when learning songs about desert animals, roadrunners, and prickly pears. They learn science when singing piggyback songs about eleven different plants and creatures, their diet, and their habitat. They choreograph dances, paint pictures, and recite poems that build their language and reading skills. Fields sees a difference in OMA students. She says, "OMA provides kids with creative learning. It helps them to understand difficult subjects. They focus better and are more engaged in their learning. OMA provides a 'roundness' of education for all children."[45]

In first grade, the OMA program emphasizes literacy and language development. It uses rhyming, sequencing, patterning, and beginning composition to strengthen that foundation. Students learn the parallels between music and verbal language: a phrase in music is comparable to a sentence. Several sentences linked together form a paragraph, which is like a cluster of musical phrases. A movement in music is like a chapter in a book, and a book is like an entire composition. Opera contains all these elements and becomes the vehicle for first graders that links writing, language, and music. Every first-grade class in OMA produces an opera.

At Kellond Elementary, first graders wrote an opera about ancient China. The children chose this theme based on a Chinese folktale their teacher had read to them about a princess who was sent from the moon to earth. Using creative writing, reading, and language arts skills, they wrote the entire script, composed the music, painted the scenery, memorized lines, and helped create costumes. Other subjects were also integrated. They studied the customs and clothing of ancient China (social studies); they studied fairytales and folk tales (reading/language arts); and they learned the elements of writing a good story, including conflict/resolution and the moral of the story (creative writing). They studied elements of meter and rhythm in order to write the musical score. Every musical line, melody, and libretto was written and composed by first graders.

Callahan has seen what happens to kids when they are actively engaged in their learning: "OMA is 100 percent student engagement. There is not a single student sitting on the sidelines bored. They experience learning in an exciting, creative, and interactive way, every single day. This type of learning is never forgotten and is so much more effective than marking off questions on a worksheet."[46]

Second grade adds movement to music. Movement is a key part of learning. It increases vocabulary, enhances listening and memory skills, and helps children to think critically as they cooperate and collaborate with others. When the rhythmic tools found in music are combined with the rhythmic movement found in dance, memory is boosted instantly. At Kellond, Callahan uses the rudiments of pantomime to teach these elements. Students learn articulation, projection, and expression along with facial expressions, body language, movement, and voice. Writing and reading fluency are also emphasized. Students work in groups of two; are given an open-ended scene and beginning lines; and create the setting, the characters, and their relationship to one another. For instance, the scenario begins with someone knocking at the door with the words, "It's me, open the door." To develop a pantomime from this, students must engage their thinking, vocabulary, listening, and collaboration skills. The tricky part: the audience has to understand the whole scene, so students must meticulously weave the right amount of detail and movement into their lines to make it interesting.

> *Movement is a key part of learning. It increases vocabulary, enhances listening and memory skills, and helps children to think critically as they cooperate and collaborate with others.*

Third graders learn to play and write music on recorders and keyboards. These activities enhance listening skills, the processing of visual information, and coordinating movement in the brain. According to Piaget, they are learning concrete reasoning skills used in phonics, music notation, and math that link auditory centers to the left and right sides of the brain. The students are also involved with creative movement, which boosts reading and writing skills. Through reading and writing poetry, choral reading, and singing simple folk songs in languages such as Japanese, Swahili, and German, they encode new sounds in the brain.

Karen Fields at Lineweaver uses recorders and the visual arts to teach the science of sound. Using soprano, alto, tenor, and bass recorders, she teaches students the differences between high and low sounds, pitch, and vibration. During one lesson, students think of a particular sound made by wind or shattering glass. They think of adjectives that describe that sound—howling, whistling, sharp, and gritty. They create movements that kinesthetically describe these sounds. They think of shapes that would represent the sounds. Combining these elements, students construct paintings reflecting the artwork of modern artist Kandinsky. They title their work "Can You See the Sound?"

In fourth grade, students develop fine motor skills by learning the violin with their teachers. Lessons are based on more abstract reasoning. Music is integrated into reading, writing, history, and science.

Julie Patrick is the OMA exploratory residency coordinator. While teaching at Cragin Elementary, she used rhythms found in music and poetry to teach students abstract concepts of fractions. Working in groups, students chose a published poem and learned about iambic pentameter and how rhythms relate to fractions. They chose words and phrases that complemented the subject of their poem. One class wrote phrases about a train going down a track. Students brainstormed and added words describing the sounds a train would make, such as "whoosh, whoosh, toot, toot, chugga chugga, and choo, choo." Combining elements of fractions— musical "straight-eights"—they created poetic phrases with a rhythm of eight beats. They could create two-beat phrases repeated four times or four-beat phrases repeated two times or any other combination that equaled eight. When the groups came together to combine their parts, they used "round singing." Each group started at a different time, continually repeating their musical phrase until every group had joined in. In music, this form of repetition is called *ostinato*. Students stood together in bee-bop fashion, using imaginative sounds, body percussion and even running motions to create the rhythm of their ostinato. The result was amazing. Without realizing it, they were learning about fractions. Patrick states, "Fractions are a difficult concept for many students, but when you take kids out of a traditional lesson, then the concept becomes more abstract. Students now look at fractions and think about them in a different, creative way. In OMA, we take the concrete and put it in the abstract. From this lesson, not only did they learn fractions, but also poetry, rhythms, music, and cooperation."[47] Abstract teaching solidifies understanding.

Fifth grade puts everything together. As in first grade, students are learning opera, but now it is on a more sophisticated scale. They connect with community arts partners. They attend professional performances. An opera team works with the class to develop writing, reading, and language arts skills. Through the use of song, they discuss voice and structure and how these relate to various elements of writing. Opera becomes the vehicle to link writing and music. Students apply what they have learned and write an original opera and compose all the songs and the libretto. In one school, students collaborated and selected a theme from American history for their opera. They chose to write their opera about the Boston Tea Party from the point of view of the fish swimming in the harbor.

The OMA program has triggered a dramatic turnaround for the Tucson Unified School District. "OMA has been integral to the success of fine arts within this large district," says Ashcraft. "It has boosted our student's understanding of core content; it has raised test scores; it has kept our kids in school; it has reduced discipline issues; and it has helped children who are shy to become more confident. In short, OMA has made learning visible."[48]

The OMA program is a success story. It is engaged learning at its best.

There are many organizations throughout the United States forging partnerships with local schools to bring music and the arts into the classroom. For example, Music and the Brain (MATB) is a nonprofit program developed by the Forty-Second Street Fund in New York City. It creates and provides schools with a comprehensive, sequential music curriculum designed for all grade levels. MATB supplies a piano keyboard lab, piano books, CDs, theory papers, rhythm cards, teachers' manuals, and invaluable training for teachers. The program is currently in 120 New York City public schools, in over fifteen schools in New Orleans, and in several countries worldwide. Education Through Music (ETM) is a nonprofit organization in New York City that brings the arts into economically disadvantaged schools. ETM serves more than fourteen thousand children in twenty-eight New York City schools. The Dallas ArtsPartners is a group of arts advocates, philanthropists, educators, and business leaders who bring arts education to the Dallas Independent School District. Today, every elementary school student in the district receives a minimum of forty-five minutes of art and music instruction each week. Additionally, Dallas ArtsPartners has coordinated efforts with the nonprofits Big Thought and Thriving Minds and has developed a curriculum that integrates the arts into traditional classroom subjects and provides professional development to educators. In Minneapolis, Minnesota, the nonprofit Arts for Academic Achievement (AAA) helps support arts specialists in schools through arts-based and arts-integrated learning. Currently, forty-five Minneapolis Schools enjoy music, drama, dance, and the visual arts through AAA. The Los Angeles Fund for Public Education and the Arts Education Branch recently launched a $200 million campaign to bring the arts into the Common Core curriculum of the Los Angeles Unified School District after having the arts gutted during their five-year budget crises. These and many other organizations share a common goal: make arts education a reality for all school children.

The Arts and At-Risk Students

Music and the arts can help a child academically, behaviorally, and with personal growth, and can be the motivating factor in keeping him or her in school. In 1995, an interesting report from the US Department of Education, *Schools, Communities, and the Arts: A Research Compendium*, found that "using arts processes to teach academic subjects results not only in improved understanding of content, but it greatly improved self-regulatory behavior."

Music and the arts can help a child academically, behaviorally, and with personal growth, and can be the motivating factor in keeping him or her in school.

Barry Oreck of ArtsConnection and Dr. Susan Baum, professor emeritus of the College of New Rochelle, observed an integration of the arts into major subjects in fourteen New York elementary and secondary public schools. They found that "student behavior improved strikingly in such areas as taking risks, cooperating, solving problems, taking initiative for learning, and being prepared. Content-related achievement also rose."[49] Elva Bolin has found this to be true in her work with at-risk students at Peoria Elementary.

Bolin works with many students who are considered at-risk: students with behavior problems, anger issues, and learning challenges. Each year, Bolin and the assistant principal identify at-risk students who would benefit from extra music in their day. Over the years, they have watched these students improve their behavior, become more engaged in their learning, cooperate better with other students, and cultivate a more positive attitude toward school. In nearly every example, they credit the school music program for these changes. Bolin believes that student success is not just about teaching music; it is about building relationships. Over the past forty-two years, she has found that if she first communicates to her students that they are important, a love for music and success in school follow. She has seen many at-risk students find success in high school and beyond through their involvement with music. Below are examples of some of her at-risk students and how music and a caring environment were keys to their success.

Joe had anger issues. His father was in jail, his mother had abandoned the family, and his older brother had been removed from the home by social services. By the time Joe entered kindergarten he had lost all the people he loved—his father, his mother, and his brother. In addition to being angry, he had trust issues and was afraid to develop close relationships with adults. When Bolin met Joe, he was living with his grandparents and was a very angry child. It took her three years to gain his trust, but eventually Bolin and Joe developed a strong rapport. Knowing that a lot of children with anger issues enjoy playing the drums, she decided to introduce him to that instrument. She was right—he fell in love instantly. Joe spent time before school and during lunchtime playing, practicing, and becoming proficient. Whenever he had anger issues in other classes, he knew he was always welcome to come to the music room and play the drums. Music became the catharsis that helped him overcome and control his anger. Bolin could see what playing the drums did for Joe, and so, through a program called

"Share the Music," she arranged for him to get him his own snare drum set. Today, Joe is in the sixth grade. He has advanced on the drums and sounds more like a high schooler than a sixth grader. He is happy, is doing well in school, and is able to control his anger.

Steven is mildly learning challenged. He came to Peoria Elementary in the fourth grade. He wanted to join the after-school music program and learn the drums. A classroom teacher voiced concerns that Steven was not smart enough to learn any instrument, even the drums. But Bolin, seeing Steven's interest, signed him up for band and introduced him to the drums. Like Joe, he fell in love and spent many hours playing and practicing. This music experience helped him to gain confidence in his abilities and opened other windows of opportunities. Eventually, Steven was asked to operate the entire sound system at his church as well as play the drums with the church band. It took time, but at age twenty-one he received, in his own words, "a real high school diploma." Today Steven is twenty-four years old and continues playing the drums and running the sound system at church. Music increased his self-worth and gave him feelings of self-reliance.

In teaching at-risk children, Bolin says, "Education is about teaching kids, not lesson plans or curriculum. Learning is a process, not a product. Every child can learn, but not all learn at the same rate and in the same manner. The teacher needs to use different ways to present a concept to the students because some students are visual learners, some aural learners, some kinesthetic learners. We, as teachers, need to break out of our comfort zone to address different learning styles. Those students who are successful have a lot that they can share with other students about the process of their own learning."[50]

Jo Ann Hood, a music teacher speaking at the Nashville Forum for the National Commission for Music Education, tells of her experiences: "I have found, during my eighteen years of teaching, that music students tend to score better on tests, have better communication skills, and are better disciplined students. They tend to be more prepared for the work force and are more readily hired by businesses. I have also seen several instances where *music kept a student in school who would have otherwise dropped out*"[51] [emphasis added]. Keeping young people in school is not only important to their educational future, but it becomes an economic issue as well. For example, in Los Angeles, 85 percent of all daytime crime in committed by truant young people. The average high school dropout costs society more than $800,000 over the course of the individual's lifetime. The yearly cost of truancy to the nation is $228 billion and rising. Later, when these young people get jobs, it costs the business community approximately $30 billion to train these workers in the basic subjects of reading, writing, and mathematics. So keeping kids in school becomes a sound investment of public funds.[52]

Music can also make a difference for young people who come from homes where the income and parental education levels are low.

Music can also make a difference for young people who come from homes where the income and parental education levels are low. In 1998, Dr. James Catterall, professor of education and co-director of the UCLA Imagination Project, conducted a study of eighth- through twelfth-grade students that showed a connection between participation in the arts and academic achievement. The study focused on the relationship between sustained involvement in instrumental music and mathematics achievement, and theater arts and human development. This was the first reported analysis of information from the NELS:88 assessment sponsored by the United States Department of Education. It included over twenty-five thousand students, who were surveyed regarding, among other things, their participation in the arts.

Of particular interest to the researchers were students from low socioeconomic status (SES). The researchers found that low SES students who took music lessons from eighth through twelfth grades increased their test scores in math and scored significantly higher than those of low SES students who were not involved in music. In addition, low SES students involved in the arts generally scored higher than their noninvolved counterparts in reading, history, geography, and citizenship. For example, math scores more than doubled for the low SES students taking instrumental music, and history and geography scores climbed by 40 percent.

Another area of interest to the researchers was in theater arts, which included acting in plays and musicals, participating in drama clubs, or taking acting lessons. Students involved in the theater arts scored higher in reading proficiency, self-concept, and motivation, and demonstrated higher levels of empathy and tolerance for others. In reading proficiency, the scores grew steadily from the eighth to twelfth grade. And by the twelfth grade, nearly 20 percent more of the low SES students involved in theater arts were reading at a higher proficiency level than those not involved in the arts. The researchers believed that the results were due to the students spending so much time reading and learning lines as actors. They concluded that music and the arts can be a catalyst for success for students in at-risk situations.[53]

This research led to a twelve-year longitudinal study of more than twelve thousand students with information taken, once again, from the NELS:88 database. The researchers had already determined that low SES students with an arts-rich education in secondary school did better academically and socially than their counterparts, but now they wanted to see how these students were doing at ages twenty and twenty-six. Data were analyzed from the following two groups of low SES students: those who had received a rich arts program in middle and high school and those students who had a deficient arts program in secondary school. They assigned the indicators *doing well*, meaning their educational attainments, and *doing good*, designating their community service and volunteer activities, to measure their success.

Overall, they found that low SES students who were intensely involved in the arts during middle school and high school had higher levels of achievement and college attainment. They were also more involved with volunteer activities and political participation. At age twenty, in the *doing well* category, nearly 20 percent more high-arts/low-SES students had enrolled in a four-year college than low arts students. In *doing good*, more than one-third of the high-arts/low-SES students reported doing some sort of volunteer work, compared to less than one-fifth of the low-arts/low-SES group. These are sizeable differences.

By age twenty-six the study accessed more information about higher education. The *doing well* area of education included the following criteria:

attended college after high school, attended a four-year postsecondary institution, grades mostly As and Bs as an undergraduate, and a degree earned. In every area, the high-art/low-SES students scored significantly higher than the low-art/ low-SES students. For example, 70.7 percent of high-art/low-SES students attended college after high school as opposed to only 48.1 percent in the low-art/low-SES students. Also, in comparing students who went further in college, spent more time in four-year colleges, and acquired more and higher degrees, the high-arts/low-SES students scored nearly 2 percent higher than their counterparts.

The *doing good* area included a variety of volunteer activities, participation in the political process, and reflections on their education. Reflections on education included that their education led to better jobs, higher pay, and more promotion opportunity, as well as more responsibility. Once again the high-arts/low-SES students continued to outscore their low-art/low-SES counterparts in every area, and in some areas by nearly 15 percent.

This research is extremely important. It clearly shows that the arts can powerfully affect students in low socioeconomic situations and that serious involvement in the arts throughout secondary schools has the potential to lead to their future, long-term success.

Last, in 2005, another study looked at a similar group of students from impoverished areas and how arts education changed the way they looked at their ability to learn and be successful. The Arts Education Partnership (AEP) conducted a three-year study of students at ten elementary and secondary schools. The schools were selected based on their success despite being in areas of high-poverty family conditions and at-risk community settings. The AEP looked at the correlation between school achievement and an arts-centered curriculum. The title of the study, *Third Space: When Learning Matters*, was couched with meaning. The researchers describe "third space" as "a metaphor that describes the positive and supportive relationships that develop among students, teachers, and the school community when they are involved in creating, performing, or responding to works of art. It is the place where connections get made." The researchers discovered that for many students, the arts had a profound impact on their learning and self-worth.

They concluded, "For many students, where school had often been a place of failure and frustration, the experience of success in the arts was a revelation that learning matters—and that they themselves matter."[54] This statement is a thought-provoking message to teachers and school administrators alike: arts education is a necessity and not a luxury in the lives of young people.

If music and the arts have such a tremendous influence on a child's ability to learn, find success in school, increase self-worth, and change his or her life, why were they ever taken out of the schools in the first place? Certainly the studies have been out there long enough to prove the value of music and arts education. Perhaps Frank Vellutino, a professor of educational psychology at State University of New York at Albany, hit on the answer when he said, "We do more education research than anyone else in the world, and we ignore more as well."[55] If this is true, then why waste the time, effort, and money to do the research in the first place?

The body of music and arts research has rarely been used in most American classrooms. Why? According to Linda Darling-Hammond, professor of education at Stanford University, "In most states, neither teachers nor administrators are required to know much about how children learn in order to be certified."

"What's worse," she adds, "decisions to cut music or gym are often made by noneducators, whose concerns are more often monetary than educational. Our school system was invented in the late 1800s, and little has changed."[56] It has been said that if someone from the 1800s was transported to the twenty-first century, the only place he or she would recognize from his or her era would be our schools.

It has been said that if someone from the 1800s was transported to the twenty-first century, the only place he or she would recognize from his or her era would be our schools.

We talk about changing curriculum and making more demands on students through higher expectations. Perhaps we should begin by making more demands on the education requirements of teachers. Teachers should be required to know and understand how children utilize the entire brain when learning music and the arts, and be able to apply those techniques to their teaching. Linda Verlee Williams, in her book *Teaching for the Two-Sided Mind*, says, "Children come to school as integrated people with thoughts and feelings, words and pictures, ideas and fantasies. They are intensely curious about the world. They are scientists, artists, musicians, historians, dancers, and runners, tellers of stories, and mathematicians. The challenge we face as teachers is to use the wealth they bring us. They come with a two-sided mind. We must encourage them to use it...so that they have access to the fullest possible range of mental abilities."[57] Music and the arts teach to both sides of the mind. Including these strategies in the curricula can help teachers meet this challenge.

During the time of Aristotle and Plato, music was considered one of the four pillars of learning, along with geometry, astronomy, and mathematics. During the late Middle Ages and throughout the Renaissance, every educated person was expected to play an instrument and read musical notation.

During the time of Aristotle and Plato, music was considered one of the four pillars of learning, along with geometry, astronomy, and mathematics. During the late Middle Ages and throughout the Renaissance, every educated person was expected to play an instrument and read musical notation. The result? Some of mankind's most revered works of art were created. In the periods that followed, the world's greatest musical compositions were written by musical giants such as Handel, Bach, Haydn, Mozart, and Beethoven. In this same period, music schools were conducted in orphanages. Orphans, abandoned children, and poor children received a complete music education, and some of these disadvantaged children became the most sought-after vocalists and musicians in all of Europe.[58] Nearly every age throughout history has recognized music to be essential to the learning process and, thus, an integral part of the education process. In this sophisticated technological age, can we consider it less?

In 1991, the National Commission on Music Education, Growing Up Complete, presented a report to Congress that discussed the intrinsic value of arts in a well-balanced education. The report, *Growing Up Complete: The*

Imperative for Music Education, said in part: "Music can make us laugh, weep and shout for joy; it can bring us to our feet or drive us to our knees. The fact that, in vast numbers of our schools, an educated understanding of this dimension of life is left to either lip-service or chance is deeply disturbing. It is a form of dehumanization by default."[59]

$\mathscr{S}$TRIKING A CHORD: MUSIC'S IMPACT ON COGNITIVE DELAYS AND PHYSICAL DISABILITIES

"Great things are not done by impulse,
but by a series of small things brought together."

Vincent Van Gogh

Joshua Villanueva did not begin to speak until he was three years old. He was diagnosed with a speech-language impairment which negatively affected his comprehension in school subjects and his socialization with his peers. Through the public schools, Joshua received additional academic support, as well as help with his speech impairment. Today he is sixteen years old and a different person. He is no longer shy. He thrives in advanced placement classes in high school and is in the International Baccalaureate program. He tutors his classmates in geometry, started a Rubik's Cube club on campus, and teaches young children how to play the piano. He is the cello section leader in the high school orchestra and has played both with the competitive Montgomery County Seniors Orchestra and the Montgomery Philharmonic for benefit concerts.

Joshua also understands the importance of service and the concept of giving back to the community. He volunteered more than four hundred hours for the Montgomery County Public Schools Service Learning program in Maryland. In 2011, he organized a piano recital that raised $1,200 for a needy family. His mother, Rose Villanueva sees the change in her son and says, "Joshua's accomplishments and success help him develop a strong confidence in himself. Joshua now believes that despite his language difficulties, he can embark on challenging endeavors in high school."[1]

India Renea Scott lives in Ebensburg, Pennsylvania. At age five she lost her sight. She learned to read and write Braille, navigate her environment with a cane, and use assistive technology. Today, at fourteen, she has succeeded both in and out of school. She is a member of her high school's marching band and plays the clarinet, piano, snare drum, and cymbals. She is also a member of the forensics team and drama club. India sets high goals for herself and wants to be valedictorian of her graduating class. Her teacher and advisor, Jessica A. Strazisar, says, "India is not a person to be weighted by a disability. While her sight may be missing, her ability to seek insight into her environment and those around her is outstanding. She is an exemplary young woman with a positive attitude and more vision than mere eyes could ever behold."

Anthony Vetere of Sayville, New York, is an accomplished musician. In elementary school, Anthony discovered music and began to play the piano. In the fifth grade, he accompanied his class as they sang in a graduation ceremony. He continued playing throughout middle school and into high school and won the "Best Student Accompanist" award three years running.

As a young child, Anthony suffered with severe language, social, and emotional issues. Socialization was a particular challenging issue. It was difficult for him to socialize with his peers, to work independently at school, and he was argumentative with his teachers. But music changed all that. Today, Anthony attends a precollege jazz program at Five Towns College and ranks in the top 10 percent of his high school class. He continues to perform in many events throughout his community. In describing his passion for music, he says, "Two years ago, I was given the opportunity to be an accompanist for the musical *13*. The experience at the Airport Playhouse made me realize I wanted to become a professional accompanist…Music is my passion. I love being a piano player and a piano accompanist." Anthony

Vetere is autistic but, as evidenced by his accomplishments, is not limited by that diagnosis.

In 2012, Joshua, India, and Anthony received the *Yes I Can* award in the arts category from the Council for Exceptional Children (CEC), which honors students with disabilities who have excelled in school.[2]

As the aforementioned examples illustrate, this chapter will discuss children who have various disabilities—cognitive, physical, and social—and how music becomes one of the catalysts for their success.

Music and Learning Disabilities

When discussing disabilities, the list is long and comprehensive. The most common classifications include cognitive delays (the skills that make it possible for us to think, remember, and learn); learning disabilities (LD), with the most common being dyslexia; attention deficit disorders (ADD/ADHD); physical and other health impairments (POHI); and intellectual disabilities that were once referred to as mental retardation (MR).

When referring to cognitive delays and learning disabilities, both terms are similar in meaning and are oftentimes used interchangeably. In a broad sense, cognitive delays include auditory and visual processing, long and short term memory, logic and reasoning, and attention skills. Specifically speaking, learning disabilities are made up of cognitive disorders that can affect speech; the ability to listen and understand; to think, read, write, spell, and understand math symbols; to follow directions; and so on.

The National Center for Learning Disabilities (NCLD) states that there are currently 2.4 million students (ages six through twenty-one) who have been diagnosed with some form of a learning disability and receive special education services in the public schools. This number represents 41 percent of all students that receive special education and translates into one out of every five people in the United States who have a learning disability. According to NCLD, learning disabilities cannot be cured and are lifelong, but, if they are identified early, a person can still learn, live, and earn successfully.

In the last ten years, school-age students identified with LD have been steadily declining, but unfortunately educational learning outcomes for students with learning disabilities remains low. The following outcomes are found on the NCLD website and indicate the seriousness of the problem.[3]

- Close to half of secondary students with LD perform more than three grade levels below their enrolled grade in essential academic skills (45 percent in reading, and 44 percent in math).

- Sixty-seven percent of students with LD graduate from high school with a regular diploma versus 74 percent of students in the general population.

- Twenty percent of students with LD drop out of high school versus 8 percent of students in the general population.

- Ten percent of students with LD are enrolled in a four-year college within two years of leaving high school, compared with 28 percent of the general population.

- Among working-age adults with LD versus those without LD, 55 percent versus 67 percent are employed; 6 percent versus 3 percent of adults are unemployed; and 39 percent versus 21 percent are not in the labor force because of lack of education.

Although these are discouraging statistics, the good news is that children who have difficulty learning in traditional ways are usually able to learn and understand when music and the arts are added to the learning process.

Although these are discouraging statistics, the good news is that children who have difficulty learning in traditional ways are usually able to learn and understand when music and the arts are added to the learning process. For example, former elementary school science resource teacher Kathleen Carroll (discussed in chapter 3) taught her students—both traditional learners and learning disabled—science concepts through songs and rhymes. Music was the catalyst for their understanding and remembering complicated science concepts such as matter, energy, classifying, and inference. Sherry Dupont, an educational researcher and teacher in south-central Pennsylvania, found that by integrating creative drama into her students' literature reading material, her remedial fifth graders retained the material better and scored higher on the Metropolitan Reading Comprehension Test.[4] Mark Jordan, retired teacher at Samuel Gompers Fine Arts Option Elementary School in Chicago, used pie pans to help his students learn music notation. A whole pie pan is a whole note and a half-note is a half a pan, and so on. He taught this method to math teachers to use with students struggling with math and fractions.[5]

To illustrate how music is a consistent vehicle for learning, no matter what the challenge, the following research studies indicate eight areas where music aids those with learning disabilities.

Music helps children with developmental dyslexia or autism. Researchers found that children with learning disabilities who have difficulty focusing with a lot of background noise are particularly helped by music lessons. Nina Kraus, Hugh Knowles Professor of Communication Sciences and Neurobiology and director of Northwestern's Auditory Neuroscience Laboratory, states, "Music training seems to strengthen the same neural processes that often are deficient in individuals with developmental dyslexia or autism or children who have difficulty hearing speech in noise."[6]

Music strengthens the auditory cortex. Most learning disabilities start as auditory processing problems. Auditory processing is the ability to understand and process what one hears and is crucial for reading and spelling. It is also referred to as "phonemic awareness." The Kraus lab at Northwestern's Auditory Neuroscience Laboratory found concrete evidence showing that playing a musical instrument significantly enhances the brainstem's sensitivity to speech sounds. The results of this study are consistent with other studies the lab has conducted and reveal that irregularities in brainstem sound encoding in some learning disabled children can be improved with auditory training that comes from learning a musical instrument.[7]

Music helps LD students with reading and vocabulary. An intensive short-term music curriculum was developed to target reading comprehension and vocabulary skills of second graders. The curriculum was then implemented in second-grade classrooms in the Southeast. Researchers discovered that when music was included into the reading process, students with a reading disability improved significantly in word decoding, word knowledge, and reading comprehension.[8]

> *Researchers discovered that when music was included into the reading process, students with a reading disability improved significantly in word decoding, word knowledge, and reading comprehension.*

Music training improves reading ability of children with dyslexia. Stanford University research found that musical training improves how the brain processes speech, which can lead to improved reading ability of children with dyslexia and other reading problems. They found that music training is especially good for children who have difficulty with rapid auditory processing, which is needed for proficient reading.[9]

Music helps speech and language impairments. Susan Sze at Niagara University in New York found that music helps students with disabilities by making difficult or impossible tasks possible. She found that music is a "sophisticated, cognitive, linguistic, social, and psychological treatment." She also found that music provides a form of compensation for students with language impairments and is a means of facilitating language development.[10]

Music helps LD children with attention and concentration. Researchers discovered that when learning-disabled children learn how to play a musical instrument, the following functions improve: attention, concentration, impulse control, social functioning, self-esteem, self-expression, motivation, and memory.[11]

Music increases temporal processing, phonological skills, and spelling skills in dyslexic children. A study of nine dyslexic boys with an average age of 8.8 years showed that music instruction improved rapid temporal processing skills, phonological skills, and spelling skills, but not reading skills. Phonological skills involve the structure or sound structure of spoken words and are a reliable predictor of later reading ability.[12]

Rhythm in music helps children with reading difficulties. The relationship between music ability and reading skills was examined in a study that showed an association between rhythmic ability and reading. The research was conducted on children with reading difficulties who were between the ages of eight and eleven. The results of the study found that the reading skills of children who received music instruction were significantly higher than those of children who did not receive the music instruction. From this study it was suggested that musical activities can help children develop a multisensory awareness and response to sounds.[13]

For the past thirty years, I have had a particular interest in music's impact on children with learning disabilities because of personal experience. In 1982 our third son, Brandon, was born. It was a traumatic birth. Born six weeks early, Brandon was too high in the birth canal, and as a result he was literally dragged out by forceps. He was an unhappy baby and cried all the time. The only thing that would calm him down, and only for a short time, was orchestral or choral music. He had constant ear infections that included a build-up of fluid in his ears, and despite being on daily doses of low-grade antibiotics, the infections persisted. Over time, this constant fluid buildup affected his hearing at a critical time in his development and caused him to experience sounds and language as if he was in a vacuum. Tubes were put in his ears, but at the age of three, he was barely talking. What he did say was unrecognizable. I was reading to him daily, playing music for him, and taking him to "mommy and me" classes, yet his language and communication skills remained poor. I had read and played music for our two older sons, and they were both early talkers and readers, so, naturally, I was concerned. He started preschool at age three and his teachers also noticed his delayed language skills. After having him tested by a professional, we determined Brandon needed speech and language intervention. I naively thought once his language problem was fixed, everything would be fine. I was wrong—this was just the beginning.

When Brandon was six, his kindergarten teacher expressed concerned about his ability to learn. He was not able to do the classroom work and seemed frustrated and distant. We had him tested both at our public school and privately by a child psychologist. The results were grim. Brandon was diagnosed with auditory processing, visual motor, visual perception, sensory motor, and attention deficit disorder. The difference between his oral IQ and written IQ was thirty-eight points, indicating severe learning disabilities.

This team of experts told us that school would be very difficult for him. We were told that he may not graduate from high school, that college was out of the question, and that a trade school would be more appropriate. They said Brandon was "high risk," meaning that as he got older, he could be a candidate for dropping out of school, experimenting with drugs, or worse. Why? Because kids need a measure of academic success. They are in school many hours each day, and they need to feel good about their abilities to learn. He needed to experience some kind of school success to increase his confidence level. But how do you help a child achieve academic success when he can't read, write or spell? When he does not understand even the simplest of math concepts? When he has difficulty paying attention and following directions, and sports confuse and frustrate him?

It was a daunting challenge, and in the beginning I was overwhelmed. I did not know the first thing about learning disabilities, but I was determined to find out and to help him because I wanted Brandon to love learning—not just for success in school, but for a rich and meaningful life.

I began researching learning disabilities: first asking questions and later aggressively networking. This was before the age of the Internet, so it required more than the flick of a wrist to find information. I observed the public school resource programs, was not satisfied, and began looking elsewhere for help. I read books. I researched at the library. I talked to parents with learning-disabled children. I talked to LD advocate organizations and attended their meetings. I took classes on learning disabilities. As the saying goes, "I left no stone unturned."

I learned that learning disabilities are layered problems—one issue is partially resolved when ten others surface—and is a slow, laborious process where progress is incremental. My research led me outside of the public schools to various programs, many of which I enrolled Brandon in. For example, the Lindamood-Bell and Tomatis Method for auditory processing, the Ayres Clinic for sensory integration, the Irlen Institute for scotopic sensitivity syndrome, and a behavioral/developmental optometrist for visual motor and visual perception issues. We also utilized the services of educational therapists and tutors. Each night, a minimum of three hours was spent with the simplest of homework assignments.

Music was a big part of his learning. We used musical games, rhymes, and songs to help him learn the material. Some children with learning disabilities have difficulty with rhyming words, but as long as the words were set to music, Brandon was able to learn them. Knowing the importance of music on brain development, we continued to play classical music for him intermittently throughout the day and evening and enrolled him in several group music classes. I was convinced that parts of his brain, rather than malfunctioning, were in need of the kind of exercise that one gets from studying a musical instrument.

Between the ages of four and eight, Brandon took group music lessons which included singing, learning the instruments of the orchestra and the composers, and playing on a little keyboard. It was frustrating because Brandon did not have any spatial sense of the musical notes on a page or their placement on the keyboard. While other children were learning simple tunes, Brandon was struggling to coordinate his fingers on the keyboard. When Brandon turned eight, he started taking private piano lessons. It was a painstaking process as he and I sat at the piano learning the notes and their location on the keyboard. Each day brought new challenges. He was unable to remember from day to day where middle C was on the piano—or any of the other notes, for that matter. The spatial arrangement of the lines and spaces of the music was most confusing for him. I decided to color-code the keyboard and his music. For instance, putting an orange dot on middle C and pointing to the orange-colored note on the music page, and then pointing to the same note on the piano gradually helped him make the association. As he slowly gained proficiency with his music, and with help from the various programs mentioned, his reading, math, and spelling improved.

When Brandon turned nine, he became fascinated with video cameras. We noticed that he had an incredibly observant eye and saw things through the camera lens that most people do not notice. When he started middle school, with permission from his teachers, he turned his homework assignments into movies which included music. As a result, Brandon went from being teased and bullied and called "stupid" by classmates to being the most popular kid in the school because everyone wanted to be in his movies.

Brandon continued taking piano lessons throughout his teen years and into adulthood. In high school, he was playing some difficult music, such as Liszt's Hungarian Rhapsody no. 2 and Beethoven's *Moonlight Sonata*. At one point his music teacher told me, "If you were bringing Brandon to me for the first time and I heard him play the piano like he plays now, I would say that you have a very musically gifted child."

Today, Brandon is thirty years old. College was a long process, but he eventually graduated with straight As and a double major in film and philosophy. He works in the film industry and is an avid writer and a voracious lover of learning. Like Einstein and many others, Brandon used music, both listening to and playing a musical instrument, throughout college to help him organize his thoughts, find patterns, and gain understanding. Today, he still uses music for the same reasons. Getting to where he is was not an easy journey, and many times it felt like climbing Mount Kilimanjaro with one leg.

In 2012, at the College Television Awards in Hollywood, California, Brandon won the award for co-producer of a film in the Best Children's Program category. It is a story about a boy who is bullied by his peers for being different, but ends up making friends and gaining self-confidence.

IMPACT OF PARENTAL INVOLVEMENT

As Brandon was growing up, I talked to and networked with many parents with learning-disabled children. We were all desperate to help our children and realized that the burden could not be left entirely to the schools to correct. Schools are faced with many challenges and can only do so much. They cannot possibly be expected to supply all the programs, money, or resources that are sometimes necessary to help a learning-disabled child. Parents must do their part as well. I believe most do.

In a recent master's thesis by Elizabeth Ron Fang of San Jose State University, Fang studied and observed two autistic boys: Mike, who was eighteen, and Ryan, who was five. Mike was musically gifted and could play a number of instruments, including the piano, drums, timpani, cello, saxophone, double bass, recorder, *Sheng* (a Chinese instrument), and *Yangqin* (Chinese hammered dulcimer). But what impressed me most about this story was not only Mike, but his mother, Wendy. Undoubtedly, Mike is where he is today because of the tenacious and indomitable spirit of his mother. When Mike started school he was placed in a mainstream classroom, and Wendy became his aide. She was with him at school every day; helping and assisting him where needed. Her approach at school was to be his teacher and not his mother. She also had a law of expectation for him regarding behavior.

At home, she stimulated his mind with different activities, including piano, abacus, Chinese language, gymnastics, cello, and drawing. Although not a musician herself, Wendy worked very hard to learn to read and play music because she understood that music

Wendy exercised his hands by having him learn piano; he learned the drums to further strengthen his wrists, he learned Sheng to develop hand-eye coordination, and so forth.

was Mike's language and talent. She used musical instruments as "therapeutic activities." When Mike started playing timpani, Wendy noticed that he played with his whole arm instead of his wrists. To correct that she taught him the dulcimer to help his wrists become more flexible. When Mike had trouble speaking, Wendy built up the muscles around his mouth and his breathing by having him learn wind instruments. She had him take saxophone lessons, "not because I want him to play, but to exercise his cheek [muscles] for speech. Practicing breathing is really helpful for his health." Rather than send him to occupational therapy (which she felt was boring), she used different wind instruments to build his motor skills. Wendy exercised his hands by having him learn piano; he learned the drums to further strengthen his wrists, he learned Sheng to develop hand-eye coordination, and so forth. Over the years, Mike has demonstrated an amazing talent for music and plays all his instruments at an advanced level. Wendy believes that his innate talent for music will be his future and open doors of opportunities. She is right. Today, Mike is doing exceptionally well. He is in four different ensembles and keeps busy by regularly performing music.[14]

Hopefully, we parents will be inspired by Wendy, as I was, and in our own way emulate her tenacity and determination when dealing with our own learning-challenged children.

As mentioned, there are many different programs available outside of school to help children with learning challenges. As you begin analyzing and researching programs, consider the following:

- Find out what each program offers.

- Find out what specific learning challenge the program helps.

- Find out how long it will take to see results.

- Find out how long it will take to complete the program, the cost, and if boosters are necessary. Sometimes after a program is complete, your child may need to go back after a few months and repeat portions of the program. These are called "boosters." Think of boosters as repeated exercise that maintains the desired result.

Below are two programs that help learning-disabled children and incorporate classical music, specifically the music of Mozart. Keep in mind that these are *sound therapies* that incorporate classical music as opposed to music therapies, which will be discussed later. Although there are many excellent programs for children with learning disabilities, I am only focusing on two sound therapy programs because of their use of classical music.

Tomatis Method (www.tomatis.com)

Alfred Tomatis, an ear, nose, and throat physician from France, developed the Tomatis Method, which helps children and adults with learning issues such as reading problems, dyslexia, auditory processing, and even autism. He found that some of these issues often stem from impaired listening, specifically the inability to perceive high frequency sounds, and can be treated by restoring listening abilities. This process focuses on retraining the muscles of the ear so that the person can distinguish the difference between high and low frequencies, among other things. It is basically a sound sensory stimulation where sound (filtered classical music) is transmitted through bone and air conduction, which stimulates the entire inner ear, particularly those areas responsible for auditory and motor functions, such as the vestibule and cochlea. The vestibule is part of the inner ear and controls balance, coordination, verticality, muscle tone, and the muscles of our eyes. It is also an important dispatch for all sensory information that our body sends to our brain. Children who have vestibular problems usually have sensory integration issues. The cochlea is also part of the inner ear and analyzes sounds important for language comprehension. Together they act as a relay station between the nervous system and the brain. Additionally, our ears play a major role in stimulating our brains. Tomatis describes it by saying, "The ear can be compared to a dynamo which transforms the stimulations it receives into neurological energy intended to feed the brain." He found that when the brain is "charged," we are able to focus, concentrate, organize, memorize, learn, and work for long periods of time. Additionally, he found that 80 percent of the energy that the brain needs is processed through the inner ear.[15]

Utilizing the music of Mozart and Gregorian chants, the Tomatis device incorporates the use of high (acute) and low (base) frequencies and sound perception contrast that strengthens the inner ear muscles through contraction and relaxation. The frequency-relative richness of the music of Mozart is "treated" with electronic gating and is called the Tomatis effect. Gating means that the music gradually shifts from an emphasis on low frequencies to an emphasis on high frequencies. A person listens to the music through headphones called an Electronic Ear. The music is programmed by a trained professional and is based on the person's specific learning challenges. The choice of music, the filtering of the music, the speed of the music, and the auditory laterality (this is a process of building neural pathways from the left to the right sides of the brain) are all selected by the professional according to the patient's specific challenges. The goal of the Tomatis Method is to restore listening function, thus making it possible for a child to learn, read, communicate, and have better motor functions.[16]

The effectiveness of Dr. Tomatis' work is told in the following story. In the early 1950s, Dr. Tomatis visited a Benedictine monastery in France following the second Vatican Council. The council decided to eliminate the traditional chanting of the monks for a more constructive use of time. Over time, the monks became more lethargic, slept more, and lost their motivation for work and study. Dr. Tomatis was invited back to evaluate the situation and determine what was happening to the monks. He found that the monks' hearing had weakened since he last saw them. He immediately began using his Electronic Ear to improve their hearing. He also suggested that the chanting be brought back into the monks' daily routine. Nine months later, the monks felt renewed and had fully returned to their vigorous lifestyle of little sleep, hard work, and vegetarian diets. Why did the music make such a difference? Because when we sing or talk, our voice acts as a battery to the brain and brings energy to our bodies, in the same way the monks singing chants affected their brains and brought energy to their bodies.[17]

The music the monks were singing is called Gregorian chants. It is a form of singing which is sung in free rhythm and without meter or time signature. The chants are sung almost entirely in Latin, and the words are from scripture. They are sung in pure melody, in unison, and without accompaniment.

In 1995, data from a meta-analysis taken from five research studies on the Tomatis Method was evaluated to determine the efficacy of this method in helping children with a wide range of learning and communication disabilities. The studies involved 231 children ages six to fifteen who were learning disabled, language-impaired, underachieving, or severely dyslexic. Each study measured the following areas: linguistic, psychomotor, personal and social adjustment, cognitive, and auditory. The children were exposed to approximately one hundred hours of the Tomatis auditory stimulation, and the control group had no music intervention. Although this is considered a small sampling of children, the results positively reflected the value of the Tomatis Method. Significant gains were shown in auditory processing, general communication, problem-solving ability, reading, and hand-eye coordination, and improvement on standardized tests of aptitude, achievement and adjustment.[18]

In 2005, the Tomatis Center in Toronto, Canada, studied the results of Tomatis Listening Therapy on over four hundred children and adolescents. Ninety-five percent of parents saw the following positive responses in their children: 89 percent had greater communication abilities, 86 percent had better attention spans; 80 percent showed a decrease in frustration levels; 74 percent showed improvement in speech quality; 73 percent showed improved memory; 69 percent had better spelling aptitude; and 84 percent showed more maturity. Six months after the program, 83 percent of those children had maintained the improvements and/or had continued to make even further gains. An additional 14 percent of the children had maintained some of the gains. Only 3 percent had maintained none of the improvements.[19]

Although the Tomatis Method has helped thousands of children and adults all over the world, another sound therapy program that uses the music of Mozart and is similar to Tomatis has emerged in the last ten years showing equal, if not greater promise than the Tomatis Method for learning disabled children.

Integrated Listening Systems (iLs) (www.integratedlistening.com)
(YouTube: http://www.integratedlistening.com/howilsworksvideo/)

Integrated Listening Sysems (iLs) was developed by Ron Minson, M.D., a psychiatrist living in Colorado. In 1990, he and his wife, Kate, were searching for a solution to their daughter's dyslexia and found success with Dr. Alfred Tomatis's sound therapy. Their daughter's success in reading was so remarkable that Dr. Minson traveled to Europe to study with Dr. Tomatis. Upon returning home, he began integrating what he learned about sound therapy into his psychiatric practice. The Minsons took what Dr. Tomatis had done and improved it. By 2007 they had developed their own sound equipment and launched Integrated Listening Systems (iLs). The iLs sound therapy program uses the same type of filtered Mozart music and Gregorian chants as does Tomatis, but is a departure from the Tomatis Method in that instead of just using sound, iLs incorporates movement and vision at the same time—very key and important additions. The person using the iLs program listens to the filtered music of Mozart while concurrently doing specific movements and engaging in visual stimulation. This network of sensory systems being simultaneously stimulated—auditory, visual, vestibular, motor, and even emotional control—produces better results with shorter training required. By 2011, iLs had trained over twenty-five hundred therapists in the United States. Many therapists using the iLs program report amazing results with children suffering from a variety of problems, including autism.

Alene Villaneda is an educational therapist from Kaysville, Utah, and uses the iLs program with her students. Since 1994 her company, Integrated Learning Strategies, has worked with children who have a variety of learning disabilities: ADD/ADHD, language issues, and autism. Specifically speaking, she helps children who suffer from issues relating to auditory processing, (both receptive and expressive language), vestibular issues (the foundational system for visual and auditory), gross and fine motor problems, and memory and concentration, as well as anyone who wants to have better listening skills. Villaneda uses a combination of different programs and has found that the iLs program addresses the needs of many of her students, but with varied outcomes. Below are some of the results her clients experienced after using the iLs program.

A nine-year-old girl came to Villaneda with severe comprehension and auditory processing problems, as well as attention issues. She also wore very thick glasses. Normally, it would have taken thirty months to fully address these problems, but by combining the iLs program with movement, the young girl experienced a remarkable turnaround in just eighteen months. She no longer has to repeatedly ask her teacher for clarification of what is said in class (auditory issues), she understands what she reads (auditory and comprehension), her attention span has drastically improved (vestibular/auditory), and even her vision has improved to where her glasses have needed adjustments.

Villaneda began working with an autistic boy when he was seven years old. Although he suffered from expressive language issues, he did understand what people said to him. At the time, he was in a special classroom at school and had difficulty with stemming—a term used to describe constant wiggling and shaking. Villaneda started him on the iLs program, and within six short months he was talking and was in a mainstream classroom. Although he is receiving additional intervention, his parents described his change as "an awakening."

When five-year-old Monica came to Villaneda, she could not sit still and could not bounce a ball or catch or throw a beanbag. She was unable to focus on an object, could not coordinate her eyes, and never noticed anything around her. Monica appeared normal, but would have severe temper tantrums and extreme bouts of anger. Additionally, she did not show any affection toward her parents or siblings. Within a few short months of being on the iLs program, Monica was transformed: she became grounded, she could throw and catch a beanbag, she became very observant of everything around her, she asked questions, and, best of all, she became a very affectionate child.[20]

Music and Selective Mutism

As illustrated, music can stimulate speech development and provide brain organization for cognitive and motor development, in addition to creating an environment that helps socialization with peers.

As illustrated, music can stimulate speech development and provide brain organization for cognitive and motor development, in addition to creating an environment that helps socialization with peers.

Miriam Choi of Melbourne, Australia, is an advanced level Suzuki music piano teacher. She works with children suffering from autism and selective mutism using music lessons and music therapy. Selective mutism (SM) is a disorder that occurs in childhood and is characterized by an inability to speak in certain settings, such as school, or in public places, as opposed to speaking at home with family members. Selective mutism is associated with anxiety, and some researchers believe that it is an extreme form of social phobia.

One of her piano students is a young boy who has been studying with Choi since he was four years old and suffers from SM. Choi describes him as a very talented young man, highly motivated, and an exceptional pianist and mathematician. Over the years, no matter the difficulty of music she gave him, he learned the pieces with detailed precision and emotional feeling. Unlike other children, his mother has never had to nag or coax him to practice the piano. He does it willingly and on his own. Not surprisingly, he has successfully completed various piano and music theory examinations with distinction. Little by little, he has gained the courage to perform in front of people. He is now fourteen years old, and when he performs at concerts, everyone marvels at both his exceptional music skills and his emotional and expressive musicality. Without a doubt, he touches the hearts of everyone who hears him play.

Choi herself has learned much from this young man. She realizes the importance of showing patience and perseverance with all of her students, particularly those who struggle with challenges. Most importantly, she has seen firsthand what happens to children with disabilities when love is combined with teaching—they blossom! Choi has watched this young man smile for the first time in his life. She says, "Teaching this young boy has helped me to see how music teachers can transform any child with any type of physical or learning issue. It is up to the teachers and parents to be willing to give lots of love when teaching them and then watching the child develop into something special." She continues, "I have helped him to explore his musical gifts through learning to play the piano, in the belief that his condition will improve through the power of music—a journey that I believe has become a vital music therapy for him as well as other children with disorders or disabilities."[21]

Music and Autism

Autism Spectrum Disorder (ASD) is a disorder characterized by abnormalities in social interactions, speech and communication, sensory perception, and restrictive or repetitive behaviors. It is the fastest growing developmental disability, with an astounding 1,148 percent growth rate over the last twenty years, and a 10 to 17 percent annual growth rate. Comparatively speaking, more children are diagnosed with autism each year than juvenile diabetes, cancer, and AIDS *combined.* In 1984, four in every ten thousand children were diagnosed with autism. Today, one in every eighty-eight births results in an autistic child, with boys being four times more likely than girls to have autism. This breaks down to one in every fifty-four boys with the disorder.[22] At this time there is no medical detection or cure for autism.[23] The American Psychiatric Association lists five subtypes of ASD: 1) autistic disorder, 2) Rett syndrome, 3) childhood disintegrative disorder, 4) pervasive developmental disorder–not otherwise specified (PDD-NOS), and 5) Asperger syndrome. (It was recently determined that Asperger's syndrome be removed as one of the autistic subtypes.)

Autism is referred to as a "spectrum" disorder because each individual on the spectrum can exhibit a range of different behaviors, and no one method or approach works for all autistic people. However, music is one area of stimulus for which almost all autistic children have a particular affinity. In fact, they respond more frequently and appropriately to music than any other auditory stimulus, and many autistic children demonstrate better music skills than cognitive skills. However, music is one area of stimulus for which almost all autistic children have a particular affinity. In fact, they respond more frequently and appropriately to music than any other auditory stimulus, and many autistic children demonstrate better music skills than cognitive skills.[24] Music therapist and researcher Michael Thaut concurs: "Children on the autistic spectrum often have a remarkable capability and responsiveness to music compared to most other areas of their behavior, as well as in comparison with typical children."[25] As a result, music therapy and music involvement for autistic children is becoming a popular treatment for helping with their self-awareness and socialization.

Bonnie and Scott Nakamoto of Torrance, California, are parents of five children. Their fourth son, Trenton, is autistic and loves and responds to music. Before he was a year old, he surprised his parents by singing in perfect pitch the "Happy Birthday" song. He did not sing the words, but had memorized the music. Later, they noticed how every time he sang, it was in key and with near-perfect pitch, often after hearing a piece of music only once. At night before he goes to bed, he never tires of hearing his mother sing the same two songs. He will join in singing with his siblings and loves when his father plays the guitar and sings to him. His teacher at school plays the guitar and sings poems that have been set to music. Trenton hears the music only once and is able to sing it back on key. Even after a year or more of hearing these poem-songs, Trenton will suddenly start singing them—word perfect and in perfect pitch. For Trenton, music unlocks the door to awareness of others and socialization.[26]

MUSIC THERAPY AND AUTISM

Using music as a method of healing began after World War II. Doctors noticed that their veteran patients who suffered from physical and emotional trauma responded positively to the community musicians who came to the hospitals to play for the patients. In fact, the patients reacted emotionally, physically, and even cognitively to the music. The doctors took note and the field of music therapy was born. Interestingly, just one year after Dr. Leo Kanner of Johns Hopkins Hospital first clinically documented autism, the first music therapy program was established at Michigan State University.[27]

Over the years, various types of music therapy have emerged, and today there are five main types. First is *receptive music therapy*, which involves listening to live or recorded music. Second is *compositional music therapy*, where the client creates music. Third is *improvisational music therapy*, where the therapist guides the client to create music. Fourth is *recreative music therapy*, where the client learns to play a musical instrument and perform a musical instrument, and fifth is *activity music therapy*, which involves musical games designed by the music therapist and may involve the use of percussion or tuned instruments or voice.[28] Often, music therapists will use a combination of the five types for their clients. A person with autism does not need musical skills to benefit from musical therapy, but the musical therapist does need a high level of musical and therapeutic skill.

> *A person with autism does not need musical skills to benefit from musical therapy, but the musical therapist does need a high level of musical and therapeutic skill.*

There are many examples of autistic children improving their social, behavioral, or communication abilities when given music therapy, but the results vary from person to person. Because autism is a spectrum disorder where each person responds differently and each result must be analyzed individually, there are several ways that autism is studied. There are *case reports*, which are also known as anecdotal examples or a study based on observations of one individual. There are *case series*, which are studies that are based on the observations of a series of individuals all receiving the same intervention. There are *cohort studies*, where a defined group of people is observed over time and then the outcomes are compared.[29] There are other types of autism research, but the ones I will be referring to below fall into one of these three categories. Each example illustrates the powerful connection between autism and music.

Ashley was diagnosed with pervasive developmental disorder (PDD), which is part of the autism spectrum, when she was twenty-one months old. She did not speak, her parents could not get her to respond to her name, and her method of communicating was grunting. Her doctor suggested a form of sound therapy which required listening to the music of Mozart for several hours each day for several weeks (much like iLs and the Tomatis Method). It paid off. One day when her parents were driving her from a therapy session, she spoke her first words, "I want cookie." From that point on she continued to make progress, and today she behaves like any normal ten-year-old, loves *Hannah Montana* and *High School Musical*, and can use language to interact with others.[30]

Researchers Dawn Wimpory, Paul Chadwick, and Susan Nash used musical interaction therapy to help a three-year-old autistic girl with socialization, interactions, and eye contact with her mother. The therapy consisted of twenty-minute sessions of musical interaction therapy twice a week for seven months. The result was increased socialization, eye contact, and initiation with her mother, but the researchers did not conclude that it was all due to the music therapy; they also postulated that the results could also be attributed to the child's maturation.[31]

Researchers Elizabeth Starr and Krista Zenker did a case study on a six-year-old boy with autism who was high functioning and verbal, but exhibited behavioral issues when there were changes to his routine or when he had to wait in line at school. His reaction was agitation and aggression. The music therapists decided that rather than having him wait in line, he could wait in the classroom. Then Starr and Zenker used an original song, "Line Up," to help him understand the importance of patiently waiting. They also used visual cue cards that showed him each step of waiting and what he was expected to do during each part of the song. He would listen to the song on the way to school and during his music therapy sessions. As a result, his anxiety and aggression associated with waiting decreased.[32]

Alexandra Raber of Birmingham-Southern College wanted to see if various music activities would help autistic children become more engaged in their school lessons. She studied twenty-two children with autism and how they responded to five different music activities: songs with movement, songs without movement, action songs, songs with full body movement, and playing instruments. Raber measured their oral response, physical response, attention, and eye contact. Of the five activities, only one resulted in full participation by all twenty-two students, and that was instrument playing.[33]

A heartwarming story of how music positively affects children with autism is illustrated in the movie *Autism: The Musical*. It is about the Miracle Project—a musical theater program that brings together a group of autistic children to perform musical theater in an atmosphere of creativity and acceptance. Elaine Hall is the director and founder of the Miracle Project. She is also the mother of Neal, who is autistic. Hall is energetic and positive and works with the children and their parents to produce a musical. The movie focuses on the process of producing the musical, and only bits and pieces of the actual musical are shown on the screen. What is powerfully illustrated, however, are the struggles and triumphs the children and their parents experience as they find ways to cooperatively come together and create something meaningful and important. The parents and children do not focus on the finish line, but rather take joy in the journey, which brings successes in improved communication, socialization, and behaviors as the children take center stage.

There are five main children featured: Neal, Adam, Henry, Wyatt, and Lexi. All five have parents who dearly love them, support them, and help them. Adam is musically gifted. At the age of two, he astounded his family by teaching himself to play blues harmonica. At the age of seven, he fell in love with the cello and began a serious attachment to that instrument. By the age of nine, he had sung opera, had performed at Disney Hall's Redcat Theater with jazz great Patrice Rushen, and had jammed at the House of Blues with his favorite "punk cello" band, Rasputina. Lexi loves to dance and sing and would like to be like Brittany Spears. Wyatt is a budding actor, writer, and musician. Henry loves dinosaurs and reptiles. Neal loves math and wants to help people better understand those with disabilities. The movie is a touching testament to music's power to reach across seemingly insurmountable barriers and profoundly affect families.

These examples and hundreds like them demonstrate how profoundly music can change the lives of children with autism. Music helps them to bond with family members, to communicate with people, and to connect to the outside world. Just as autism seems to lock them out of society, music draws them back in. It becomes the key to their social, emotional, and physical awareness.

Music and Physical Disabilities

Children and adolescents who have physical disabilities, such as hearing or sight issues or cerebral palsy, can also be positively affected by music.

Evelyn Glennie was born on a farm in Northeast Scotland. At the age of eight she began taking piano lessons. Glennie fell in love with music, did extremely well on the piano, and received the highest mark in the United Kingdom when she took the Associated Board Grade One piano exam. By the age of ten she was performing for people in local assisted living homes.

Children and adolescents who have physical disabilities, such as hearing or sight issues or cerebral palsy, can also be positively affected by music.

During primary school, she realized she was missing things like homework assignments and was becoming "slow" in some areas of school. At the beginning of secondary school, her hearing was tested, and the audiologists found that Glennie had significant hearing loss. They labeled her "profoundly deaf." The doctors said she would need hearing aids and would do better in a school for the deaf. They also explained to her parents that because of her deafness, music would no longer be an option. In response to this comment, Glennie later remarked, "It was so strange… thirty minutes before walking through that door, I could do whatever I wanted to do, and thirty minutes later, the medical profession was telling me I could not do some things." Undaunted, her father believed that—hearing or not—Evelyn would do what she wanted to do and be successful.

Glennie attended mainstream schools and classrooms, and her teachers wore microphones so that she could hear them more easily. The secondary school she attended had a strong music department, and she decided to try playing percussion. For Glennie, percussion was the perfect choice. This was the beginning of a lifelong passion with percussion instruments.

Today, instead of relying on her ears to hear sounds, Glennie relies on her other senses, such as "touch" and "feel," to experience music. For instance, she takes off her hearing aids so she hears less through her ears and more through her body. "I can literally reach out to that sound and *feel* that sound," she says.

Glennie has a fascination for anything she can hit or produce a sound with, such as rocks, stones, metal, and things made of clay. She even appeared on *Sesame Street* and played garbage cans with Oscar the Grouch. Her collection of percussion instruments is over eighteen hundred and growing.

Today, Evelyn Glennie is considered a world-class percussionist and is the first person in musical history to successfully sustain a full-time career as a solo percussionist. She has performed all over the world and has inspired many musicians struggling with physical disabilities. In 2007, she was awarded Dame Commander of the British Empire.[34]

Hamid Ala was born in London, England, and at the age of twelve moved to the United States. As a young child he loved classical music and began voice training. He eventually began studying under Professor Hedley Nosworthy, author of *Singing: The Truth Be Told*. What makes his story so remarkable is that Ala was born with cerebral palsy—a neurological condition which affects muscle coordination and motor skills. When other music teachers refused to teach him, Professor Nosworthy gave him a chance and taught him to sing classical music. Ala has shown exceptional determination and focus and was recently accepted to the Bob Cole Conservatory of Music at California State University at Long Beach to continue his voice studies. For Ala, his journey in becoming a classically trained vocalist has been difficult, with many lessons learned along the way, including patience and helping others who have misconceptions about people with disabilities. He states, "People with disabilities want to be seen as human beings, as individuals, and not as having cerebral palsy or other disabilities. We want to be seen as equals, and music has done that for me."[35]

Josie I. Nielson is an accomplished violinist and is legally blind. At the age of five, she began taking violin lessons and fell in love with music and the sounds of the violin. She began wearing glasses in kindergarten, but during puberty her eyesight started to deteriorate very quickly. In fact, the doctor would change her prescription and one to two weeks later her eyesight had significantly worsened. Concerned, her parents took her to the Casey Eye Institute in Portland, Oregon, where she was diagnosed with a rare form of macular degeneration that would eventually rob her of her sight. She was thirteen years old. "That was hard for a thirteen-year-old to be told," says Nielson, who is majoring in family studies with an emphasis in social work and a minor in violin performance at Brigham Young University in Provo, Utah. "One of my first concerns was how I would learn music when I'm blind." But she believes that her trials can also be gifts. "I have discovered that as my vision worsens, my other senses become sharper, especially my hearing. My memory has also quickened, and I'm able to memorize more music in a shorter amount of time." Nielson has trained her ear to the point that she is able to listen to a recording of symphony music where multiple instruments are playing and can clearly hear her violin part. Additionally, she is able to correctly visualize, through her acute sense of hearing, the exact note being played and the finger position.

Nielson has trained her ear to the point that she is able to listen to a recording of symphony music where multiple instruments are playing and can clearly hear her violin part.

Her method of learning music is to listen to recordings with her heightened sense of hearing. "A particular time when I couldn't detect my parts was when the BYU Philharmonic Orchestra played Mahler's Symphony no. 5. My professor, Monte Belknap, recorded my violin part—about forty pages—slower so I could memorize the music for the performance." She adds, "There were other times when I was learning a lot of music in a short amount of time: music for the Philharmonic, string ensembles, and solo pieces. I was able to memorize the music very quickly after spending many hours listening and memorizing."

Despite her challenges, Nielson has high goals. After graduation in 2014, she is planning a career in social work. Eventually, she wants to develop the methodology and tools that will help her teach music to others with visual impairment. "Music is my passion," she says. "I like helping those with or without disabilities to motivate and help them pursue their life dreams." She continues, "Although being visually impaired is an obstacle, I know that it builds my character. I refuse to let my impairment dictate what I accomplish in life, or the goals I pursue. My music brings me insurmountable joy. Through my music, I am able to bring joy to others as well. I believe music speaks to people in ways that words cannot. I understand that I have a unique situation being legally blind, but I believe this sets me apart from others in a positive way. I have developed skills that make it possible for me to be successful with my music. I generally have to work harder and longer to memorize and master a piece of music. However, I believe this makes me a better musician."[36]

Josie Nielson is not a person waiting for the final note to fade before enjoying the music. She is actively and positively participating in and enjoying the journey of life. Her indomitable spirit is an example to everyone—with or without physical handicaps—that life is a miraculous experience no matter the challenge.

Choosing Musical Instruments for Children with Physical and Cognitive Challenges

As illustrated, children experiencing physical, emotional, or intellectual challenges respond to music and can play music, but one important question remains—what instruments are best for these children and why? A few years ago, I read an article in *Music Educators Journal* discussing this very topic and giving suggestions. Here is a brief synopsis of that article and what instruments they suggest for children with specific physical and learning challenges as well as what instruments may be more difficult to play.[37]

Physical Disabilities

Strings: The violin, viola, cello, and bass are all good for children with physical challenges and are particularly well suited for children where breathing is difficult, such as with cystic fibrosis.

Woodwinds: The bass clarinet and the saxophone work well for children with various physical disabilities because the neck strap and bass clarinet pin help support the instrument.

Brass: The French horn is a great instrument because the child can partially support the instrument on one leg.

Percussion: These instruments are particularly good for children with cystic fibrosis, nasal irregularities, or severe asthma.

DEAF OR HARD OF HEARING

Strings: The violin or viola work well because the child can feel the vibrations from the instrument to the jawbone.

Woodwinds: Clarinet and saxophone are also great instruments because children can feel the vibrations through their teeth on top of the mouthpiece.

Brass: These instruments are difficult for children who are deaf or hard of hearing because they cannot hear the right overtones.

Percussion: Bass drum is a great instrument for children with hearing impairments. They can feel the vibrations by standing on a wooden floor with shoes removed or playing with their left hand on the drum head. They can also lean against the drum and feel vibrations while watching the director.

GROSS MOTOR SKILLS IMPAIRMENTS

Strings: The cello or bass is a good choice for children having difficulty with gross motor skills because there is room to maneuver uncoordinated fingers.

Brass: The trombone is a good instrument because children can coordinate the slide on the trombone more easily than valves (such as on wind instruments) and only two working fingers are required.

Percussion: Mallet percussion instruments can be challenging for children with gross motor disabilities. They require shifting back and forth between diatonic and chromatic bars and playing all bars in the center, which can cause frustration.

FINE MOTOR SKILLS IMPAIRMENTS

Woodwinds: These instruments are difficult for children with fine motor control problems.

SPEECH IMPAIRMENTS

Woodwinds: These instruments may be difficult for children with speech problems because they may have difficulty coordinating their tongue.

LEARNING OR COGNITIVE IMPAIRMENTS

Brass: The brass family of instruments is a good choice for children with learning difficulties because the player does not use as many fingers as when playing wind instruments.

Percussion: Mallets can be difficult for children with visual tracking problems (visual motor) because they need to see the music and look for the correct bar to strike. It is hard for them to read, then look, then hit, then read, and so on.

Percussion: A child with processing delays will have difficulty playing the drums in good time.

ATTENTION DEFICIT DISORDER (ADHD/ADD)

String Instruments: The string bass is a good choice for children with ADHD/ADD because the child can stand while playing and it allows him or her to move, which helps with his or her ability to focus.

Woodwinds: The saxophone is a good choice because it allows the child to stand up as much as possible.

Percussion: Mallet instruments allow students with ADHD/ADD some freedom to stand and move.

Despite challenges, children with various disabilities can and do learn to play musical instruments and can be involved in school music programs, as illustrated by the many stories in this chapter. Music teacher Stephen Zdzinski, in his article "Instrumental Music for Special Learners," states, "Instrumental music teachers can successfully teach learners with a variety of disabilities to play band and orchestral instruments by making minor modifications to traditional instrumental teaching techniques and by employing techniques used primarily in special education."[38]

Music: A Far-Reaching Impact

Music's impact is far reaching. It touches and influences everyone, from the learning and physically disabled to the average person on the street. It opens doors and makes learning easier; it changes the lives of people struggling with disabilities and unlocks windows of opportunities while making people with challenges feel accepted and part of society. It provides a niche where people who struggle can still find acceptance and achievement, many for the first time.

Recently, I heard a remarkable story of a deaf man who, after being fitted with state-of-the-art hearing aids, could hear for the first time. This dramatically changed his world, and for the first time in his life he could hear music. Austin Chapman is a twenty-three-year-old freelance filmmaker whose life, up until now, has largely been visual. He was born profoundly deaf and was diagnosed when he was a year old. Chapman can read lips and communicate in American Sign Language, but was never able to hear the music behind his own award-winning films. After getting his new, improved Phonak hearing aids, the first piece of music he listened to was

Mozart's "Lacrimosa," causing him to literally weep with joy. He described the experience of hearing music for the first time as the sensation of being exposed to a color you've never seen before or seeing a high-resolution photograph for the first time. He posted his audio breakthrough on the social network reddit.com, asking people what he should listen to. Within days he had more than fourteen thousand suggestions with everything from Beethoven to the Beatles. He says that he has always been a happy person, but the prospect of hearing music had brought an incalculable happiness to his life.[39]

Music can change our lives, our environment, and our world— no matter our challenges. Poetically speaking, human beings are made of music. It has been postulated that the smallest parts of our cells are made up of strings. Strings vibrate. Vibrations produce tones. And tones produce music. Human beings are made of music! Is it any wonder that people everywhere and in every circumstance respond to music?

It has been postulated that the smallest parts of our cells are made up of strings. Strings vibrate. Vibrations produce tones. And tones produce music. Human beings are made of music! Is it any wonder that people everywhere and in every circumstance respond to music?

$\mathcal{I}$MPROVISATION: CREATIVITY AND THE TWENTY-FIRST CENTURY

"I think, at a child's birth, if a mother could ask a fairy godmother to endow it with the most useful gift, that gift should be curiosity."

Eleanor Roosevelt

Jack Andraka seems like any ordinary sixteen-year-old high school sophomore. He enjoys science, mountain biking, whitewater rafting, and kayaking. Appearances, however, can be deceiving: Andraka is no ordinary high school student. He recently won the $75,000 grand prize at the Intel International Science and Engineering Fair for his biochemical test that can detect a protein in blood linked to pancreatic cancer. His test is 168 times faster and twenty-six thousand times less expensive (costing about three cents) and over four hundred times more sensitive than the current diagnostic tests. It can even be used to detect ovarian and lung cancers. He has an international patent pending and has talked to large pharmaceuticals in hopes of bringing the test to market in the next three to five years. Currently, he is collaborating with high school students all over the world on a device that, when passed over the skin, detects disease instantly.

Andraka is from Maryland, reads academic journals such as *Science, Nature,* and the *Journal of Clinical Neurology* for fun, and has a mentor at

Johns Hopkins University who calls him the "Edison of our times."[1] He is a problem solver and experimenter, a pattern recognition specialist and expert in synthesizing seemingly unrelated pieces of information. To be precise, he is a creative genius.

Today, as in years past, there are problems in education that are negatively affecting the global marketplace: unqualified teachers, overcrowded classrooms, too much "drill and kill," the disappearance of art and music programs, and students graduating with a lack of proficiency in reading, writing, and math. One problem of particular concern is the spiraling downward trend of creativity. In May 2010, Kyung Hee Kim at the College of William and Mary discovered that creativity scores have been falling since 1990. What is alarming, according to Kim, is, "It is the scores of younger children in America—from kindergarten through sixth grade—for whom the decline is most serious."[2] Our children are less and less creative in the very moment that the global marketplace demands more innovative thinking. What is truly disconcerting is that we indirectly and inadvertently encourage this demise of the creative mind.

What is creativity? Why is it important, and how is it tied to the realities of the global economy in the twenty-first century? What I intend to examine in the following chapter is how creativity can be taught, what parents can do to nurture creativity at home, what the schools can do to foster creativity in the classroom, and the fundamental role of music in the creative process.

Creativity is learning how to think in different ways; it is being able to problem-solve and produce something original, useful, and meaningful. Creative thinkers look at and approach the world differently than other people, they open themselves up to new possibilities and change, and they combine seemingly incongruent ideas together to solve perplexing problems. To be creative in a certain subject requires knowledge in that subject. In other words, in order to be creative in the field of neuroscience, you must have a certain level of expertise. Creativity is ageless; its potential belongs to everyone, and it can be learned, developed, fostered, and ignited both at home and in the classroom. Creative and critical thinkers are important to our economy and world because they seek solutions to complex issues, such as poverty, health care, education, world peace, environmental concerns, and many others. Creative people are an undisputed necessity for a thriving economy. Recently, an IBM poll of fifteen hundred CEOs acknowledged creativity as the number one "leadership competency" of the future.[3] Many

Creativity is ageless; its potential belongs to everyone, and it can be learned, developed, fostered, and ignited both at home and in the classroom.

believe that a lack of creative thinkers will undermine our ability to compete as a nation in a global marketplace. Dr. Arthur Costa, former president of the California Association for Supervision and Curriculum Development, warns, "We're facing a critical time in history. For our nation to survive we have to realize that what's coming up is the smallest work force we've had in a long time; we've had a big population dip and our industries have a much smaller pool of talent. This small group is one of the most undertrained with the largest number of dropouts. At the same time, industry has the greatest demand for problem solvers and thinkers, entrepreneurs, and craftsmen—creative people whose products are so excellent and whose thinking is so forward that we can match the other countries for survival. We're at a time of great competition for creativity and thinking—we've got to develop these skills in all our students."[4]

The Problem

The home is where creativity must begin. Sadly, it is where creativity is dying. Kim's study on creativity was based on the Torrance Tests of Creative Thinking (TTCT). This test was developed by Professor E. Paul Torrance, an American psychologist. It is considered the most respected, tested, and applied creativity test in the world. In applying the Torrance Test, Kim speculates that the decline in creativity owes much more to the home than the schools because personality development is most influenced by the home. She believes that instead of children being engaged in creative activities at home, they are spending too much time "interfacing with machines instead of people." She lists the following as potential culprits: computers, cell phones, handheld Internet devices, DVD players in cars, talking GPS, hundreds of channels on increasing numbers of televisions, and long hours spent playing video games. Kim believes that these machines serve as a distraction rather than an enhancement for a child's creative development.[5]

The criticism is not new. Educators and critics alike have long decried the oversaturation of certain technologies as a hindrance to creative development. As a parent, I agree wholeheartedly. These myriad machines have their place, but they also need parental controls. For instance, it is amusing when parents tell me video games improve hand-eye coordination and help children problem-solve because video games require decision making. Children naturally learn hand-eye coordination by playing a musical instrument or playing group sports. Furthermore, video games are limited in the number of choices the player can make, and this kind of problem solving does not foster creativity. If a child was to actually create and develop a video game—that would be creative—but playing a video game does not increase creativity.

The mind-numbing effects of television need no introduction. Spending hours watching mindless television can destroy creativity. Parents have been cautioned for many years about children watching too much television. In the 1980s, Jim Trelease's *The Read-Aloud Handbook* was my bible. He talks about television and lists sixteen reasons to keep this machine under wraps. In a nutshell, too much television, he says, disrupts a child's language development and ability to think, stifles the imagination, and discourages creative play.[6] On the other hand, learning a musical instrument develops inventive thinking, builds language, teaches problem-solving skills, and fosters communication and socialization—all components of creative thinking.

On the other hand, learning a musical instrument develops inventive thinking, builds language, teaches problem-solving skills, and fosters communication and socialization—all components of creative thinking.

More recently, we have witnessed a rise in global positioning satellite (GPS) technologies. Certainly, GPS makes for convenient traveling, but you might consider teaching your child how to read a map. The process of learning to read a map, navigating directions and developing a sense of where he or she is in a city or neighborhood will increase his or her spatial awareness—another core component of creativity. Learning a musical instrument, as we discussed in previous chapters, dramatically increases spatial ability.

I know many parents who put controls on the amount of time their children may spend playing video games or watching television. One parent required that for every five minutes her children spent playing video games or watching television, they had to practice their musical instrument the same amount of time. As a result, they thought twice about the time they spent on these machines, which in turn taught them the importance of making choices, being disciplined, and understanding sacrifice. Bottom line: if parents want to nurture and ignite a creative spirit and awareness in their children, give them music lessons. Along with music lessons, read to them each day; ask them questions; and get them involved with activities that encourage them to think and problem-solve. When buying toys, purchase ones that spark creativity, such as blocks, Tinkertoys, Legos, Lincoln Logs, science toys, and so forth. Cultural critic Roland Barthes lamented in the 1970s that the wooden blocks children used to play with were in decline, and it was sad because now children were taught to be users, not creators.

Jack Andraka was not taught to be a user—he was taught to be a creator. At the age of three his parents did not answer his questions directly, but rather encouraged him to think and figure things out for himself. Instead of mind-numbing video games and television, they provided books, encyclopedias, and math and science toys for Andraka to explore and problem-solve with. He particularly loved a toy "river" that had a circulating hydraulic pump. He spent hours playing with this toy, rearranging rocks to make rapids, throwing in twigs to make strainers, floating foam kayaks down the river, and experimenting with changes in the flow of the water when making the river narrow or wide. On weekend river rafting trips with his family, Andraka made comparisons between his toy river and the actual river. Through creative play, he figured out the hydraulics of the river. As a teen his fascination with rivers grew into an intense interest in low-head dams and how to retrofit them for safety.

Growing up, he was also enthralled with mathematical calculations. He spent time figuring out how tall a dinosaur was; if the reptile could peek into his bedroom window; and how many strides it would take for the dinosaur to walk around the house or neighborhood. His parents encouraged his interest in mathematics and signed him up for Kumon math. Later he joined a math team, competed with the Montgomery Blair Regional Math team, and studied with the Fairfax Math Circle in Virginia.

Instead of the family spending dinner time in front of the television set watching mindless shows, they gathered around the kitchen table and, while eating, discussed various topics, such as physics, chemistry, and mathematics. From these lively conversations, Andraka spent hours researching different subjects on the Internet and following threads to more and more interesting ideas.[7] In every way—books, science toys, stimulating questions, family conversations, and even piano lessons—Jack Andraka's parents fostered, ignited, and encouraged curiosity in their son. Clearly, it paid off.

Schools: Failing to Develop Creativity

Outside of the home, schools are where most children are *supposed* to develop creativity. So, why are schools failing our students? What are the flawed methodologies currently employed by our educational systems which produce the undertrained workforce that lacks creative problem-solving skills?

As children learn reading, writing, and arithmetic, they are exercising the logical and rational parts, or the left side, of their brains. But there is more to learning and intelligence than merely thinking rationally and logically and coming up with the one "correct" answer.

First, most instruction methods in school target primarily left-brain learning. As children learn reading, writing, and arithmetic, they are exercising the logical and rational parts, or the left side, of their brains. But there is more to learning and intelligence than merely thinking rationally and logically and coming up with the one "correct" answer. Challenges at work are not "true or false," "fill in the blanks," or "circle the correct answer." In today's world there is never just one way to solve a problem, or one way to respond to a situation, and workers need to use imagination and imagery, parts of the creative thinking process, to solve challenging problems. Confirming the importance of creative thinking, the late Mary Alice White of Teachers College stated, "It is quite possible that linear thinking, as opposed to imagery thinking, has been one of our handicaps in trying to solve pressing worldwide problems. The mode of thinking we need…must help us to visualize the connections among all parts of the problem. This is where imagery is a powerful thinking tool, as it has been for scientists, including Einstein."[8] Imagery thinkers—those who are able to formulate three-dimensional pictures in the mind's eye and thereby solve perplexing problems—are exactly the kinds of creative thinkers needed in this century.

Ms. White's statement points out yet another problem—the current educational practice of fragmented instruction. This kind of instruction gives students bits and pieces of information—a little history, a little English, a little math—but for the most part there is no connection between subjects. Rarely, if ever, are students encouraged to find interdisciplinary relationships. Peter Senge, an expert on the "learning organization," says, "From a very early age, we are taught to break problems apart, to fragment the world. This apparently makes complex tasks and subjects more manageable, but we pay an enormous price. We can no longer see the consequences of our actions; we lose our intrinsic sense of connection to a larger whole…After a while, we give up trying to see the whole altogether."[9]

To understand and see the whole or big picture, students need to connect information, look for patterns, and then apply that knowledge to the past, present, and future events. *All* subjects in school contain connecting patterns, and students need to be able to see how all knowledge is like a puzzle with each piece being important and interrelated to the finished "big" picture. Being able to find overarching patterns, as well as minute details, and apply them to macrocosmic problem solving and reasoning not only equips students for their future work, but also helps to make sense of their education, especially for those students who often lament, "How is learning this ever going to help me?" Speaking to the importance of patterns, Priscilla Vail, author of *Smart Kids with School Problems* and *Clear and Lively Writing*, says, "The ones who have kept alive their ability to play with patterns, to experiment—they will be the ones who can make use of what technology has to offer. Those whose focus has been on getting the correct answers to get a high score will be obsolete."[10] Information is not a paint-by-numbers exercise. The beauty of information is its malleability: how once discovered it is adjusted, reconceptualized, amended, and reconfigured. Information is not scribbling on a stone tablet; it has the fluidity of hypertext.

Information is not a paint-by-numbers exercise. The beauty of information is its malleability: how once discovered it is adjusted, reconceptualized, amended, and reconfigured. Information is not scribbling on a stone tablet; it has the fluidity of hypertext.

Jack Andraka understands all too well the importance of playing with information, finding patterns, and applying knowledge through diverse experiences. He was in his freshman biology class half listening to his teacher lecture on antibodies while at the same time reading a scholarly article on applications for nanotubes. It was that eureka moment when suddenly the two ideas collided in his mind: "What if I could lace a nanotube network with mesothelin-specific antibodies and then introduce a drop of a pancreatic cancer patient's blood? The antibodies would bind to the mesothelin and enlarge…"[11] In a rather understated fashion, Andraka's mentor, Dr. Anirban Maitra, professor of pathology, oncology, and chemical and biomolecular engineering at Johns Hopkins School of Medicine, called his experience "connecting the dots." Highly creative people understand that connecting the dots of information can yield fascinating, if not revolutionary, results. "He's ahead of his time in many ways," says Maitra. "Taking one idea and seeing how to extrapolate something even more expansive, that's the difference between being great and being a genius."[12] The problem is we're not encouraging greatness, let alone genius.

Steve Jobs understood how to connect the dots. He said, "Creativity is just connecting things. When you ask creative people how they did something, they feel a little guilty because they didn't really do it, they just saw something. It seemed obvious to them after a while. That's because they were able to connect experiences they've had and synthesize new things. And the reason they were able to do that was that they've had more experiences or they have thought more about their experiences than other people."[13]

In the past as in the present, the main responsibility of education has been to teach our children the skills necessary to be able to live, grow, and compete in the world, to enjoy life through their talents and abilities, and to prepare them for the future workplace. The problem with this model is that our workplace is changing rapidly and the education system is outdated. The Industrial Age, with its emphasis on manufacturing and trade, is over. We are now in the Information or Digital Age, working with information and technology coming toward us at warp speed. As in the past, workers of the twenty-first century still need to be competent in reading, writing, and math, but now more than ever, they need to be flexible thinkers and skilled in evaluating, analyzing, and synthesizing knowledge. Collaborative work ethic, excellent communication, and acute decision making are essential skills in this increasingly complex society. Companies need individuals with imaginative vision, those who seek and find solutions to problems, and those with innovative personalities and dual creative-critical thinking. In sum, people with a wide range of higher-order thinking skills.

Finding Solutions

The problems associated with the lack of creative development are well documented. The larger, more important question is this: What can our schools do to produce students proficient in creative, imaginative thinking?

Certainly, there is a need for many schools to look at a variety of solutions, from the way their basic skills are taught to employing more effective teaching methods to hiring more qualified and better-trained teachers. What is often overlooked, however, is that schools must model their educational practices on those of other institutions that are producing competent students. What are some of these practices? Exceptional teachers who are using a variety of effective and creative strategies appropriate for their different classes to meet their clearly stated objectives. Students who are being held to a higher standard. Students actively involved in the learning process and who know not only the expectations but have a vested interest in their own accountability. These teachers and classrooms do exist, despite the myriad of problems created by the No Child Left Behind Act, which relegated the arts to the sidelines and fostered "drill and kill" learning.

One such teacher who continues to teach creatively and holds his students to a high standard is Rafe Esquith, who has taught at Hobart Elementary School in Los Angeles for over twenty-five years. Mr. Esquith is one of those teachers that every school wants to employ and every parent wants for his or her child. Not only does he teach his students the three *R*s in exciting, interesting ways, but he teaches them life skills, such as how to be good decision makers, the importance of a good character, and how to enrich their lives through education and upstanding behavior. He has a law of expectation in his classroom and challenges his students to think critically, expand their learning, and shun mediocrity.

Early in his teaching career he began using Shakespeare's plays as a means to help his students learn English and increase their vocabulary. Shakespeare, he quickly realized, was also a tool to encourage problem solving. He started the Hobart Shakespeareans group, where each year his fourth- and fifth-grade students perform an unabridged production of one of Shakespeare's plays. For anyone even remotely familiar with Shakespearean drama and its complicated diction and subject matter, this is no easy feat. The students volunteer to come throughout the summer to dissect the play's intricate language, learn accompanying parts on musical instruments, and foster a genuinely collaborate spirit. After eleven months of rehearsals, the students perform the production to an awed public. His goal is to take his students' natural gifts and turn them into something extraordinary—character qualities and creative gifts that will benefit them in the future workplace. Rafe Esquith is a teacher who changes lives. His accolades are numerous. He is the only teacher to have been awarded the president's National Medal of the Arts. He also received the American Teacher Award, *Parents* magazine's As You Grow Award, Oprah Winfrey's Use Your Life Award, and *People* magazine's Heroes Among Us Award.[14]

The foundation of any good educational system is competent, dedicated teachers trained in teaching methods developed from the knowledge of how children learn best. However, schools need to recognize that there is something missing from their current curricula. That "something" is the conduit needed to connect basic skills with higher-order thinking skills, to connect learning to both right and left sides of the brain, and to connect those "bits and pieces of information" now taught in isolated parts as separate subjects. What, then, is missing in our school system today that can help our students meet the demands of the business world tomorrow? A few prominent business leaders believe they have the answer to this question. Here is what four have to say.

The foundation of any good educational system is competent, dedicated teachers trained in teaching methods developed from the knowledge of how children learn best.

According to Richard Gurin, former president and CEO of Binney and Smith,

> "After a long business career, I have become increasingly concerned that the basic problem gripping the American workplace is not interests rates or inflation; those come and go with the business cycle. More deeply rooted is…the crisis of creativity. Ideas…are what built American business. And it is the arts that build ideas and nurture a place in the mind for them to grow. Arts education programs can help repair weaknesses in American education and better prepare workers for the twenty-first century."[15]

Likewise, Helge W. Wehmeier, president and CEO, Bayer Corporation, believes,

"A good well-rounded education must include the study of both the arts and the sciences. As a company we explore the synergies between arts and science. Of all subjects, the arts and sciences are the closest and most interrelated. They offer complementary ways of understanding the same object or event…They also teach critical thinking, creativity, and curiosity—skills that make for an educated and innovative workforce."[16]

Fred Behning, retired from IBM Corporation after a thirty-two year career that included assignments in systems engineering, product development, management, and customer technology briefings:

"I have made a career doing things that weren't even invented when I graduated from high school forty years ago. It will be the same for today's graduates, only on a sharply accelerating timeline. Much of what I learned in the classroom is obsolete or, at best, only marginally useful. What has made a difference in my life has been the ability to learn as I go, to adapt to new ideas, to have the courage to take risks, and to feel confident I will be able to perform and successfully meet the challenges of new situations. These skills I learned through participation in band and drama."[17]

And finally, Joyce Hergenhan, president, G.E. Fund, states,

"Tomorrow's workforce—and especially its leaders—will need broad abilities beyond technical skills. There will be a demand for people who can solve problems, communicate ideas, and be sensitive to the world around them. Children who receive an elementary foundation in the arts; ongoing comprehensive, sequential education in music, drama, dance, and the visual arts; who are afforded opportunities for higher levels of achievement—these are children who will step into tomorrow's world, 'the arts advantage.' They will bring to it a quick mind, focus, discipline, imagination, judgment, personal drive, experience in teamwork, attention to detail, grasp the big picture, and an essential urge to continue learning."[18]

The commonality between these statements is easily observed: a fundamental emphasis on the arts to encourage creative thinking. Perhaps it seems too simplistic to think that by merely adding music and the arts to the curricula, the schools will churn out students ready to accept and meet the challenges of the workplace in our twenty-first century. But when we consider the information gained through the scientific studies on brain development, we can see that this simple idea provides the method by which the complex process of developing optimal brain function can be achieved. The research speaks loudly and clearly—learning must include activities that exercise the whole brain for students to reach their full creative potentials. The parts of the brain that our schools fail to develop are the creative areas, which we use for the imagination, for postulating innovative ideas, and for dealing with complexity and ambiguity. Creative abilities eventually lead us to the generation and discovery of new ideas, vital qualities that our nation was built on and will continue to be needed in this century. Yes, as simple as it may seem, when a child receives a comprehensive sequential education in music and the arts, the creative areas of the brain are stimulated and higher-order thinking skills develop naturally. Esquith concurs: "Music is crucial for a child's complete development no matter his aptitude. …Music must not be optional. Reading music is as important as reading itself. Music training should be required as part of a complete

> *Yes, as simple as it may seem, when a child receives a comprehensive sequential education in music and the arts, the creative areas of the brain are stimulated and higher-order thinking skills develop naturally.*

education. If your child reads music, plays music, and makes it a part of his daily existence, his life will be better for it."[19]

Countries around the world, understanding the need for more creative thinkers and problem-solvers and concerned about the significant decline of student's creativity scores, are developing programs to teach and foster creativity. In 2008, secondary schools in Great Britain changed their entire curricula—from science to foreign languages—to emphasize idea generation; an important creative thinking skill. The European Union named 2009 as the European Year of Creativity and Innovation. They held conferences on the neuroscience of creativity, offered teacher training, and instituted problem-based learning programs that included real-world issues. Chinese schools have also joined in and are adopting a problem-based learning approach. Recently, Jonathan Plucker of Indiana University toured some of the schools in Shanghai and Beijing using problem-based learning. What he saw was creativity at work: a boy for his class science project rigged a tracking device for his moped with parts from a cell phone. [20]

Creative Thinking Skills in the Classroom

Many teachers use a variety of creative techniques in their mainstream classrooms, but others believe that creativity belongs solely in the art or music classroom. Nothing could be further from the truth—creativity belongs in *every* classroom. Why? Because creativity is more than drawing a picture or composing a piece of music, and every student will need to use creative thinking skills in his or her future job. Creative theorist Donald Treffinger suggests the following creative thinking skills that can be used in all classrooms and at work: fact finding, problem finding, idea finding, solution finding, and a plan of action. Incorporated within these skills are divergent thinking—generating many unique ideas and brainstorming— and convergent thinking—combining those ideas to formulate a single result or solve a problem.

In the creation of El Sistema—the famous music organization in Venezuela talked about in chapter 6—we see Treffinger's simple creative formula at work. In 1975, Dr. José Antonio Abreu, economist, musician, and social reformer, started El Sistema. He had a vision which started with *fact finding*. Abreu saw the gulf between the rich and poor in Venezuela. He saw that many young people, because of their poverty, became involved in crime and drugs, and he believed that music could change their lives and put them on a positive course. Next was *problem finding*—how should he go about creating, organizing, and structuring such a system? Then, *idea finding*: as a musician and social reformer himself, he believed that all Venezuelan children would benefit from participating in classical music; that music could be the catalyst to change people and societal structure. *Solution finding:* he decided to structure this program as a social program as opposed to a cultural program; one that would develop values of solidarity, harmony, and mutual compassion and garner government support. A *plan of action* took place in 1975 when he launched El Sistema, which became a musical opportunity for all children regardless of their economic situation. Today, nearly forty years later, El Sistema is a nationwide organization with over 250,000 musicians, 102 orchestras, sixty children's orchestras, and 270 music centers.[21] People and organizations in the United States have taken note and copycat programs are being established across our nation. It is a model of success, and it all started with one man who had a creative idea.

The creation of this music program that affects thousands of children illustrates that creative thinking solves the seemingly unsolvable through small, simple adjustments.

Part of understanding and teaching creativity is for educators to recognize creative tools when they see them. In December 1999, an article appeared in the *Los Angeles Times* titled "L.A. IMAX Says No, So Disney Builds Its Own Huge Screen." The California Science Center refused to show *Fantasia 2000* on their IMAX screen because they questioned the "educational merits of *Fantasia 2000*." Joe DeAmicis, vice president of marketing for the California Science Center, stated, "We're an educational institution, and we had real questions about whether this would meet the mandate of the school groups we serve."[22] When educators miss the obvious and do not recognize something that can be used as both an educational and creative tool in the classroom, it should come as no surprise why the creative quotient (CQ) of our children has taken a dive.

Fantasia and Fantasia 2000 are educational masterpieces that inspire and ignite creative thinking and can be used as a tool in both the classroom and at home to teach principles and skills found in the creative spectrum.

Fantasia and Fantasia 2000 are educational masterpieces that inspire and ignite creative thinking and can be used as a tool in both the classroom and at home to teach principles and skills found in the creative spectrum. Many people who watch these films come away only seeing classical music and Disney animation. But that is seeing the obvious. Part of thinking creatively is looking beyond the obvious or being able to see "outside the box." Albert Szent-Györgyi, a Nobel Prize-winning physician, said, "Discovery consists of looking at the same thing as everyone else and thinking something different."[23] If you look beyond what is portrayed on the screen, you will see how these movies teach imaginative thinking of the scientific, the educational, and the aesthetic with vital interlocking connections and fascinating patterns.

Imagine *Fantasia* and *Fantasia 2000* as wordless books supported by classical music that tell enchanting stories while providing multiple layers of ideas and useful information. When books or movies use a wordless format, it puts the observer or reader in the powerful position of being responsible for creating the meaning of a story. The observer must imagine diction, tone, inflection, and subtext. This, in turn, increases vocabulary, expressive language, and creative thought. According to Jim Trelease, "One excellent means of building the confidence, imagination, and vocabulary of pre-readers is through the use of wordless books."[24] Along with *Fantasia* and *Fantasia 2000*, introduce your children to the enchanting wordless books *The Silver Pony*, by Lynn Ward, and *Noah's Ark*, by Peter Spier, and watch their imaginations and vocabulary soar.

Bringing *Fantasia* and *Fantasia 2000* into the classroom becomes a useful exercise in creative dissection. Educators can make the films relevant to students and what they are learning in the classroom by taking apart each film segment, analyzing it, and associating it with and connecting it to subjects they are learning, such as literature, language arts, math, science, social studies, and history. This exercise will stretch their imaginations, compel them to look beyond the obvious, critically think, dig deeper for hidden nuggets of knowledge, and connect bits and pieces of information—all necessary skills of creative problem solving that can be used in their future jobs. As students use their critical thinking skills, they will find that the far-reaching impact of these films lie just below the surface. Again, it is like putting a puzzle together; fitting all the pieces and watching a picture emerge.

You may ask, how exactly do I use this film in my classroom or at home? How do I make connections from the movie to subjects I am teaching? How do I spur *my* imagination?

All classroom lessons plans contain strategies. Begin by using the strategy of word association. One of the segments in *Fantasia 2000* is about death and rebirth and uses the element of fire. Ask yourself what words remind you of fire—destroys, hot, devastating, cleansing, ashes, burns, fire extinguisher, and Prometheus. Next use the strategy of idea generation. As you watch the segment, jot down every random idea that comes to you. Even if the ideas seem ridiculous, write them down; editing will come later. For instance: it's telling a story, how many ways are stories told? Is fire always bad? What would it cost if an entire forest burned down? Who started fire? Is there a story about fire in literature? Are their examples in history where something bad like fire turns into something good? How do you treat a burn? Use this time to rid yourself of mental blocks—preconceived attitudes that do not allow you to think something different. One idea will lead to other ideas and then to many ideas and eventually to connections to subjects in school. If you watch the segment and nothing comes to you, then you need to watch it until something does. Creative thinking doesn't just happen; you must work for it.

> *Creative thinking doesn't just happen; you must work for it.*

Last, ask other people to watch the movie with you. Explain to them what you are doing and looking for. Most people catch on very quickly, and it becomes a contest of who can generate the most creative and interesting ideas.

Here is one example from *Fantasia 2000* that I developed using word association and idea generation. (These films are currently in the Disney vault and not available for purchase. Either rent them or purchase them used from amazon.com because this exercise is more powerful if you are actually watching the films).

The last segment in *Fantasia 2000* uses Igor Stravinsky's *Firebird Suite* (1919 version), which was originally presented as a ballet in 1910. The Disney theme is death and rebirth portrayed by a sprite, firebird, and elk. The sprite represents nature, and she awakens spring in the forest, only to have it destroyed by the firebird, who lives in a volcano. Afterwards, the elk and sprite work together to bring life back to the ravaged forest and reawaken what lies beneath the ashes.

Look at the connections below (they are in simple outline form) and add your own ideas. You will also see interconnections between subjects. For instance, when you are generating social studies ideas, a literature idea may pop into your head.

- LITERATURE: Look for the literary theme of good triumphing over evil (the sprite is good and overcomes the evil destruction of the firebird). Compare this with other examples from literature, as there is always a protagonist and antagonist. Fairytales and fantasy—such as *The Chronicles of Narnia*, by C. S. Lewis; *Harry Potter*, by J. K. Rowling; or *Snow White*, by the Brothers Grimm—are particularly good and easy for younger children to identify. This segment also illustrates how Disney comes full circle with the first segment in *Fantasia 2000* demonstrating the forces of good and evil and this last segment showing how good triumphs over evil.

- LANGUAGE ARTS: This segment tells a story through music, dance, and mime. Discuss the various forms of storytelling and how storytelling has been a part of civilization since the dawn of time. Before the written word, stories were oral traditions and were passed down verbally from generation to generation (hence the nine hundred versions of *Cinderella*!). Discuss how ballet communicates a story through dance or movements of the body. Mimes tell stories through body movements in the same way people tell stories when playing the game charades. Art tells a story through paintings and sculpture (you've all heard the saying "every picture tells a story"). Literature weaves stories through words and music sings a story. Students can create their own stories using dance, art, mime, or the written word.

- MATH AND ESTIMATION: In the segment, the entire forest is burned to the ground. Estimate the yearly amount of damage in dollars created by fires, both by arson and natural forces. Consider the damage to homes, property, animals, forests, businesses, and lives. Do a statistical and comparative analysis of the damage created from different fires in local neighborhoods and the nation.

- SCIENCE—SEASONS AND CYCLES: This segment illustrates seasons and cycles of the earth. Learn about the cycles and seasons found in nature: spring represents the renewal of life while winter represents death. Learn what happens to trees, flowers, animals, and insects during the four seasons. If possible, plant a flower, vegetable, or herb garden on a plot at the schoolyard or at home. Let children experience firsthand the different growing seasons and required climate conditions of plants, flowers, vegetables, and herbs. If you plant a garden, section off a portion and grow milkweed and buddleias which will attract butterflies and will open up new learning experiences.

- SCIENCE: This segment shows the devastation created by natural disasters. Learn about natural disasters in nature and how seemingly devastating events can have positive outcomes—just like what is illustrated in this movie segment. Some examples are the fires in Yellowstone National Park, the eruption of the Mount St. Helens volcano in Washington, and the landslide in Yosemite National Park in California. In all three instances these disasters created a cleansing effect on their surroundings.

- SCIENCE: Because this segment deals with fire, explain how a fire extinguisher works and have the students make a simple fire extinguisher (see *Science Wizardry for Kids*, by Margaret Kenda and Phyllis S. Williams). Fire extinguishers contain carbon dioxide, which throws out an invisible blanket over the fire and extinguishes it. Create carbon dioxide from vinegar and baking soda and use it to extinguish a candle flame. Discuss why it is a good idea to keep a fire extinguisher at home, in the car, and at school, and teach children/students how to actually use a real extinguisher (they are not as easy as you may think!).

- SOCIAL STUDIES: This segment powerfully illustrates the power of fire. Discuss fire and who possibly discovered it. There is a myth in Greek mythology about Prometheus stealing fire/knowledge from the gods and giving it to human beings. He was punished for doing this by being chained to a rock; an eagle devoured his liver during the day and it regrew during the night. There are also hundreds of artistic representations of Prometheus in classical and Renaissance art. What are the uses of fire that are both good and bad? Discuss the frightening aspects of fire when it is out of control. Talk about forest fires, the damage they can do to the forest, how fires can destroy lives, property, and communities. Explore the history and background of Smokey Bear. How does Disney create fire as something very frightening, overpowering, and destructive?

- HISTORY: Discuss the bubonic plague or the black death. Explain that like the movie where an entire forest is destroyed, the black plague caused the death of twenty-five million to forty million people. In terms of percentages, it is considered to be the worst disaster in the history of mankind. Also like the movie, something good did happen despite its horrifying devastation to lives. The survivors inherited money, lands, property, and hundreds of pounds of useless cloth. Eventually, they used the cotton cloth to manufacture cotton rag paper, and, with the advent of the printing press, the cotton rag paper was used to produce books. Cotton rag paper was much easier to work with than the vellum and parchment they were currently using. This seeming catastrophe produced cotton rag paper and, coupled with the printing press, books were published and education became available to the masses.[25]

- FIRST AID KIT: If you talk to your students about treating burns, here are two suggestions that work amazingly well: therapeutic lavender oil or an egg white applied directly on the burn.

This is one example. Now, put on your creative thinking hat, watch the entire movie, and have fun stimulating your children or students' creative juices.

SCANS: The First Steps

In 1991, as a result of the growing concern for educating our future workers adequately, representatives from education, business, labor, and the government met to discuss the needs of the future workplace. From this meeting, *What Work Requires of Schools* was published by the Secretary of Labor's Commission on Achieving Necessary Skills (SCANS).[26] The report stated that students, to meet these needs, must achieve these specific skills:

- Have the ability to use resources.

- Have interpersonal skills.

- Be able to manipulate information.

- Use appropriate technology.

- Understand systems.

The foundation of these skills is proficiency in the basic skills— reading, writing, mathematics, speaking, and listening—as well as thinking skills; that is, being able to think creatively, make decisions, solve problems, see things in the mind's eye, and know how to learn and reason. Also, the development of the personal qualities of individual responsibility, self-esteem, sociability, self-management, and integrity is needed. What I will demonstrate in the following sections is how each of these SCANS skills can be acquired through music and arts education.

Ability to Use Resources

The ability to use resources is defined in part as workers being able to allocate time, materials, and space.

Although there are other activities, such as sports, that will teach a child how to allocate and organize time, materials, and space, music is a consistent, ongoing activity that habitually perfects these skills. Students involved in music and the arts learn very early the importance of balancing their time effectively. A music student needs sufficient time to practice his instrument each day; meet rehearsal schedules; go to music lessons; and fit in other activities of community, home, school, and friends. Musicians learn the necessity of careful planning, which enables them to juggle many assignments at once. Rafe Esquith says this about music's ability to teach children how to organize time: "Through music, a student will learn to literally play with others, and without realizing it will develop time management skills that will be useful throughout the day, even when the instrument is not being played."[27]

Additionally, students involved in drama or dance learn how to organize, divide, and choreograph space on the stage as they plan and prepare for a performance. Mural artists must be able to organize a variety of materials as they design and proportion space in creating large murals that will be viewed by many in the community. These qualities of organization and planning of one's time and space, when developed in childhood, become skills in adulthood that will carry over to their future jobs.

Interpersonal Skills

Interpersonal skill is defined as the ability to work in teams, teach others, and work well with people from culturally diverse backgrounds.

For the most part, it takes the talents of many to accomplish most "great" ideas. Very few ideas are realized through the efforts of one person, so being able to work well with others, share and communicate opinions, and collaborate on issues become essential assets in the workforce today. Teamwork is being able to acknowledge and integrate multiple points of view—realizing that two, three, or four heads are better than one. It is also the ability to set aside one's ego in order to see alternate approaches to a situation or problem. A music and arts education trains children in teamwork skills. Whether you are singing in the school choir, playing in the band, painting a group mural, or performing on stage, you are engaging in teamwork skills.

A music and arts education trains children in teamwork skills. Whether you are singing in the school choir, playing in the band, painting a group mural, or performing on stage, you are engaging in teamwork skills.

Because most teams work toward a standard of excellence, mediocrity is never acceptable. Collaborators want the finished product to reflect excellence, attention to detail, and the work of both an individual and group. For those that decry collaboration as the weak subsisting on the strong, there is nothing like the competitive, supportive nature of a team to keep everyone working at his or her highest capacity. For example, students in a high school drama class need to individually know their parts *and* work closely together to achieve a polished theater performance that flows. Students in the band or orchestra must listen carefully to one another to achieve a harmonious and balanced sound. It takes team effort, cooperation, and communication for an orchestra to achieve performance-level competency. There is an intense team effort that is expended when a school produces a musical. Singers, musicians, artists, dramatists, dancers, and stagehands work as a unit as they develop a musical masterpiece. As this process evolves, students learn about the power of communicating and cooperating as a team, that there is strength in numbers, and that it takes rigorous hard work and perseverance to achieve a standard of excellence. These lessons become valuable personality assets, no matter what the student chooses to do in life.

Our youngest son, Trevor, played percussion in our community orchestra, as well as his high school band and drumline. All of these activities taught him the importance and necessity of teamwork, which he has transferred to his college studies. He is a business major and in May 2012 joined with other students in the business department on an Asian study abroad. The students were from various backgrounds, and most did not know each another. One day, in preparation for the trip, the instructor put a series of large tarps on the floor. Groups of twenty-five students were asked to crowd together on each tarp. Then the instructor gave the assignment: turn the entire tarp completely over onto the other side without anyone in the group stepping off the tarp at any time. The students looked at each other quizzically, wondering how this could possibly be done. Eventually though, ideas began to formulate: what if some of the students held other students on their backs or in their arms while others in the group slowly rolled the tarp to the other side? Some groups tried it and immediately found that it was not going to work because people were losing their balance and falling. Other ideas were generated, discussed, and tried, but most failed. Ultimately, each group completed the task successfully amid laughter, some tears, and obvious teamwork. The instructor then explained that on study-abroad trips—no matter how well planned and organized—the unforeseeable can happen such as people getting lost, people getting left behind at train stations, lost luggage, companies canceling appointments at the last minute, and so forth. This exercise, she said, was to illustrate to each of them the importance of teamwork, camaraderie, getting along, flexibility, communicating, problem solving, and solution finding, no matter how difficult the situation. The instructor could have easily stood up and given a tedious lecture on the importance of all of the above, but she was creative and allowed the students to experience firsthand something that necessitated these skills. It worked...the one-hundred-plus students who began the trip as strangers from different backgrounds became close friends who were there to help each other whenever and wherever a need arose. When Trevor was relating the experience to us, he remarked that the very teamwork and problem-solving skills which were required to do this exercise were the same skills he learned when performing music with his peers in high school.

Additionally, music serves as a powerful universal language that crosses all race barriers because it draws on the culture and history of nations all over the world. In this century the United States will be a country of "majority minority," meaning the minority population will become the majority population.[28] An education in music and the arts will bridge the gaps between nationalities and will give people a greater understanding of one another as they learn, understand, and appreciate the cultural and artistic talents of other people and countries. Not to mention it allows for the sharing of musical and artistic cultures. The African American blues of the Deep South have been musicologically traced to Sephardic Jewish folk music, Brazilian samba, Spanish cante jondo, and Cuban rumba and dazon.

An education in music and the arts will bridge the gaps between nationalities and will give people a greater understanding of one another as they learn, understand, and appreciate the cultural and artistic talents of other people and countries.

MANIPULATION OF INFORMATION

Manipulation of information is defined in part as acquiring and evaluating data, interpreting and communicating, and using computers to process information.

Today in the workforce, it is imperative to stay abreast of information that changes daily. Bruce O. Boston, author of "Educating for the Workplace Through the Arts" in *Business Week*, talks about a new job that has been defined in corporate America—chief knowledge officers (CKOs)—who are being hired by companies to help them maintain a competitive edge.[29] As the name implies, their job is to keep the company aware of the latest knowledge and technology in the world—a daunting task! Once again, this job requires creative thinkers and lifelong learners; people with the ability to analyze, synthesize, evaluate, and interpret information, understand and relate important facts, and solve problems. The following true story from *Innovation and Entrepreneurship*, by Peter Drucker, illustrates how the innovative thinking of a musician and his ability to evaluate and interpret new information turned a company into a multimillion-dollar enterprise.

In the mid-1920s, Hoffmann-LaRoche was a small, struggling company that made a few textile dyes, but was overshadowed by huge German dye makers and other large firms. About this time, vitamins were discovered. The scientific world could not quite accept the whole concept surrounding vitamins and questioned their necessity. Although no one wanted the patents for these new substances, Hoffmann-LaRoche took a gamble and purchased them. The company then hired the Zurich University scientists who had discovered the vitamins, offering them several times what they were currently making as professors. The company then invested all possible funds into the manufacturing and marketing of the vitamins. Over eighty years later, Hoffmann-LaRoche owns almost half of the world's vitamin market, amounting to billions of dollars in sales each year.

The man behind the success of the venture was a family member of LaRoche—a musician with an orchestra he could not support. According to Drucker, "In creating something truly new, something truly different, nonexperts and outsiders seem to do as well as the experts, in fact, often better. Hoffmann-LaRoche did not owe its strategy to chemists but to a musician who had married the granddaughter of the company's founder and needed more money to support his orchestra than the company then provided through its meager dividend. The company, in picking the vitamins in the early twenties, exploited new knowledge. The musician who laid down its strategy understood the 'structure of scientific revolutions' a full thirty years before a philosopher, Thomas Kuhn, wrote the celebrated book by that name."[30]

In the process of studying music, this young musician developed both his creative and logical sides of his brain, thus enabling him to draw on all of his mental capabilities. Hence, he understood:

- The complexity and uncertainty of solving problems that involve calculated risk.

- The power of new and innovative knowledge (by picking vitamins to market he was testing new knowledge).

- How to see the "big" picture of what was happening (he envisioned the success before it happened).

- The importance of visionary thinking—seeing the potential of vitamins when even scientific experts of the time did not see it.[31]

Each year more and more companies are spending millions of dollars to foster creativity and imagination in their employees. Manipulating information demands ingenuity, not mediocrity. Companies find that those who are the most creative are those who are willing to think in unpredictable ways. Creative people operate outside their comfort zones by eliminating those rules that no longer work or apply. Because learning music requires using the entire brain, children involved in the arts exercise those areas of the brain that allow them to have the confidence in their ability to take calculated risks, come up with new ideas, and look for innovative ways to accomplish tasks.

Because learning music requires using the entire brain, children involved in the arts exercise those areas of the brain that allow them to have the confidence in their ability to take calculated risks, come up with new ideas, and look for innovative ways to accomplish tasks.

Today, some of the most innovative companies realize that people get some of their best ideas when their minds are relaxed and when they are doing repetitive activities such as showering, shaving, driving in a car, listening to soothing music, or just before going to sleep. These activities tip us from our logical brain to our more creative brain, which is where ideas hatch and take flight. As a result, many companies are offering their employees a certain percentage of time during working hours to relax, listen to music, think random thoughts, and spin new ideas. Google offers a 20 percent program, Gore & Associates (Gore-Tex) offers a "dabble time," and 3M has a 15 percent program. Google's 20 percent factor has paid off. Alec Proudfoot used his daydreaming time and came up with RechargeIT—a project which is working to produce affordable and efficient hybrid cars. With Krishna Bharat's 20 percent time, he envisioned Google News, which is up-to-date news coverage taken from stories all over the world. Today, millions of people use Google News the way Bharat envisioned.[32] This concept of creative daydreaming at the office is being noticed in corporate America as more and more visionary ideas are being conceptualized during employee downtime while simultaneously increasing the bottom line.

Also included within this competency is the ability to use computers to process information. The key word here is *process*. In 1997, *Atlantic Monthly* reported that by the year 2000, 60 percent of the nation's jobs will demand computer skills and pay an average of 10 to 15 percent more than jobs requiring no computer work. It is now 2013, and most jobs today require computer literacy. It is also a fact that having advanced computer skills and high-level proficiency in various computer programs may give a person employment advantages, leadership opportunities, and job promotions. But the late Joseph Weizenbaum, a professor of computer science at MIT, stated that even in his technology-heavy institution, new students can learn all the computer skills they need "in a summer."[33]

Unfortunately, schools are choosing to hear only of the future demand for computer-literate workers and are outfitting computer labs at a frenzied pace, often at the expense of dropping music and arts programs. Each year, millions of dollars are poured into the latest computer technology in school districts nationwide. Millions more are spent as the computers break down or become obsolete. Despite this futile outpouring of funds, schools continue to bemoan the fact that they need better and more sophisticated systems for their students in order for them to compete in the workforce. The fact is, computers were *never* meant to be the answer to education's problems. Yet, examples abound of the venerable position given computers in schools.

When it comes to schools purchasing the latest in computer technology, the money miraculously appears, but when a music or arts program needs money to stay alive at a school— a program that is known to be a crucial part in developing higher-level thinking skills, problem-solving skills, and creativity (and which, it is also known, a computer is not)—the money is nowhere to be found.

In February 2013, Los Angeles Unified School District (LAUSD) announced the school board's approval to spend $50 million on computer tablets for students on forty-eight campuses in fall 2013. Their long-range plan is to provide all six-hundred-thousand-plus students with a computer tablet, which will cost the district over $500 million.[34] LAUSD has suffered under dire financial stress and has been "forced" to eliminate almost 50 percent music and arts programs, resulting in a 50 percent decline in student involvement with music programs. Yet they are able to find $50 million for a bunch of computer tablets. This is not something new for LAUSD. A few years ago, Kittridge Street Elementary School in Los Angeles dropped its art, music, and physical education programs and then spent $333,000 on computers.[35] Think about this: if computers really did ignite creativity and problem-solving skills, then we should have a nation filled with creative, problem-solving geniuses. But we do not—in fact, we have the opposite.

Certainly the administrators of schools have good intentions to provide their students with the benefits of modern technology to enhance their education, but it is important to carefully review the findings of research, reports, studies, and experts, which *clearly* point out that computers are not education's panacea. To the contrary, research shows that music and arts programs in our schools are needed to produce students competent in the skills to succeed in the future work force of our nation. For example, Drs. Gordon Shaw and Frances Rauscher, in a follow-up to their groundbreaking studies we discussed in chapter 2, found no significant increase in spatial reasoning when children were exposed to the computer each day, as compared to a 34 percent increase when the students were exposed to a piano keyboard daily. Also as mentioned in chapter 2, although a later study using a specifically designed computer program for increasing spatial intelligence showed a 100 percent increase in spatial intelligence, Dr. Shaw still

Newsweek reported that both music and physical education programs feed the brain and make it easier for kids to learn.

believed that over the long term, the music lessons will have a greater impact. *Newsweek* reported that both music and physical education programs feed the brain and make it easier for kids to learn.[36] A study found that Reader Rabbit, a reading program used in over one hundred thousand schools, caused students to suffer a 50 percent drop in creativity. Forty-nine students used the program for seven months and were no longer able to answer open-ended questions and showed a significantly diminished ability to brainstorm with fluency and originality.[37] Although this study was conducted a few years ago, the findings were ignored and Reader Rabbit is still used in schools across the nation. Corporations and businesses find that employees who use computers a lot "grow rusty in their ability to think." The reason—because computers use only two senses—hearing and sight—and children and adults need an integration of all their senses to learn, understand, and connect information. And Larry Cuban, emeritus professor at Stanford University and an authority on the history of technology in American education, says, "Anyone who tells you computers are more effective than anything else is either dumb or lying."[38] Cuban also states, "Schooling is not about information. It's getting kids to think about information. It's about understanding and knowledge and wisdom."[39]

Dr. John H. Lienhard, professor emeritus, University of Houston, has written and lectured about how computers compromise creativity and curtail certain learning processes. From the outset, he makes it clear that computers are a marvelous tool for many applications, but on the downside they have created memory issues, fragmented learning, divorced knowledge from its appropriate context, and decreased spatial visualization—all skills that develop and support creativity. According to Lienhard, students no longer need to memorize spelling words, understand the geographical location of cities and countries, commit to memory important dates that keep historical events in context, or work out mathematical numbers in their minds—the computer does it for them. Former habits that students used to develop memory—looking words up in a dictionary, noticing information on adjacent pages, memorizing the spelling and meaning of those words, or committing to memory decimal placements and math calculations in their minds—are no longer necessary; computers do all those tasks as well. He believes memorization is important because it helps students with association and recollection as they connect vital pieces of unrelated information which, in turn, spurs invention. Likewise, he is gravely concerned about the loss of spatial visualization which is the ability to solve problems in the mind's eye. Rather than mentally working through three-dimensional problems, students see only the results on a two-dimensional screen. As Lienhard puts it, "Creative thought means building in our minds. We erect strings of logic and we frame poetic images. We sift and rearrange recollection. We construct every kind of relation among objects or shapes or quantities. What will become of generations who've never formed the *habit* of visualizing—to math students who've never built graphs in their minds, to medical students who've learned gross anatomy on a 2-D computer screen?"[40] As we lose our ability to think three dimensionally, we will also compromise our abilities to visually perceive the world, which is important to learning. Without visual perception children cannot accurately learn to read, give or understand directions, copy from a blackboard, have good hand-eye coordination, or integrate visual information with other senses. In short, it compromises our capacity to learn, understand, and create.

The areas where Lienhard believes computers compromise learning and creativity are actually increased when a child learns a musical instrument. Music students memorize music, see the spatial relationships of black and white keys, connect passages, interpret style and tempo, and construe the composer's meaning when learning a piece of music. And all of these skills are developed as a three-dimensional experience.

Most people will agree that computers are an amazing invention, but we must realize what they do and do not do. They are a *tool* used for creative endeavors—they are not the catalyst for developing creativity. We learn the skills necessary to operate a computer without being creative or learning creativity. We develop creative ideas in our minds before ever turning on the computer to execute the idea. On the contrary, the very process of learning a musical instrument builds and strengthens creative processes in the brain.

If a school wants to be unique and a model for other schools, then *first* offer an extensive music program. If a school has a computer lab, then offer classes that require imagination and creative thinking before turning on the computer to execute the idea. Computer animation, motion graphics, typography (which is designing a book, inside and out), communication design, environmental design, sound design, video design, interactive programming, and web design are all subjects that require creative thinking and planning *first*. For students interested in the various aspects of film production offer classes that teach pre-production, production, and post-production processes (writing a script, writing music, casting, costuming, lighting, shooting, editing, and so forth) and how to transfer these skills to produce content for a YouTube channel. These artistic projects are conceived through pre-drawing, pre-planning, mental conceptualizing, creative problem solving, storyboarding, video shooting—all *three-dimensional*, hands-on creations— *before* they are transferred to the *two-dimensional* computer. These types of activities will require students to think, evaluate, and interpret vast possibilities and ideas as they create something truly exciting, increase their creative abilities and, at the same time, gain marketable skills for whatever they choose to do in college and their future occupations.

USE OF APPROPRIATE TECHNOLOGY

Use of appropriate technology is defined as selecting equipment and tools, applying technology to specific tasks, and maintaining and troubleshooting technologies.

Technology has been a part of the arts since the beginning of time. But the place the arts hold in the technological world is, more often than not, misunderstood. Some feel that as man was able to make better things through improved skill and pace, it gave him more time to pursue creative and artistic endeavors. But to the contrary, history shows us that the arts generated the improved skills and that, in turn, this led to the advancement of technology. Many anthropologists believe that it was solving creative problems that ultimately led to inventions with utilitarian purposes. For example, early man learned that clay could be used to make art objects such as bison, deer, foxes, bears. Later, he discovered that baking the clay turned it into a hard material that eventually led to the making of ceramic pots and dishes used for food storage, preparation, and serving. Knives dating back to Cro-Magnon times show that, perhaps, they were first created as objects of beauty before they were used in a practical application.[41]

Musical instruments were made for producing sound to allow man to extend his sound production capabilities beyond what could be projected by his voice. From this came the science of acoustics, furthered by the Greeks in their dramatic performances. In studying the development of man's skills, it becomes apparent that art and technology cannot be separated.

Today, the arts and technology continue to be a team. Steve Jobs was an artist, and an artist who recognized what happens when art and technology merge. The devices he built were not just for technology, but for the creation of art. In March 2011, at the launch of the iPad2, Jobs said, "Technology alone is not enough…It's technology married with liberal arts, married with the humanities, that yields us the result that make our hearts sing."[42]

> *Today, the arts and technology continue to be a team.*

With the computer technology of Musical Instrument Digital Interface (MIDI), students were able to write and orchestrate their own music. Now Universal Serial Bus (USB) is used for most music applications. The use of interactive media combines art and technology, thus creating highly sophisticated special effects and animation. This artistic technological medium has become an enormous opportunity for students to express their creative and inventive ideas, while demonstrating to them the vast possibilities of technology combined with their own imaginations.

The compact disc market is another example of the interrelationship between technology and art. Compact discs were originally produced as a way to create excellent sound quality in a musical application. Next they were linked with computers to store information for hundreds of uses. Our current digital age now produces Blu-ray, high definition (HD), digital video recordings (DVR), MP3 downloads, and many others. Philip Elmer-Dewitt, former science and technology writer for *Time* magazine and currently a contributor to *Fortune* magazine, said, "Without the CD music market, data CDs would not exist…Every time Bruce Springsteen and Stevie Wonder sell a compact disc, it's good news for the data side."[43]

Over twenty years ago, Steven Spielberg could not have created *Jurassic Park,* with its phenomenal special effects, but with media arts pushing for more complicated computer technology, the creation of *Jurassic Park* became a reality, with other technically brilliant films following it, such as Larry and Andy Wachowski's *The Matrix* and Peter Jackson's *The Lord of the Rings* trilogy. Film animation has also taken a technological leap with Pixar, the company responsible for the mind-boggling animation found in *Toy Story* and *Finding Nemo.* Students educated in the arts and sciences will have no trouble understanding, utilizing, and applying the vast possibilities of technology in their future occupations.

UNDERSTANDING SYSTEMS

Understanding systems is defined as understanding social, organizational, and technological systems, monitoring and correcting performance, and designing or improving systems.

Several years ago, the University of Washington required a course called "Creative Dramatics" for elementary teacher certification. It was recognized as an effective teaching/learning strategy or system that brought almost any subject to life for students. Because of budget cuts, the program no longer exists, but while it was in place, it provided students an opportunity to work within such systems through the medium of artistic expression. For example, in a drama lesson the students both listened and read stories and poems, analyzed a painting, or listened to a piece of music. From this, they organized themselves into groups as they planned a dramatic presentation around a particular art form. Designing a plot, creating characters, setting, dialogue, and action were all a part of the presentation. Other students not in the play critiqued and monitored the performance, suggested changes, and gave the artists a chance to make adjustments. Afterward, the students changed roles. As you can see, social, organizational, and technological skills were all brought into play.

Dee Dickinson, author of *Learning Through the Arts*, explains the success of the program: "Clearly this process is a highly collaborative one, develops quick-witted spontaneous thinking, problem solving, poise and presence, concentration, and both conceptual and analytical thinking skills. Making a piece of theater with students encourages, in fact demands, cooperation, compromise, and commitment." She further states, "Formal theater demands additional skills, including the coordination and creation of sets, costumes, props, lighting design, scripts or script-writers, and possibly musicians and dancers. Memorization of lines and action are essential to the process, and great dramatic literature may enrich the actor's memory throughout life."[44]

On a lighter, fictional note, the movie *School of Rock*, with Jack Black, is an amusing example of how social, organizational, and technical skills come together and generate creativity and fun. In some ways it parallels the nonfiction Creative Dramatics experience. Jack Black (a.k.a. Dewey Finn) plays the part of a wannabe-rock-star-turned-substitute-teacher that discovers musical talent in his fourth-grade students. He selfishly seeks to turn them into a rock band so that he can perform in a "battle of the bands" competition which will solve his financial problems and put him back in the rock-band spotlight. He organizes the students into groups— singers, guitarists, pianists, costume designers, graphic artists, managers, and so forth—and capitalizes on their musical, technical, and leadership skills to create the band. It is heartwarming and inspiring to watch the students collaborate to manage and problem solve. They hone their musical instruments, improve their singing voices, fashion costumes, and create live video graphics, all the while monitoring and correcting their performance under the guiding hand of their eccentric teacher. In the end, although they do not win the battle of the bands competition, they win skills of teambuilding, developing inner confidence while having fun.

As young people work within these systems—social, organizational, and technological— a certain amount of conformity to basic rules and standards is necessary; however, within that framework, the flow of imagination and new ideas, which are essential to success, is unrestricted. If a person can imagine it, they can make it happen. Imagination causes people to seek and find solutions to problems, as well as to recognize and act on presented opportunities. August Kekule's dream of six encircling snakes led to the discovery of the benzene molecule. Scientists say that "the benzene molecule is so complex that no amount of logic could have conceived it."[45] It was Kekule's imagination that gave him the idea that led to this scientific breakthrough.

> *Imagination causes people to seek and find solutions to problems, as well as to recognize and act on presented opportunities.*

There are many examples in our history of designing systems through the use of imagination. Alexander Graham Bell created the design for the telephone by imitating the ear.[46] Through the use of his imagination, Einstein worked out formulas to explain what his mind was experiencing and, as a result, came up with one of the most significant theories of all time. Military designers borrowed Picasso's cubist art to create more effective camouflage patterns for tanks. Tim Berners-Lee, the visionary inventor of the World Wide Web, used his imagination and expanded a system that was initially set up as a way for physicists to store and access information in a hyperlinked environment over the Internet. It was the addition of pictures (a strong visual medium) that caused it to take off among a wider audience, and thus our present-day information highway, or World Wide Web (www.), was created in just three short years![47] (Berners-Lee also happens to be a pianist.)

As in the Creative Dramatics program and *School of Rock* film, children who are involved with music and the arts projects, where imagination reigns, will develop proficiency in social, organizational, and technological systems. Paul Griffiths, a journalist for the *New York Times*, wrote that "a child involved in musical performance is confronted with challenges that will be of lifelong benefit: how you present yourself in public, how you argue a case, how you interpret a document, what evidence you accept and what you will question, where you draw the line between what you are told and what you want, and how you work with others toward a common goal."[48]

Stephanie Perrin, former head of the Walnut Hill School in Natick, Maryland (an international boarding high school for the arts), sums it up succinctly when she says, "If you want a motivated, organized, hardworking, flexible, smart, creative worker, able to work well alone or in groups—hire a young violinist!"[49]

Our Future

The SCANS report, given over twenty years ago, gave our nation's schools a mandate to produce students proficient in the five skills just examined. It was hoped that school administrators would realize that providing a comprehensive sequential music and arts program was the way to develop these skills and prepare students by making them more creative and hence more marketable for future employment. Despite numerous studies, research and reports authenticating the need for the arts to develop creativity in students, increase test scores, and keep our nation competitive in a global marketplace, it has primarily fallen on deaf ears. Many school administrators fail to see the writing on the wall, because they fail to think creatively themselves. Instead, we got the No Child Left Behind Act, which seeks to standardize education and narrow our nation's school curricula, leaving the arts for privileged schools. In 2005, Sir Ken Robinson, senior advisor, education policy, Getty Foundation, said, "Standardization is the enemy of innovation." He went on to say, "I speak to a lot of corporate audiences and they mostly want the opposite of standardized employees...They want people who can think for themselves, adapt and be creative."[50] While Jonathan Plucker was visiting China he was asked by university faculty to identify trends in American education. Plucker described our focus on standardized curriculum and rote learning, to which the Chinese laughed and said, "You're racing toward our old model. But we're racing toward your model, as fast as we can."[51] American standardized education is swiftly turning back the clock on progress, innovation, and our ability to be the leaders in a global marketplace. The costs will be devastating.

American standardized education is swiftly turning back the clock on progress, innovation, and our ability to be the leaders in a global marketplace. The costs will be devastating.

As we have discussed, prominent business leaders and chief executive officers are keenly aware that having employees who are literate in the arts adds value to their business. In 2001, McKinsey & Company, Inc., published a study, "The War for Talent." Over six thousand executives from four hundred companies were asked what they considered their biggest challenge in the future. Their answer: finding people who can make good decisions in uncertain times, people who can adapt to new opportunities and respond to creative change.[52] In other words, they need creative thinkers and problem solvers. But they are having difficulty finding these people because of our education system. Judith A. Fuller, assistant professor of art education at Daemen College, stated in a forum on public policy, "The threat to arts, humanities, and science education has now reached crisis proportions, and it is up to teachers, administrators, artists, parents, cultural organizations, and other advocates of liberal arts education to make it known to policymakers that it is imperative to provide our youth with a well-rounded education that appeals to all students' intelligences."[53] I agree with Fuller. And speaking as a parent and educator, I believe the first place for music and arts exposure is in the home. Home is the grounding, foundational place to begin. Second, schools have a responsibility. They are accountable to the children and parents of this nation. To ensure a successful future for our children in this century and help our nation maintain a competitive edge in a global marketplace, nothing less than an education in the arts will suffice. When we ponder the significance of the arts to the future of our nation, it is impossible to view them as frills or easily expendable subjects. In 1994, John Goodlad, in *A Place Called School*, concluded, "The arts are not an educational option; they are basic."[54]

PART FOUR

A CULTURAL HERITAGE

CHAPTER 10

ℐOICES IN UNISON: SUPPORTING THE ARTS IN YOUR COMMUNITY

"While there can be no greater introduction to music than through singing or playing an instrument, the fact remains that the overwhelming majority of our pupils will be neither singers nor players. Whatever contact they will have with music in their adult life will be as listeners. We therefore have to teach them how to listen if we are to make them true music lovers."

Joseph Machlis

In *Megatrends 2000,* it was predicted that "during the 1990s the arts will gradually replace sports as society's primary leisure activity."[1] It was also predicted that in the twenty-first century, people would attend museums, ballets, symphonies, and operas more than ever before, and, as a result, many new jobs would open up. Authors John Naisbitt and Patricia Aburdene made these predictions by analyzing thousands of printed stories in newspapers, journals, and magazines. However, critics questioned their predictions because their prophetic methods were unscientific and did not use the more reliable sophisticated modeling techniques used in official economic forecasting. Despite their calculation methods, the question remains: have any of their predictions come true? The answer is yes and no.

Between 1982 and 2002, a window of success regarding arts attendance was reported by the National Endowment for the Arts (NEA). For example, total attendance at live opera performances grew at a staggering 46 percent, representing the largest increase of all performing arts disciplines. In fact, the annual number of people attending opera performances was estimated at twenty million, or roughly the same attendance at NFL football games. Opera was booming! As a result, the United States became one of the global leaders of opera with the formation of 125 professional opera companies. Translation: today the United States has more opera companies than Germany or Italy—the birthplaces of opera. The Metropolitan Opera in New York is the largest opera company in the United States and boasts an annual attendance of eight hundred thousand people. In 2005, OPERA America reported that forty-four states saw 3,012 performances of 420 different opera productions.[2]

Then a few short years later the house of cards came tumbling down. In June 2009, the NEA released the results of a study, *"Arts Participation 2008: Highlights from a National Survey,"* showing that the number of American adults who attended arts and cultural events had sunk to its lowest level since 1982, when the study began. Among the types of arts events the report measured were museum shows, classical music concerts, ballet, opera, theater, and jazz concerts. The survey asked adults ages eighteen and older about their patterns of arts participation over a twelve-month period. They found that groups that were formerly dependable audiences had reduced their participation levels. They discovered that college-educated Americans were attending at lower rates, and that forty-five- to fifty-four-year-olds were curbing their attendance. Additionally, a long-term trend toward aging audiences was noted. Economics were cited as a possible cause for the decline in 2008 and included deteriorating economic conditions, rising gas prices, and a drop in consumer spending. But the researchers did not believe that economic problems were the main issue. Sunil Iyengar, the NEA's director of research and analysis, in his summary of the report said, "Although NEA research has identified a close relationship between changes in the US gross domestic product and performing arts ticket sales, one cannot attribute the lower attendance rates solely to economic conditions with any degree of certainty."[3]

In his 2012 book, *The Perilous Life of Symphony Orchestras: Artistic Triumphs and Economic Challenges,* Stanford Emeritus Professor Robert J. Flanagan agreed about the decline in at least one area of arts participation—classical music concert attendance. Like the NEA, Flanagan discovered that the public is attending classical music concerts less frequently, and for reasons other than economic. He says, "The decline in attendance at classical music concerts may reflect broad social shifts in the use of leisure time that have little to do with orchestra policies."[4]

As it turns out, Iyengar and Flanagan were right. Diminishing audiences pointed to more than an economic downturn. While the 2008 survey revealed dwindling audiences for virtually every art form (except musical plays), it also captured new data on Internet use and other forms of arts participation. Figures showed that nearly 40 percent of adults in the United States used the Internet to view, listen to, download, or post artworks or performances as opposed to actually attending concerts.[5] A decrease in arts education was also noted. From 1982 to 2008, it was found that the number of eighteen- to twenty-four-year-olds who said they had had any music education in their lives had dropped by more than a third. For visual arts education, the number had decreased by half.[6]

These studies shed light on some important information: if we are going to enjoy the arts in all their varied forms *and* have them around to enjoy, there are several things we must do. First, for young people to support the arts as adults, they need arts education in school (see chapter 7). Iyengar concurs: "We know that prior education, including exposure to arts education, are critical factors associated with high levels of adult participation in the arts."[7]

Second, we need to support the arts community by actually purchasing tickets and attending concerts. Tuning into the Internet and watching a YouTube video of *Phantom of the Opera* or the *Nutcracker* is not the same as seeing a live performance. There is something memorable about dressing up, going to a concert hall, and watching a staged production of a musical, opera, or symphony. The ambiance, the excitement, the whole sensory experience cannot be replicated on a computer screen—not even close. When I was growing up our family had a stereo, but that didn't stop us from attending the symphony. We didn't allow technology to replace an actual experience.

Third—affording the tickets. Parents may complain, "We'd love to expose our children to the arts programs, but the tickets are too expensive." Okay, I agree, the tickets can be expensive, but keep a list of all the "extras" you purchase for your children: expensive video games, tickets to high-priced theme parks and sporting events, designer clothes, movies, toys, incessant eating out, and the list goes on. Bottom line: people will spend money on things they value. Are the arts something you value and want your children to be exposed to? If so, when grandparents and other relatives ask what they can give your children for birthdays and holidays, tell them, "Tickets to a musical or symphony or an opera." Also, keep in mind that there are many free musical programs and reduced-priced tickets for arts events in communities all over the country. So, take advantage of as many concerts as your budget will allow.

By exposing your children to a variety of musicals, ballets, symphonies, grand opera, chamber music concerts, and choral music recitals, you are building a future concert supporter and creating memorable musical experiences together.

Supporting the arts community does one more very important thing: it builds a cultural heritage. Sunil Iyengar says, "Such [arts] experiences are important not only for producing an inspired and imaginative citizenry, but also for preserving and articulating our cultural *heritage* [emphasis added] as Americans."[8] The definition of *heritage* is "something that is passed down from preceding generations; a tradition." My maternal grandparents were from Germany. They both loved music. My grandmother had a beautiful singing voice and my grandfather was a talented mandolin player. They immigrated to America in the 1920s, and in 1932 my grandfather died, leaving my grandmother to raise two small children under the age of eight—my mother and her brother. Grandma Schutz was not fluent in English and cleaned houses to support her family. Despite her situation, music was important to her and she was determined that her children would have music in their lives. She carefully saved money from her meager earnings and eventually was able to purchase a used piano and violin so my mother and her brother could have the opportunity of learning musical instruments. My grandmother believed no sacrifice was too great to keep the tradition of music alive. It was her sacrifice, dating clear back to the 1930s, that has kept alive and influenced five family generations (thus far) of music lovers: my grandparents, my parents, my husband and I, our children, and now our grandchildren.

If music and the arts are important to you and are something you want to preserve as part of your family's cultural heritage, then consistent exposure and an education in the arts is the place to start. In this chapter, we will discuss some of the musical programs available in communities around the world; what to expect from each; how to prepare your children before, during, and after a concert; and ideas to make it a lasting and positive legacy.

Finding Events in Your Community

Musical events can be found in communities everywhere. The following list offers suggestions on how to find them:

- The Internet: The Internet is a treasure trove of information, and Google just made surfing easier. "Google-Local-Search" will pinpoint all the available visual and performing arts activities in the area you live in. It changes daily and keeps you updated on all the latest offerings.

- Newspapers: Check your local newspapers, particularly on the weekends. Look for programs that are especially designed for children. As your child gets older (around fifth or sixth grade) critically consider *all* the musical programs offered.

- CLASSICAL RADIO STATIONS: Listen to the classical radio stations for any advertisements on upcoming programs. Some stations may even offer special deals or discounts.

- COMMUNITY COLLEGES: Check community colleges and universities for what they offer in the way of children's musical programs. Oftentimes, they will offer a children's series that will be both affordable and excellent in content. For years, we took our sons to a children's classical music series offered at our local community college. The programs were wonderful, affordable, and best of all—close! (In Los Angeles "close" is a big deal!)

- RELIGIOUS ORGANIZATIONS: Check with the religious organizations in your area. Oftentimes they will sponsor guest performers and musical groups throughout the year, particularly during holidays. These concerts tend to be reasonably priced, the right time length for children, culturally expanding, and very entertaining. Expose your child a broad sampling of music from different cultures, religions, backgrounds, and nationalities. For example, take your child to hear the music of churches other than your own—such as gospels, cantors, Gregorian chants—or to cultural festivals in your community where she will hear music from diverse peoples.

- NETWORK: Network with other parents who expose their children to musical concerts. Ask your children's private music teacher and school music teacher about concerts they would recommend. Generally, these people are up to date on enjoyable children's programs that are offered in your area.

- LOCAL LIBRARIES AND COMMUNITY PARKS: Check the bulletins, advertisements, and flyers at your local library. You will find this to be an excellent source for concerts presented by local talent. Summer concerts held at community parks are a great way to see and experience local performers.

- **Concert subscriber:** Become concert subscribers with matinee tickets. Not only are you committing your family to a certain number of concerts a year, but you are also communicating to your children that music and the arts are important, and that attending concerts is a cultural and educational family routine and a fun family outing.

If you are on a tight budget, search for affordable or free concerts in your community. When Kevin and Tracy Bergen of Torrance, California, were raising their children money was tight, but they still found ways of taking their four daughters to musical concerts. Here's what they did:

> *If you are on a tight budget, search for affordable or free concerts in your community.*

- When their piano teacher performed a free recital at the local college, the Bergen children attended. It gave them an opportunity to hear wonderful music and, at the same time, see their piano teacher in a performance setting.

- They called local colleges and universities, found out their musical offerings, and attended the rehearsals, which were usually free.

- During the summer, their city offered an outdoor concert series on a weekday night for free. The Bergens enjoyed all kinds of music at these concerts—jazz, country, bluegrass, big band, and classical.

- Tracy called the local elementary schools and inquired about school music assemblies. She put those dates on her calendar and took her two younger children to those—once again for free.

- Through a flyer at the local library, they discovered a series entitled "Musical Circus," held at the Pasadena Civic Auditorium in

Pasadena, California, for children three to eight years of age. Four free events are offered yearly on Saturday afternoons and include an instrument "petting zoo," where the children actually see, touch, and play the instruments of the orchestra, plus enjoy a half-hour recital, usually featuring the guest soloist for that evening's performance. Through attendance at this series, the Bergens found that children could attend the symphony for a reduced rate when accompanied by a full-paying adult. They would buy one adult ticket and two children's tickets, and the parents would trade off taking the children throughout the year.

No matter what your financial constraints are, you can always find something to fit your budget—so don't let cost hold you back from exposing your children to the arts.

Preparing Your Children for Concerts

Whether you have subscribed to a series of concerts or purchased tickets for a single concert, the next step is to prepare your children for what they will experience. The following are practical suggestions that will help make the experience memorable.

Listen to the Music

Whether you are taking your child to a ballet, opera, symphony, or musical, get a copy of the music that will be performed, either at the library, online, or at a bookstore. About two weeks before the concert, start playing the music for your child. You can do this while they are getting ready for school in the morning, during the day, or while they are going to sleep at night. Point out the interesting parts of the music, the lively parts, the slower parts, and the instruments playing each. Ask them what they like and don't like about the music and why. After listening to the music for a few days, bring out some rhythm instruments and let them beat out the rhythm of the music, or let them dance and move to the music.

Another fun thing is to have your child sit at the kitchen table; provide her with paper, markers, crayons, and paints; and encourage her to "draw what she hears." It is exciting to watch your child's imagination flow. You will be amazed at the creative artwork your family will produce. Hang the pictures up on your bulletin board and entitle them: "Our Interpretations of the Music from *The Nutcracker* (or *The Magic Flute*, or Vivaldi's *Four Seasons*). By doing these activities, your child will become very familiar with the music and, as a result, enjoy the concert more.

GET TO KNOW THE COMPOSER AND THE PERIODS OF MUSIC

Talk to your children about the composer and include the period in which he or she composed (baroque, classical, and so on), and some interesting facts about his or her life. An excellent children's book about composers is *Lives of the Musicians: Good Times, Bad Times (And What the Neighbors Thought)*, by Kathleen Krull. It gives meaningful facts and stories about the composer, as well as humorous happenings in their lives. As you take a few minutes each day to read stories about the composers to your children, the composers will become real people for them and not just names on a page.

Also, introduce your children to the four periods of music—baroque, classical, romantic, and twentieth century—by letting them listen to familiar music that is played in the particular style of these eras. Two highly recommend recordings that will help you are *Heigh-Ho! Mozart* and *Bibbidi Bobbidi Bach*. They are a compilation of Walt Disney songs recorded in the style of individual composers from the various musical eras. You will hear "Can You Feel the Love Tonight" (from *Lion King*) in the style of Tchaikovsky (romantic period), "Little April Showers" (from *Bambi*) in the style of Handel (baroque), and "Heigh Ho!" (from *Snow White and the Seven Dwarfs*) in the style of Mozart (classical). When your children hear these familiar songs repeatedly, they will begin to recognize the various styles and nuances of each composer and the musical era. While listening to these CDs, you might find the following information helpful regarding each of these musical eras.

Baroque

The *baroque period* lasted from approximately 1600 to 1750, with the main composers of this period being Bach, Vivaldi, and Handel. The music of this era was very ornate, very orderly, flowery, and had lots of emotional contrasts of feelings (high/low, loud/soft, fast/slow). The composers of this era conveyed through their music a wide range of emotions: passion, heroism, sacrifice, reverence for religion, and feelings of ecstasy.

Classical

The *classical period* was marked by music that was for the masses and not just the royalty or wealthy. It lasted from approximately 1750 to 1820. The main composers of this period were Mozart, Haydn, and Beethoven. The musical forms of the symphony, sonata, and string quartets were used extensively during this era.

Romantic

The *romantic period* lasted from approximately 1820 to the end of the century. The expression of emotions and feelings is typical of this era, with the composers being inspired by the flora and fauna of nature, sunrises, sunsets, the sea, and thunderstorms. The composers of this era included Schubert, Schumann, Mendelssohn, Chopin, Liszt, Brahms, and Tchaikovsky.

Twentieth Century

The *twentieth century period* comprises the music of Mahler, Debussy, Strauss, Stravinsky, and Shostakovich. This music is varied—with some composers seeking to create a mood or atmosphere, others wanting to express the inner feelings of man, and still others wanting to incorporate the folk tunes from their countries—but one thing is for sure: most just wanted to do things their own way.

Get to Know the Orchestra

Part of your preconcert preparation should include becoming familiar with the instruments of the orchestra and the musicians who play those instruments. Check out books from the library that show your children pictures of each instrument of the orchestra, so they can see what they look like. If possible, take them to a music store, so they can actually see, touch, and hear some of these instruments. This would be a good time to play Benjamin Britten's *A Young Person's Guide to the Orchestra,* as it will help them become familiar with each instrument's distinctive sound. Then when you play the CD for the upcoming concert, have your children listen carefully for each instrument.

Check out a general music book from the library that will show your children where everyone in the orchestra sits. When the musicians are seated on stage or in an orchestra pit, they form a large half circle. Each group of musicians is seated in a specific area, with the violins to the left of the conductor, the violas in the center, and the cellos to the right of the conductor. Behind the cellos are the double bass; and behind the violas are the piccolos, flutes, oboes, bassoons, English horns, and clarinets. Behind the violins is the harpist. In the back row (going from left to right) are the percussionists, then the horns, the trumpets, the trombones, and finally the tubas. There are usually ninety to one hundred musicians in a symphony orchestra, and, on the day of the performance, they are dressed in formal attire. There are many wonderful books available to use in explaining the orchestra and each orchestra member to your child. Some favorites include *The Philharmonic Gets Dressed*, by Karla Kuskin, and *Meet the Orchestra*, by Ann Hays.

The life of the musician is not always glamorous or exciting; in fact, it can be very stressful at times. Professional musicians give enormous amounts of time, effort, and dedication to their art. They want the music to sound beautiful

Professional musicians give enormous amounts of time, effort, and dedication to their art. They want the music to sound beautiful and flawless for their audiences.

and flawless for their audiences. To do so, they must put in long hours of practicing and rehearsal time with the other musicians. Most orchestras typically have seven to nine rehearsals each week where each rehearsal is two-and-a-half hours long. This doesn't include the time they spend practicing their instruments each day, or the amount of new music they must learn in a week. Within seven days, they can perform up to four different concerts, which translates into a lot of music that needs to be learned. When people go to hear a symphony, they usually do not realize the dedication that has gone into making the performance sound perfect and polished. It is usually an "eye opener" to find out the amount of time expended to accomplish what they do. One famous pianist, after performing a concert, was told by a woman, "I would give my life to play like you." To which he replied, "I have, madam."

GET TO KNOW THE CONDUCTOR

Prior to taking your children to a concert, explain to them some of the responsibilities of the conductor. Early orchestras did not have conductors. The first violinist did the job; he started everyone together and saw to it that everyone finished together. As the music became more complicated, a leader was needed, and the role of the conductor was born. Jean-Baptiste Lully was one of the first conductors during the baroque era. He would stand in front of the musicians pounding out the beat on the floor with a heavy staff. Once as he was beating out the time, he mistakenly pounded his foot instead of the floor. Unfortunately, the wound proved fatal because his foot became infected with gangrene. Today, this is obviously not a hazard because conductors no longer pound out the beat of the music with a staff. They employ their arms, hands, and baton movements to communicate to the orchestra the rhythm of the music.

    The conductor is a very important part of the orchestra. He is literally the leader of the group—guiding each musician through the music; controlling the delicate balance of speed, volume, and note length of the musical score; and getting everyone to play with a sense of musicality. Musicality is the ability of the musicians to play with emotional expression, creativity, knowledge, and technical ability. To have this come off well takes enormous skill on the part of the conductor. He must be a confident tour de force! All of the musicians must be able to read his every gesture, his body language, face, eyes, and baton movements, as each has meaning and importance to the success of the music. Stored in his brain is the entire score of the piece, as well as every part, nuance, and musical interpretation for each instrument. He must be able to bring in the violins, clarinets, trumpets, and percussionists at just the right time, with the right volume, expression, and feeling that causes the music to drive us to tears. When you are at a symphony, carefully observe the conductor. He or she is as interesting to watch as listening to the music itself. A fascinating story is told of Felix Mendelssohn, who, when conducting the premiere performance of Bach's *The Passion According to St. Matthew,* discovered at the podium that he had the wrong musical score! But, because the show must go on, Mendelssohn lifted his baton and began to conduct Bach's *Passion.* Every so often, he would turn the pages of the score, so as not to alarm the musicians, but in reality he conducted the entire two-hour score from memory and with no noticeable mistakes! It was a phenomenal success, and only the most talented of conductors could pull off such a feat successfully.

GET TO KNOW THE STORY

If you are going to an opera, musical, or ballet where a story is involved, check out books from the library and read the story to your children. Explain the plot, the characters, and the setting. The more information and preparation you can give them the better, for obvious reasons—we enjoy that which we understand and can easily follow. Many years ago, we took our boys to the stage production of *Beauty and the Beast.* Even though they had seen the Disney movie, we still checked out the fairy tale from the library to read. We found more than one version of *Beauty and the Beast* and ended up having fun comparing different variations on the same theme. If you see the ballet, *Cinderella,* you will find over nine hundred written versions of that fairy tale. Before we saw *Phantom of the Opera,* we read the book and listened to the music many times. It was a spectacular production, and even though our youngest was only in the second grade at the time, he loved it because of our preparation. If you have lots of creative energy, you can even "act out" the ballet, opera, or musical at your house with each member of the family playing one or more parts. Resurrect the costumes from your Halloween supply and improvise. Who knows, this may be the beginning of a new career for your family. Over the years, as you take your children to these productions, you will end up with a marvelous collection of books on ballets, operas, and musicals that will become a treasure trove and can be used for future generations.

PLAN A BACKSTAGE TOUR

Prior to the performance, call and arrange a backstage tour. Many places will do this, especially if you have a large group of children. These tours can be a valuable educational experience and will make the performance come to life on many levels. Many years ago, our son, Ryan, had the opportunity to go on a backstage tour for *Phantom of the Opera.* A mother in his class called the theater and arranged a tour for the whole class, which turned out to be a fascinating experience for everyone. Ryan came home very excited, as he shared with us intricate details of how this spectacular opera was choreographed and produced. We learned that there are usually fifteen backstage people to run the lights, make scenery changes, and so on, in most productions, but with *Phantom* there were so many special effects that it took more than sixty backstage people to see that everything came off perfectly. The fabrics for the masquerade ball came from Europe, and the weekly cleaning bill for all the gorgeous costumes was enormous. Although there was only one person playing the part of the phantom, there were others dressed up as the phantom to help create certain special effects and illusions. Two weeks later when we went as a family to see *Phantom,* Ryan's extra information helped everyone to appreciate and understand what went into the production of this musical. A few years later, our son Brandon went on a backstage tour of another musical. He saw how the backstage people change the scenery, but he also learned how a sound system works. All of the principal actors' voices are pumped through a PA system back to a computer that analyzes the pitch, volume, and sound levels of the voice. Corrections are made so that on the night of the performance, the singing and speaking voices of the actors sound perfect. Even on the night of the performance, if adjustments are necessary, they can be made right on the spot so that the voices sound flawless—and all because of the wonders of technology. This was several years ago when Brandon went on this tour. Today, the sound systems are even more sophisticated. Backstage tours can be very informative and educational for your children. For that reason, do not be afraid to *ask* if backstage tours are available—the worst thing they could tell you is no, but it is definitely worth a try.

Going to the Concert

The next step is actually going to the concert. It is important to make this event special and fun. The following ideas will help to ensure that it is both.

- ATTIRE: As far as what your children should wear, the rule is comfort. I've been to many concerts in Southern California and, believe me, I've seen *everything*. Dress your child in comfortable clothes, such as slacks and polo or dress shirts for boys and a soft dress or nice pants for girls. Boys in tight ties and girls in scratchy, fluffy dresses can be very uncomfortable. It is important for children to be comfortable throughout the concert, but it is equally important for them to know that going to a concert is a special occasion and wearing something a little nicer communicates respect for the event and the performers.

- CONCERT ETIQUETTE: Let your children know that you expect proper concert etiquette from them. This means that during the performance, they must be absolutely quiet out of respect for others who have paid money to see the performance and want to be able to enjoy it without hearing interfering noise of any kind. In most concert halls, the acoustics are incredibly sensitive, and even a sneeze, cough, or whisper can resonate throughout the hall. Also, instruct your children on the appropriate time to clap for the musicians, as well as the time not to clap, such as in between movements. Many *adults* make the mistake of clapping too soon, so follow this rule of thumb—don't clap until you see the conductor put his hands and arms down to his side and all the musicians have put down their instruments. A wonderful book written for children on this very subject is *When Can I Clap, Daddy?*, by Margaret Keith. Unfortunately it is out of print, but check out your local library or used bookstores for a copy.

> *Many adults make the mistake of clapping too soon, so follow this rule of thumb—don't clap until you see the conductor put his hands and arms down to his side and all the musicians have put down their instruments.*

- Arrive on time: Most places have strict rules on late seating, and if you arrive late you may not get seated until the intermission, which is only fair to the other people around you. By arriving early, you don't feel rushed, you can get to the restroom one last time, and you will have an opportunity to look over the program and point out any last bits of interesting information about the performers or musical numbers to your child.

- Intermission: During intermission, if you are at an opera, ballet, or a musical, take your child down to see the orchestra pit. It is always interesting for a child to see where the music is coming from. This is also a good time to evaluate if your child can last through the second half of the performance. I remember when we took our oldest son to his first big concert. He was barely four and we took him to see the Austrian Boys Choir (not a great choice for a first concert). By intermission, he had had enough and was ready to leave. So, that's exactly what we did. We decided that by leaving early and not forcing him to stay until the end, we could still leave with a good feeling—and that was our main goal. So, when you buy those expensive tickets, remember that you may see only half of what you have paid for. That is another important reason to invest in children's series; they tend to understand a child's limited attention span and produce concerts that are just the right time length.

After the Concert

After the concert you can either make a beeline for the nearest exit, or stay and go backstage to meet the artists. We've done both. We have taken our children to places where, after the performance, the artists come out into the foyer to shake hands with the children, sign autographs, and pose for pictures. When you are booking tickets, ask if they offer this wonderful perk. Postconcert is also a great time to go to dinner, lunch, or dessert, because everyone is usually famished. While you are eating, discuss what everyone liked best about the concert, the performers, the music, and so on. If you saw a ballet, opera, or musical, talk about the actors, the story, the scenery, and the music.

If there is a performance that you take your children to year after year—such as the *Nutcracker, A Christmas Carol*, or a favorite musical—compare performances from year to year. What changed, what is the same, which of all the performances did they like better, and why? What is their opinion of the artistic abilities of the principal performers or musicians? Did they like their performance better this time or not as well? Why or why not? What made this performance more special than the others? By asking open-ended questions, you will get your children thinking, analyzing, comparing, and expressing ideas about their musical experiences.

Some friends of ours took their children to see *Phantom of the Opera* twice, each with different men performing the role of Phantom. It was very interesting for the parents to hear everyone's opinion on which Phantom they liked better and why. Another memorable activity you might want to add to your list of family traditions is to write down each of your children's feelings about the concert in a special family journal saved just for musical experiences. It is fun to look back and read everyone's thoughts and feelings about the concert and to see how your children grow and mature in their ideas and responses as the years progress. This book also can be a great place to put programs and pictures of each event as a visual memory. As the years go by, your family will enjoy reliving those special musical memories.

Good Concert Choices for Children

Not all concerts are appropriate for children. Consider the following before purchasing tickets.

THE SYMPHONY ORCHESTRA

Most symphony orchestras provide children's programs that introduce them to the wonder and excitement of live orchestral music. For children to learn from and enjoy these presentations, they should be visually colorful, short, lively, and entertaining. You will find that many of these geared-for-children-programs are centered on a theme with appropriate classical music that complements the subject. For instance, if the theme is animals, the orchestra may present Saint-Saëns's *Carnival of the Animals*. If the theme is seasons, the orchestra might play Vivaldi's *Four Seasons,* or if the theme is musical stories, they may perform *Peter and the Wolf*. Orchestras also like to introduce music from other countries or music from a particular ethnic group to help children understand and appreciate the songs and music from other countries and people.

Most community orchestras understand the importance of building future audiences by engaging children when they are young, and, as a result, the majority of orchestras offer children's programs.

If your community has a symphony orchestra, find out if it offers children's concerts and the appropriate age they recommend a child to be. Most community orchestras understand the importance of building future audiences by engaging children when they are young, and, as a result, the majority of orchestras offer children's programs. Some orchestras present concerts that can be appropriate for children as young as three. For over eighty years, the Los Angeles Philharmonic has been committed to kids. They spend $4.5 million a year on a broad range of programs geared toward educating and exposing young people to musical experiences. One of their most popular children's programs is the Toyota Symphonies for Youth family concerts at Walt Disney Concert Hall. This series includes four concerts for children between the ages of five and eleven and introduces children to music old and new. Different themes are introduced each season, with the classical repertoire presented with a clever twist. For instance, Prokofiev's *Peter and the Wolf* is presented with projections and puppetry and transports the tale from a Russian forest to urban Los Angeles.

Another wonderful symphony series that combines a dramatic story, a bit of history, and magnificent classical music is "Classical Kids LIVE!" These magically staged concerts use professional actors and acclaimed symphony orchestras that bring to life the extraordinary lives and music masterpieces of the great classical composers. They follow Susan Hammond's best-selling audio stories, such as *Vivaldi's Ring of Mystery*, *Beethoven Lives Upstairs*, and *Mozart's Magnificent Voyage*. For over twenty years these concerts have brought children a unique blend of music entertainment, adventure, education, and classical music. Check their website to see if they will be performing in your area: www.classicalkidslive.com. These fifty-minute productions are adventures the whole family will enjoy.

Today, many symphony orchestras, realizing how visually oriented children of the twenty-first century are, use interactive, interdisciplinary, and hands-on experiences. You will find the use of video enhancements, screens around the hall where closeups of the instruments can be shown while they are being played on stage, as well as crafts and activities that will make the experience memorable. Most of these concerts last anywhere from thirty minutes to one hour—the perfect amount of time for a young child's attention span.

Actually seeing the symphony orchestra "up front and personal" can be thrilling to young children. They are able to see and observe (and many times talk to) the musicians playing the pieces that they have previously only heard on a CD. It adds a whole new dimension to their musical experience, and suddenly they realize how music is produced by a large group of people working together.

Chamber Music

Chamber music is music that is written for small, intimate groups of instruments or vocalists and is performed in rooms rather than theaters or large public areas. It usually comprises somewhere between two and ten performers, and there is no conductor. Considering this definition, a family of musicians could conceivably perform chamber music and, as a matter of fact, many of the "privileged" of Europe did just that. Haydn is credited with establishing the string quartet as the crowning chamber music form. Nearly all of the composers wrote some chamber music, but originally most of the chamber music was written for only the wealthy of Europe. It was not until the nineteenth century that chamber music was written for the masses.

Today, chamber music is performed more than any other kind of music because the musicians love the small, intimate settings, where they can be close to their audience and at the same time engage in a wonderful discourse among their fellow players. It is fun to take your child to experience chamber music for this reason. The cozy setting makes it easier to talk and mingle with the musicians afterward. They are usually extremely friendly and anxious to answer questions and talk about their musical experiences.

Pianist Leif Ove Andsnes said this about chamber music: "Playing chamber music feeds my solo performing," he said. "You get so close to others you're playing with—it's like a marriage, musically and personally."[9] Before going to hear chamber music, anticipate that your children will be able to talk with the musicians afterward, so think about some questions they could ask. For instance, what part does music play in their lives; is this a hobby or their regular occupation; how long have they been playing with this group; how long do they practice each day; and what have they sacrificed to reach this level of music proficiency? If you have a child who is wavering and wants to quit playing his instrument, take him to hear chamber music and let them talk to the musicians. It might be just the right experience he needs to help him over a difficult period and inspire him to continue with his musical studies. Among some favorite pieces of chamber music, suitable for children are Schubert's, Piano Quintet in A Major (the *Trout*), Mozart's Quintet for Clarinet and Strings, Dvořák's String Quartet in F (*American*), and Brahms Trio for Violin, Horn, and Piano.

Choral Music

If you have ever sung in a choir at church, a chorus at school, or a choral group in the community, you know how rewarding and fun it is to be a part of these singing ensembles. I remember one Christmas when I was fourteen years old, singing Handel's *Messiah* with our church choir. It was an amazing experience, and those songs will be etched forever in my memory. Even today, when I hear choruses sing *Messiah*, it gives me goose bumps. Apparently, many people feel the same way, because during the holidays, many music centers throughout the United States offer to the public an opportunity to be a part of a massive sing-along choir performing *Messiah*. If your community offers an opportunity like this, take advantage of it with your entire family. Whether you are a participant or spectator, it is a thrilling experience and can add a memorable tradition to your holiday season.

Seek out opportunities for your children to hear choral music, and keep in mind that most of it will be of a religious nature. In preparing them, do the same activities you would to prepare them for any other kind of concert. First, get the music and let them listen to it, repeatedly. You want them to become familiar with both the words and the music because the words give additional meaning to the music. Second, tell your children a little of the history behind choral music and what exactly choral music is. Choral music is music with words and is performed by a combination of solo singers, choruses, and orchestras. It is usually associated with religious or sacred music and has been around longer than orchestras—in fact, centuries longer. Recorded history states that a "School for Singers" existed during the time of Pope Silvester's reign over sixteen hundred years ago.

Choral music includes oratorios, cantatas, and chants. An oratorio is a very large work of music and can last several hours. It is written for a chorus, orchestra, and vocal soloists, and usually tells a story from the Bible. Probably the most famous oratorio ever written is Handel's *Messiah*. Bach also wrote several spectacular oratorios, including *The Passion According to St. Matthew*, which is referred to by his own family as "the Great Passion."[10]

A cantata is a short oratorio. Bach wrote more than two hundred cantatas—including one that was meant as a joke, the *Coffee Cantata*, or Cantata no. 211. It is about a father and his daughter who love coffee (also Bach's favorite drink) and was written as a result of coffee just being introduced into Europe by the Turks.[11]

Chants are melodies that have been around since Pope Gregory the Great (540 to 604 AD), and legend has it that he received them from the Holy Spirit. Today, these chants are known as Gregorian Chants.

Choral music also can be found in symphonies. In Beethoven's Ninth Symphony, he uses a chorus for the "Ode to Joy." Hector Berlioz used anywhere from three hundred to nine hundred singers in his "Mass for the Dead" (or what is jokingly referred to as "Mass to Wake the Dead") from *Symphonie Fantastique*.[12]

When introducing your child to choral music, choose programs that are short and have a variety of different songs, such as school choruses, choirs of various religions, and community choirs singing a variety of songs.

When introducing your child to choral music, choose programs that are short and have a variety of different songs, such as school choruses, choirs of various religions, and community choirs singing a variety of songs. By doing so, you will help them become familiar with this wonderful art form, gain an understanding and appreciation of it, and instill within them a desire to experience a whole oratorio or cantata when the time comes. Some favorites to include are "Jesu, Joy of Man's Desiring" (Cantata no. 147), by Bach; *Messiah*, by Handel; the final chorus of *The Passion According to St. Matthew*, by Bach; and *Requiem*, by Mozart.

BALLET

Ballets are enchanting stories told through colorful dancing and music and are enjoyed by boys and girls. Many years ago, the dancing was the most important part of a ballet, and the music was used for the background. Then famous composers such as Peter Tchaikovsky began writing ballet music that was as beautiful as the dancing. Today, we go to see a ballet as much to hear the music as to see the dancing. In fact, the music is usually so breathtaking that it can be enjoyed on its own.

Music in a ballet is considered programmatic, which means that the music itself tells a story, and each note corresponds to the action on the stage. One of the most popular ballets that children of all ages enjoy is Tchaikovsky's *Nutcracker Ballet*. The story, similar to a fairy tale, is about a young girl named Marie (in some versions her name is Clara) who discovers that the nutcracker she received from her godfather for Christmas is real. Through a series of exciting events, he proves to be a young man who has been put under a spell by an evil mouse king. Throughout the story, Marie and the nutcracker visit many lands, including the land of the Sugarplum Fairy and Toyland. The *Nutcracker* ballet is both beautiful and visually exciting and is a must for all children to see and experience. It is usually presented in December around holiday time, but the music should be included in every child's CD collection and enjoyed year round. With the DVD version of Mikhail Baryshnikov and the American Ballet Theater performing the *Nutcracker* ballet, you can enjoy this ballet year-round.

Before going to the ballet, explain to your child that the ballet dancers tell a story and express their feelings through their hand movements, gestures, and dancing. Each movement of the dancers communicates the story to the audience. Besides the *Nutcracker*, some other wonderful ballets to take your children to include *Sleeping Beauty* (Tchaikovsky), *Swan Lake* (Tchaikovsky), and *Cinderella* (Prokofiev). For older children, try *Firebird Suite* (Stravinsky), *Romeo and Juliet* (both Prokofiev and Tchaikovsky), and *Petrushka* (Stravinsky).

GRAND OPERA

Grand opera is considered the most perfect of all the art forms because it includes the visual arts (scenery and costumes), singing (vocalists), music (orchestra), drama, literature (the story), and dancing (corps de ballet). Grand opera has no spoken parts— everything is sung. The singing is composed of arias—songs that express the deep feelings and emotions of the character; recitative—chanting the words instead of singing them; and leitmotif—a series of musical notes or theme played each time a certain character comes on stage. Because it takes four times longer to sing something than as it does to say the same thing, operas tend to be lonnnnng! In fact, the word "opera" means "work"—and work it is, particularly for the vocalists, whose voices must hold up for four or more hours.

Opera can be a wonderful experience for a child, but there are specific ideas and suggestions that will help your children understand this art form better before they are exposed to it.

Once again, the first thing to do is get the music from the opera and play it every day. Next, get the book that tells the story, and read it to your children, explaining any parts they might not understand. A wonderful children's book about opera is *Sing Me A Story*, by Jane Rosenberg. Operas can get very confusing because there are so many characters. To help your children keep all the characters straight (and if you are feeling industrious), make paper dolls of the characters and let them act out the scenes.

Look for an opera company in your community that performs opera geared to children. There are a plethora of opera programs for children of all ages in cities and states across North America. For example, the Santa Fe Opera in Santa Fe, New Mexico, has an exceptional children's opera program called Opera Makes Sense. This series allows children to explore the world of opera using a variety of activities and games. Through the five senses, opera's art forms are introduced using poetry

> *Look for an opera company in your community that performs opera geared to children. There are a plethora of opera programs for children of all ages in cities and states across North America.*

and song, music and dance, costumes, and art activities. In 1973, the Santa Fe Opera introduced the Pueblo Opera Program (POP), which reaches more than two thousand Native American children from New Mexico's twenty-one pueblos and reservations. Through POP, children participate in the Youth Nights at the Opera program and write and produce their own operas as part of the Student-Produced Opera project.

The Houston Grand Opera in Texas offers a wonderful children's opera series called "Opera to Go!" This professional touring company produces fully staged portable operas in English for students in kindergarten through eighth grade. It also offers opera geared to high school students and opera matinees for children from ages nine to fourteen.

Children's Opera Theatre (COT) is a subsidiary program of Fort Worth Opera. Each year, this professional touring company produces two children's operas and performs them in elementary schools across the state of Texas. All of the productions are sung in English; are forty-five minutes in length; are fully costumed and staged; and are presented by professionals. One of their productions, "The Three Little Pigs," incorporates music from famous operas by Wolfgang Amadeus Mozart and promotes reading and problem-solving skills. Their goal is to open the minds of millions of young people to the colorful and exciting world of opera.

The Canadian Opera Company (COC) is located in Toronto, Ontario, Canada, and is the third largest producer of opera in North America. For the past twenty years, their touring group, Xstrata Ensemble Studio School Tour, has brought a one-act opera into schools all across Ontario. The ensemble performs in full costume with sets, props, and piano accompaniment to delighted young audiences. The operas are performed in English and an informal question-and-answer period with the cast follows each performance.

LA Opera in Los Angeles, California, is the fourth largest opera company in the United States. Working in partnership with the County of Los Angeles Public Library, LA Opera has developed Opera Tales, an exciting, energetic show that tours to various county libraries for free family performances. The show features five professional opera singers performing musical moments from favorite opera stories. Opera Tales is a perfect way to introduce young audiences to the excitement of story and music linked together. In 2011, through their Domingo Family Program, LA Opera introduced half-price tickets for children nine to seventeen years of age, as well as special family packages to make it more affordable to introduce children to opera. Each one includes themed activities for families to enjoy while learning more about opera.

When your children get older, you can take them to opera written by the classical masters. Opera companies realize that to capture children's attention and help them understand this artistic medium, exposure needs to be gradual. Expecting a child to sit through hours of singing in a foreign language is not the way to endear a child to opera. Most children end up bored and hating every minute of it. When I was ten years old, my grandmother took me to my first opera. It was Richard Wagner's *Tännhauser*—a terrible choice for a young child's first opera experience! It was so long—four-and-a-half hours—that I just about died from boredom, and even at that tender age, I decided I would never go to see another opera again. (But I did.) So, when choosing an opera for your child to see, remember, "less is more."

Remember, too, that most of the grand operas are not written in English, and they are not translated into English because the poetic meaning of the words gets lost in the translation and the words don't fit the music. Today, most opera companies feature English subtitles above the stage to enhance the experience. But, one *musical* that has all the elements of grand opera (arias, recitative, corps de ballet) and is exciting, spectacular, *and* is sung in English is Andrew Lloyd Webber's *Phantom of the Opera*. Your children will love it, and so will you. The purists do not consider it grand opera, but it will start your child on the path to enjoying "pure" opera later on.

It is important to know that many operas deal with sex, violence, and murder—or everything that you find in the popular movies of today. The difference is, at the end of some operas, mainly Mozart's operas, one of the characters comes out on stage and lets the audience know that there is always a price to pay for vice or wrongdoings.

There are some delightful operas to introduce your children to that they will enjoy. Some favorites are Mozart's *Magic Flute,* Menotti's *Amahl and the Night Visitors,* Humperdinck's *Hansel and Gretel,* Prokofiev's *The Love for Three Oranges,* and Ravel's *L'Enfant et Les Sortileges.*

If you want your family to experience opera, but can't afford it, or it's inaccessible where you live, consider tuning into the Metropolitan Opera radio broadcasts. Launched in 1931, the Metropolitan Opera's Saturday matinee broadcasts are the longest-running classical music program in radio history and have won several Peabody Awards for excellence in broadcasting. The series is transmitted on over three hundred stations in the United States and on stations in forty countries. The broadcasts are also available to listen to online via streaming audio, through the Met Opera on Demand service, and on the free online service Rhapsody.

During the long intermissions between acts, the radio broadcasts offer informative and entertaining opera-related features, including discussions about the opera being performed, quizzes, and interviews with opera performers. Since 2006, these entertaining features have included interviews with the lead singers as they leave the stage. In December 2009 a new program was added called Talking Opera, which explains terminology used in the opera world.[13]

My six sisters and I all remember these radio broadcasts when we were children, cleaning our grandmother's house every Saturday. My sister Jeannette recalls, "Grandma sat in a chair next to the radio mesmerized by the music and story. I remember times when she started to cry, and, seeing my concern, she explained to me that it was the beauty of the music that caused her to cry. Each Saturday, she talked to me about the opera and explained the characters and story. My grandmother was my first link to opera, and those broadcasts were my *only* link to actually hearing opera as a child."

The Metropolitan Opera has also enjoyed a rich history on public television. In 2006 and 2007, the Met partnered with *Great Performances* for the premier of *Great Performances at the Met. Great Performances* is a television series devoted to telecasting the performing arts on Public Broadcasting Service (PBS). These high-definition video presentations of six operas were shown in movie theaters around the United States, Canada, Japan, and Europe with views of the Met's lavish productions. With the help of English subtitles, they have played a major role in increasing the public's awareness and enjoyment of opera.[14]

MUSICALS

The main difference between an opera and a musical is that opera is entirely sung and usually tells a serious story, while musicals have both singing and dialogue, and the story line can be light, comical, or serious. For example the musical *Les Miserables* has a more serious storyline, while *Mary Poppins* is fun and comical. Most of the Broadway plays are classified as musicals.

Musicals tell a story through singing, dancing, colorful settings, and costumes. This art form grew out of the old American minstrel shows popular in the 1840s.

Musicals tell a story through singing, dancing, colorful settings, and costumes. This art form grew out of the old American minstrel shows popular in the 1840s. *Showboat,* produced in 1927, brought together the traditions of the European operetta with distinctive American themes and folk elements. It became a classic of the American stage, and the American musical as we know it today was born. Some of the best musicals have been adapted from works of literature. For instance, Rogers and Hammerstein's *Carousel* was based on a play by Ferenc Molnar, *South Pacific* was from stories by James Michener, and *My Fair Lady* was from George Bernard Shaw's play *Pygmalion.* Musicals are a delightful way to introduce your children to longer stage productions—and because they are so lively and entertaining and the music is so appealing, children love them.

In preparing your child for a musical, the same rules we discussed earlier apply. Get the music for them to listen to, and make certain they are familiar with the story. If you have exposed your children to symphonies, short operas, chamber music, and choral groups, they will be able to easily sit through a musical by the time they are six or seven. Some musicals that children enjoy include *Mary Poppins, Lion King, Beauty and the Beast, Annie,* and *Sound of Music.* When they are older, take them to musicals with a more sophisticated storyline, such as *Wicked, Evita,* and *Les Miserables. Les Miserables* is a powerful musical story of love and forgiveness—and once you see the stage production and read the book by Victor Hugo, it will become one of your favorites. Both before and after seeing this moving performance, take the time to discuss and analyze this unforgettable story and its characters with your children.

If our children are to enjoy these various art forms when they are adults, as well as derive the benefits to the intellect and the psyche that arts education brings, they will need to have someone show them the way when they are young. That someone can be a parent, teacher, caregiver, or anyone who knows that a child's soul and mind are enriched by the beauty of the cultural and educational experiences they are exposed to. Hungarian composer Zoltán Kodály is certainly one who knows. He said, "Music is the manifestation of the human spirit, similar to language. Its greatest practitioners have conveyed to mankind things not possible to say in any other language. If we do not want these things to remain dead treasures, we must do our utmost to make the greatest possible number of [children] understand their idiom."

Exposure to these various art forms over many years will make them living treasures for our children.

If our children are to enjoy these various art forms when they are adults, as well as derive the benefits to the intellect and the psyche that arts education brings, they will need to have someone show them the way when they are young.

CHAPTER 11

$\mathcal{T}$HE "DO RE MIS"
OF STARTING AN ORCHESTRA

*"If one advances confidently in the direction of his dreams,
and endeavors to live the life which he has imagined,
he will meet with success unexpected in common hours."*

Henry David Thoreau

In January 1999, after spending sixteen years researching and studying the effects of music on the brain, I decided it was time to switch from research-theory mode to practical-application mode and start a community orchestra. I'm convinced this idea was born from inspiration because I had no prior experience of starting even a string quartet. The vision came to me one night as a very distinct and clear idea while I was pondering. Meditative pondering is when we get our best, most creative ideas because the brain is relaxed. In this relaxed state, the brain can harmonize and integrate all the information and data it has accumulated. During this mulching period, the gigantic powers of the parabrain—the 99% of our unused mental ability that includes the subconscious—are released. Once this happens, a person can have highly accurate perceptions that can become the basis of important decisions. Louis Pasteur said, "Chance favors only the mind that is prepared," and I believe my mind was prepared and ready to capitalize on this orchestra insight.

That night I wrote an outline of the goals I wanted to accomplish. I was certain of one thing: this was going to be an orchestra—not a chamber orchestra, but a full-size symphony orchestra. I jotted down a rough mission statement that included the following objectives: an orchestra (1) where both young and older musicians in the community could experience playing together in an orchestra setting; (2) where seasoned and/or professional adult musicians would share their musical talents, knowledge, and expertise with other musicians of varying skill levels; (3) where musicians of all races and cultures would come together to play music regardless of any personal beliefs or practices; (4) where family members could join and play alongside one another; and, last, (5) to support the concept of lifelong learning. Today, the orchestra still follows and adheres to the original goals I wrote down fourteen years ago.

Well, it is one thing to come up with an idea, but it is an entirely different set of skills to develop it and see the idea become a living, breathing reality. It was an exciting journey, albeit a difficult and time-consuming one. Nonetheless, the orchestra has become one of my most gratifying accomplishments.

In the beginning stages, because I did not know what I was doing, I did not organize a governing board—that came later. There were no "how-to-start-an-orchestra" books in the library. The Internet was too new to supply the information I needed. I was literally left to forge ahead and acquire all the "on the job training" I would need. Several years before, I had started a very small company so I understood the basics of building something from the ground up. That experience became my foundation. My favorite motto, "leap and the net will appear," became my wings. With a healthy dose of fear and trepidation, I began.

If you have even the slightest inkling or desire to start an orchestra in your community, your church, or your school, hopefully this chapter will give you helpful tips to accomplish that goal. Below are the steps I took, the things I learned, and the mistakes I made along the way. If you experience feelings of fear and angst, rest assured you are in good company. Chuck Jones, the animator of Bugs Bunny, Wile E. Coyote, and Daffy Duck, said, "Fear is a vital factor in any creative work. Anxiety is the handmaiden of creativity."[1] Anyone who has ever been involved with creative endeavors—

Leonardo da Vinci, Albert Einstein, Steve Jobs—understands that apprehension, anxiety, and fear are the building blocks of creative achievement.

Step One: Structuring the Orchestra

Orchestras can be organized in a number of different ways. They can be structured as nonprofits, for-profits, or under the umbrella of a larger organization, such as a school or religious group. Orchestras can be completely volunteer, where none of the participants are paid, or can be orchestras where only the principal people, such as the conductor, the president, and certain key individuals, are paid. The orchestra I started—the Palos Verdes Regional Symphony Orchestra—was structured under the auspices of a religious organization, but later a separate nonprofit component was added which enabled us to raise tax-deductible money. In the beginning, it was designed as a volunteer orchestra, where every person involved—president, conductor, assistant conductor, musicians, board members, audiovisual technicians, and so forth—served as volunteers. Today, it is a semivolunteer orchestra where only the conductor is paid. Because the position of conductor requires a high level of expertise, he is compensated. The overall concept and spirit of volunteerism has been key to the success of the orchestra and follows what many great leaders of our nation have said—that volunteerism and service have reshaped our country and have made it great.

> *Anyone who has ever been involved with creative endeavors—Leonardo da Vinci, Albert Einstein, Steve Jobs—understands that apprehension, anxiety, and fear are the building blocks of creative achievement.*

> *The overall concept and spirit of volunteerism has been key to the success of the orchestra and follows what many great leaders of our nation have said—that volunteerism and service have reshaped our country and have made it great.*

Step Two: Finding a Sponsor

From the outset, an orchestra needs three basic things to function: a venue in which to practice, coverage for the cost of the music, and compensation for the conductor. Hence, a sponsor is needed. Sponsors can be found just about anywhere—in the private or public sector, in religious or nonreligious organizations, businesses, and schools. Ideally, a sponsor needs to be willing to cover the costs of the music, a conductor, and, if necessary, rent for a practice facility. At times sponsors can provide only part of what you need; perhaps they can pay for the costs of music and a conductor, but cannot provide you with practice facilities. If so, contact places that may offer complimentary rooms, such as local libraries or schools, performing arts studios, the YMCA, banks, or even grocery stores with extra rooms. In return, offer to perform gratis at a function they may sponsor. As mentioned earlier, our sponsor is a religious organization. Religious sponsors are relatively common. Many different religious organizations sponsor small chamber orchestras that perform with their church choirs. In the beginning, our sponsor paid for the music, provided a place for us to practice each week, and paid for overhead expenses of programs, advertisements, photocopying, and so forth. The musicians were then, and still are today, responsible for providing their own music stands and instruments. In return, we perform four concerts per year for the church and the community. Today, although the church still generously sponsors the orchestra and provides a place for practices, additional expenses are now covered by private donors.

A word about private donors: our private donors started out as both audience members and the orchestra members themselves. The orchestra is fortunate to be surrounded by very generous people. For example, when it became necessary to hire a professional conductor, a family generously agreed to pay the yearly stipend. Our harpist, Dianne Callister, seeded a tax-deductible fund that her husband (a lawyer) set up for the orchestra. From that point on, we were able to raise money that would give donors a tax benefit. Robert Pilmer, our senior cellist, purchased a high-quality cello for our principal cellist to play, which improved the tone quality of the cello section. Christel Wagner, a spunky German woman who loved the orchestra, donated the cost of desperately needed percussion instruments. With her contribution we purchased three tympani, an authentic Chinese orchestra tam-tam, a concert bass drum, chimes, a rosewood xylophone, crash cymbals, sleigh bells, a slapstick, and a triangle—giving this orchestra a very sophisticated percussion section! Prior to her donation, all of our percussion instruments were borrowed from the local high schools. Although the schools were always very generous, there were times when our need conflicted with theirs, so Wagner's donation was a godsend. Because of this, we named the percussion section "The Leoni and Hans Wagner Percussion Section," after her parents, who instilled within her a love of music.

Grants are also an option for raising money. But this requires someone with expertise to write the applications and submit them to funding institutions. For our orchestra, grant writing was not necessary, as our needs were answered in the charitable donations of generous individuals who believed in the orchestra and saw its benefit to the community. Keep in mind, the structure of your orchestra will determine the amount of funds you will need to raise. Because our orchestra is primarily a volunteer organization, our monetary needs are considerably smaller than an orchestra where all the musicians and key people are paid.

Step Three: Soliciting Musicians

Before soliciting musicians, make certain you are organized and ready to launch, which means having a sponsor, a venue to practice, music to play, and a conductor. This will project a feeling of confidence to potential members. Prior to our first orchestra meeting, I sent out flyers and made phone calls inviting musicians to attend. I do not know what I was expecting, but seven musicians showed up: one violin, two clarinets, one tuba, one French horn, and two trumpets—hardly enough to start an orchestra, but start it we did! Over the ensuing weeks, months, and years the orchestra grew exponentially. The phrase from the movie *Field of Dreams*, *"If you build it, they will come,"* certainly applied here and by January 2003—just four years after starting—we had eighty-five members with all instrumentation represented. We also had performed in several venues throughout Southern California, including the Cerritos Center for the Performing Arts, the Ronald McDonald House, and the now defunct Borders Books and Music, and had been professionally recorded.

Starting an orchestra today with flyers and phone calls would probably be considered archaic—there are much better options—but both then and now the concept of networking, networking, and more networking is still considered king. Below are some ideas to solicit musicians that utilize twenty-first-century technology.

Social media in all its varieties can be extremely powerful and was not available when our orchestra was initially started. For instance, there is enormous potential for attracting musicians through a website, YouTube videos, Facebook advertising, and regular blogging and twittering. Here are a few social media options:

- FACEBOOK: This social networking site is intended to connect friends, family, and business associates. It is also a place where you can "advertise" for musicians through assertive networking. Make frequent posts to keep friends and family informed about upcoming events and concerts.

- BLOGGING: The word "blog" is short for web log and is used for advertising and passing on information about your organization, website, and so forth. It can be done through Blogger and Wordpress, but you must do more than just advertise for musicians—you want to inform orchestra members and potential members about upcoming concerts, auditions, practices, and the everyday comings and goings of the orchestra.

- TWITTER: Use this social networking and microblogging service to send and read text-based posts of up to 140 characters. It is a valuable, quick, and easy tool for staying in touch with the members of the orchestra and sending important messages about practices and upcoming events.

- YouTube: If you are trying to attract musicians to your orchestra, a powerful way is to videotape concerts and interviews with current members. Then, upload the videos to YouTube. As the saying goes, "seeing is believing!" You can also create a YouTube channel which allows your audience to subscribe (free) and receive notifications of new videos you have added.

- Pinterest: This pinboard-style website is for photosharing. Users are allowed to create and manage theme-based image collections. The site seeks to "connect everyone in the world through the 'things' they find interesting." This could be a valuable tool for stimulating all kinds of interest in the orchestra. Take photos of venues, concerts, and promotional flyers to recruit both new musicians and audience members.

- Flickr: Another great photo management and sharing application is Flickr. Use it to post pictures of the orchestra members and performances.

- Quora: This site is a collection of questions and answers created and edited by people who use it. You can both post and answer questions about the orchestra.

- Slideshare: You can use this online hosting service to upload PowerPoint, PDF, or OpenOffice documents. If you want to compile a PowerPoint of the orchestra, this is a great place to host it.

- LinkedIn: Make friends with other likeminded musicians and engage in professional networking with this business-oriented social media site.

Below are additional ways of attracting musicians that were successful when I used them, but may need tweaking according to your particular goals and circumstances now.

* E-mail/Flyers: Design a colorful solicitation flyer and e-mail it to private music teachers and school music teachers. Also, post it on library bulletin boards and in music stores.

* Enlist Music Teachers to Recruit Students: Contact music teachers directly via phone, e-mail, or, if appropriate, a personal visit. Keep the conversation short. Explain to them that you have started an orchestra with both seasoned and intermediate musicians, and would like their students to join. Savvy teachers will recognize the golden opportunity for their students. Supply them with flyers for their students and invite them to an orchestra practice or a concert. Meeting you and the conductor, observing the other musicians, and scrutinizing the setting can boost their confidence in the orchestra and help them to feel at ease in recommending their students. When I started the orchestra, one of the music teachers I contacted was Elmer Su, a famous violinist and string teacher from China. He had many students of varying skill levels and was thrilled to have an ongoing venue for his students to perform in. He understood that one way of keeping a budding musician dedicated to their craft is becoming part of an orchestra. Today, Elmer Su is the conductor of the orchestra.

* Recruit Music Teachers: If you are having difficulty building an instrument section or the proficiency level of the section is lacking, consider inviting a music teacher that teaches that particular instrument to join and act as principal of that section. Our orchestra was having difficulties in the viola section. I found a viola teacher, called her

If you are having difficulty building an instrument section or the proficiency level of the section is lacking, consider inviting a music teacher that teaches that particular instrument to join and act as principal of that section.

regularly, and convinced her and her students to join. Because of her expertise and background, she made an indelible impact on the viola section.

- PERSONAL VISITS TO POTENTIAL MEMBERS: Sometimes a personal visit to a potential musician can have a positive outcome. If you find a musician who is qualified for a section that needs strengthening, call and set up an appointment. Take the music you are currently working on, a schedule of practices and performances, a member roster, and rules of the orchestra. Even though this represents extra time on your part, the results can be well worth the effort. In the beginning stages of the orchestra, I made a personal visit to Michelle Whitesides, a talented violinist I was hoping to recruit. She later said that her "love of music and my *personal invitation*" were the motivating factors that convinced her entire family to join. Her impact on the orchestra has been far-reaching; Michelle instigated and oversaw the music library, was the section leader for the second violinists, and is currently serving as the Young Violinists chairperson.

  Another personal visit that reaped rewards occurred when I was building the cello section. I heard about a gifted adult cellist, so I made a visit. She joined, became the section principal, and had an indelible influence on the young cellists.

- USE ORCHESTRA MEMBERS TO RECRUIT: Encourage members of the orchestra to invite friends, co-workers, and acquaintances that play a musical instrument to join. Oftentimes people are more apt to join when someone they know is a part of the group.

- WEEKLY CALLS: The beginning stages of building an orchestra are crucial. During this time have someone call each member weekly to remind him or her of practices. A hassle? Yes, but worth it. I called each musician every week for the first six months. I let each one know he or she was important to the success of the orchestra and was needed at every practice.

Last, be aware that not every person that initially attends the orchestra will become a permanent member. One woman joined our orchestra for two weeks, then decided to quit. The idea of a mixed group of young people and adults was not was she was looking for. I gave her information about an adult orchestra that was forming and left the door open if she ever wanted to return. Another family of three joined, but the mother wanted an authoritarian conductor who put pressure on any child who did not pay strict attention. She also informed me that her daughter had perfect pitch and our amateur orchestra made her daughter's ears hurt. In these situations, recognize that your orchestra concept is not for everyone.

Step Four: Auditions or Not?

In the beginning stages of the orchestra, auditions were not required as they are now. But it was mandatory that each musician play at an intermediate level. During the launching period we wanted the orchestra to grow quickly, so we accepted just about anyone who owned an instrument, could read music at an intermediate level, was willing to learn, and would remain dedicated to our effort. At times, we had both adults and young people join that had difficulty with some of the music. They were also determined to persevere and learn the pieces. Because of their willingness, we took the time to rewrite some of the orchestration and encouraged them to get additional music lessons. This approach always paid off and these individuals became some of the most dedicated musicians in our orchestra. There may be situations where young people or even older adults want to join, but the music is too difficult. Do not write these people off. Put them on a waiting list and have them check back periodically as their skill level increases.

Step Five: Staying True to Your Orchestra Concept—Cultural Diversity

One of the goals of the orchestra was to organize it as an ethnically diverse group of people. Over the past fourteen years numerous nationalities have been represented in the orchestra, including Caucasian, Japanese, Chinese, Korean, Thai, Filipino, Malaysian, Vietnamese, Hispanic, African American, Jewish, Indian, Palestinian, and a mixture of European descent.

One of the goals of the orchestra was to organize it as an ethnically diverse group of people.

Dean Simonton, a University of California psychologist, believes that the development of creativity depends on exposure to cultural diversity. After researching the great civilizations in Europe, India, China, and the Islamic world, he found that the most creative periods in world history occur when there is an infusion of diversity. New ideas and cross-cultural encounters propel societies into a golden age of inspiration and creativity. Simonton believes that America, because of the growing numbers of cultures within its borders, is poised for such a leap. By drawing upon the strength of this plurality into a unified vision, America has the potential of becoming one of the most creative nations in the world.[2]

In a small, but significant way, this is precisely what the Palos Verdes Regional Symphony Orchestra seeks to accomplish. Our ethnic diversity and altruistic goals are what continue to spark and foster our creativity.

Step Six: Staying True to Your Orchestra Concept—Mentoring

In the PVRSO, we employ a unique mentoring concept where the professional and seasoned musicians help and support the younger musicians. There are many examples throughout the world where professionals mentor talented, young musicians. However, the concept of having an orchestra comprised of musicians ranging in age from seven to seventy with varying levels of experience is novel and unique. In the beginning, the orchestra had the following mix of musicians:

* Professional and seasoned musicians playing alongside and mentoring young musicians (seven to eighteen years old) who had varying levels of orchestra experience.

- Professional and seasoned musicians playing alongside other adults (eighteen to seventy-five years old) who wanted to improve and/or reawaken their musical skills by playing in an orchestra.

- Young, talented high school or college musicians that raised the level of confidence of older musicians with whom they were paired.

In short, we strategically placed musicians together in a way that gave them the best musical experience and opportunity available. An orchestra structured like this has its challenges, but if the musicians agree to *unselfishly* work together and to lay aside egos, everyone benefits and the results are astounding. Here are some of the reasons why this concept works:

- ADULT MUSICIANS MENTOR YOUNG MUSICIANS. In the beginning stages of the orchestra, we had musicians as young as seven and those approaching seventy. The payoff—adults sharing their musical expertise with young musicians. Within each instrument section, adults were paired with youth. They helped with the bowing, intonation, embouchure, the art of listening to one another, how to watch the conductor, and the fine points of performing in an orchestra setting. This adult/young person pairing can be beneficial for any orchestra employing this concept. We also had situations where older musicians did not feel as confident in their playing, and so we paired talented high school students with them. The result—a boost in confidence of the older musician. For example, we had a very talented "young-at-heart" trumpet player whose lip was cracking in some of the pieces. He tried a number of remedies—lip exercises, taking additional lessons, and so on—but with little success. He was considering quitting when we paired him with a very talented high school trumpet player. Playing the same parts increased his confidence level, knowing that if he could not make the high notes, she could and would. He is still an active and an important member of the orchestra.

- GREAT SOUND IN A SHORT TIME. Using the combination of adults and youth helps the orchestra sound wonderful almost immediately.

The reason is twofold: adults with more advanced music experience perform at a higher level, which immediately helps the orchestra to sound better, and additionally, when the musically seasoned adult plays alongside a youth, it boosts the level of confidence and playing ability of the young musician. A win-win situation!

Step Seven: Sharing the Responsibility

In a volunteer orchestra, everyone's help is vital. Members who actively participate have a greater investment in the success of the orchestra. Below are some of the job categories and duties that our orchestra utilized. Add, subtract, and rotate the responsibilities and duties to fit the needs of your orchestra.

PRESIDENT

This is a key position in the orchestra. The president of the orchestra does not need extensive musical training or background, but he or she does need organizational skills, perseverance, determination, and unending energy. He or she needs to know how to implement and execute ideas, to have strong interpersonal skills, and to have a passion for the orchestra and its members. Most importantly, he or she needs to have a vision of what the orchestra can accomplish and believe completely in the orchestra's ability to accomplish that vision. Sometimes the president of the orchestra is also the founder.

Duties and Responsibilities of the President

- Organize the orchestra into a functional entity by using the ideas contained in this chapter.

- Assign orchestra members and parents various positions of responsibility within the orchestra.

- Work closely with others without becoming a micromanager. For instance, work closely with the conductor and event coordinator to arrange, organize, and execute musical programs for the orchestra to perform, and to secure performance venues.

- Conduct regular meetings, including board meetings, with persons holding key positions in the orchestra.

- Listen to and implement any feasible advice, concerns, ideas, or input from orchestra members and parents. Keep in mind that everyone has an invested interest in the orchestra and the mark of a good leader is willingness to actively listen to others,

- Constantly look for creative ways for the orchestra members to improve and enhance their activities.

CONDUCTOR/MUSIC DIRECTOR

The conductor/music director is vital for any orchestra. Obviously, your conductor needs to be experienced in performance and knowledgeable about all musical instrumentation. In this type of an orchestra, he or she needs to enjoy working with both young people and adults. It also helps if he or she has infinite patience and a sense of humor.

Duties and Responsibilities of the Conductor/Music Director

- Works closely with the president and assistant conductor.

- Plans the practices and performances and conducts them.

- Picks out music to be performed.

- Selects section principals.

- Calls sectional practices when needed.

Assistant Conductor:

The assistant conductor should understand how to read and conduct music. Ideally, he or she should be a member of the orchestra and attend weekly practices.

Duties and Responsibilities of the Assistant Conductor

- Assist and support the conductor.

- Conduct at practices and performances if the conductor is not available.

- Help the conductor select principals for instrument sections.

- Help select music for the orchestra.

Secretary

This position requires a very responsible person who regularly attends practices and has access to a computer.

Duties and Responsibilities of the Secretary

- Take roll each week.

- Alert section principals when musicians miss practice for follow-up.

- Design, photocopy, distribute, and e-mail any communication pertinent to the orchestra and members.

- Keep track of budgetary items, such as costs associated with sheet music, programs, photocopying, and so forth.

- Support and work closely with the president.

Music Librarians

This position requires a very organized individual. It is advisable to have up to three people sharing this responsibility.

Duties and Responsibilities of the Music Librarians

- Work closely with the president and conductor.

- Photocopy music when needed and adhere to copyright laws.

- Count and categorize music. (All music dispersed should be individually counted and categorized. This number should be in pencil on the corner of each piece of music. For instance, if you are passing out forty copies of music to the first violin section, the first person to receive the music should have a 1/40 in the corner; the second person should have a 2/40 in the corner, and so forth.)

- Distribute all music to the musicians.

- Collect and count all music from musicians after performances.

- When distributing new music, have each musician sign a paper designating they have received that piece of music.

- When collecting music, have each musician sign the sheet indicating he or she has returned the music.

- Catalog each piece of music by instrument section and musical piece.

Section Principals

The section principals are individuals in each musical division that are seasoned musicians who are willing to attend weekly practices and who are patient and kind to people of all ages.

Duties and Responsibilities of Section Principals

- Work closely with the president, conductor, and assistant conductor.

- Mentor and nurture the musicians in the instrument section by giving help and correction when needed.

- Coordinate the rotation of chairs in the instrument group.

- Rotate the first, second, and third instrument parts so that everyone in the section has an opportunity to play various parts. Obviously, this needs to be based on their music level and desire to play different parts.

- Call, e-mail, or text people in the section regarding practices or performances.

- Alert the president, conductor, or assistant conductor about concerns regarding the section.

Event Coordinator

The event coordinator is responsible for finding suitable venues for the orchestra to perform. It is important for the orchestra to have places to display the talents of the members. When the orchestra is rehearsing for a performance, the musicians are working toward a goal. Their motivation and excitement level remains high. If you cannot find venues in your community, then create your own events. Talk to everyone about possible venues, even if a person may have no connection to music. Mark Granovetter, author of *Getting a Job*, talks about an interesting study conducted in 1974 about how people make contacts and find work. He discovered that people do not get jobs through their friends, but rather through their acquaintances. This is because "weak ties" are more important than strong ties. In fact, he coined the phrase "the strength of weak ties."[3] Musicians occupy pretty much the same world, but acquaintances or strangers occupy different worlds and are more likely to know of venues that are not readily apparent.

> *It is important for the orchestra to have places to display the talents of the members. When the orchestra is rehearsing for a performance, the musicians are working toward a goal. Their motivation and excitement level remains high.*

Duties and Responsibilities of the Event Coordinator

- Work closely with the president and conductor.

- Find performance venues. Check local hospitals, retirement and assisted living homes, women's shelters, children's centers, libraries, bookstores, music stores, schools, religious organizations, community and performing arts centers, and so forth.

- Create venues for performances (see "Creating Performance Venues").

- Network, network, network!

PUBLIC RELATIONS/SOCIAL MEDIA COORDINATOR

The public relations/social media coordinator is responsible for orchestra publicity and building relationships online and in the community. This position requires strong writing and communication skills. Public relations activities include creating and sending press packets to specific journalists assigned to the arts section of local newspapers and magazines. I visited Meredith Grenier, a writer at our local newspaper, *The Daily Breeze*, which had a circulation of almost five hundred thousand weekly. Because of that visit, she came to an orchestra practice, interviewed members and parents, took pictures, and wrote a very impressive front-page article complete with color photographs. It gave us amazing coverage and publicity, which in turn brought us new musicians. To show our appreciation, all the orchestra members wrote her thank-you notes. She loved them and, as a result, *The Daily Breeze* did another half-page article on the orchestra highlighting the thank-you notes.

Social media is a powerful advertising tool that has the possibility of reaching millions of people in nanoseconds. Responsibilities for establishing a website, Facebook, Twitter, and other online accounts are under the auspices of the public relations/social media coordinator. However, the maintenance of the sites could be shared by the members of the orchestra. Frequent, timely posts are the key to keeping these sites relevant. Assign a group of young people (with adult supervision) to be responsible for all aspects of social media that can be used to promote the orchestra and orchestra events.

Duties and Responsibilities of the Public Relations and Social Media Coordinator

- Create press packets with the following: a business card with contact information; links to the orchestra website, Facebook page, Twitter account, and other online sites; a concise history of the orchestra; member bios; performance programs; and photographs.

- Contact journalists and distribute press packets.

- Write press releases for each performance and other news about the orchestra.

- Distribute press releases to journalists.

- Follow-up press packets and press releases with a personal contact via phone, e-mail, or an invitation to meet.

- Send thank-you notes to the editors who feature the orchestra in their magazines, newspapers, or online news sites.

- Establish and manage social media, including supervising members who are authorized to post news, photos, and events on orchestra sites.

VIDEOGRAPHER, PHOTOGRAPHER, AUDIOVISUAL COORDINATORS

Each of these should be a separate position, handled by different people.

The videographer needs to be talented and knowledgeable about videotaping performances; someone with an artistic eye who understands focus, camera angles, lighting, and editing. If someone associated with the orchestra has expertise in this area, definitely use him or her. If not, check local high schools and colleges for someone involved with film and video production. You may want to use multiple people to act as videographers. In the beginning, we had three young men from the local high school and community college that assisted us. Your videographer may double as your photographer, but if not, a photographer is needed to take photos of individual members and group shots of the orchestra. You will also need photographs of performances and other orchestra events. The audiovisual coordinator is extremely important. He or she must be willing to attend all performances and set up any audiovisual equipment that may be needed, such as sound and recording systems. For twelve years, the orchestra was extremely fortunate to have Ben Savagian as our volunteer audiovisual coordinator. Ben is a rare find—he is amazingly talented with great mastery and understanding of the audiovisual world. He was always willing to bring his own equipment when needed. He never missed a performance, and the orchestra never encountered an audio problem he could not solve.

Duties and Responsibilities of the Videographer, Photographer, and Audiovisual Coordinators

- Work closely with the president regarding scheduled performances.

- Have expertise in videotaping, photography, and audiovisual coordination.

- Have access to all the equipment needed.

- Be available for performances and concerts.

- Maintain a library of recordings, photographs, and DVDs of the orchestra and orchestra events.

- Coordinate all archival materials with the orchestra historian.

HISTORIAN

Each day your orchestra exists, it is creating history. Who can predict the influence your orchestra will have on future generations and to your community? Therefore, the history of your orchestra needs to be preserved. There are many ways of preserving history—written, recorded, and videotaped—and all should be utilized for the most comprehensive documentation.

Duties and Responsibilities of the Historian

- Keep a written journal of all the activities and performances of the orchestra; include interesting stories and experiences of orchestra members.

- Work closely with the videographer and photographer in securing copies of any videos, photographs, and so forth for historical preservation.

- Keep memorabilia of the orchestra's performances—handbills, programs, flyers, photographs, film, and so on—and preserve it using archival quality materials into a readable and savable format.

Refreshment Coordinator (optional)

This optional job is fun and does not require a lot of time. Our orchestra serves light refreshments during practice breaks because food is always a great social icebreaker.

Duties and Responsibilities of the Refreshment Coordinator

- Coordinate weekly refreshments.

- During practices, have people sign up to bring refreshments.

- Each week, remind the people bringing refreshments.

- Each week, set up and take down a refreshment table.

Room Set-Up Coordinator

Prior to each practice, chairs need to be set up. This is an easy job that takes about fifteen minutes and creates an organized atmosphere for the musicians.

Duties and Responsibilities of Room Set-Up Coordinator

- Work closely with the conductor and set up the chairs exactly how he wants them to be placed. Chairs will be arranged this way each week unless otherwise specified.

- Post instrument signs until the younger musicians know exactly where to sit.

Creating Performance Venues

It would be wonderful if your orchestra was in constant demand, making regular appearances throughout your community, but the reality is, you will more than likely have to create your own performance venues. It takes work, coordination, and organization, but can be fun and allow for creative expression. For instance, one year we created a music lecture series entitled "Fine Arts Distinguished Speakers and Music Series." The programs featured a speaker and appropriate music played by the orchestra. One program, "A Tribute to Henry Mancini," featured the music of the popular composer. Mancini's daughter Felice, the executive director of the Mr. Holland's Opus Foundation, graciously came and spoke about her father and his musical accomplishments. The orchestra performed several of Mancini's works. Another program featured Alan Williams—an Academy Award nominee for the IMAX movie *Amazon*. He spoke about composing music for film and television and conducted the orchestra performing several of his works. Another program featured Laurie Olsen Schnoebelen, a synesthete painter who discussed her art inspired by the music of Johann Sebastian Bach. It was a fascinating look into synesthesia, the brain's ability to meld the senses of sight and sound. The orchestra performed several Bach Inventions to make this an unforgettable program. Last in this series, an entire evening was dedicated to music from America. Various representatives from the United States Armed Forces and interfaith choirs joined the orchestra in singing and performing patriotic numbers. On another occasion, we joined with the Los Angeles Chinese Musicians Ensemble Chorus and performed a classical concert.

Keep in mind that if you want record numbers of people attending your performances, you need to vary your programs and include other groups to perform along with you. For example, one of our programs featured the music and dancing of various ethnic groups living through-

Keep in mind that if you want record numbers of people attending your performances, you need to vary your programs and include other groups to perform along with you.

out Los Angeles—the Kyodo Taiko Drummers (Japanese), Groupo Folklorico Xanath (Mexican), the BEN Gospel Choir (African American), the Great Plains Indians (Native American Indian), Le Polynesia Productions (Pacific Islander), the West Los Angeles Children's Choir (multiethnic America), and the PVRSO. To increase the number of people attending the event, we displayed student artwork from local schools with artwork from famous and not-so-famous artists. The result—approximately fifteen hundred people were drawn to the program. Because it was so well-received, many of these people became concert "regulars."

Staying with this same approach, our holiday concerts featured not only the orchestra, but other local talent, such as three octave handbell choirs, a jazz quintet, a musical saw, chorales, and vocalists.

Another idea is to write and develop musical programs for children ranging in age from three to eight. If you want to build an audience of people who will support the arts when they are adults, you must start when they are young. Begin to expose them to fun and exciting programs featuring a mixture of classical music. We arranged with Borders Books and Music to have the orchestra perform two Saturday morning concerts geared for this age group, and I wrote a program entitled "Vibrations and Music." It included everything you wanted to know about vibrations, using rubber bands, kazoos, balloons, and sand blocks. The children carefully stretched rubber bands between their front teeth and fingers and strummed them, creating a vibration they could feel with their teeth and lips. They held balloons in their laps and felt the vibrations of the orchestra music through the balloons. They blew into kazoos, creating musical vibrations, and, using sand blocks, they joined the orchestra playing the "Sandpaper Ballet," by Leroy Anderson. The children left with a balloon and kazoo and the parents left with a list of upcoming performances, tips on how to prepare their children to attend one of our concerts, and music books to purchase.

In 2008 the orchestra performed at Disney Concert Hall, home of the Los Angeles Philharmonic. There are a number of prestigious performing arts buildings throughout the country where your orchestra can perform, but keep in mind that there are substantial costs to this: renting the hall, ticket sales, and miscellaneous expenses. In addition, you are responsible for attracting an audience to fill the space.

In Their Own Words: Orchestra Members Describe Their Experiences

One of the original seven to join the orchestra was Fred Virgo of Palos Verdes, California. Fourteen years later, Fred is still an active member and one of the stalwarts of the orchestra. His musical experience began in the fifth grade, where, with encouragement from his mother, he learned both the piano and trumpet. This musical foundation later led him to play in the University of Southern California (USC) marching band, and eventually he joined the orchestra, first as a trumpet player and then as a euphonium player. His love for music has been passed down to his son and grandchildren, thus creating a legacy in the Virgo home. Summing up his experience with the orchestra, he says, "I joined the orchestra because I love music and had never played in a symphonic setting. I thought it would be fun and therapeutic, and it certainly has been. It is wonderful to be a part of a unique orchestra with both youth and adult members who have a broad range of experience and talent. I have enjoyed broadening my musical repertoire. Music has provided me with a great deal of enjoyment. It is totally engrossing and healing—when I am playing or practicing I don't think about anything else."

Another unique aspect of the orchestra is the opportunity

Another unique aspect of the orchestra is the opportunity family members have to join and create music together.

family members have to join and create music together. We have many different combinations of musical families that have joined the orchestra such as mother/son, mother/daughter, father/son, father/daughter, cousins, sisters, brothers, and whole families. It has provided a great opportunity for parents to engage in a rewarding, worthwhile, side-by-side activity with their child/children. Many parents comment how this experience strengthened their parent-child bond. One father remarked, "This is the first time I've been able to actually play in an orchestra with my son. It has been the best experience of my life!"

An example of an entire family joining is the Whitesides family of San Pedro, California. Rob plays the tuba, Michelle the violin, their son Andrew plays the French horn, and their daughters Karyn and Sarah play the violin. Rob and Michelle have witnessed the impact it has had on their family: "Our family is in a unique situation, as all five of us play an instrument and have been able to participate in the orchestra together. One of the sweetest rewards is that we all share in a common activity that we enjoy both individually and as a family. It has drawn us closer together and has allowed us to develop musically and has broadened our spectrum of friends. A sym-phony 'puts sound together.' It also puts people and families together beautifully." The Whitesides continue to make an indelible impact on the orchestra through their musical expertise, their creative and practical ideas for improvements, and their willingness to take on numerous responsibilities that support our efforts. Not only have Rob and Michelle given their time and talents to the orchestra, but they have involved their children at every level. As a result, their family has had an amazing musical experience and has learned firsthand the joy that comes from dedicated service.

Starting an orchestra in your church, your community, or your school can be an exciting musical journey toward a rewarding destination where the lives of many people are positively affected along the way.

Orchestras have been around since the seventeenth century and have been enjoyed by communities the world over. Bringing together a group of musicians for the purpose of learning uplifting and inspiring music to be shared with a receptive audience is both satisfying and fulfilling. Starting an orchestra in your church, your community, or your school can be an exciting musical journey toward a rewarding destination where the lives of many people are positively affected along the way.

PART FIVE

FINALE

CHAPTER 12

ℬuilding A Legacy: A Parent Responsibility

"We are so much like violins
Frames, with sensitive strings
The touch of the hand
That holds the bow
Determines the music it brings."

Edna Machesny[1]

On July 4, 1952, Florence Chadwick was attempting to swim twenty-one miles from the southern California mainland to Catalina Island. The water was a freezing forty-eight degrees, the fog was thick and dense, and the visibility was nil. She was only one-half mile from her destination when she became discouraged and quit. The next day reporters asked her if she quit because of the cold water or the distance. "Neither," she replied. "I was licked by the fog." She then recalled a similar experience while swimming the English Channel. The fog was equally impenetrable, the water was cold, and she was exhausted and ready to quit. As she reached for her mother's hand in a boat next to her, her mother quietly pointed to the shore. Florence raised her head out of the water, saw the land ahead, and, with that new vision, pressed forward and became the first woman to conquer the English Channel.[2]

This story illustrates that with increased vision can come increased motivation. Hopefully the data, research, reports, and ideas found in this book have given you increased vision of the power of music and, in turn, increased motivation to get your child involved with music. But, before you make the plunge, please consider three ideas that when implemented *consistently* will be the vehicle for success when bringing music into your child's life.

Hopefully the data, research, reports, and ideas found in this book have given you increased vision of the power of music and, in turn, increased motivation to get your child involved with music.

These ideas work. They will be the keys to starting music traditions, or any other traditions, in your home. Before presenting these ideas, let me explain how they were formulated.

Without a doubt, the most inspiring and memorable experiences of most couples is the birth of their children. For most parents, no other event comes close in terms of emotions and pure joy. I have captured forever in my mind the memory of gazing down with wonder and awe at each of my five sons right after birth and being amazed at the miracle of life. For those brief moments, the huge responsibility that lay before me did not enter my mind or occupy one single thought. But that didn't last long, and today, I know and understand all too well the enormously challenging, time-consuming, and, yes, rewarding responsibility that comes with raising children. It has been difficult, but as with *all* challenges that life presents us, I have learned many things along the way. Unfortunately, children do not come with an instruction book—one unique to their personality—and so the *art* of raising children demands on-the-job training (if this book has illustrated anything, it is that parenting is an artistic performance).

A few years ago, a news release from Los Angeles related the story of a blind father who rescued his tiny daughter from drowning in the new swimming pool that had been installed in the neighborhood. The father heard a splash as his daughter, who could not swim, fell into the pool. It was evening, and he became frantic, knowing that there was no one but him to save his child. He got on his hands and knees and crawled around the outside edge of the pool, listening for the air bubbles that came from the little girl as she was drowning. Through his heightened sense of hearing, he followed the sound of the air bubbles, and in one desperate attempt and with overwhelming love in his heart, he jumped into the pool and grasped his precious daughter and brought her to safety.[3]

Parenthood is fraught with challenges, and many times we really are "blind"—groping to find the best way to "save" our children and to do the right thing because of our love for them and because of our desire to see them evolve into happy, well-adjusted adults. Dr. Mihaly Csikszentmihalyi, a psychologist and former head of the department of psychology at the University of Chicago and author of *Flow*, confirmed the power of love in raising healthy children in a twenty-year study he conducted. He found that the most gifted and happiest of individuals are those who come from families that communicate high expectations and have clear rules, but also offer early opportunities for meaningful choices within a *warm, loving,* and *supportive* environment[4] (emphasis added). His findings are illustrated in the true story of Sarah Edwards, an early colonial woman. Sarah raised eleven children while her husband, Jonathan Edwards, a minister, was busy with church duties, writing, and becoming famous himself. She stayed in the background as a very nurturing and loving homemaker and mother. She valued each child's individuality and intelligence and saw to it that all of her three sons and eight daughters were educated. Sarah taught them to work and act responsibly as well as serve others. Many years after she died, genealogical research was performed on the Edwards' family tree, and fourteen hundred descendants were tracked. If we consider her impressive progenitors, it becomes obvious that Sarah Edwards had raised her children to be extraordinary. Her descendants include thirteen college presidents, sixty-five professors, one hundred lawyers (including a dean of an outstanding law school), thirty judges, and sixty-six physicians (including a dean of a medical school). There were also eighty public officials: three United States senators, mayors of three large cities, governors of three states, a vice president of the United States, a controller of the United States Treasury, and countless others who were successful in business, the arts, and sciences. Of the fourteen hundred, only two were considered "black sheep," which eloquently testifies to the power of one woman who understood the importance of raising children with expectations within a warm, loving, and supportive environment. Likewise, it illustrates the magnitude of motherhood—which has been devalued in our society—to powerfully influence future generations.

For years, my husband and I studied the concepts of child rearing as we examined our priorities, methods, motives, and goals regarding this task. Along the way, we made many mistakes that forced us to stand back and look for better ways and approaches to situations, mistakes that encouraged us to rethink ideas and expectations. We learned to carefully consider our children's feelings and interests when choosing family, school, community, and religious and spiritual activities we hoped would mold them into well-rounded, independent, and confident human beings. But through this experience called "parenthood," we discovered one very important element in raising our children that, when missing, anything else we did with them and for them became almost inconsequential. This element, oftentimes a difficult task, was establishing and maintaining a close personal relationship with each of our sons and making their emotional health and development our highest priority. We found that our sons responded to the things that were important to us (e.g., good music, literature, the arts) when *first* we worked at getting to know and appreciate them as people with thoughts, feelings, and opinions. As parents, we can give our children the best education, provide material possessions, afford a myriad of lessons, and expose them to all kinds of exciting experiences—but if they do not know and feel that we care about them simply for being who they are, and that we love them despite inappropriate and embarrassing behavior at times, the best formulated plans and goals can backfire. When they get to be teenagers, there is always the possibility they will rebel against the very things that are important to us, if we haven't shown through our actions that we value them first as human beings. It is as though our children are saying to us, "Don't tell me how much you know until you show me how much you care."

We live in one of the most exciting times in the history of this world, a time filled with countless electronic and technological conveniences. We have access to more information than ever before, and in a myriad forms: the Internet, computers, books, e-books, e-faxes, magazines, television, radio, cellular phones, satellite transmissions, and digital video recordings, to name a few. Although the possibilities of all these inventions make our lives easier in one sense, they can complicate matters in our relationships with our children as our attention is stretched in many different and varied directions. With all of these outside influences and demands on our time, raising children becomes a delicate balancing act, and sometimes we can't help but fall off the beam—as shown by many reports and studies of parents too busy to raise their children with needed guidance. In 1995, the Carnegie Commission presented an alarming picture of a society that neglects and discounts adolescents. American parents were seen as preoccupied and dismissive, unable to cope with the problems of their children. These were adolescents from both poor and economically advantaged homes, who only saw their parents while they were taking them from swimming lessons to dance class to tutoring.[5] Sadly, many parents believe that these many activities make up for the time they cannot, or will not, spend with their children on a personal level. Children need to have more from their parents than the cost of yet one more lesson or activity.

Little has changed since 1995. All we have to do is read the newspapers to know there are serious problems with the youth of today, but if we carefully analyzed the reasons why, we would find that the greater problem lies with the parents. In the past, it was assumed that kids with emotional problems usually came from impoverished or disadvantaged homes, but not so today. Madeline Levine, PhD and author of *The Price of Privilege*, states, "It is now clear, children of privilege are exhibiting unexpectedly high rates of emotional problems beginning in junior high school and accelerating throughout adolescence."[6] Studies show that whether kids succeed or fail, socioeconomic status of a family makes little difference—the difference lies in parents showing a genuine interest in their children by giving them both quantity and quality time as they establish an emotional bond with them. Deborah Fallows, author of *A Mother's Work*, understands the importance of quality and quantity time in constructing an emotional bond with each child. She says, "To meet my standard of responsible parenthood, I have

Studies show that whether kids succeed or fail, socioeconomic status of a family makes little difference—the difference lies in parents showing a genuine interest in their children by giving them both quantity and quality time as they establish an emotional bond with them.

to know [my children] as well as I possibly can and see them in as many different environments and moods as possible in order to know best how to help them grow up, by comforting them, letting them alone, disciplining them, enjoying them, being dependable, but not stifling. What I need is time with them—in quantity, not [just] 'quality.'"[7] Yes, more than anything, children need our time. They want our time. Really, they want little else.

Lauren Greenfield spent four years photographing kids from Los Angeles. The result was *Fast Forward, Growing Up in the Shadow of Hollywood.* The pages show kids with every advantage in life—money, fame, and material possessions—but dramatically illustrate what can happen when children are given everything but parental time: early experimentation with drugs, sex, and/or gang affiliation, and a haunting look of oldness. Despite all of their indulgences, these young people are very much alone, left only with the "things" money can buy. Robert Jones, in "Fast Forward Kids," sums it up by saying, "They jump from one indulgence to another, spending ever more money, trying to fill the alone-ness."[8] Technology has made it possible for young people to communicate with each other in fast, easy, and convenient ways—Facebook, Twitter, texting, and e-mails—but all of these are accomplished in isolation. They connect to thousands of "friends" without having to face a single one of them. Something is awry when young people's principal method of communicating and socializing is through texts and e-mails, which are oftentimes loaded with *mis*communications and contribute to their "alone-ness." An educator friend of mine said, "You can never get full on things you don't need, and all else obtained, the emptiness remains."

Material possessions, these "things" that permeate our culture, ultimately do not make children *or* adults happy or fulfilled. When we lose the *things* in life that really mean something—like a warm relationship with our children—nothing else matters. Even MGM's Louis B. Mayer, the once powerful, wealthy king of Hollywood, knew money couldn't buy everything. As he lay dying in his hospital bed, he despairingly said, "Nothing matters. Nothing matters."[9] Likewise, Thomas Griffith, a former editor for *Time* magazine, in writing about our era said, "We are so caught up in the complexity and clamor of our way of life that we do not realize how much all of these powerful efforts to attract or divert us are a tax on our spirit: they do a double harm, in the triviality of what they offer and the fatigue which they engender, that keeps us from doing something more profitable with our time."[10] And that "profitable something" should be *time* spent with our children: building a bond, strengthening a relationship, and expressing our love.

Over the years, I have observed what it is that parents and children of successful families have in common. What do I mean by a "successful" family? I see it as families that are emotionally balanced as opposed to extraordinarily talented. *All* families have numerous talents, but not all have emotional stability. In my search, I have found that although parents of emotionally functional families are busy trying to balance home, work, family, and community, they take the time to do those simple acts such as talking and listening to their kids, expressing their love for them, making them feel special and valued, and making their homes a place of refuge from the storms of life. They understand the importance of prioritizing, putting their children as their top priority, and knowing full well that "no other success can compensate for failure in the home."[11] They take primary responsibility for their children, aware that they will not learn all they need to learn in school, and that the home is the first and most effective place for them to learn the lessons of life. They see themselves as the master teachers in their children's lives and realize that *their* example is the most effective teaching tool. They do not acquiesce their parental responsibilities to the next-door neighbor, the school, or the state or federal government; they consider themselves the primary caretaker and take their responsibility as parents seriously. In short, their lives and the lives of their children are filled with mutual purpose and direction.

Sounds like a family right out of a fairy tale, right? Not quite. There are many such families throughout the world, but for whatever reason, we just do not hear about them very often. One woman who singlehandedly built a successful family based on these qualities is Sonja Carson. She was married at thirteen, had two children by the time she was fifteen, and then was deserted by her husband to raise two young sons in poverty. Despite being a single mother with overwhelming challenges, Sonja took her responsibility of parenting seriously and had a strict law of expectation for her sons. They were expected to do well in school, read a book each week, study their math facts daily, and could only watch two TV programs a week. They did all this with her constant support, help, encouragement, and love. In spite of her strong parental presence, one day her son, Ben, then fourteen, tried to resolve an argument at school by stabbing a classmate with a knife. A metal belt buckle the boy was wearing saved his life, and essentially saved Ben's, too. Instead of blaming her financial situation, the school, not having a husband in the home, or the lack of opportunities, she put the responsibility where it belonged—on her son. Sonja sat him down and, with gentleness and firmness, let him know his behavior was intolerable, and in life more can be accomplished with kindness than with violence. Today, Ben Carson is the director of pediatric neurosurgery at Johns Hopkins Hospital and a world-renowned neurosurgeon. Sonja's other son, Curtis, is a successful engineer. Both are accomplished musicians and are raising thriving families of their own. What made a difference for Curtis and Ben was the example of their mother, who took the necessary time to build a loving relationship with them, who communicated with them, and who let them know they were important and valued. She keenly understood the importance of providing emotional stability for her sons. Sonja Carson's motto for raising children is, "Every mom knows that a child isn't going to hear too much of what she says. It's what she does that is important."[12]

Providing emotional balance in the home is not just psychobabble, but an actual physical reality. As mentioned in chapter one, it has been scientifically demonstrated that our body is filled with

Providing emotional balance in the home is not just psychobabble, but an actual physical reality.

emotional cells. The limbic system is the emotional center of our brain and comprises 15 percent of brain mass. Our gut is overflowing with emotional cells and produces 95 percent of the serotonin in our body— the neurotransmitters that contribute to our emotional well-being. Our emotions are so powerful that they can override any of our intellectual functions. We all know that when we are emotionally distraught, those feelings cloud everything else in our lives and can, at times, immobilize our ability to function at home and at work. The same happens with our children. When they experience emotional trauma, it affects how they do in school, how easily they make friends, and how they feel about themselves. Daniel Goleman, author of *Emotional Intelligence*, confirms the importance of our emotions and talks about young children that experience depression as early as five years of age. He said the cost to these children goes beyond the suffering caused by depression itself. They do poorly in school; depression interferes with their memory and concentration, making it harder to pay attention in class and retain what is taught. They also have poor social skills and are often ostracized by other children.[13] Levine found similar issues with adolescents and their relationship with their parents. Wealthy parents were emotionally distant from their children but insisted on high levels of achievement, which created emotional issues of "intense feelings of shame and hopelessness" in their children.[14] Dr. Marian Diamond found in her studies on the brain that our "emotional well-being may be more essential for survival than intellectual." In her book *Enriching Heredity*, she talks about Nathaniel Hawthorne's story "Ethan Brand" and how essential emotions are in the development of the "whole" or complete person. She says,

> *Dr. Marian Diamond found in her studies on the brain that our "emotional well-being may be more essential for survival than intellectual."*

His main character is searching for the unpardonable sin. He concentrates to such an extent on his intellectual pursuit that he becomes emotionally starved. He eventually becomes dismayed and throws himself into his fiery kiln. When others discover the remains, all that is left is his charred rib cage enclosing a cold marble heart. He had discovered the unpardonable sin by neglecting to integrate the warm, emotional heart, in a metaphorical sense, with his intellectual pursuit.[15]

The handwriting is on the wall. If parents want to raise children that do well intellectually and emotionally—at school, at home, with their peers, and in life—they need to make the time to build an emotional bond with each of their children. Levine agrees, "It is emotional closeness, maternal warmth in particular, that is as close as we get to a silver bullet against psychological impairment."[16] By doing so, parents will be rewarded with their child's emotional well-being and stability—a most important and powerful element essential for a successful parent-child relationship and for their child's lasting success in life.

I have asked many parents of successful families what specific ideas they use to establish and maintain a personal relationship with their children. From the varied answers, I compiled the three most often-repeated suggestions. As you consistently implement these ideas with your children, you may find the following happening in your home: mutual respect and consideration between family members growing, contention diminishing, and your children more responsive to your counsel, particularly in situations where it is most important that they listen to you and heed your advice. Barbara Bush, when addressing a Wellesley College graduating class, said, "Your success as a family, our success as a society, depends not on what happens at the White House, but on what happens inside your house." With that in mind, consider these relationship-building ideas that can change a struggling relationship into a strong parent-child bond, and how you can implement them into your family.

Date Nights

Once a month, take each one of your children on his or her own "Date Night." This does not have to be an expensive activity. It can be as simple as playing at a park, going on a walk or hike, visiting the library or a bookstore, or going to the ice cream store. The main purpose is to have one-on-one time with your child and to interact and have fun with him away from his other siblings or other stresses of life. Date nights communicate to your child that he is important enough to have special time alone with his parent or parents. One important rule to remember is no criticism or preaching. Do not bring up issues that are sensitive—grades, homework, sports performance, not practicing a musical instrument, or any other subject that can create negative feelings and ruin the atmosphere of the date. The most important goal is to have fun, laugh, enjoy one another's company, and experience open communication. Be sure to put all the date nights on the family calendar by the first day of the month; if not, the month slips away before you know it. If you do not have a family calendar, this may be a good time to purchase one and keep family activities scheduled and organized.

Family Night

Each week, set aside a specific day and time for the purpose of spending one hour together as a family. Make it the same day and time each week, so members of the family can plan for it on their schedules. Do not allow any other activities to interfere. Our family nights always began with plugging in everyone's weekly activities on the calendar, which helped keep everyone organized. Other possible suggestions on what to do during the month include:

- WEEK ONE, RELIGION OR SPIRITUAL NIGHT: Share and discuss with your children your religious or spiritual beliefs. It is important for them to know what you believe and why. Also, make certain that your beliefs match your behavior, or your child will see your deceit. Spending time at church, synagogue, or mosque listening to sermons about loving your neighbor and then coming home and criticizing and gossiping about neighbors and people that do not meet your moral criteria is nothing more than hypocrisy. The same holds true for parents who advocate personal spirituality, but are involved in the same double-standard behaviors. Example is everything, and if your children see you as a hypocrite, they will not trust what you say. Religious and spiritual training also brings a sense of hope to children, which gives them comfort amid difficulties. Martin Seligman, a psychologist at the University of Pennsylvania, said, "For the last thirty or forty years, we've seen the ascendance of individualism and a waning of larger beliefs in religion, and in support from the community and extended family. That means a loss of resources that can buffer you against setbacks and failures. To the extent you see a failure as something that is lasting and which you magnify to taint everything in your life, you are prone to let a momentary defeat become a lasting source of hopelessness. But if you have a larger perspective, like a belief in God and an afterlife, and you lose your job, it's just a temporary defeat."[17] Clearly, a spiritual or religious foundation creates feelings of stability amid challenges.

This may also be a good time to formulate a family mission statement, design a family flag, write a family cheer, motto, or newsletter, make family goals, and plan family vacations.

- WEEK TWO, GAME NIGHT: Bring out your collection of board games, and for the next hour play as many different games as possible. Board games are fun, require social interaction, and build thinking skills (especially chess). Games are such a fun way for families to interact that some schools have opened up the cafeteria for families to come and play games together in the evening. Years ago, Michele Clayton, a third-grade teacher at Leland Elementary in San Pedro, California, started a family night because "we need to play together—inside, outside, and upside-down!...The more involved parents are, the more successful children are...They have better verbal skills, they learn quicker, and they cooperate better with other people." She believed that many of these skills can be developed through playing games, so each week at Leland Elementary, eighty families filled the school cafeteria to plan games together.[18] School game nights are becoming popular, and there is now a website that will give you tips and instructions on how to make this happen. Peggy Epstein writes that a school game night can provide an evening of fun for parents, teachers, and students, and that the goal is to promote positive interaction between the kids and their parents. It also gives parents a chance meet the parents of their children's classmates.[19] (Check out this website for more information: http://www.ehow.com/how_5675401_plan-school-game-night.html.)

- WEEK THREE, CULTURAL NIGHT: Use this night to expose your children to the vast elements of culture: music, art, literature, history, and government. This is a great time to incorporate the musical ideas discussed in this book—attend a musical concert; study the lives of composers; listen to a symphony, sonata, or concerto; or compose a family song. Visit an art or science museum, paint a still-life, or draw a caricature of each family member. Read a book, write poetry, or compose a short story together; or write them individually and then share them with each other. Take the opportunity to learn about other cultures. Study another country, and assign each family member to research an interesting fact about the country. One person can draw the country's flag; one can relate some intriguing facts about the people—their customs, music, and food. Another child can plan an imaginary trip complete with cost and itinerary. Invite a family or individual from another country to come to your home and share their customs with your family. Afterward, serve a dessert from that country. Make the world come alive for your children with these hands-on activities and turn learning into a family affair. If feasible, plan a trip to visit the countries you study.

- WEEK FOUR, SPORT NIGHT: Exercise is good for the body and the brain. In our obesity-laden society, it is important to teach children the importance of good eating habits and regular exercise. Invite other families, and meet at the local park for a game of baseball, flag football, or basketball. Take the family ice skating, sleigh riding, bowling, miniature golfing, billiard playing, swimming at the beach, or hiking in the mountains. At home, teach your children some old-fashioned games: tag, jacks, hide-'n'-go-seek, or one of the newer games, stacking cups, and do not forget that it is always fun to attend a professional sporting event.

- WEEK FIVE, FAMILY SERVICE PROJECTS: In many states across the nation, high school seniors are required to give a certain number of hours of community service before they graduate. Many of the students have commented on their life-changing experiences as a result of unselfish giving. When children take opportunities to give of themselves, their time, talents, or even their finances, they learn early in life that lasting happiness comes when we give to others. A religious leader was asked by a mother, "What is the most important thing I can teach my children?" He replied, "Teach them to deny themselves." This is sage advice considering most of the problems with teens, in marriages, and in the world are rooted in self-centered behavior.

Many presidents throughout the ages have talked about how volunteerism has made our country great and how it strengthens communities and enriches lives. Families can strengthen their local communities and improve their own lives as they voluntarily give service in their neighborhoods. Choose those activities that are appropriate with the ages of your children. For instance, when your children are young, make goodies for a neighbor or someone with special needs, and drop them off anonymously on their porch. Write notes and letters, or have your children draw pictures for someone who is lonely. As they get older, take them to a hospital, a retirement home, or assisted living facility to visit people unable to leave their surroundings. Volunteer at an animal shelter and help groom and care for the animals. Join other families and give musical performances for the elderly around the holidays

Families can strengthen their local communities and improve their own lives as they voluntarily give service in their neighborhoods.

or for other occasions throughout the year. Go to a local park or community facility and pick up garbage and debris. Mow an elderly neighbor's lawn or shovel snow. Offer to babysit free of charge for a young mother in need. Heifer International is an excellent organization for individuals and families to give of their time and resources. One year for Christmas, instead of giving our children more "things," we had them pick animals they wanted to give to families of other countries through Heifer International. A wonderful children's book that explains the success of this program is *Beatrice's Goat*, by Page McBrier.

Teach your children to give service within the family unit as well. They need chores and responsibilities that are not tied to an allowance because it is important for them to do their part as a contributing member of the family. Check your local newspapers for additional ideas for service projects in your community. Youth Service America is a wonderful organization that offers thousands of volunteer opportunities for young and old alike. Check out their website at www.SERVEnet.org. By entering your zip code, you can find organizations in your area that are looking for help. There are also many books that give ideas for service projects. One of my favorites is *The Spirit of Service*, with various contributing writers. It is important to remember that giving of oneself is *never* convenient—sacrifice is a big part of service—so, if you are waiting for the perfect time to fit service into your schedule, it will never happen.

Other families have adopted family nights with slightly different agendas and goals but with the same results: increased communication and stronger child-parent relationships. For instance, the Starr family of Hidden Springs, Idaho, has a weekly family night based on a program used in the business world called agile development, which includes working as teams, daily progress sessions, and weekly reviews. The central focus of agile development is accountability. For the Starrs, this means having a morning checklist of chores that each of their four children is responsible for. It also means the family works together for common goals, such as more efficient conflict resolution, time-shifting meals, and flexibility. At their weekly family night they discuss three questions: 1) What went well in our family this week? 2) What didn't go well? 3) What will we agree to work on this week? Each family member gives input and ideas and solutions are voted on.

The goal: work together to improve the following week. David and Eleanor Starr explains that their family has experienced "increased communication, improved productivity, [and] lowered stress, and [it] made everyone much happier to be part of the family team."[20]

A weekly family night will bond children and parents to one another and give children a heightened sense of belonging, security, and self-worth. The gains are so great that it is worth any sacrifice to make it happen.

Personal Interviews

Each week set aside a specific day and time to have a personal interview with your child. Parent-child interviews are a very powerful way to strengthen your relationship with your child because they give you an opportunity to actively and compassionately listen to their concerns, worries, how school is progressing, and their friendships; understand their feelings; and lovingly teach and counsel when necessary. It is a perfect time for parents to help the child set goals. For your child to feel comfortable to freely discuss any problems, fears, concerns, or experiences, this time together must be void of damaging criticism. But it is also an appropriate time to discuss behavioral issues that need changing and topics that require the child to choose another course of action than the one she is pursuing. When we had to discuss a difficult or controversial issue with our children, we prefaced the conversation by telling them we needed to talk about the "hard sayings." This way, they immediately knew we would be discussing a topic requiring a possible change of behavior.

Interviews also provide an excellent opportunity to teach children how to problem solve. Challenges and hardships happen to everyone, and children need parents to show them how to recognize, confront and overcome problems. In the process, children will learn that challenges are stepping stones to growth, rather than stumbling blocks, and are necessary if they want to become independent, confident adults. Since every problem requires making decisions and weighing options, we taught our children this simple exercise. Take a piece of paper, fold it in half, at the top of one side write "Pros," and on the other side write "Cons." Then have your child write down on the "Pro" side all the positive reasons for doing a particular action, and on the other side write down all the negative reasons for doing the same action. The key to this exercise is taking the time to go through the process of writing down each reason. Why? Because the choices will be more clear. The consequences will be clearer. And they will make more responsible decisions. Although this seems ridiculously simple, it is very powerful and can apply to many situations young people face, such as issues with family, friends, school, drugs, alcohol, college, a career, a job, a future companion, and so on. Or it can be as simple as deciding whether or not to practice a musical instrument. Will they still make mistakes along the way? Absolutely! And they will learn from the consequences.

When our son Ryan applied to doctorate programs in English, he carefully evaluated each school and its program and applied accordingly. He was accepted into four universities, two of which were Vanderbilt University and the University of Missouri at Columbia. Everyone in the family assumed that since Vanderbilt was rated as a top-ten school for English and was offering him more fellowship money, it would be a slam-dunk decision. Surprisingly it was not. Ryan went through the exercise above, which allowed him to carefully weigh the pros and cons of each school and its surrounding community. Neither did he consider it a strictly personal decision—his wife and children were also part of the quotient. He was concerned about the well-being of the *family*. After careful soul searching with himself and his wife, he accepted the offer in Missouri. He has never been happier. Ryan was young when we taught him this exercise, and it is still working for him as an adult.

Interviews are also a good time to express your love to your child. To reinforce this, every few months give your child a paper that answers the following statements: "I Love You Because," "I Like You Because," "I Admire You Because," "I Have Fun with You When," "I Respect You Because," and "I Find You Humorous Because." Try to make goals for the week—including those areas where both child and parent can improve. Use this time to teach your child basic principles on how to live meaningful lives so that their decisions in life will be based on these principles and not on circumstances. (Remember the example of Yo-Yo Ma's father, who wanted his children to be good people first and musicians second.) Most importantly, take the time to apologize to your child for any behavior you regretted during the week. Doing this simple act conveys to the child that even Mom and Dad make mistakes, and no one is too big to say "I'm sorry!"

Some people have said to me, "Why do I have to have a formal weekly interview with my child—I'm available to talk to him anytime—what's the big deal about a set time?" It is true that we should be available to talk to our children at any given time, but think about this: every child, like every adult, communicates differently. Some children are very open and bold, other children are more quiet and shy, and other children are somewhere in between. It is during this set interview time where communication differences emerge, where personality differences surface, and where parents can observe and seek to understand these differences and the best ways to reach their child. Strong and open communication between people does not just happen—it has to be planned for and worked at. (Think marriage.) We found these interviews became the catalyst for developing an open communication and a strong emotional bond that flowed into our weekly interactions with them.

> *It is during this set interview time where communication differences emerge, where personality differences surface, and where parents can observe and seek to understand these differences and the best ways to reach their child.*

As you conduct these weekly interviews, you will become in tune with your children as they confide and express their innermost feelings. Opportunities to teach will arise naturally as you encourage your child to share his or her experiences. It will amaze you how open and receptive he or she will be to your counsel and advice. Noted author and psychologist M. Scott Peck wrote this regarding the far-reaching influence a parent has when he or she takes the time to communicate with his or her child: "The parents who devote time to their children even when it is not demanded by glaring misdeeds will perceive in them subtle needs for discipline, to which they will respond with gentle urging or reprimand or structure or praise, administered with thoughtfulness and care. They will observe how their children eat cake, how they study, when they tell subtle falsehoods, when they run away from problems rather than face them. They will take the time to make these minor corrections and adjustments, listening to their children, responding to them, tightening a little here, loosening a little there, giving them little hugs and kisses, little admonishments, little pats on the back."[21]

We started interviews with our children in 1980 after attending a local lecture. The speaker and his wife had conducted personal interviews with their children for many years and shared how, as a result, they had not only established strong bonds of love and trust with each child, but when serious situations arose, their children listened to parental advice, even as teenagers. Years later, we had an opportunity to put this to the test with our own son.

Our son was a typical sixteen year-old. When his teenage friends began to pursue what we felt was a self-destructive path, we decided to intervene. We talked to our son about the choices he was making, his responsibilities, and the consequences involved. We stressed that while some choices may seem harmless, even insignificant, they can have far-reaching and often unanticipated effects. At the same time, my husband and I told him that, ultimately, the choice was his, but so were the consequences.

As is often the case, the situation proved to be a difficult and stressful balancing act. On the one hand, as parents, there is the urge to forcefully compel our children to act in accordance with our desires—to mandate obedience to parental authority. On the other hand, a contrasting impulse to allow our children to make their own choices. There is no easy solution. The former risks alienating our children into an emotional state of arrested development, while the latter opens the door for our children to make ill-advised decisions replete with potentially devastating consequences. It is easy to demand obedience and deny our children agency. However, if children are not allowed to make choices and suffer consequences, they will very likely become submissive, dependent, and weak-willed adults, incapable of necessary problem-solving skills to navigate the harsh realities of society.

For six months, we watched the situation get worse with our teenage son. During this time we maintained an open line of communication. At one particular interview, we asked him if he would be willing to give up these friends and find new ones. It was not an easy request. These were his lifelong friends and the basis of his social life. What we were asking seemed unfair, but we felt it necessary for his long-term wellbeing. With great difficulty, he eventually made the break. Some people might say we were lucky, but I believe luck had nothing to do with it. Interviews work. They work for you as a parent, and they work for the child. Interviews give you a time to *analyze* your present parenting goals, to *discover* new and better ways to approach each individual child, and to *change* and *refine* your methods of parenting to complement the uniqueness of each of your children. I can say with certainty that if you consistently, week after week, interview your children with love and kindness, when the day comes that they need to listen to you on important, life-threatening issues—they will.

The formula for starting musical traditions in your home includes: a compass to give direction, a map to guide the way, and a plan to make it all happen.

The formula for starting musical traditions in your home includes: a *compass* to give direction, a *map* to guide the way, and a *plan* to make it all happen. The pages of this book have given you the compass—you now know and understand the powerful direction music can make in your child's life. You have the map—practical ideas, suggestions, and examples to guide you in this endeavor. And you have the plan to make this all happen—the ideas to use to mold and shape a relationship between you and your child. This formula will ensure success in making music a strong force in your home and in the lives of each family member, and, by doing so, you will be a part of making classical music, in all its beauty, a tradition in our nation and a legacy for future generations.

ℛESOURCES

Classical Music for Your Children to Enjoy

In choosing classical music for young children, choose orchestral works over single-instrument selections and fast, lively, entertaining pieces over slow, sedative music. There are hundreds of wonderful classical pieces of music that your children will enjoy, but when introducing them to a symphony, play the movement that is livelier first. This method of exposure will draw them into the music and get them excited about what they are hearing. After they are familiar with the lively movement, introduce them to the entire score.

The following is a list of classical music geared specifically for children. There are also websites that will allow you to preview the music before purchasing it. By doing so, your family can hear and experience the music first, before deciding which ones to purchase for your collection.

JOHANN SEBASTIAN BACH

Brandenberg Concerto no. 2, third movement
Brandenberg Concerto no. 4, first movement
Keyboard Concerto in D Minor, 1052 (Schieff, pianist)
Fugue in G Minor, "The Little"
Gavotte
Cantata no. 147, choral prelude: "Jesu, Joy of Man's Desiring"
Suite no. 2 in B Minor for Flute and Strings
Rondeau
Toccata and Fugue in D Minor
The Passion of St Matthew, final chorus

LUDWIG VAN BEETHOVEN

"Fur Elise"
Symphony no.1, third movement
Symphony no. 5, first movement
Symphony no. 6 in F, op. 68, first movement ("Pastorale Symphony")
(You can also see the first movement of this symphony performed on Walt
Disney's *Fantasia.*)
Symphony no. 9 in D Minor, op. 125, "Choral," second and fourth
movements ("Ode to Joy")
Violin Concerto in D, last movement

HECTOR BERLIOZ

"March to the Scaffold" from *Symphonie Fantastique*, op. 14
"Dream of the Witches Sabbath" from *Symphonie Fantastique*, op. 14
"Damnation of Faust," op. 24 ("Rakoczy March")
Roman Carnival Overture

Georges Bizet

L'Arlesienne Suite no. 2—Carillon, Farandole, Minuetto
Carmen, Prelude, Act I, Entr'acte III
Children's Games
"Soap Bubbles"
"The Top"
"Toreadors" (from *Carmen*)

Johannes Brahms

Hungarian Dance no. 5 in G Minor
Cradle Song
Concerto for Violin and Cello, last movement
Symphony no. 4, third movement

Benjamin Britten

The Young Person's Guide to the Orchestra
Simple Symphony, "Playful Pizzicato"
Serenade, Prologue

Frédéric Chopin

Waltz, op. 64, no. 1, "Minute Waltz"
Prelude in C-Sharp Minor, op. 28, no. 10
Polonaise in A Major, op. 40, no. 1
"Raindrop Prelude"
Nocturne in E-Flat, op. 9

AARON COPLAND

Rodeo, "Hoedown"
The Red Pony
Old American Songs
Appalachian Spring, "Variations on Simple Gifts"
Billy the Kid, "Street in a Frontier Town"
Symphony no. 3, "Fanfare for the Common Man"

CLAUDE DEBUSSY

Children's Corner Suite: "Jimbo's Lullaby," "Golliwog's Cakewalk," "The Snow is Dancing"
Gardens in the Rain
Pagodes
La Mer, "Play of the Waves," "Dialogue of the Wind and the Sea"
"Clair de Lune" from *Suite Bergamasque*
Preludes, Book 1, Voiles

ANTONIN DVOŘÁK

Slavonic Dance, op. 46, no. 1, and no. 8 in G Minor
Humoresque, op. 101
Symphony no. 9, (*New World Symphony*), third movement
Symphony no. 6, third movement

SIR EDWARD ELGAR

Enigma Variations—Nimrod
Pomp and Circumstance, March no. 1

GABRIEL FAURÉ

Dolly Suite, "Berceuse"
Pavane

CHARLES GOUNOD

Faust, "Soldier's Chorus"
"Funeral March of a Marionette"

EDVARD GRIEG

Peer Gynt Suite no. 1: "Anitra's Dance"
Peer Gynt Suite no. 1: "Morning"
Peer Gynt Suite no. 1: "Ase's Death"
Peer Gynt Suite no. 1: "In the Hall of the Mountain King"

FERDE GROFE

Grand Canyon Suite, "On the Trail"
Grand Canyon Suite, "Cloudburst"
Death Valley Suite, "Desert Water Hole"

GEORGE FRIDERIC HANDEL

Water Music, Alla Hornpipe
Music for the Royal Fireworks
Xerxes, Largo
Solomon, "Arrival of the Queen of Sheba"
Messiah, "Hallelujah Chorus"

JOSEPH HAYDN

Symphony no. 45, "Farewell," last movement
Symphony no. 94, "Surprise," second movement
Trumpet Concerto in E-Flat Major, finale
Cello Concerto no. 2 in D Major, last movement
String Quartet in C, "Emperor's Hymn"

GUSTAV HOLST

The Planets, "Mars," "Jupiter"

ENGELBERT HUMPERDINCK

Hansel and Gretel, "Brother, Come and Dance with Me," "Nibble, Nibble, Mousekin," "Prayer,"
"Prelude," "Susie, Little Susie," "Tra-la-la"

ZOLTÁN KODÁLY

Hary Janos Suite, "The Viennese Musical Clock"

FRANZ LISZT

Hungarian Rhapsody no. *2*

FELIX MENDELSSOHN

A Midsummer Night's Dream, "Scherzo," "Wedding March"
Symphony no. 4, "Italian,"
Spring Song

WOLFGANG AMADEUS MOZART

Symphony no. 40, first movement
Symphony no. 41, "Jupiter"
Eine Kleine Nachtmusik (*A Little Night Music*)
Horn Concerto no. 4, last movement
Clarinet Concerto in A Major, last movement
Quintet for Clarinet and Strings in A Major, first and fourth movement
Rondo alla Turca
The Sleigh Ride
Magic Flute
The Marriage of Figaro, overture

MODEST MUSSORGSKY

Night on Bald Mountain
Pictures at an Exhibition: "Ballet of the Unhatched Chicks," "Promenade,"
"The Old Castle"

JACQUES OFFENBACH

Tales of Hoffman, Barcarolle

JOHANN PACHELBEL

Canon in D

NICCOLÒ PAGANINI

Perpetual Motion

SERGEI PROKOFIEV

Peter and the Wolf
Lieutenant Kije Suite, "The Birth or Kije," "The Wedding of Kije," "Troika"
Summer Day Suite, march
Love for Three Oranges, march
Classical Symphony, first movement
Classical Symphony, Gavotta
Romeo and Juliet, ballet suite

GIACOMO PUCCINI

Madam Butterfly, Un bel di Vedremo
Turandot, "Nessun Dorma"

MAURICE RAVEL

Mother Goose Suite: "Conversations of Beauty and the Beast," "Laideronette,"
"Empress of the Pagodas"
String Quartet in F, last movement
Bolero
Le Tombeau de Couperin, minuet

Ottorino Respighi

The Birds, Preludio
The Pines of Rome, last movement

Nicholas Rimsky-Korsakov

The Tale of Tsar Sultan, "Flight of the Bumblebee"
Scheherazade, first movement
Russian Easter Overture
Mlada, Cortege

Gioacchino Rossini

Barber of Seville, Largo al factotum
Barber of Seville, overture, *William Tell Overture*
The Thieving Magpie Overture

Camille Saint-Saëns

Carnival of the Animals

Franz Schubert

Symphony no. 8, "Unfinished," first movement
Symphony no. 9, "The Great," third movement
The Erlking
March Militaire no. 1
Piano Sonata in A, Rondo
Trout Quintet

ROBERT SCHUMANN

Album for the Young, Book 1: "The Happy Farmer," "Soldier's March"
Album for the Young, "The Wild Horseman"
Scenes from Childhood

DMITRI SHOSTAKOVICH

The Gadfly

JEAN SIBELIUS

Finlandia

BEDRICH SMETANA

Dance of the Comedians
The Bartered Bride Overture

JOHN PHILIP SOUSA

"The Thunderer March"
"Semper Fidelis"
"The Liberty Bell"
"Washington Post"
"The Stars and Stripes Forever"

Johann Strauss

"Radetzky March"
"Tritsch Tratsch Polka"
"The Blue Danube"
"Wine, Woman, and Song"

Richard Strauss

Also Sprach Zarathustra
"Vienna Blood Waltz"
Till Eulenspiegel's "Merry Pranks"

Igor Stravinsky

The Firebird, "Berceuse," "Infernal Dance"
Petrushka, "Coachmen's Dance," "Russian Dance"
Pulcinella Suite, "Tarantella"
Rite of Spring (This is on Walt Disney's *Fantasia*)

Peter Ilyich Tchaikovsky

The Nutcracker
1812 Overture
Sleeping Beauty
Romeo & Juliet, overture
Swan Lake
Serenade for Strings in C Major
Symphony no. 4, fourth movement
Symphony no. 6, "Pathetique," third movement
Violin Concerto, third movement

GIUSEPPE VERDI

Il Trovatore, "Anvil Chorus"
Rigoletto, "La Donna e Mobile"
Rigoletto, "Questa o quella"
La Traviata, "Libiamo ne'lieti"

HEITOR VILLA-LOBOS

Bachianas Brasileiras no. 2, "The Little Train of the Caipira"

ANTONIO VIVALDI

The Four Seasons
Concerto for Guitar D Major
Concerto in C for Two Trumpets
Oboe Concerto in D Minor, first and third movement

RICHARD WAGNER

The Flying Dutchman Overture
Die Walkure, "Ride of the Valkyries"
The Mastersinger Overture
Tannhauser, overture, "Arrival of the Guests at Wartburg"
Lohengrin, prelude

Favorite Classical Lullabies to Play for Your Unborn and Newborn (CDs, MP3 Downloads)

Baby Needs Lullabies (Delos Records)

Bach at Bedtime: Lullabies for the Still of the Night (Philips)

Bach for Babies: Fun and Games for Budding Brains (Philips)

Bedtime Mozart: Classical Lullabies for Babies (Classical Lullabies)

Beethoven at Bedtime: A Gentle Prelude to Sleep (Philips)

Billboard Presents Family Lullaby Classics (Rhino Records)

Brahms at Bedtime: A Sleepytime Serenade (Philips)

Celtic Baby Lullabies (only available as an MP3 download)

Daydreams and Lullabies (BMG Music)

Goodnight Guitar: Classic Guitar Lullabies (Penney)

Kids Classical Music: Baby Dreams Vol. 1 (Marken Sound Records)

Kids Classics: Lullabies (EMI Classics)

Mozart for Mothers-to-Be, Tender Lullabies for Mother and Child (Philips)

Mozart for Meditation: Quiet Music for Quiet Times (Philips)

Perchance to Dream (Delos), features pianist Carol Rosenberger

UltraSound: Music for the Unborn Child (BMG)

Musical Stories about Composers (CDs and MP3 Downloads)

"Classical Kids"—This is a wonderful series for children. It weaves enchanting stories with real drama and superb music from the lives of the composers. (Appropriate for children preschool to grade six.) The titles include:

Beethoven Lives Upstairs (also available as a DVD)

Mr. Bach Comes to Call

Mozart's Magic Fantasy

Vivaldi's Ring of Mystery

Hallelujuh Handel

Tchaikovsky in America

Mozart's Magnificent Voyage

Classical Kids Christmas

Another worthwhile series about music and composers is:

"Music Masters CD Series: *The Stories of the Composers in Words and Music*"

Each one-hour CD features thirty minutes of engaging narration of the composer's life and thirty minutes of music only. The series includes composers from the baroque, classical, romantic, and twentieth century. They are lively and entertaining and are a perfect way for children to become familiar with the composers and their music. Each CD comes with a six-page booklet with program notes, additional reading, and audio references. These can be purchased at Music in Motion, 1-800-445-0649. I played these for my own children for many years, and I highly recommend them.

Excellent Classical Titles for Children (CDs and MP3 Downloads)

Baby Dance (Warner Brothers)

Baby Needs Series (Delos)—series includes *Baby Needs Baroque, Baby Needs Bach, Baby Needs Beethoven, Baby Needs Brahms, Baby Needs More Mozart, Baby Needs Tchaikovsky*

Beethoven For Babies, Brain Training for Little Ones (Philips)

Beethoven's Wig: Sing Along Symphonies (Rounder/Umgd)—four different volumes available

Bibbidi-Bobbidi! Bach—Favorite Tunes in the Style of Great Classical Composers (Delos)

Child's Celebration of Classical Music (Music for Little People)—includes narrations by Meryl Streep, Carol Channing, Danny Kaye, and Bobby McFerrin.

25 Children's Favorites (Vox)

Classical Child Series (Metro Music, Sophia Sounds)—series includes *Classical Child is Born, Classical Child Dreams, Classical Child at Play, Classical Child at the Ballet, Classical Child at the Opera,* and *The Classical Child Early to Bed.*

Classical Dreams for Kids (Rhino Flashback)

Classical Zoo (Telarc Release). Itzhak Perlman narrates these new poems for *Carnival of the Animals* and Respighi's *The Birds.*

Classics for Children (BMG Classics). The Boston Pops with Arthur Fiedler conducting. This wonderful CD has Saint-Saëns's *Carnival of the Animals,* as well as Benjamin Britten's *YoungPerson's Guide to the Orchestra* and several other great pieces of children's music, and is a *must* for your family collection.

Classics for Kids, Boston Pops (BMG Classics). A wonderful variety of classical music for children on one CD, including Ravel's *Mother Goose Suite,* Bizet's *Childhood Games,* Schumann's *Dreams.*

Fiedler's Favorite Marches (RCA)

G'night Wolfgang (Music for Little People)

Heigh-Ho! Mozart—Favorite Tunes in the Style of Great Classical Composers (Delos)

Jazz-A-Ma-Tazz (Baby Boom). A wonderful jazz series for children.

Moving with Mozart (Kimbo Educational). Perfect for children ages three to seven. Combines music and movement to the music of Mozart.

Mozart for your Mind and *More Mozart for your Mind* (Philips Classics). Great music to listen to while studying.

Mozart TV Favorite TV tunes in the style of great classical composers (Delos)

My Favorite Opera for Children: Pavarotti's Opera Made Easy (London). This is an excellent CD to introduce your child to the exciting world of opera.

Peter and the Wolf (Sony). The Boston Symphony Orchestra with narrator Melissa Joan Hart. This is a delightfully fresh version of not only *Peter and the Wolf*, but also *Carnival of the Animals* and *The Young Person's Guide to the Orchestra*.

Peter and the Wolf is offered in a number of CDs and narrated by various people, including Sting, Patrick Stewart, David Bowie, Ben Kingsley, Boris Karloff, and Itzhak Perlman.

Piano Rags: Scott Joplin/George Gershwin (Quintessence)

Power Classics (RCA Records). A variety of artists and music styles.

The Mozart Effect: Music for Children (Children's Group)

The Power of Classical Music (Twin Sisters). Classical music perfect for naptime, playtime, or travel time.

The World's Very Best Opera for Kids...in English! (Children's Group)

This is My Country (RCA). Wonderful selections of patriotic classical music, including Copland's *Fanfare for the Common Man*, Grofe's *Grand Canyon Suite*, and Gershwin's *Strike Up the Band*.

Thunderous Classics (Vox). The ultimate in bombastic music.

Music to Study By

Most of the following selections are suggested by Dr. Georgi Lozanov, who found that music aids in the absorption, retention, and retrieval of information (see chapter 2).

JOHANN SEBASTIAN BACH

Brandenburg Concertos
Fantasy for Organ in G Major
Fantasy in C Minor
Prelude and Fugue in G Major
Organ Fugue in E Flat Major

Ludwig van Beethoven

Emperor Concerto for Piano, no. 5
Violin Concerto in D

Johannes Brahms

Concerto for Violin, D Major, op. 77

Archangelo Corelli

Concerti Grossi, op. 2, 4, 5, 8, 10, 11, 12

George Frideric Handel

Water Music
Concerto for Organ in B Flat Major, op. 7, 6

Joseph Haydn

Concerto no. 1 for Violin
Concerto no. 2 for Violin
Symphony no. 101, *The Clock*
Symphony no. 94 in G Major

Wolfgang Amadeus Mozart

Mozart for Your Mind (This CD contains the Piano Concerto in D used in the University of California, Irvine, study to enhance spatial-temporal reasoning.)

Concerto for Piano no. 18 in B Flat Major
Concerto for Piano no. 23 in A Major
Concerto for Violin no. 5 in A Major
Symphony in A Major
Symphony no. 40 in G Minor
Symphony no. 35 in D Major, "Haffner"
Symphony in D Major, Prague

PETER ILYICH TCHAIKOVSKY

Concerto for Violin, op. 35
Concerto for Piano, no. 1

ANTONIO VIVALDI

The Four Seasons, no. 8

Reinforcing Your Child's School Experience

Below is a list of twelve different subjects. When your child studies these subjects in school, reinforce his or her learning at home by playing the classical music and using the books listed. (The books are geared for preschool through elementary.) For instance, if he or she is studying bees, Rimsky-Korsakov's *Flight of the Bumblebee* is a perfect piece to get his or her imagination visualizing a bee buzzing.

   If he or she is studying animals, play Saint-Saëns's *Carnival of the Animals*. As you play this music, have your child try to guess which of the thirteen animals is being musically described. If he or she is studying planets or the universe, Gustav Holst's *The Planets* will get your child's mind soaring through space. When introducing the music, have your child follow these four steps:

first, *listen* to the music; second, use rhythm instruments to *beat out* the rhythm; third, *dance* or move to the music; and fourth, *draw* what you hear.

Animals

Music

Carnival of the Animals (Saint-Saëns)
Animal Planet Presents: Sing With the Animals (use Raffi's "Old McDonald Had a Band")
Trout, Quintet (Schubert)
The Birds (Respighi)

Books

Carnival of the Animals, by Jack Prelutsky (book and CD)
Brown Bear, Brown Bear; and *Polar Bear, Polar Bear*, by Bill Martin
Why Mosquitoes Buzz in People's Ears: A West African Tale, by Verna Aardema
Wild About Books, by Judy Sierra
Old McDonald Had a Farm, by Kathi Ember
Barnyard Dance, by Sandra Boynton

Insects/Bees/Ants

Music

Flight of the Bumblebee (Rimsky-Korsakov)
Perpetual Motion (Paganini)
Minute Waltz (Chopin)
Moto Perpetuum (Johann Strauss, Jr.)

Books

Buzz, Said the Bee, by Wendy C. Lewison
The Tale of the Tsar Sultan, by Alexander Pushkin
Insectlopedia, by Douglas Florian

TRAINS

Music

"Little Train of the Caipira" with Villa Lobos, on *Bachiana Brasileira* no. 2.
All Aboard, by John Denver. Use this nonclassical CD for compare/contrast.
Mostly Railroad Music, by Eldon Rathburn (Crystal Records). Uses the calliope.

Books

Freight Train, by Donald Crews
The Little Engine that Could, by Watty Piper
Polar Express, by Chris Van Allsburg

WEATHER/STORMS

Music

Pastoral Symphony no. 6 in F, op. 68 (Beethoven)
Thunder and Lightening Polka (Johann Strauss)
Grand Canyon: "Cloudburst" (Grofe)
Appalachian Spring (Copland)

"Hall of the Mountain King" (Grieg)
"The Thunderer March" (Sousa)
"March to the Scaffold" from *Symphonie Fantastique*, op. 14 (Berlioz)
Damnation of Faust, op. 24 ("Rakoczy March") (Berlioz)
Mlada, Cortege (Rimsky-Korsakov)

Books

Cloudy With a Chance of Meatballs, by Judi Barrett
Rainbabies, by Laura Krauss Melmed
Nimby, by Jasper Tomkins

SEASONS

Music

The Four Seasons (Vivaldi)
Spring Song (Mendelssohn)
Sleigh Ride (Mozart)
"Snow is Dancing" (Debussy)

Books

The Weather (My First Discoveries), by Sarah Matthews
Oh Say Can You Say What's the Weather Today? All about Weather, by Tish Rabe
Flash, Crash, Rumble, and Roll, by Franklyn M. Branley
The Cloud Book, by Tomie DePaola

Nature

Music

"Morning Song" from *Peer Gynt* (Grieg)
Raindrop Prelude (Chopin)
"Snow is Dancing" (Debussy, from *The Children's Corner Suite*)
Spring Song (Mendelssohn)
Symphony no. 6, in F, op. 68 *(Pastorale Symphony)* (Beethoven)
Gardens in the Rain (Debussy)
Also Sprach Zarathustra (Strauss). This is great music to conjure images of sunrise.

Books

Rainbabies, by Laura Krauss Melmed
I Love Dirt! 52 Activities to Help You and Your Kids Discover the Wonders of Nature, by Jennifer Ward
Fun with Nature: Take Along Guide, by Mel Boring, Diane Burne, and Leslie Dendy
Swirl by Swirl: Spirals in Nature, by Joyce Sidman

Sea/Sky/Moon

Music

La Mer (sea) (Debussy)
Clair de Lune (moon) (Debussy)
Calm Sea (Mendelssohn)
Trout, Quintet (Schubert)
Pachelbel Canon with Ocean Sounds (Real Music)

Books

Grandfather Twilight, by Barbara Berger
Goodnight Moon, by Margaret Wise Brown
Moongame, by Frank Asch
The Sky is Full of Stars, by Franklyn Branley
Over in the Ocean: In a Coral Reef, by Marianne Berkes

SOLAR SYSTEM/PLANETS/EARTH/CREATION

Music

The Planets (Holst). The music from *Star Wars* is very similar to this.
Rite of Spring (Stravinsky). Featured in Disney's *Fantasia*.

Books

The Magic School Bus Inside the Earth, by Joanna Cole
My First Book about Space, by Dinah Mocke
There's No Place Like Space: All about Our Solar System, by Tish Rabe
Me and My Place in Space, by Joan Sweeney
If You Decide to Go to the Moon, by Faith McNulty, illustrated by Steven Kellogg

COWBOYS/AMERICA/HORSES/WILD WEST

Music

"Hoedown" from *Rodeo* (Copland)
The Red Pony (Copland)
Appalachian Spring, "Variations on Simple Gifts" (Copland)

Billy the Kid, "Street in a Frontier Town" (Copland)
The Wild Horsemen (Schumann)
William Tell Overture (Rossini)
"The Entertainer" (Joplin)
"Sweet and Low Down" (Gershwin)

Books

Pecos Bill, by Steven Kellogg
The Silver Pony, by Lynn Ward
The Toughest Cowboy: or How the Wild West Was Tamed, by John Frank
Why Cowboys Sleep with Their Boots On (*Why Cowboys* series), by Laurie Knowlton
The Gingerbread Cowboy, by Janet Squires

Marches/Fourth of July/America/Patriotism

This music is great to play in the morning while your children are getting ready for school.

Music

"Toreadors" (Bizet)
"Stars and Stripes" (Sousa)
"Grand March" (Verdi)
"Colonel Bogey" (Alford)
"Pomp and Circumstance" (Elgar)
"March of the Toys" (Herbert)
"March of the Soldiers" (Tchaikovsky)
"Funeral March of a Marionette" (Gounod)
March Militaire no. 1 (Schubert)

Books

Where the Wild Things Are, by Maurice Sendak. Great to get up and march to.
The Story of America's Birthday, by Patricia A. Pingry
The Scrambled States of America, by Laurie Keller
America: A Patriotic Primer, by Lynne Cheney
If America Were a Village: A Book about the People of the United States, by David J. Smith

HOLIDAYS/HALLOWEEN

Music

Danse Macabre (Saint-Saëns). Part of the CD *Bernstein Conducts for Young People*.
"March to the Scaffold" in *Symphonie Fantastique*, op. 14 (Berlioz)
"The Hut of Baba Yaga" (Mussorgsky, *Pictures at an Exhibition* with Ravel)
Toccata and Fugue in D Minor (Bach)
Hungarian Dance No. 5 in G Minor (Brahms)

Books

It's Halloween, by Jack Prelutsky
Scary Stories to Tell in the Dark, by Alvin Schwartz
The Widow's Broom, by Chris Van Allsburg
The Little Old Lady Who Was Not Afraid of Anything, by Linda Williams

MUSICAL STORIES/OPERA/BALLETS

Music

Peter and the Wolf (Prokofiev)
Peter and the Wolf Play Jazz (Crosse)

The Nutcracker (Tchaikovsky)
The Magic Flute (Mozart)
The Sorcerer's Apprentice (Dukas)
Babes in Toyland (Herbert)
Scheherazade (Rimsky-Korsakov)
Hansel and Gretel (Humperdinck)
Cinderella (Prokofiev)
Peer Gynt Suites (Grieg)
Sleeping Beauty (Tchaikovsky)
Swan Lake (Tchaikovsky)

Books

Sing Me a Story, by Jane Rosenberg
Dance Me a Story, by Jane Rosenberg
The Magic Flute, by Anne Gatti
Babes in Toyland, by Victor Herbert
Swine Lake, by James Marshall and Maurice Sendak
Sergei Prokofiev's Peter and the Wolf (with orchestrated CD), by Janet Schulman

Fiction about Music

A is for Alliguitar: Musical Alphabeasts, by Nancy Raines Day

Abiyoyo, by Pete Seeger

Animal Orchestra, by Nick Sharratt

Bat Boy and His Violin, by Gavin Curtis

Ben Franklin's Glass Armonica, by Bryna Stevens

Ben's Trumpet, by Rachel Isadora

Berlioz the Bear, by Jan Brett

Carnival of the Animals: Classical Music for Kids, by Barrie C. Turner

Carnival of the Animals, by John Lithgow

Ellison the Elephant (with audio CD), by Eric Drachman

Freddie the Frog and the Thump in the Night: 1ˢᵗ Adventure Treble Clef Island, by Sharon Burch

Gobble, Quack, Moon (with audio CD), by Matthew W. Gollub

Hip Cat, by Jonathan London

I Have Another Language: The Language is Dance, by Eleanor Schick

Irving the Frog and His Violin, by Michelle Zwirn

I See A Song, by Eric Carle

Lady Treble and the Seven Notes, by Eliyana Biklou

Lentil, by Robert McCloskey

Little Pig Joins the Band, by David Hyde Costello

Lullabies and Night Songs, by William Engvick

Maestro Mouse and the Mystery of the Missing Baton, by Peter and Cheryl Barnes

Mandy and Brother Wind, by Patricia McKissack

Max Found Two Sticks, by Brian Pinkney

Mole Music, by David McPhail

Moses Goes to a Concert, by Isaac Millman

Nana Hannah's Piano, by Barbara Bottner

Over the Rainbow, by E. Y. Harburg

Song and Dance Man, by Karen Ackerman

The Banza, by Diane Wolkstein

The Carnival of the Animals (book and CD), by Jack Prelutsky

The Ding-Dong Bag, by Polly Peters

The Jazz Fly, by Matthew Gollub

The Maestro Plays, by Bill Martin and Vladimir Radunsky

The Music Teacher from the Black Lagoon, by Mike Thaler

The Remarkable Farkle McBride, by John Lithgow

The Whales' Song, by Dyan Sheldon

This Jazz Man, by Karen Ehrhardt

When Louis Armstrong Taught Me Scat, by Muriel Harris Weinstein

Yolonda's Genius, by Carol Fenner

You Are My Wonders, by Maryann Love

Zin! Zin! Zin! A Violin, by Lloyd Moss

Books about Composers

Bach to Rock: An Introduction to Famous Composers and Their Music, by Rosemary Kennedy

Beethoven for Kids: His Life and Music with 21 Activities, by Helen Bauer

Charlie Parker Played Be Bop, by Chris Raschka

For the Love of Music: The Remarkable Story of Maria Anna Mozart, by Elizabeth Rusch

Gershwin's Rhapsody in Blue, by Anna Harwell Celenza

Getting to Know the World's Greatest Composers, by Mike Venezia

If I Only Had A Horn: Young Louis Armstrong, by Roxane Orgill

Lives of the Musicians: Good Times, Bad Times (And What the Neighbors Thought), by Kathleen Krull

Magic of Mozart, by Ellen Switzer

Pictures at an Exhibition (CD included), by Anna Harwell Celenza

Satchmo's Blues, by Alan Schroeder and Floyd Cooper

Stories of the Great Composers (CD included), by June Montgomery and Maurice Hinson

Who Was Wolfgang Amadeus Mozart? by Yona Zeldis McDonough

Books about Ballet

Dance Me a Story, by Jane Rosenberg

Swine Lake, by James Marshall and Maurice Sendak

Tale of the Firebird, by Gennady Spirin

The Firebird, by Brad Kessler

The Story of the Nutcracker Ballet, by Diane Goode

Books about Opera, Musicals, and Choral Music

Amahl and the Night Visitors, by Gian Carlo Menotti

Bravo! Brava! A Night at the Opera: Behind the Scenes with Composer, Cast, and Crew, by Anne Siberell

Opera Cat, by Tess Weaver

Phantom of the Opera, by Gaston Lerous

Sing Me a Story: Metropolitan Opera's Book of Opera Stories for Children, by Jane Rosenberg

The Magic Flute, by Anne Gatti

The Magic Flute: An Opera by Mozart, by Kyra Teis

Books about Instruments, the Orchestra, and General Music

Can You Hear It?, by William Lach

Do Re Mi: If You Can Read Music, Thank Guido D'Arezzo, by Susan Roth

Kids Can Listen, Kids Can Move! (CD included), by Lyn Kleiner

Kids Make Music! Clapping and Tapping, from Bach to Rock, by Avery Hart, Paul Mantell, and Loretta Trezzo Braren

M Is for Melody: A Music Alphabet, by Kathy-jo Wargin

M Is for Music, by Kathleen Krull

Making Musical Instruments with Kids: 67 Easy Projects for Adults Working with Children, by Bart Hopkin

Meet the Orchestra, by Ann Hayes

Musical Instruments from A to Z (Alphabasics), by Bobbie Kalman

My First Classical Music Book, by Genevieve Helsby

Rhythm Band Instruments BWDG Boomwhackers C Major Diatonic, by Rhythm Band Instruments

101 Rhythm Instrument Activities for Young Children, by Abigail Flesch Connors

Rubber-Band Banjos and Java Jive Bass, by Alex Sabbeth

Story of the Orchestra: Listen While You Learn About the Instruments, the Music and the Composers Who Wrote the Music!, by Robert Levine

The Big Book of Music Games, Grade 1–5, by Debra Olson Pressnall and Lorilee Malecha

The Orchestra, by Mark Rubin

The Philharmonic Gets Dressed, by Karla Kuskin

Those Amazing Musical Instruments! with CD: Your Guide to the Orchestra Through Sounds and Stories, by Genevieve Helsby

Folk Tune Stories

These books, based on folk tunes, are wonderful to use with rhythm instruments. Help your child beat out the sing-song rhythm interwoven in the text.

All God's Critter's Got a Place in the Choir, by Bill Staines

Commotion in the Ocean, by Giles Andreae

Dancing Feet, by Lindsey Craig

Dem Bones, by Bob Barner

Five Little Monkeys Sitting in a Tree, by Eileen Christelow

Going to the Zoo, by Tom Paxton

Hush, Little Baby, by Shari Halpern

I Know a Shy Fellow Who Swallowed a Cello, by Barbara Garriel

I Know an Old Teacher, by Anne Bowen

If You're Happy and You Know It: Jungle Edition, by James Warhola

I'm a Little Teapot, by Iza Trapani

It's Raining, It's Pouring, by Rob Gilbert

Little Drummer Boy, by Jack Keats

Mama Don't Allow, by Thacher Hurd

Mary Wore Her Red Dress and Henry Wore His Green Sneakers, by Merle Peek

Miss Mary Mack, by Mary Ann Hoberman

Old Black Fly, by Jim Aylesworth

Over in the Jungle: A Rainforest Rhyme, by Marianne Berkes

Over the River and Through the Wood, by Lydia Maria Child

Roll Over!, by Merle Peek

Silent Night: The Song from Heaven, by Linda Granfield

Simple Gifts, by Chris Raschka

The Itsy Bitsy Spider, by Iza Trapani

The Marvelous Toy, by Tom Paxton

There Was an Old Lady, by Pam Adams

There Was an Old Lady Who Swallowed a Pie, by Alison Jackson

There Was an Old Lady Who Swallowed a Trout, by Teri Sloat

This Land is Your Land by Woody Guthrie

We're Going on a Lion Hunt, by David Axtell

What a Wonderful World, by George Weiss and Bob Thiele

You Are My Sunshine, by Jimmie Davis

You're Adorable, by Martha Alexander

Classic Music DVDs for Children

The following DVDs can be ordered through Amazon or Music in Motion (1-800-445-0649), or purchased through your local bookstores or music stores.

- *A Young Person's Guide to the Orchestra.* This DVD visually illustrates Benjamin Britten's music by the same title. It focuses on the unique qualities of each instrument and each individual playing it—from the instrument maker who created it to the musicians who creates its sound. The narrator is conductor Andrew Davis, with commentary from Yo-Yo Ma and others.

- *Alice's Adventures in Wonderland Ballet.* The Royal Ballet brings to life Lewis Carroll's popular story. Captivating designs, an engaging and passionate score, and breathtaking choreography combine to produce the best dance adaptation of this children's classic.

- *Amahl and the Night Visitors*, by Menotti. A wonderful opera for children about a crippled boy, Amahl, who is visited by the Three Wise Men en route to Bethlehem.

- *Amazing Music DVDs.* Andrew Litton and the Dallas Symphony bring to children the wonderful world of classical music. The four-part series includes *Emotions in Music* (the expressive power of music), *Pictures in Music* (how music creates images in the mind), *Families* (includes the families of instruments), and *Jazz* (features the Billy Taylor Trio). (Available at Music in Motion.)

- *Beethoven Lives Upstairs.* This story is taken from the *Classical Kids Series.* It is about Beethoven as seen through the eyes of ten-year-old Christoph and includes twenty-five excerpts of Beethoven's most famous works.

- *Behind the Scenes with Julie Taymor!* Taymor is the director of *The Lion King* and creates a visual theater using puppets, masks, and music.

- *Carnival of the Animals. Bugs & Daffy's Carnival: Looney Tunes Golden Collection.* Bugs Bunny and Daffy Duck act as duo pianists and perform *Carnival of the Animals* with a live orchestra. Includes four DVDs.

- *The Composers' Specials.* Includes the life and times of Bach, Bizet, Handel, Liszt, Rossini, and J. Strauss. These are fictionalized episodes based on actual events with examples of the composer's music interwoven throughout the stories.

- *Disney's* Peter and the Wolf/*Make Mine Music.* Includes the famous tale by Prokofiev and other mini classics, including *Willie the Operatic Whale, Mickey Mouse's The Band Concert, Farmyard Symphony*, and more.

- *Elmo's Musical Adventure: The Story of* Peter and the Wolf. The Boston Pops perform *Peter and the Wolf* with friends from Sesame Street posing as the characters. They discover the secret to making beautiful music.

- *Hansel and Gretel: An Opera Fantasy.* This Grammy Award-winning production uses over thirty-five hand-sculpted Kinemen dolls. The story is set to Englebert Humperdinck's 1893 opera and is sung by acclaimed performers. A delightful classic fairytale!

- *Miracle of Mozart.* This Babyscapes video series teaches children ages eighteen months to five years about numbers and shapes using computer graphics and Mozart's music.

- *Nutcracker.* This is the American Ballet Theater version of the Tchaikovsky classic, featuring Mikhail Baryshnikov as the Prince/Nutcracker. It is the traditional story of a girl's dream on Christmas Eve.

- Peter and the Wolf: *A Prokofiev Fantasy.* Narrated by Sting. A hilarious production showing life-sized Spitting Image puppets and the Theatre de Complicite, along with live musicians and characters. Also includes two works for children by Prokofiev: *Overture on Hebrew Themes* and *The Classical Symphony*, where Peter upsets a banquet attended by Bach, Beethoven, Mozart, and others.

- *Reading Rainbow DVD Series.* This series includes *Abiyoyo, Barn Dance, Berlioz the Bear, Follow the Drinking Gourd, Hip Cat, Mama Don't Allow, Mufaro's Beautiful Daughters, The Paper Crane, Sophie and Lou, Uncle Jed's Barber Shop,* and *Zin! Zin! Zin! A Violin.* Suitable for pre-kindergarten to age three. Introduces children to the many varieties of music through children's literature. This is a two-time Emmy Award-winning series and is hosted by LeVar Burton. Celebrities narrate many of the stories. (Available at Music in Motion.)

- *The Story of "Silent Night."* Features the Vienna Boys Choir. Live action retelling the story of how this Christmas carol was written in 1818.

Classic Music DVDs for Young Adults

These DVDs can be ordered through Amazon or Music in Motion (1-800-445-0649), or purchased through your local bookstores or music stores. These productions are more sophisticated and more appropriate for older children.

- *Amadeus*: A dramatic film directed by Miloš Forman and written by Peter Shaffer. It chronicles the life of Wolfgang Amadeus Mozart as seen through the eyes of composer Antonio Salieri. It won eight Academy Awards, including Best Picture. The music is performed by the Academy of St. Martin in the Fields with Sir Neville Marriner conducting. (Watch the YouTube trailer: http://www.youtube.com/watch?v=yIzhAKtEzY0.)

- *Meet the Musicians*: Dennis Kobray is an accomplished pianist and actor who dresses up in full costume and portrays five different composers: Bach, Mozart, Beethoven, Gershwin, and Joplin. This DVD series gives young people an opportunity to meet the composers, listen to their music, and learn of their hardships, triumphs, and sacrifices made to compose their music.

- *Opera Stories*. This five-DVD set introduces young people to music, drama, characters, and the vision of opera. Charlton Heston narrates the stories from their original locations with excerpts from major opera productions. For instance, *Aida* is told from the pyramids of Egypt and *La Boheme* from the sidewalk cafes of Paris. There are ten programs in all, each telling the story of a single opera, and including *La Boheme, Manon Lescaut, Falstaff, Die Fledermaus, Il Trovatore, Aida, Tosca, Otello, Andrea Chenier*, and *Ernai*.

- *Stories of Famous Composers*: This biographical DVD series features portraits, music, commentary, and rare archival material of thirteen different composers. Music is performed by the Elysian Ensemble. This series is a wonderful introduction to classical music.

- *Swan Lake: Guangzhou Acrobatics Troupe*: This is Zhao Ming's stunning production of Tchaikovsky's acclaimed *Swan Lake*. It is a breathtaking mix of ballet and acrobatics. The Prince's sea voyage is made of acrobats on poles, creating the ship's sails, and dancers are like ocean waves. In the *pas de deux*, the swan is *en pointe* on the head and shoulders of the prince—a spectacular creation! (Available at Music in Motion.)

- *The Music Instinct: Science and Song.* This DVD brings together scientists, musicologists, anthropologists, researchers, and psychologists to explore the *how* and *why* of music found in different cultures and even the animal kingdom. Hosted by Bobby McFerrin and neuroscientist Daniel Levitin with musicians YoYo Ma, Evelyn Glennie, and Daniel Barenboim.

- *Young People's Concerts by Leonard Bernstein*: These concerts performed with the New York Philharmonic stand as one of Bernstein's greatest achievements. He led a total of fifty-three Young People's Concerts in fourteen years and covered a broad range of musical subjects, including "Jazz in the Concert Hall," "Folk Music in the Concert Hall," "What Does Music Mean," "Musical Atoms: A Study of Intervals," and so forth.

Inspiring DVDs of Music's Influencing Power

These movies and/or documentaries are inspiring. They illustrate in a very personal way how music impacts people struggling with varying challenges, difficulties, or hardships. You will witness how music transforms seemingly ordinary lives into something extraordinary.

- *Autism: The Musical.* This movie will change the way you look at autism. It follows acting coach Elaine Hall, five autistic children, and their parents as they courageously prepare for a life-changing event: staging a full-length original musical. Through insurmountable odds, parents and children learn to communicate their feelings in song and performance and find joy in the act of creating. This film should not be missed.

- *Blind Tom.* This "Gold Apple" award-winning film documents the true story of the life of Thomas Bethune, a slave born blind in 1849 in

Georgia. An autistic savant, Bethune had an amazing ear and memory for music. At a very young age, he began accurately echoing the sounds of nature around him. He learned piano by ear, composed music, and eventually learned seven thousand pieces of music, including hymns, waltzes, and classical repertoire. He toured extensively throughout the world, performed as often as four times a day, and became the nineteenth century's most highly compensated pianists.

- *El Sistema: Music to Change Life.* "El Sistema" is Venezuela's unique system of music education that removes children from slums and turns them into world-class musicians. This documentary chronicles the lives of children taken from the streets of violence and gang warfare into music schools and eventually to the finest concert halls, powerfully illustrating how music builds better people and a better society.

- *Mr. Holland's Opus.* This is a fictionalized film of how a music teacher impacts the lives of his students through music. Glenn Holland is a composer and musician who teaches music at a local high school to support his family while he dreams of composing one memorable piece of music. He finds that his dreams must be put aside to help a son who is deaf and students with challenges. Eventually he discovers that his real passion is teaching and reaching his students with music and witnesses the impact he leaves on generations of young people.

- *Music of the Heart.* This film is the story of Roberta Guaspari, who teaches violin to students in a tough inner-city neighborhood school. Despite the music program's success, Guaspari and her students must fight to keep the program alive when budget cuts are aimed at shutting it down for good. This film will resonate with any and all teachers and parents who have fought for quality music education programs in their schools.

- *The Singing Revolution.* This film is about the tiny nation of Estonia and their struggle for independence from the Soviet Union through the rich tradition of song. Between 1987 and 1991, hundreds of thousands of Estonians gathered in the fields to sing forbidden patriotic songs and rally for independence. Free speech became song, and songs became their anthem of independence. This film commemorates a people who revolted with no weapons but their songs and, as a result, survived.

- *The Soloist.* This deeply moving film is about Nathaniel Ayers, a homeless street musician who plays on a battered two-string violin. At one time, he attended the Juilliard School of music before mental illness changed his life. Ayers is discovered by Steve Lopez, a *Los Angeles Times* columnist who writes about people of Southern California. Lopez befriends Ayers and follows his journey of how he battles mental illness through the power of music.

- *Touch the Sound: A Sound Journey with Evelyn Glennie.* Profoundly deaf since childhood, Evelyn Glennie, a Grammy-winning classical and jazz solo percussionist, uses all of her senses and "hears" and feels with her entire body. This documentary follows her to a variety of locations—a Scottish farm, Grand Central Station, a rooftop, an airport, a beach—where she uses the vibrations she feels throughout her body to create music. Watching her teach hearing-impaired students in her native Aberdeenshire is one of the highlights of the film.

Unique Music Programs and Musical Materials for Home and Classroom

Below are some examples of musical material appropriate for home and classroom discussed in more detail. I have personally owned and used everything listed and find them to be exceptional in every way. Where possible, I've included a YouTube site for you to witness firsthand each of these musical items. Also, included is an outstanding music program for very young children.

Let's Play Music
Shelle Soelberg
480-840-1969
Website: www.letsplaymusicsite.com

Let's Play Music is the brainchild of music education major, Shelle Soelberg. Unable to find a suitable music program for her daughter, she began writing her own curriculum and a year later, Let's Play Music, was born. Using the concepts found in Orff-Schulwerk, Dalcroze, and Kodály, the program introduces young children, between the ages of four through six, to music, movement, and singing. The curriculum is organized into three sequential years. The first year incorporates games, songs, and tone bells to teach staff awareness and rhythm reading skills. The second year, they transfer these skills to playing the piano, where the children learn chord notation, intervals, and harmonic improvisation. By the end of the third year, students are playing the piano at level one or two, transposing music, composing their own music, sight-reading music, and are prepared to excel in further private piano instruction. Recently, "Sound Beginnings," was added to the curriculum. The program, for children ages two to four, includes singing, movement, games, stories, and activities. *Let's Play Music,* is offered in twenty-six states and in Canada. Check out their website for a program in your neighborhood.

Baby Einstein (DVDs, CDs, and toys)
The Walt Disney Company
Website: www.babyeinstein.com
(YouTube: http://www.youtube.com/user/babyeinstein)

In 1996, Julie Algner-Clark shot her first *Baby Einstein* video in her basement in Georgia. It was an instant hit with babies and parents. Many videos followed, including *Baby Mozart, Baby Bach,* and *Baby Beethoven.* In 2001, the Walt Disney Company acquired the Baby Einstein Company and today the *Baby Einstein* DVDs, books, and toys can be found in over thirty countries and in over twenty-five languages. These DVDs are a playful, imaginative introduction to the music of several composers in "video board book" style. Children will love the images of brightly colored toys and visually captivating objects, and little ears will love the carefully selected and charmingly arranged music of Mozart, Bach, Beethoven, and others. These videos have been featured on the Oprah Winfrey show and CNN and are a must for every baby to experience.

Bad Wolf Press (Musical Plays)
John Heath and Ron Fink
888-827-8661
E-mail: contact@badwolfpress.com
Website: www.badwolfpress.com

Bad Wolf was started in 1995 by lyricist John Heath and composer Ron Fink. They met in the sixth grade and started writing songs together in high school. What emerged from that relationship was Bad Wolf Press. The company produces excellent musical plays for nonmusical teachers. They are designed to be integrated into kindergarten through high school curricula and include a wide range of subjects, including Africa, ancient Greece, ecology, folk tales, literature, oceanography, science, math, US history, character education, and holidays. Kids love the catchy tunes and stories that are filled with curriculum facts. In 2011, Heath and Fink had created fifty shows that had been performed in over one hundred thousand schools worldwide. Their patented formula for why these plays work so well in the classroom is: Entertaining Story + Music/Rhyme = Subject Mastery.

Boomwhackers (Rhythm Band Instruments, LLC)
Website: www.boomwhackers.com
(YouTube: http://www.youtube.com/watch?v=Yd-CldfiS2o)
(YouTube: http://www.youtube.com/watch?v=1l6Engk7IMQ)

Boomwhackers are eight musically tuned percussion tubes designed and created by MIT graduate Craig Ramsell. To play, each person holds one or two of these colorful and perfectly tuned percussion tubes and whacks them against his arm, thigh, or any hard surface to produce the sound. The harder the surface, the brighter the sound will be. The gradations in length of the tubes (the tubes are twelve to twenty-four inches long) help players arrange themselves in sequential notes to understand the relationship between length and pitch and the color gradations provide an additional way to visualize the sequence of notes. Boomwhackers are available in the diatonic and chromatic scales as well as treble extension, bass diatonic, pentatonic, and with octavator caps (put the cap on the tube to lower the pitch one octave). Learning to play Boomwhackers is amazingly fun for children of all ages. They can be played individually, but it is recommended that the tubes are played as a group, which means they are great for families and classrooms.

Author Tom Anderson, in his book *Music of the Masters for Boomwhackers Musical Tubes and Other Instruments*, shows how Boomwhackers can be used to play classical music with piano accompaniment and with eight-note handbells. In 2009 Boomwhackers was named the "Top Toy of the Year" by *Creative Child* magazine, and in 1999 they received the Parents' Choice Gold Award. They are sold all over the world.

Sing a Song of Science (CDs)
Kathleen Carroll
Brain Friendly Learning
Website: http://kathleencarroll.com/sing-a-song-of-science

Sing a Song of Science is a classroom-tested CD with songs, raps, stories, and activities that get children excited about science and help them to understand scientific vocabulary and concepts. Children will learn about matter, layers of the earth, energy, classifying, observation and inferences, sound symmetry, weather, the water cycle, the tropical rainforest, and George Washington Carver. *Sing a Song of Science* helps children love science. My youngest son was introduced to the songs when he was ten years old and can still recite from memory many of the lyrics and was able to transfer the concepts to his science classes. *Science Songs and Stories for the Big Questions* is a seventy-three minute CD that helps learners find an emotional connection to science while providing an effortless way to learn scientific vocabulary and concepts. Included are topics such as "Scientific Method Blues Song," "Autobiography of a Sound Wave," "The Story of a Plant Song," and many others.

The Alphabet Operetta and My Favorite Musical Numbers (CDs, MP3 download)
Mindy Manley Little
Sold on www.mvorecords.com and www.amazon.com

The Alphabet Operetta is absolutely addicting! Your children will love Little's voice and the catchy alliteration and sing-along tunes for each letter of the alphabet. The songs are recorded in a variety of musical styles, including jazz, blues, and rock n' roll. In 2002, *The Alphabet Operetta* received the Parents' Choice Award. Her other recording, *My Favorite Musical Numbers*, starring numbers zero to ten, is spirited and humorous and a perfect blend of entertainment and education. These CDs are a must for your family's collection.

The Great Courses (DVDs, CDs for parents and teachers)
800-832-2412
Website: www.thegreatcourses.com

If you are a parent or teacher, love to learn, and want to be an example of lifelong learning to your children or students, then *The Great Courses* are for you. For more than twenty years, *The Great Courses* have produced engaging college-level courses taught by the top 1 percent of college professors from major universities across the United States. Each course is crafted and designed to make learning come alive. Literally hundreds of subjects are offered, from math to science, literature, philosophy, religion, business, economics, history, health, and, of course, music. The music courses taught by Professor Greenburg, a music historian-in-residence with San Francisco Performances and a Princeton graduate, are some of my favorite. Spending thirty minutes a day listening to a lecture will transform your life. If we want our children to be lifelong learners, they need to see their parents live that example by actively engaged in learning, and *The Great Courses* allow parents and teachers to do just that.

Arts Resources for Parents and Educators

These are organizations with a national impact. It is by no means a complete list.

Arts Education Partnership

1 Massachusetts Ave. NW, Suite 700
Washington, DC 20001
202-326-8693
Website: www.aep-arts.org

This group is a private, nonprofit coalition of education, arts, business, philanthropic, and government organizations that demonstrates and promotes the essential role of arts education in enabling students to succeed in school, life, and work.

ARTSEDGE

Website: http://artsedge.kennedy-center.org
(YouTube: http://www.youtube.com/user/ArtsEdge)

ARTSEDGE is an all-inclusive arts program of the Education Department of the John F. Kennedy Center for the Performing Arts. It is one of the nation's leading creators of free arts education materials. It offers a wide range of educational media resources that are available in multiple platforms, such as video, audio, interactive, and print. Its interactive guides and podcasts are free and can be used as standards-based lessons and materials for educators. ARTSEDGE serves teachers, students and families by supporting teaching and learning about the arts.

Meet the Composer (now part of "New Music USA")
90 John St., Suite 312
New York, New York 10038
212-645-6949
Website: www.newmusicusa.org

Meet the Composer, a national organization, was founded in 1974 by the New York State Council on the Arts. The goal is to bring music to rural communities, small towns, suburban centers, and urban neighborhoods across the United States.

Mr. Holland's Opus Foundation
4370 Tujunga Ave., Suite 330
Studio City, California 91604
818-762-4328
Website: www.mhopus.org

Mr. Holland's Opus Foundation was inspired by the motion picture *Mr. Holland's Opus*, the story of a dedicated music teacher and the impact he had on hundreds of students. The foundation donates new and refurbished instruments to school music programs across the United States lacking the resources to purchase their own due to attrition, loss, and wear. They also provide instruments to students on waiting lists or who share instruments. Each year approximately ten thousand young people across the country are helped with instruments and are thus able to experience the benefits of learning to play music.

National Association for Music Education
1806 Robert Fulton Drive
Reston, VA 20191
703-860-4000 or 1-800-336-3768
Website: www.nafme.org

The National Association for Music Education (NAfME) is one of the world's largest arts education organizations and is the only association that addresses all aspects of music education. Its website states, "NAfME advocates at the local, state, and national levels; provides resources for teachers, parents, and administrators; hosts professional development events; and offers a variety of opportunities for students and teachers. The association orchestrates success for millions of students nationwide and has supported music educators at all teaching levels for more than a century." This is a marvelous organization and is willing to help in any way to make music a reality for every child across America.

National Endowment for the Arts
1100 Pennsylvania Ave. NW
Washington, DC 20506
202-682-5400
Website: www.arts.gov

The National Endowment for the Arts (NEA) is an independent agency of the United States federal government and was created by the United States Congress on September 29, 1965. As a public service agency, its purpose has been to offer support and funding of projects exhibiting artistic excellence and to further the artistic and cultural aspects of this country.

VH1 Save the Music
1515 Broadway, 20th Floor
New York, New York. 10036
212-846-7600
Website: www.vh1safethemusic.com

This nonprofit organization is dedicated to improving the quality of education in America's public schools by restoring and supporting instrumental music education programs in cities across the county and by raising public awareness about the importance of music participation for our nation's youth.

Young Musicians Foundation
195 South Beverly Drive, Suite 414
Beverly Hills, CA 90212
310-859-7668
Website: www.ymf.org
(YouTube: http://www.youtube.com/watch?v=4CNvn9QG7PU)

This nonprofit organization provides encouragement and recognition to gifted young musicians ages eight to twenty-five through financial assistance and performance opportunities.

The centerpiece of YMF's programs is the Debut Orchestra, which comprises seventy of Los Angeles's most talented musicians who perform four free public concerts each year, including performances for underserved and low-income children in public schools in Los Angeles County. Nearly every orchestra in the United States today has a member that started his/her training in the Young Musicians Foundation program. There is also a similar program in Colorado.

Weekend Warriors: The National Association of Music Merchants (NAMM)
5790 Armada Drive
Carlsbad, CA 92008
760-438-8001
Website: www.namm.org

The National Association of Music Merchants (NAMM) sponsors Weekend Warriors, which targets people who enjoyed playing a musical instrument when they were younger, but put it aside for family, college, and career responsibilities. Inactive musicians can become active players again when they are hooked up with other musicians in their area. A person is grouped by musical interest and compatibility. In just four short rehearsals, their band, along with others, can be ready for a performance at a local venue.

Internet Sources for Music Information and Research, Music Materials, Music Catalogs, and Retail Stores

CAIRSS for Music
Website: http://webapp.lib.utsa.edu/Databases/index_more.
php?ername=CAIRSS

"CAIRSS (Computer-Assisted Information Retrieval Service System) for Music is a bibliographic database of research literature in music education, music psychology, music therapy, and music medicine. CAIRSS contains citations to every article published in eighteen primary journals, as well as citations from selected articles from more than one thousand additional journals. CAIRSS is produced by the faculty and staff of the University of Texas at San Antonio."

Clarus: Words and Music for Young People K-12
(in association with Stanton Sheet Music)
Website: www.clarusmusic.com/
Stanton's Sheet Music
330 South Fourth St.
Columbus, OH 43215
614-224-4257

Clarus Music, Ltd., is a premier worldwide music dealer and has been a major source of enriching quality materials for educators since 1975. The materials listed on their website have been carefully researched, tested and chosen from the marketplace for their superior quality. You will find a wide range of diverse, quality music materials on their easy-to-use website.

Classic Cat
Website: www.classiccat.net

The goal of Classic Cat is to make classical music more popular by making it more accessible. It does this by providing an index of over five thousand free links to download classical performances on the Internet which are sorted by composer and work. The site is specialized in audio files, but also contains video, sheet music, lyrics, and MIDI links.

Classical Net
Website: www.classicalnet.com

Classical Net is a website offering a comprehensive collection of information and news on classical music subjects and resources relating to classical music. It is a treasure trove of information, giving a guide to classic masterworks of the past one thousand years, information on composers from medieval to modern, books and scores, reviews and articles, a buying guide for the classical collector, and a catalog of classical music websites.

MMB Music
9051 Watson Road, Suite 161
St. Louis, Missouri 63126
314-531-9635
800-543-3771
Website: www.mmbmusic.com

Write or call for a catalog on music books, materials, and instruments for home and the classroom. They specialize in Orff instruments.

Music in Motion
PO Box 869231
Plano, Texas 75086-9231
800-445-0649
Website: www.musicmotion.com

This company offers an amazing catalog filled with everything musically imaginable. It is the perfect music education and gift catalog for all ages. Music teachers, parents, and students will find music items here that cannot be found anywhere else—including Amazon.

The Piano Companies
800-726-9109
Local: 703-771-8119
Local: 703-777-7789
Websites: www.pianoco.com; www.thepianoco.com

The Piano Companies are family-owned businesses that sell the highest quality pianos for the best possible price. With locations in Northern Virginia, The Piano Company facility located in Leesburg has one of the largest single piano showrooms on the East Coast. They specialize in helping their customers purchase pianos that later become personal and family heirlooms. They also reach out to the community and offer various classes and seminars to help the public with their musical choices. For example, free seminars are offered to professionals, amateurs, teachers, and students, such as, "How to Properly Choose the Piano of Your Dreams," and "Acoustic or Digital, it's Your Choice." They also offer many free community outreach events featuring local, national and international professional talent, including solo and ensemble performances and teacher resources such as recital space. Young students performing recitals at the Piano Company have the privilege of playing on an Italian Fazioli Model 308 ten-foot-two-inch grand piano which was played at the Kennedy Center, the White House, and other popular venues, as well as the new, high-quality Shigeru Kawai pianos from Japan. Additionally, they provide grand pianos, rehearsal space, and technical service to the annual Ensemble Festival sponsored by the Fairfax-Loudoun Music Fellowship. The Piano Company provides recording areas where high-quality pianos are available to record in broadcast quality. General Managers Robert and Antoinette Purdon believe that music is as important as breathing and they are dedicated to bringing pianos and music to the greater Washington, DC, area.

The Woodwind & Brasswind
PO Box 7479
Westlake Village, CA 91359
800-348-5003
Website: www.wwbw.com

The Woodwind & Brasswind was founded in 1978 by a music instructor that was supplementing his teaching income selling musical instruments and accessories at a fair price. More than thirty years later, it is still committed to offering the right product at the right price. It offers more than fifty thousand products to people in ninety-one countries.

West Music Company
PO Box 5521
Coralville, IA 52241
800-397-9378
Website: www.westmusic.com

When West Music started in 1941, it was a one-room retail and instrument repair shop in Iowa City, owned and operated by Pearl West. Today, over seventy years later, it is a booming family-owned music retail business with numerous locations throughout Eastern Iowa and Western Illinois. West Music offers every type of musical instrument, including pianos and keyboards, band and orchestra instruments, guitars and amplifiers, drums and percussion, software, elementary general music materials, early childhood instruments, and music therapy products. Since 1984, they have imported piccolos from Germany, guitars from Spain, percussion instruments from Mexico, China and Germany and ethnic instruments from Africa. Their West Music Education Catalog Department boasts a yearly 170-page catalog that is sent to schools, universities and churches throughout the United States and abroad. In 1995, they started West Music Therapy to address the physical, emotional, cognitive, and social needs of individuals of all ages. Their partnership with the University of Iowa Music Therapy program has grown, and today they employ thirteen music therapists, which has fulfilled West Music's goal of "enriching all people's lives through the participation in music." In 2005, realizing the importance of introducing children to music at an early age, they introduced a new line of children's exploratory instruments called *Sounds Like Fun*. Their goal is to provide an opportunity for people everywhere to experience the power of making music.

Notes

Chapter 1

1   Ian Crofton and Donald Fraser, *A Dictionary of Musical Quotations* (New York: Schrimer Bros., 1985).

2   Donald Hodges, "The Influence of Music on Human Behavior," *Handbook of Music Psychology* (San Antonio: IMR Press, 1996), 497.

3   Ibid., 474.

4   Ibid., 44, 476, 477.

5   Jon-Roar Bjorkvold, "Canto-ergo sum: Musical Child Cultures in the United States, the Soviet Union, and Norway," in *Music and Child Development*, eds. Frank R. Wilson and Franz L. Roehmann (St. Louis, MO: MMB Music, Inc., 1996), 118.

6   David Tame, *The Secret Power of Music* (Rochester, VT: Destiny Books, 1984), 237.

7   Ibid., 236.

8   Ibid., 239.

9   K. C. Cole, "Scientist Trace Cosmic Blast to Unusual Star," *Los Angeles Times*, September 30, 1998.

10   "The Sun Sings: Musical Sounds from the Atmosphere Revealed," *Scientific Computing* online magazine, June 22, 2010.

11   Richard Huber, scientist, interview with author, August 20, 1998.

12   William F. Allman, "The Musical Brain," *US News & World Report*, June 11, 1990.

13   "Icebreaker Rescues Trapped Whales," *National Geographic World*, February 1986.

14   Stewart H. Hulse, "Comparative Psychology and Music Perception," in *Music and Child Development*, eds. Frank R. Wilson and Franz L. Roehmann (St. Louis, MO: MMB Music, 1990), 153.

15   Ibid., 139.

16   Glenn Oeland, "Emperors of the Ice," *National Geographic*, vol. 189, no. 3 (March 1996):64.

17   Alex Sabbeth, *Rubber-Band Banjos and a Java Jive Bass* (New York: John Wiley & Sons, Inc., 1997), 11, 20.

18   Tony Mickela, "Does Music Have an Impact on the Development of Students," prepared for the 1990 state convention of California Music Educators Association. Barbara L. Stein, C. A. Hardy, and Herman Totten, "The Use of Music and Imagery to Enhance and Accelerate Information Retention," *Journal of the Society for Accelerative Learning & Teaching*, vol. 7, no 4, 341. Laura Saari, "The Sound of Learning," *The Orange County Register*, February 6, 1997.

19   Sally J. Rogers, "Theories of Child Development and Musical Ability," in *Music and Child Development*, eds. Frank R. Wilson and Franz L. Roehmann (St. Louis, MO: MMB Music Inc., 1990), 3. *Profile of SAT and Achievement Test Takers*, College Entrance Examination Board, Princeton, New Jersey, 1995. Hodges, "Influence of Music," 542. *What Work Requires of School: A SCANS Report for America 2000* (Upland, PA: Diane Publishing Co., 1993). Also found in *Visual and Performing Arts Framework* (Sacramento: California Department of Education, 1996), 13.

20   Hodges, "Influence of Music on Human Behavior," 536.

21   Doc Childre and Howard Martin, *Heartmath* (New York: HarperCollins, 2000), 28.

22   Ibid., 27.

23   Michael D. Gershon, MD, *The Second Brain* (New York, HarperCollins, 1998), xiii.

24   Marian Diamond, *Enriching Heredity* (New York: The Free Press/Simon & Schuster, 1988).

25   Dee Dickinson, "Music and the Mind" (Seattle: New Horizons for Learning, 1993).

26   Robert Lee Hotz, "Study Suggests Music May Someday Help Repair the Brain," *Los Angeles Times*, November 9, 1998.

27   Diamond, *Enriching Heredity*.

28   Holtz, "Music May Someday Help Repair the Brain."

Chapter 2

1   Alison Motluk, "Can Mozart Make Math Add Up?" *Science*, March 15, 1997.

2   Frances H. Rauscher, Gordon L. Shaw, Linda J. Levine, and Katherine N. Ky, "Music and Spatial Task Performance," *Nature*, vol. 365, October 14, 1993.

3   Frances H. Rauscher, Gordon L. Shaw, Linda J. Levine, Eric L. Wright, Wendy R. Dennis, and Robert L. Newcomb, "Music Training Causes Long-Term Enhancement of Preschool Children's Spatial-Temporal Reasoning," *Neurological Research*, vol. 19, February 1997.

4   Rauscher et al., "Music and Spatial Task Performance."

5   Amy B. Graziano, Gordon L. Shaw, and Eric L. Wright, "Music Training Enhances Spatial-Temporal Reasoning in Young Children: Toward Educational Experiments," *Early Childhood Connections,* Summer 1997.

6   Kimberly Kindy, "Piano, Games May Multiply Math Skills," *The Orange County Register*, March 15, 1999.

7   F. H. Rauscher and M. T. LeMieux, "Piano, rhythm, and singing instruction improve different aspects of spatial-temporal reasoning in Head Start children," Cognitive Neuroscience Society, New York (April 2003).

8   Frances H. Rauscher, "Can Music Instruction Affect Children's Cognitive Development?" ERIC Digest; ERIC Identifer: ED480540, September 2003.

9   Wendy S. Boettcher, Sabrina S. Hahn, and Gordon L. Shaw, "Mathematics and Music: A Search for Insight into Higher Brain Function," *Leonardo Music Journal,* vol. 4, 1994.

10   G. J. Allman, *Greek Geometry from Thales to Euclid* (New York: Arno, 1976).

11   A. J. S. Rayl, "Striking A Neural Chord: Musical Links for Scientists and Mathematicians of Tomorrow," *OMNI*, 1995.

12   Marcia Davenport, *Mozart* (New York: Avon Books, 1979).

13   E. Anderson, *The Letters of Mozart and His Family* (New York: W. W. Norton Co., 1985).

14   Martha B. Denckla, "The Paradox of the Gifted/Impaired Child," in *Music and Child Development*, eds. Frank R. Wilson and Franz L. Roehmann (St. Louis, MO: MMB Music, Inc., 1990), 228.

15   Donald A. Hodges, "Neuromusical Research," *Handbook of Music Psychology* (San Antonio: IMR Press, 1996), 242.

16   "Neurology: Musical 'Maps' May Grow With Experience," *Washington Post*, April 1998.

17   R. Butzlaff, "Can Music be Used to Teach Reading?" *Journal of Aesthetic Education*, 34(3-4), 167-168.

18   Laura Saari, "The Sound of Learning," *The Orange County Register*, February 6, 1997.

19   Ibid.

20   Graziano et al., "Music Training."

21   Boettcher et al., "Mathematics and Music."

22   Ben Carson, *Gifted Hands* (Grand Rapids, MI: Zondervan Publishing House, 1990), 110.

23   Victor Goertzel and Mildred George Goertzel, *Cradles of Eminence: A Provocative Study of the Childhoods of Over Four Hundred Famous Twentieth-Century Men and Women* (Boston: Little, Brown, 1962), xii.

24   Eric Oddleifson, "The Case for Sequential Music Education in the Core Curriculum of the Public Schools" (East Hampton, NY: Center for the Arts in the Basic Curriculum, Spring 1989).

25   Walter Isaacson, *Einstein* (New York: Simon & Schuster, 2007), 14.

26   Elizabeth Murfee, "Eloquent Evidence: Arts at the Core of Learning" (Washington, DC: Assembly of State Arts Agencies, 1995).

27   Thomas Armstrong, *Seven Kinds of Smart* (New York: Penguin Group, 1993), 59.

28   Anne C. Roark, "How US Failed in Science," *Los Angeles Times*, November 8, 1990.

29   "Mathematics Conference Focuses on Encouraging and Aiding Doctoral Students," Morehouse College: *Campus News,* March 4, 2008.

30   Robert D. Atkinson and Merrilea Mayo, "Refueling the US Innovation Economy: Fresh Approaches to Science, Technology, Engineering, and Mathematics (STEM) Education," *The Information Technology & Innovation Foundation,* December 2010.

31   "Tapping America's Potential," US Chamber of Commerce, July 2005.

32   Elizabeth Craig, Robert J. Thomas, Charlene Hou, and Smriti Mathor, "No Shortage of Talent: How the Global Market is Producing the STEM Skills Needed for Growth," 2011.

33   Atkinson, "Refueling the US Innovation Economy"

34   Anne C. Roark, "Classroom Changes Give a 'Feel' for Math, Science," *Los Angeles Times*, November 9, 1990.

35   Brendan Borrell, "Speaking Out on the Quiet Crisis," *Scientific American*, December 2011.

36   Sandra Johnson, interview with author, April 9, 2013. See also: Rob Kuznia, "Kids find science is fun in lab," *Daily Breeze*, July 23, 2012. See also: www.experiumscienceacademy.com.

37   Rob Kuznia, "Kids find science is fun in lab," *Daily Breeze*, July 23, 2012. See also: www.experiumscienceacademy.com.

38   *The Midland Chemist (American Chemical Society)*, vol. 42, no. 1, February 2005.

39   Hodges, "Neuromusical Research," 242.

40 Robert Lee Hotz, "Study Suggests Music May Someday Help Repair Brain," *Los Angeles Times,* November 9, 1998.

41 Tony Mickela, "Does Music Have An Impact on the Development of Students?" Prepared for the 1990 state convention of California Music Educators Association.

42 Ibid.

43 Howard Gardner, *Art, Mind, and Brain, A Cognitive Approach to Creativity* (New York: Basic Books, 1982), 329-330.

44 Dee Dickinson, "Music and the Mind" (Seattle: New Horizons for Learning, 1993). Also see www.newhorizons.org.

45 Mickela, "Does Music Have An Impact?"

46 Hotz, "Music May Someday Help."

47 Mickela, "Does Music Have An Impact?"

48 Sara Martin, "Music Lessons Enhance Spatial Reasoning Skills," *Monitor,* 1994.

49 Barbara L. Stein, C. A. Hardy, and Herman L. Totten, "The Use of Music and Imagery to Enhance and Accelerate Information Retention," *Journal of the Society for Accelerative Learning & Teaching,* vol. 7, no. 4.

50 Shelia Ostrander and Lynn Schroeder, *Superlearning* (New York: Delacorte Press, 1979).

51 Ibid.

52 Ibid.

53 J. Ormrod, *Educational Psychology* (New Jersey: Prentice Hall, 2000).

54 Y. C. Ho, M. C. Cheung, and A. Chan, "Music training improves verbal but not visual memory; cross-sectional and longitudinal explorations in children" (2003), *Neuropsychology*, 12, 439-450.

55 J. Madeleine Nash, "Fertile Minds," *Time*, February 3, 1997.

56 Ibid.

57 Ibid.

Chapter 3

1 Thomas Armstrong, *Seven Kinds of Smart* (New York: Penguin Group, 1993), 73.

2 L. Salk, "Mothers' heartbeat as an imprinting stimulus," *Transactions: Journal of the New York Academy of Sciences*, vol. 24, no. 7:753-763.

3   Donald J. Shetler, "The Inquiry into Prenatal Musical Experience: A Report of the Eastman Project 1980-1987," in *Music and Child Development*, edited by Frank R. Wilson, and Franz L. Roehman (St. Louis, MO: MMB Music, Inc., 1990), 46.

4   Peter F. Ostwald, "Music in the Organization of Childhood Experience and Emotion," in *Music and Child Development*, eds. Frank R. Wilson and Franz L. Roehmann (St. Louis, MO: MMB Music, Inc., 1990), 12.

5   Donald Hodges, "Neuromusical Research," *Handbook of Music Psychology* (San Antonio: IMR Press, 1996), 210.

6   S. G. Lopez, "The Effects on Infants of Empathy and Resonance as Reflected in Lullabies and Playsongs: A Musical Developmental Theory" (PhD dissertation, University of California, San Diego, 1991).

7   Shetler, "Prenatal Musical Experience," 50.

8   Ibid., 55.

9   "Babies Remember Music Heard in the Womb: The New Pedagogy, An Interdisplinary Model," *Educational CyberPlayGround, Inc.*, July 2001. See: http://www.edu-cyberpg. com.

10   Thaddeus Baklinski, "Newborns Remember Music Heard in the Womb," *Birth & Parenting News,* March 8, 2011.

11   Ibid.

12   Frances H. Rauscher, K. D. Robinson, and J. J. Jens, "Improved Maze Learning Through Early Music Exposure in Rats," *Neurological Research.*

13   "New Musical Pacifier Helps Premature Babies Get Healthy," *ScienceDaily*, May 21, 2012.

14   "Mozart's Music Mellows Out At-Risk Preemies," admin., ISRAEL21c, January 4, 2010.

15   Robert Preidt, "US in Top 10 for Premature Births," *HealthDay News*, June 8, 2012.

16   "Music May Improve Feeding, Reduce Pain in Premature Babies, *ScienceDaily*, May 27, 2009.

17   Tiffany Field, *Touch* (Massachusetts: MIT Press, 2001), 119.

18   Sharon Heller, PhD, *The Vital Touch* (New York: Henry Holt and Company, LLC), 131.

19   Donald Hodges, "Human Musicality," *Handbook of Music Psychology* (San Antonio: IMR Press, 1996), 47.

20   Ostwald, "Childhood Experience and Emotion."

21   John Baily and Veronica Doubleday, "Patterns of Musical Enculturation in Afghanistan," in *Music and Child Development,* eds. Frank R. Wilson and Franz L. Roehmann (St. Louis, MO: MMB Music, Inc., 1990), 88.

22   Hodges, "Human Musicality," 47.

23   W. Kessen, J. Levine, and K. A. Wendrich, "The Imitation of Pitch in Infants," *Infant Behavior and Development* 2, 1979, 931-99.

24   Robert Lee Holtz, "The Language of Learning," *Los Angeles Times*, September 18, 1997.

25   Marcel R. Zentner, Jerome Kagan, "Perception of Music by Infants," *Nature*, 383/6595, 1996, 29.

26   Robert Garfias, "Thoughts on the Processes of Language and Music Acquisition," in *Music and Child Development*, eds. Frank R. Wilson and Franz L. Roehmann (St. Louis, MO: MMB Music, Inc., 1990), 100.

27   Dee Dickinson, "Learning Through the Arts" (Seattle: New Horizons for Learning, 1997), 7. See also www.newhorizons.org.

28   Sally J. Rogers, "Theories of Child Development and Musical Ability," in *Music and Child Development*, eds. Frank R. Wilson and Franz L. Roehmann (St. Louis, MO: MMB Music, Inc., 1990), 2.

29   Ibid., 3.

30   Carla Hannaford, *Smart Moves* (Arlington, VA: Great Ocean Publishers, 1995), 107.

31   "Music and Your Child: The Importance of Music to Children's Development," American Music Conference, 1988.

32   Gordon Shaw, interview with author, April 13, 1999.

33   Jane M. Healy, *Endangered Minds* (New York: Touchstone Books/Simon & Schuster, 1990), 93.

34   Hannaford, *Smart Moves*, 83.

35   Baily and Doubleday, "Patterns of Musical Enculturation in Afghanistan," 97.

36   *Profile of College-Bound Seniors National Reports from 2006-2010.* College Entrance Examination Board, Princeton, New Jersey, 2010.

37   *Voices in the Arts: Perspectives on the Importance of the Arts in Education*, "Five-Year SAT Score Comparison: Texas All-State Musicians Compared to the National and State Average," Texas Music Educators Association, www.tmea.org, 2011.

38   Christopher M. Johnson and Jenny E. Memmott, "Examination of Relationship between Participation in School Music Programs of Differing Quality and

Standardized Test Results, University of Kansas. *MENC Journal of Research in Music Education,* Winter 2006, vol. 54, no. 4, 293-307. Used with permission.

39   Harris Interactive poll of high school principals conducted spring 2006; funded by MENC and NAMM. Analysis conducted by the Texas Coalition for Quality Arts Education and the Texas Music Educators Association (www.tmea.org). Used with permission.

Chapter 4

1   International Music Products Association and US Census, December 8, 2011.

2   "What is Orff Schulwerk." See: http://www.aosa.org/whatis.html.

3   Shinichi Suzuki, *Nurtured by Love* (New York: Exposition Press, 1964).

4   Sharon Begley, "Your Child's Brain," *Newsweek,* February 19, 1996.

5   John Holt, *Never Too Late, My Musical Life Story* (New York: Delacorte Press/Seymour Lawrence, 1978), 4.

6   Begley, "Your Child's Brain."

7   "Gallup Poll Reveals Piano and Guitar Still Top the Charts in Popularity," *Music USA* 1994, NAMM, International Music Products Association.

8   Madeau Stewart, *The Music Lover's Guide to the Instruments of the Orchestra* (New York: Van Nostrand-Reinhold Co., 1980), 12.

9   Helen Colijn, *Song of Survival: Women Interned.* (Ashland, OR: White Cloud Press, 1995).

10   Ibid.

11   "America's Performing Art: A Study of Choruses, Choral Singers, and Their Impact" (*Chorus Impact Study,* 2003). See: www.chorusamerica.org.

12   Sondra Harnes, interview with author, April 11, 2013. See also: www.worldchildrenschoir.org.

13   Marg Kruse, e-mail correspondence, April 13, 2013. See also: www.alaskachildrenschoir.net.

14   William A. DeGregorio, *The Complete Book of US Presidents* (Fort Lee, NJ: Barricade Books, 2005).

15   "America's Performing Art."

16   Thomas H. Maugh, "Study Finds Piano Lessons Boost Youths' Reasoning," *Los Angeles Times*, February 28, 1997.

17   Jane Webb, interview with author, August 1, 2012, See also: www.flmf.org.

18   Roger Von Oech, *A Whack on the Side of the Head* (New York: Warner Books, 1990).

19   DeGregorio, *The Complete Book of US Presidents.*

20   Stewart, *The Music Lovers Guide.*

21   Duane Noriyuki, "Secrets Wonderful and Cruel," *Los Angeles Times Magazine*, August 31, 1997, 8.

22   Ted Libbey, *The NPR Guide to Building a Classical CD Collection* (New York: Workman Publishing, 1994), 133.

23   Bob Pool, "Singular Act Makes Him a Triple Threat," *Los Angeles Times*, April 15, 1999.

24   DeGregorio, *The Complete Book of US Presidents.*

25   Libbey, *The NPR Guide,* 74.

26   DeGregorio, *The Complete Book of US Presidents.*

27   Libbey, *The NPR Guide,* 44.

28   Maurice Summerfield, *The Classical Guitar, Its Evolution, Players, and Personalities Since 1800* (Newcastle-Upon-Tyne, England: Ashley Mark Publishing Company, 1991).

29   DeGregorio, *The Complete Book of US Presidents.*

30   Loralee Shoffner, interview with author, August 21, 2012.

31   Chris Niswonger, interview with author, August 20, 2012.

32   Barry Trobaugh, interview with author, August 2, 2012. See also: www.munfordband. com and www.sbomagazine.com.

33   Helen Epstein, *Music Talks* (New York: McGraw-Hill Book Company, 1987), 75.

34   Ibid., 69.

35   Ibid., 87.

36   Ibid., 93.

37   Dorothea Alpert, interview with author, August 23, 2012.

Chapter 5

1   Eric Oddleifson, "The Case for Sequential Music Education in the Core Curriculum of the Public Schools" (East Hampton, NY: Center for the Arts in the Basic Curriculum, 1989), 29.

2   Jenny Oaks Baker, interview with author, July 16, 2012. See also www.jennyoaksbaker. com.

3   Kevin Hsieh, interview with author, July 7, 2012.

4   Mikel Poulsen, interview with author, August 22, 2012.

5   Melissa Healy, "Fathers at School Give Children an Edge, Study Finds," *Los Angeles Times*, October 3, 1997.

6   Sally J. Rogers, "Theories of Child Development and Musical Ability," in *Music and Child Development*, eds. Frank R. Wilson and Franz L. Roehmann (St. Louis, MO: MMB Music, 1990), 3.

7   Patrick Kavanaugh, *Raising Musical Kids* (Grand Rapids, MI: Servant Publications, 1995), 124.

8   Lauren A. Sosniak, "From Tyro to Virtuoso: A Long-Term Commitment to Learning," in *Music and Child Development*, eds. Frank R. Wilson and Franz L. Roehmann (St. Louis, MO: MMB Music, 1990), 274-289.

9   Ibid., 281.

10   Helen Epstein, *Music Talks* (New York: McGraw-Hill, 1987).

11   "Talking With David Frost," Burrelle's Information Services, April 25, 1997.

12   Oddleifson, "The Case for Sequential Music Education," 44.

13   K. Anders Ericsson and Neil Charness, "Expert Performance: Its Structure and Acquisition," *American Psychologist*, vol. 49, no. 8, August 1994.

14   Todd Stout, "The Four Utah Varieties of *Papilo indra*," *Utah Lepidopterist*, February 1997, 6.

Chapter 6

1   Thomas Stanley, Ph.D., and Willam D. Danko, *The Millionaire Next Door: The Surprising Secrets of America's Wealthy* (Atlanta, GA: Longstreet Press, 1996).

2   Character Education Partnership, *Performance Values: Why They Matter and What Schools Can Do to Foster Their Development* (Washington, DC: Character Education Partnership, April 2008).

3   Patrick Kavanaugh, *Spiritual Lives of the Great Composers* (Grand Rapids, MI: Zondervan Publishing House, 1992), 31.

4   Lucinda Hahn, "Maestro of Their Dreams," *Reader's Digest*, August 1996.

5   See: http://www.odessaphilharmonic.org/index.php.

6   Suzanne Chazin, "She Heard the Music," *Reader's Digest*, February 1997.

7   Stan Miller and Sharon Miller, *Especially for Mormons* (Provo, UT: Kellirae Arts, 1973), 69.

8   Tina Tom, interview with author, June 12, 2012.

9   Anita Bartholomew, "Music Was His Passport," *Reader's Digest*, March 1997, 41-48.

10 Christine Gilbert, "Love at First Sound," *The Beat*, Spring 2010. Accessed on August 27, 2012: www.uwe-thebeat.org/dat.html.

11 From "Growing Up Complete: The Imperative for Music Education." Copyright 1991 by Music Educators National Conference. Used with permission.

12 Carol Lynn Pearson, "My Story," from the play *My Turn on Earth*, lyrics and music by Carol Lynn Pearson.

13 Sarah Jo Ciotti, "Bundit Ungrangsee," 76-77, 2012 copyright Deseret Book Company. Used by permission.

14 Tony Mickela, "Does Music Have an Impact on the Development of Students?" Prepared for the 1990 state convention of California Music Educators Association. Used with permission.

15 Ibid.

16 DVD: *The Promise of Music*. See also http://www.elsistemausa.org.

17 Christina Hoag, "Maestro Leading the Way," *Los Angeles Times*, November, 14, 2011.

18 Melanie Grayce West, "Inspiring Music Teachers, Young Students," *The Wall Street Journal*, April 29, 2011.

19 Sterling W. Sill, *The Majesty of Books* (Salt Lake City, Utah: Deseret Book Company, 1974), 121.

20 Mickela, "Does Music Have an Impact?"

21 Dan Rather, "Silencing the Sound of Music," *San Diego Union-Tribune*, March 20, 1998.

22 *War Dance*, 2007 documentary film, written and directed by Sean Fine and Andrea Nix Fine (DVD). See also: www.wardancethemovie.com.

23 From "Growing Up Complete: Used with permission.

24 Norman Lebrecht, "More heartbreak at the Landfill Harmonic," *Slipped Disc*, December 10, 2012, accessed December 29, 2012.

25 "A Way out of the landfill: Paraguay kids play Mozart with violins made from trash," *World News on NBCNews.com*, December 17, 2012, accessed December 29, 2012.

26 Dee Dickinson, "Lifelong Learning for Business: A Global Perspective." Presented at a conference on lifelong learning for European business, Oxford University, October 1992.

27 Daniel Golden, "Building a Better Brain," *Life*, July 1996.

28 Robert Lee Hotz, "Active Mind, Body Linked to Brain Growth," *Los Angeles Times*, February 23, 1999.

29 Don Heckman, "Recalling a Master of Violin Versatility," *Los Angeles Times*, December 2, 1997.

30 Ibid.

31 Marissa Epino, "Eleven Decades of Harmony," *Los Angeles Times, South Bay Weekly*, December 4, 1997.

32 Carolyn Allen, interview with author, February 28, 2013.

33 Melanie Grayce West, "Inspiring Music Teachers, Young Students," *The Wall Street Journal*, April 29, 2011.

34 Golden, "Building a Better Brain."

35 Carla Hannaford, *Smart Moves* (Arlington, VA: Great Ocean Publishers, 1995), 83.

36 Elaine Dutka, "Eighty-Eight Keys to Success," *Los Angeles Times*, January 16, 1998.

37 Paul Sullivan, "The Cellist of Sarajevo," *Reader's Digest*, November 1996, 57-59.

38 Matea Gold, "The Chord of Life," *Los Angeles Times*, April 9, 1997.

39 Ibid.

40 Barbara Sande Dimmitt, "Silent Night," *Reader's Digest*, December 1997, 67.

Chapter 7

1 Lauren Blevins, interview with author, June 2012.

2 *No Child Left Behind Act of 2002*, Title IX, Part A, Sec. 9101 (11).

3 Scott Schuler, "Music Education for Life: Core Music Education: Student Civil Right," *Music Educators Journal*, May 2012, vol. 98, issue 4, p. 7-11. Used with permission.

4 Fran Smith, "Why Arts Education is Crucial and Who's Doing it Best," *Edutopia* (The George Lucas Foundation), January 28, 2009.

5 *The Value and Quality of Arts Education: A Statement of Principles*, copyright January 1999 by MENC: The National Association for Music Education. Used with permission

6 Smith, "Why Arts Education is Crucial and Who's Doing it Best."

7   Schuler, "Music Education for Life." Used with permission.

8   Lara Pellerinelli, "Music Education in Public Schools Gets a Passing Grade," *The Record*, April 6, 2012. See also: http://www.npr.org/blogs/therecord/2012/04/06/150133858/music-education-in-public-schools-gets-a-passing-grade.

9   Ibid.

10 Smith, "Why Arts Education is Crucial and Who's Doing it Best."

11 "California Public School Music Programs at Stake at September 9 Public Hearings in Los Angeles," *PR Newswire Association*, 2004.

12 Smith, "Why Arts Education is Crucial and Who's Doing it Best."

13 Schuler, "Music Education for Life." Used with permission

14 Donald Hodges, *Handbook of Music Psychology* (San Antonio: IMR Press, 1996).

15 Jeffrey T. Schnapp, "Art in Schools Inspires Tomorrow's Creative Thinkers," *Edutopia*, January 28, 2009.

16 R. R. Konrad, *Empathy, Arts, and Social Studies*, 2000.

17 Dr. Laurel Trainor, professor of psychology, neuroscience, and behavior at McMaster University, 2006. See also: www.psychology.mcmaster.ca/ljt/.

18 "The Impact of Arts Education on Workforce Preparation," May 2002, the National Governors Association. See also: www.nga.org/cda/files/050102ARTSED.pdf.

19 James Catterall, Richard Chapleau, and John Iwanaga, "Involvement in the Arts and Human Development: Extending an Analysis of General Associations and Introducing the Special Cases of Intensive Involvement in Music and Theater Arts," 2002. Found in R. Deasy, *Critical Links: Learning in the Arts and Student Achievement and Social Development,* Washington, DC: AEP.

20 E. Skoe and Nina Kraus, "A Little Goes a Long Way: How the Adult Brain is Shaped by Musical Training in Childhood," *Journal of Neuroscience*, 32 (34) 11510.DOI: 10.1523/JNEUROSCI.1949 12-2012.

21 Carrie Sturrock, "Playing Music Can be Good for Your Brain: Stanford Study Finds it helps the Understanding of Language," *San Francisco Chronicle*, November 2005.

22 Sol Jang, interview with author, June 2012.

23 *Critical Links: Learning in the Arts and Student Academic and Social Development*, Arts Education Partnership, 2002.

24 "The Impact of Arts Education on Workforce Preparation," May 2002.

25 Harris Interactive poll of high school principals, spring 2006, funded by MENC and NAMM.

26 Christopher M. Johnson and Jenny E. Memmott, "Examination of Relationship between Participation in School Music Programs of Differing Quality and Standardized Test Results," *MENC Journal of Research in Music Education,* Winter 2006, vol. 54, no. 4, pgs. 293-307. Used with permission.

27 James S. Catterall, "Different Ways of Knowing: 1991-94 National Longitudinal Study Final Report" (Tucson: the Morrison Institute of Public Policy,1995).

28 The College Board, Profile of College-Bound Seniors National Report for 2006. See also: www.collegeboard.org.

29 Harris Interactive poll of high school principals, spring 2006.

30 Eric Oddleifson, "A Fifty School Arts Education Demonstration Project," *On the Beam,* vol. XI, no. 1, Fall 1990.

31 Jaye T. Darby and James S. Catterall, "The Fourth R: The Arts and Learning," from *Schools, Communities, and the Arts: A Research Compendium,* 1994.

32 Dee Dickinson, "Learning Through Many Kinds of Intelligence" (Seattle: New Horizons for Learning, 1997).

33 Oddleifson, "A Fifty School Arts Education Demonstration Project."

34 Dickinson, "Learning Through the Arts."

35 Anne Green Gilbert, e-mail correspondence with author, March 15, 2013.

36 Kristin Leidig-Sears, interview with author, March 14, 2013.

37 Allison Hickmann, interview with author, January 23, 2013.

38 Nicolas Ferroni, "Using Music in the Classroom to Educate, Engage, and Promote Understanding," *Huffington Post,* November 11, 2008.

39 Kanda Hill, interview with author, March 25, 2013.

40 Darlys Lickliter, interview with author March 15, 2013.

41 Elva Bolin, interview with author, March 13, 2013.

42 Elizabeth Tummons, interview with author, March 25, 2013

43 Laura Brino, interview with author, March 22, 2013

44 Paul DeRoo, interview with author, March 22, 2013.

45 Karen Fields, interview with author, April 1, 2013

46 Melissa Callahan, interview with author, April 1, 2013.

47 Julie Patrick, interview with author, April 1, 2013

48 Dr. Joan Ashcraft, interview with author, March 22, 2013.

49 Dickinson, "Learning Through the Arts."

50 Elva Jean Bolin, interview with author, March 13, 2013.

51   From *Growing Up Complete: The Imperative for Music Education,* copyright 1991 by Music Educators National Conference. Used with permission.

52   Jay Smink and Joanna Zorn Heilbrunn, "Legal and Economic Implications of Truancy," *Truancy Prevention in Action Series,* 2005. Bruce O. Boston, "Educating for the Workplace Through the Arts," *Business Week,* October 28, 1996, 6.

53   James S. Catterall, Richard Chapleau, and John Iwanaga. "Involvement in the Arts and Human Development: Extending an Analysis of General Associations and Introducing the Special Cases of Intensive Involvement in Music and in Theater Arts." Monograph Series No. 11, (Washington, DC: Americans for the Arts, Fall 1999).

54   L. M. Stevenson and R. J. Deasy, *Third Space: When Learning Matters* (Washington, DC: Arts Education Partnership, 2005).

55   Sharon Begley, "Your Child's Brain," *Newsweek,* February 19, 1996.

56   Ibid.

57   Eric Oddleifson, "To Perceive, and to Imagine" (East Hampton, NY: Center for the Arts in the Basic Curriculum, 1996).

58   Roger Kamien, *Music, An Appreciation* (New York: McGraw Hill Book Company, 1988), 142.

59   From *Growing Up Complete: The Imperative for Music Education.* Used with permission.

Chapter 8

1   Rose Villanueva, e-mail correspondence, April 2, 2013.

2   Cathy Scott and Donna Vetere, interview with author, April 10, 2013.

3   "Learning Disability Fast Facts," National Center for Learning Disabilities editorial team. See: http://www.ncld.org/types-learning-disabilities/what-is-ld/learning-disability-fast-facts.

4   Sherry DuPont, "The Effectiveness of Creative Drama as an Instructional Strategy to Enhance the Reading Comprehension Skills of Fifth-Grade Remedial Readers," *Reading Research and Instruction,* vol. 31(3), 1992, 41-52.

5   From *Growing Up Complete: The Imperative for Music Education,* copyright 1991 by Music Educators National Conference. Used with permission.

6   Nina Kraus and Bharath Chandrasekaran, "Music Training for the Development of Auditory Skills." *Nature Reviews Neuroscience,* vol. 11, August 2010, 599-605.

7   "Music Training Enhances Brainstem Sensitivity to Speech Sounds" (Chicago: Northwestern University, February 22, 2010).

8   D. Register, A. A. Darrow, J. Standley, and O. Swedberg, "The Use of Music to Enhance Reading Skills of Second Grade Students and Students with Reading Disabilities," *Journal of Music Therapy*, vol. 44(1), 2007, 23-37.

9   Carrie Sturrock, "Playing Music Can be Good for Your Brain: Stanford Study Finds it helps the Understanding of Language," *San Francisco Chronicle*, November 2005.

10 Susan Sze, PhD, Sanna Yu, "Effects of Music Therapy on Children with Disabilities," *International Conference on Music Perception and Cognition,* Evanston, IL, 2004, 342.

11 Ibid., 342.

12 K. Overy, "Dyslexia and Music: From Timing Deficits to Music Intervention" (England: University of Sheffield, 2002).

13 S. Douglas, P. Willatts, "The Relationship Between Musical Ability and Literacy Skills," *Journal of Research in Reading*, vol. 17(2), 1994.

14 Elizabeth Ron Fang, "Music in the Lives of Two Children with Autism: A Case Study" (San Jose, CA: San Jose State University, 2009). See also: *scholarworks.sjsu.edu/cgi/viewcontent.cgi?article=4344&context.*

15 Pierre Sollier, MFT, "Overview of the Tomatis Method" (Lafayette, CA: Lafayette Tomatis Center).

16 Pierre Sollier, MFT, "How Tomatis Treats Learning Problems" (Lafayette, CA: Listening and Learning Center).

17 See: http://www.tomatis.com/add.html.

18 Timothy M. Gilmor, PhD., "The Efficacy of the Tomatis Method for Children with Learning and Communication Disorders: A Meta-Analysis," *International Journal of Listening*, vol. 13, 1999, 12-23.

19 Peter Sollier, "Studies on Effects of Learning and Communication Disorders," Tomatis Center, Canada, 2005.

20 Alene Villaneda (Integrated Learning Strategies), interview with author, October 2012.

21 Miriam Choi, interview with author, September, 2012.

22 "Prevalence of Autism Spectrum Disorders — Autism and Developmental Disabilities Monitoring Network, 14 Sites, United States, 2008." Department of Health and Human Services, Centers for Disease Control and Prevention. *Morbidity and Mortality Weekly Report, March 2012.*

23 See: www.autismspeaks.org. Accessed November 21, 2012.

24 Elizabeth Starr and Krista Zenker, "Understanding Autism in the Context of Music Therapy: Bridging Theory and Practice," *Canadian Journal of Music Therapy*, vol. 6, no. 1, 1998, 1.

25 William B. Davis, Kate E. Gfeller, and *Michael H. Thaut, An Introduction to Music Therapy (Boston: McGraw-Hill, 1999).*

26 Bonnie Nakamoto, interview with author, December 18, 2012.

27 Jacqueline Peters, *Music Therapy: An Introduction* (Springfield, IL: Charles C. Thomas Publisher, LTD, 1987), 41.

28 R. Accordino, et al., "Searching for music's potential: A critical examination of research on music therapy with individuals with autism," *Research in Autism Spectrum Disorders* (2006), doi:10.1016/j.rasd.2006.08.002. Accessed November 12, 2012.

29 S. Green and J. Higgins, "Cochrane Handbook for Systematic Reviews of Interventions," May 2005, 4, 2, 5. Available online: "Types of Autism Research Study," *Research Autism*, http://www.researchautism.net/pages/autism_research_journal_articles_publications_studies/autism_research_study_types (accessed November 15, 2012).

30 Elizabeth Aguila, "Music and the Mind: Can Music Benefit Those with Autism?" *The Triple Helix Lent*, Carnegie Mellon University, 2011.

31 D. Wimpory, P. Chadwick, and S. Nash, "Musical interaction therapy for children with autism: An evaluative case study with two-year follow-up," *Journal of Autism and Developmental Disorders,* vol. 25, 1995, 541–552.

32 R. Accordino, "Searching for music's potential."

33 "Teaching Children with Special Needs: Music, Movement, and Autism: The Trials and Triumphs of Working with Special Needs Populations," blog, April 30, 2010, http://specialneeds.achievement-products.com/2010/04/music-movement-and-autism.html (accessed November 12, 2012).

34 DVD *Touch the Sound* and website: http://www.evelyn.co.uk/evelyn-glennie.html#evelyn-glennie.html.

35 Zachary Fenell, "Unlikely Similarities: Classical Music and Cerebral Palsy," *Share Your Voice on Yahoo*, September 2, 2011.

36 Josie I. Nielsen, interview with author, February 6, 2013. See also "Playing by Ear and by Heart," *BYU Magazine*, Summer 2010, 59.

37 Kimberly McCord and Margaret Fitzgerald, "Children with Disabilities Playing Musical Instruments," *Music Educators Journal*, March 2006, vol. 92, issue 4, 46-52. Used with permission.

38 Linda K. Damer, "Children with Special Needs," *Music Educators Journal*, 2001, 87:17. Used with permission.

39   John Rogers, "Deaf man hears music—and can't stop listening," *Daily Breeze*, August 26, 2012.

Chapter 9

1   Jack Andraka, interview with author, April 6, 2013. See also: Abigail Tucker, "The Prodigy," *Smithsonian*, December 2012, 69. Wikipedia: http://en.wikipedia.org/wiki/ Jack_Andraka, and TED Talks: TED 2013, The Young, The Wise, The Undiscovered, "Jack Andraka Detecting Pancreatic Cancer."

2   Po Bronson and Ashley Merryman, "The Creativity Crisis," *Newsweek*, July 19, 2010, 45.

3   Ibid.

4   Jane M. Healy, *Endangered Minds*, (New York: Simon & Schuster, 1990), 279.

5   Britannica Editors, "Explaining the Decline of Creativity in American Children: A Reply to Readers," *Encyclopedia Britannica Blog: Facts Matter*, December 23, 2010.

6   Jim Trelease, *The Read-Aloud Handbook* (New York: Penguin Books, 1982), 94-96.

7   Jane Andraka, e-mail correspondence with author, April 8, 2013.

8   Healy, *Endangered Minds*, 338.

9   Bruce O. Boston, "Educating for the Workplace Through the Arts," *Business Week*, October 28, 1996, 8.

10   Healy, *Endangered Minds*, 338.

11   Tucker, "The Prodigy," 71.

12   Ibid.

13   *Wired*, February 1996

14   Rafe Esquith, *Lighting Their Fires* (New York: Penguin Group, 2009).

15   Boston, "Educating for the Workplace."

16   Michele and Robert Root-Bernstein, "Artsmarts: Why Cutting Arts Funding Is Not a Good Idea," *Imagine That!*, *Psychology Today* online, February 14, 2011.

17   http://www.supportmusic.com.

18   Joyce Hergenman, president, GE Fund, "Gaining the Arts Advantage." www.aep-arts. org/files/publications/WhyYourChildNeedstheArts.pdf. Accessed January 1, 2013.

19   Esquith, *Lighting Their Fires*, 29-30.

20   Bronson, "The Creativity Crisis," 45.

21   See: http://elsistemausa.org/el-sistema/venezuela/. Accessed December 18, 2012.

22   Christopher Noxon, "LA IMAX Says No, So Disney Builds Its Own Huge Screen," *Los Angeles Times*, December 7, 1999.

23   Roger von Oech, *A Whack on the Side of the Head* (New York: Warner Books, 1983). 7.

24   Trelease, *Read-Aloud Handbook*, 47.

25   Charles Van Doren, *A History of Knowledge* (New York: Ballentine Books, 1991), 154.

26   *What Work Requires of Schools: A SCANS Report for America 2000* (Upland, PA: Diane Publishing Co., 1993).

27   Esquith, *Lighting Their Fires*, 30.

28   Elizabeth Murfee, "Eloquent Evidence: Arts at the Core of Learning" (Washington, DC: National Assembly of State Arts Agencies, 1995).

29   Boston, "Educating for the Workplace," 2.

30   Peter F. Drucker, *Innovation and Entrepreneurship—Practice and Principles* (New York: Harper & Row, 1985), 216.

31   Eric Oddleifson, "The Case for Sequential Music Education in the Core Curriculum of the Public Schools" (East Hampton, NY: Center for the Arts in the Basic Curriculum, 1989).

32   Erin Hayes, "Google's 20 Percent Factor," *ABC World News with Diane Sawyer*, May 12, 2008.

33   Todd Oppenheimer, "The Computer Delusion," *Atlantic Monthly*, July 1997, 54.

34   Barbara Jones, "LAUSD Approves $50M for Computer Tablets," *Daily Breeze*, February 15, 2013.

35   Oppenheimer, "The Computer Delusion."

36   Sharon Begley, "Your Child's Brain," *Newsweek,* February 19, 1996.

37   Oppenheimer, "The Computer Delusion."

38   Romesh Ratnesar, "Learning By Laptop," *Time*, March 2, 1998.

39   Oppenheimer, "The Computer Delusion."

40   John Lienhard, "Children, Literacy, and the Computer," see: http://www.uh.edu/engines/alatalk.htm, accessed December 28, 2012.

41   Donald Hodges, "The Influence of Music on Human Behavior," *Handbook of Music Psychology* (San Antonio: IMR Press, 1996), 478.

42   Steve Rosenbaum, "The Explosive Power of Art+Science," *Magnify.net*, November 11, 2011.

43   Hodges, "The Influence of Music," 480.

44   Dee Dickinson, "Learning Through the Arts" (Seattle: New Horizons for Learning, 1997), 9. See also: www.newhorizons.org.

45   Oddleifson, "The Case for Sequential Music," 28.

46   Von Oech, *A Whack on the Side of the Head.*

47   Robert Wright, "The Man Who Invented the Web," *Time*, May 19, 1997.

48   Paul Griffiths, "Don't Blame Modernist for the Empty Seats," *New York Times*, March 22, 1998.

49   Eric Oddleifson, "To Perceive, and to Imagine: Unleashing the Talent and Energy of Teachers and Students" (East Hampton, NY: Center for the Arts n the Basic Curriculum, 1996), 6.

50   Sir Ken Robinson, "How Creativity, Education, and the Arts Shape a Modern Economy," *Arts and Minds: Conversations about the Arts in Education,* April 2005.

51   Bronson, "The Creativity Crisis."

52   Robinson, "How Creativity, Education, and the Arts Shape a Modern Economy."

53   Judith A. Fuller, "No Child Left Behind Strikes the Arts: How Can We Restore a Balance Among the Studies in the Arts, Sciences, and Humanities?" *Forum on Public Policy*, edweek.org, 2006.

54   John I. Goodlad, *A Place Called School* (New York: McGraw Hill, 1983).

Chapter 10

1   John Naisbitt, and Patricia Aburdene, *Megatrends 2000* (New York: Morrow, 1990).

2   Jonathan Leaf, "America's Opera Boom," *The American,* July/August 2007. See also: http://www.american.com/archive/2007/july-august-magazine-contents/america2019s-opera-boom.

3   "National Endowment for the Arts Announces Highlights from 2008 Survey of Public Participation in the Arts," June 15, 2009. See also: http://www.arts.gov/news/news09/sppa-highlights.html. Accessed on September 12, 2012.

4   Sarah Lutman, "The Perilous Life of Symphony Orchestras," January 1, 2012. Accessed September 12, 2012. See also: http://www.artsjournal.com/speaker/2012/01/the-perilous-life-of-symphony-orchestras/.

5   "National Endowment for the Arts Announces Highlights from 2008 Survey."

6   David Ng, "NEA report shows declining attendance in arts events nationwide," *Los Angeles Times*, December 10, 2009.

7   "National Endowment for the Arts Announces Highlights from 2008 Survey."

8   Ibid.

9   Elaine Dutka, "Eighty-Eight Keys to Success," *Los Angeles Times*, January 16, 1998.

10   Ted Libbey, *The NPR Guide to Building a Classical CD Collection* (New York: Workman Publishing, 1994), 406.

11   Ibid., 405.

12   Ibid.

13   See: http://en.wikipedia.org/wiki/Metropolitan_Opera_radio_broadcasts.

14   See: http://en.wikipedia.org/wiki/Great_Performances, accessed September 18, 2012.

Chapter 11

1.   Daniel Goleman, Paul Kaufman, and Michael Ray, *The Creative Spirit* (New York: Plume, 1993), 44.

2.   Ibid., 173.

3.   Malcolm Gladwell, *Tipping Point* (Boston: Little, Brown, and Company, 2002), 54.

Chapter 12

1   Edna Machesny, "Different Strokes," *Good Housekeeping*, February 1988, 206.

2   Sterling W. Sill, Conference Report, 1955, 117. See also Randy Alcorn, "Florence Chadwick and the Fog."

3   "A Blind Father Rescues His Daughter from Drowning," *Los Angeles Times* (UPI), June 6, 1973.

4   Mihaly Csikszentmihalyi, *Flow: The Psychology of Optimal Experience* (New York: Harper & Row, 1990).

5   Eric Oddleifson, "To Perceive, and to Imagine" (East Hampton, NY: Center for the Arts in the Basic Curriculum, 1996).

6   Madeline Levine, Ph.D, *The Price of Privilege* (New York: HarperCollins, 2006), 21.

7   Deborah Fallows, *A Mother's Work* (Boston: Houghton Mifflin, 1985), 16.

8   Robert A. Jones, "Fast Forward Kids," *Los Angeles Times*, June 22, 1997.

9   *The Lion in Winter*, Part 3 of the documentary *MGM: When the Lion Roars*, Turner Pictures, Inc., 1992.

10   Thomas Griffith, "The Waist-High Culture," *Time*, 1959, 188.

11   David O'McKay, *Improvement Era* magazine, June 1964, 445.

12   Michael Ryan, "If You Can't Teach Me, Don't Criticize Me," *Parade*, May 11, 1997.

13   Daniel Goleman, *Emotional Intelligence* (New York: Bantam Books,1997), 243.

14   Levine, *The Price of Privilege*, 30.

15   Marian Diamond, *Enriching Heredity* (New York: The Free Press/Simon & Schuster, 1988).

16   Levine, *The Price of Privilege*, 31.

17   Goleman, *Emotional Intelligence*, 241.

18   Susan Salter Reynolds, "The Family That Plays Together…Is the Goal of This Special School Program," *Los Angeles Times*, June 12, 1997.

19   Peggy Epstein, "How to Plan a School Game Night," http://www.ehow.com/how_5675401_plan-school-game-night.html.

20   Bruce Feiler, "Family Inc.," *The Wall Street Journal*, February 9-10, 2013.

21   M. Scott Peck, *The Road Less Traveled* (New York: Touchstone. 1978), 23.

Index

A

A+ Schools, 172–73, 174–75
AAA (Arts for Academic Achievement), 189
Abdelazer (Purcell), 86
Abravanel, Maurice, 36
Abreu, José Antonio, 117, 131, 132, 245
academic success, need for, 206
Acholi children, 136–39
activity music therapy, 219
ADD (attention deficit disorder), 227–28
ADHD (attention deficit hyperactivity disorder), 227–28
Adolphe, Bruce, 76
adversity
    confidence through, 136–39
    overcoming, 122–23, 145–47
agile development, 347
Ala, Hamid, 223
Alaska Children's Choir, 74
Alexander, Jane, 151
Allen, Carolyn, 143
Alpert, Dorothea, 94–96
Alphabet Operetta (Manley), 53
alpha mode, 27
Andraka, Jack, 231–32, 235–36, 238
Andsnes, Leif Ove, 144, 293
animals, response of, to music, 5–7
A+ Schools, 172–73, 174–75
appreciation, learned through music, 145–47
arithmetic. *See* math
Armstrong, Thomas, 20
arts. *See also* community arts; school music programs
    and ability to use resources, 252
    at-risk students and, 189–97
    creative thinking and, 241–44
    future of, 268–69

government mandates regarding, 154–55
    importance of, 157–62
    learning through, 162–71
    love of, 145–47
    Opening Minds through the Arts (OMA) program, 183–88
    organizations encouraging, in classroom, 188–89
    successful integration of, 171–83
    technology and, 263–64
Arts Education Branch, 189
Arts Education in Public Elementary and Secondary Schools, 1999-2000 and 2009-2010, 155–56
Arts Education Partnership (AEP) study, 194–95
Arts for Academic Achievement (AAA), 189
Ashcraft, Joan, 182, 188
assistant conductor, responsibilities of, 317
at-risk students, 189–97
attention, learning disabled students and, 204–5
attention deficit disorder (ADHD/ADD), 227–28
attire, for concert attendance, 287
audiovisual coordinators, responsibilities of, 322–23
auditions, 312
auditory cortex, 16–17, 203–4
autism
    Integrated Listening Systems and, 215
    music's impact on those with, 203, 217–18
    music therapy and, 219–22
    parental involvement and, 209–10
Autism: The Musical, 221–22

429

ABOUT THE AUTHOR

Sharlene Habermeyer, MA, has spent over twenty-five years researching the effects of music in the brain development of young children. She holds a masters degree in Education from Pepperdine University in Malibu, California. In 1999, she started the Palos Verdes Regional Orchestra (now the Palos Verdes Regional Symphony Orchestra). It currently boasts over one-hundred members. A college instructor, a frequent lecturer, and a consultant, she is the mother of five boys and lives with her husband in Torrance, California.

Contact Information:
sharlene@goodmusicbrighterchildren.com

Made in the USA
Lexington, KY
25 June 2014